Educational
Statistics

EXPLORATION SERIES IN EDUCATION
Under the Advisory Editorship of
John Guy Fowlkes

Educational Statistics

Use
and
Interpretation

Second Edition

W. JAMES POPHAM
Associate Professor
University of California, Los Angeles
KENNETH A. SIROTNIK
University of California, Los Angeles

Harper & Row, Publishers
New York · San Francisco · Evanston · London

EDUCATIONAL STATISTICS: Use and Interpretation, Second Edition

Standard Book Number: 06-045252-8

Library of Congress Catalog Card Number: 72-87881

CONTENTS

APPENDIX

EDITOR'S
INTRODUCTION

Over the last fifty years, observers of efforts to measure the behavior of human beings quantitatively, particularly with respect to mental and social behavior, have had an exciting and enlightening experience. Yule, E. L. Thorndike, Rugg, Helen Walker, Truman Kelly, Thurstone, Guilford, Cattell, Ralph Tyler, Lindquist, Cronbach, Chester Harris, and Julian Stanley are distinguished examples of a relatively small but highly significant group of individuals who have exerted a marked influence on the study of human ability and achievement. Their efforts have resulted in the increasing application of quantitative methods of measuring intellectual capabilities and achievements, particularly of students. Data on individuals enrolled in schools, colleges, and universities have been increasingly subjected to statistical treatment.

Statistical analysis has been commonplace among researchers in biological and physical sciences for a considerably longer period of time than among those primarily concerned with human behavior. With increasing frequency, researchers in social and psychological studies are utilizing statistical techniques similar to those used by physical and natural scientists. As noted by the authors of this book, these statistical procedures are unfamiliar to many of those engaged in educational activity, including not only elementary and secondary teachers but indeed often the staffs of colleges and universities. Although the Ph.D. includes the writing of a doctoral thesis, usually involving data which must be treated by highly involved statistical methods, many doctoral candidates lack the background to use such techniques with understanding and interpret them with discrimination.

To all engaged in the study of intellectual and social phenomena and the identification of relatively effective or ineffective classroom practices, this book should prove to be of great help. As the authors succinctly state, "The emphasis throughout the text will be upon the common-sense rationale *underlying the statistical methods described.''* In other words, the authors proposed to write a book that readers who are not mathematically oriented can understand. This is indeed a laudable intent, and one that they have achieved.

John Guy Fowlkes

PREFACE TO THE SECOND EDITION

In our revision of Educational Statistics, *we have attempted to preserve the spirit in which the first edition was written, as expressed in the opening paragraphs of the original preface. We remain dedicated to the proposition that the beginning student in statistics need not be traumatized by algebraic and symbolic complexities, ultimately (and necessarily) encountered when a more advanced understanding of the topic is pursued. Thus, we attempt to provide the student with a working knowledge of the utilitarian aspects of statistical methodology, even though he may not necessarily be prepared to hold his own at the annual meeting of the American Statistical Association.*

We have, however, recognized a number of problems inherent in the original text, including a number of potential student misconceptions, probably resulting from our overzealous attempt to simplify the statistical procedures. This second edition then, is an attempt to correct these problem areas while at the same time maintaining the relative simplicity and applicability of the material. In some cases, chapters have been substantially modified (see, for example, the chapters on Correlation and Regression). In addition, a new chapter (17) has been added to familiarize the student with the great number of statistical and practical considerations involved in improving experimental and nonexperimental (ex post facto) research designs where analysis of variance procedures are typically employed.

We reiterate our expression of gratitude to those individuals who were involved in the previous edition and also thank Ward Keesling, who was kind enough to review Chapter 17 of this edition, and Rosemary Spencer, who suffered through the typing, cutting, and pasting. Beyond these individuals, a number of colleagues and students were kind enough to examine various sections of the manuscript.

K.A.S—W.J.P.

PREFACE TO THE FIRST EDITION

This book was written primarily in reaction against my own experience as a student in educational statistics classes. It was evident that many of my fellow students in those classes were essentially going through the motions necessary to pass the course but were acquiring little real understanding of the statistical concepts which were treated. Subsequent conversations with numerous educators from all parts of the country confirmed my opinion that only a small collection of professional educators possess real confidence regarding their ability to use and interpret statistical methods. In the field of education which, fortunately, is increasingly relying upon empirical research findings to guide the decision-maker, such deficiencies in statistical understanding are disturbing.

Many of the unfortunate experiences of education students in statistics classes can be traced to the highly mathematical treatments of statistics in the most commonly used textbooks. Although the precise language of mathematics provides a most incisive method of explaining statistics to those who are mathematically oriented, it may prove awesome to many students in education. I decided to try to prepare an educational statistics text which would sidestep mathematical exposition whenever possible, relying instead on verbal or graphic explanations. To the extent that this goal has been achieved, the volume may be of value to the student of educational statistics.

In the preparation of this text I have appreciated the opportunity at a number of points to seek the counsel of Dr. T. R. Husek of the University of California, Los Angeles. Dr. Henry Kaiser of the University of Wisconsin was kind enough to examine and offer helpful criticisms of the chapter on factor analysis. I am grateful to Mrs. Eva L. Baker, who read the manuscript and offered a series of excellent suggestions for improvement. The responsibility for deficiencies in the text, of course, is solely mine.

I am indebted to the literary executor of the late Sir Ronald A. Fisher, F.R.S., Cambridge, and to Dr. Frank Yates, F.R.S., Rothamsted, also to Messrs. Oliver and Boyd Ltd., Edinburgh, for permission to reprint Tables III and IV from their book Statistical Tables for Biological, Agricultural and Medical Research, *and for permission to reprint Tables VA and VB from their book* Statistical Methods for Research Workers.

W.J.P.

Introduction

Any professional practitioner, whether he is a physician, an attorney, or an educator, should be interested in improving himself. In medicine, for example, the outstanding surgeon is constantly seeking knowledge which will enable him to perform more effectively his delicate tasks. Professionals in education, too, are usually eager to improve their instructional procedures. But whereas the surgeon consults his medical journals to learn of new discoveries regarding human anatomy or operating procedures, where does the educator turn?

Suppose an elementary school teacher has heard that particular films may provide a remarkably efficient tool for teaching children about the U.S. Constitution and that evidence regarding their effectiveness is contained in a recent issue of an educational research journal. If the teacher wishes to explore the suitability of the films for her own purposes, she should obviously read the research report which describes their value. But what if she refers to the report and finds that the discussion is centered on the following sentence? "The analysis of covariance yielded an F value of 4.62 which, with 1 and 38 degrees of freedom, is significant beyond the 0.05 level." How many educators can make sense out of such statements? Yet, this is the language of statistics—a language that is employed in most educational research studies. If members of the teaching profession really intend to benefit from the newer discoveries of their field, they should become adept in comprehending at least the most commonly used statistical procedures.

Statistical formulations will be encountered by the inquiring teacher at almost every turn. For example, imagine that a high-school English instructor is deciding whether to use a standardized achievement test and wishes to know something about the test. He reads the manual accompanying the test and finds that "the standard deviation of the normative sample was 16.24," "split-half reliability $r = 0.89$ ($p < 0.01$)," and "subtest intercorrelations ranged from 0.52 to 0.71." Will the teacher be able to interpret the data properly or will this be another instance where a lack of statistical understanding forces him to over-look relevant data? Without understanding the statistical methods employed in much educational writing, the reader must "skip over" a crucial segment of such material. This is analogous to fitting a jigsaw puzzle together without one of the important pieces. Only through statistical understanding can an educator really become professionally literate, that is, be able to read and comprehend the primary sources of new knowledge in his field of specialization.

One should not ignore the possibility that some researchers, either unwittingly or through deliberate intellectual dishonesty, misuse statistical methods in certain instances. The astute student of statistics need not look far in educational research journals to find rather serious errors in the application of statistical techniques. Just because a research article is in print is no assurance that the author's conclusions are accurate. The competent educator must be prepared to evaluate the validity of all the researcher's methods, including the statistical techniques which are employed.

There are encouraging signs that educators are placing increasing emphasis on empirical methods in evaluating their endeavors. Instructional specialists, for example, are more frequently assessing the merits of teaching procedures in terms of changes in learner behavior rather than subjective impressions of a teacher's competence. With so much attention given to empirical evidence, the educator needs to be even more conversant with the statistical language used so often in reporting such evidence.

THE TEXT AND THE READER

A few words regarding the general scheme used in this text may assist the reader. First, the emphasis throughout the text will be on the *common-sense rationale* underlying the statistical methods described. It is hoped that by learning *how* a statistical technique operates, the reader will be able to understand the purpose of the technique and in what types of educational situations it should be used. Further, many examples of appropriate tasks for different statistical techniques are supplied so that the reader will be able to see, not only *why* a technique can perform certain functions, but also when it should be used. Whenever possible, statistical concepts are described in a verbal or graphic fashion. Mathematical explanatory techniques are reduced to an absolute minimum. No derivations of formulas are included. For statistical techniques involving considerable computation, such as correlation, an initial chapter dealing with the general function of the technique is presented. This is followed by a companion chapter that explains the computational procedures of the same technique. The reader's purposes will necessarily dictate whether the computational chapters should be read. For example, a student in an educational statistics course would probably be required to read them, whereas other readers might not choose to do so.

It will be necessary to deal with some statistical symbols and with a certain amount of mathematical calculation. Statistical symbols, however, are merely a shorthand method for identifying certain mathematical operations or quantities. If the symbols in statistical formulations were replaced by the verbal explanations of the operations they represent, few readers would view them with alarm. However, if this were done, the number of pages in statistics books would probably have to be doubled in order to accommodate such a clarifying, but highly uneconomical, elaboration. By dealing with only a few symbols at a time, the reader should be able to master those needed for the more commonly used techniques in educational statistics.

At the close of many chapters, exercises are presented which most readers should undertake. These vary in nature since some exercises require only verbal or "thinking" responses while others demand a certain amount of mathematical computation. In either instance, the reader's knowledge of the topic under discussion should be increased by his completion of these exercises. Answers to all exercises are presented on pages 342–351.

A final chapter allowing the reader an opportunity to practice the selection of appropriate statistical techniques has also been provided. This section, organized in a manner similar to that employed in "branching" self-instructional programs, should prove helpful to most readers.

THE USES OF STATISTICAL METHODS

Most statisticians agree that there are two primary purposes of statistics as applied to education. The first purpose involves the *description* of data. Statistical techniques which are used to describe data are referred to as *descriptive statistics*. Descriptive statistics are used to summarize sets of numerical data such as test scores, ages, and years of education. Through the use of descriptive statistics one conserves the time and space necessary to describe data.

The second principal use of statistics in education is to allow the researcher *to draw better inferences* as to whether a phenomenon which is observed in a relatively small number of individuals (a sample) can be legitimately generalized to a larger number of individuals (a population). This use of statistical methods is usually termed *inferential statistics.*

In inferential statistics one is frequently concerned with relationships between variables. The educator attempts to discover relationships among such variables as student intelligence, achievement, and attitudes so that he may take these relationships into consideration in order to improve school programs. Suppose a researcher observes a clear relationship between two important variables, for example, reading ability and test performance, in a relatively small sample of fifth graders. He is far more interested in the presence of the relationship for fifth-grade pupils in general, since he undoubtedly wishes to make future decisions regarding other pupils on the basis of his findings. To what extent can his findings be generalized to a larger population of fifth-grade youngsters? Inferential statistics can be employed to determine the degree of confidence one can place in inferences about such sample relationships.

Consequently, inferential statistics serve an important function in the design of educational research. The research planner should organize his studies carefully so that the data yielded from the investigation can be analyzed meaningfully. Therefore, to a considerable degree, the availability of suitable statistical techniques is a crucial factor in the design of a well-conceived research investigation.

The research neophyte who attempts to plan a study without due consideration of statistical methods will find to his dismay that he cannot simply turn over his data to a statistician for appropriate analysis. Even a highly sophisticated statistical analysis can rarely salvage a poorly designed research study in which the investigator has paid scant attention to possible procedures of data analysis.

The fields of testing and test construction also rely heavily upon descriptive and inferential statistics. The test developer has obvious need of descriptive statistics, for example, when he summarizes the performance of normative groups on his test. He may use inferential statistics when he attempts to generalize to a population on the basis of a student sample's performance on a predictor test (such as music aptitude) and a predicted criterion measure (such as music performance). In a variety of ways the educator who deals with measurement and evaluation procedures, even in the classroom, will find it helpful to employ statistical procedures.

STATISTICAL RESULTS AND EDUCATIONAL JUDGMENT

There is, unfortunately, no one-to-one relationship between the results of statistical operations and the judgments which should be rendered by the educational decision-maker. Statistics provide a tool whereby educational data can be parsimoniously described and more precisely analyzed than by merely "inspecting the scores." The results of these statistical analyses should undoubtedly influence the decisions reached by the educator and make such decisions far more enlightened. But statistical results should not be equated with the final conclusions of scientific judgment. For one thing, statistical questions and research design considerations can be considered separately. One can, of course, apply the proper statistical procedures to a research study which is poorly designed. But even with a skillfully designed study and the judicious use of statistical methods, the wise decision-maker must weigh factors other than statistical results prior to reaching a conclusion.

For example, a research study may reveal that a new method of teaching foreign languages yields results which are slightly, but consistently, higher than those produced by conventional methods. A difference favoring the new method has, therefore, been found. Is the educator obliged to adopt the new method? Perhaps the new approach is particularly expensive, or demanding of teacher time and energy. If the results favoring the new method, however reliable, are not of great magnitude, the educator may justly decide against the new instructional approach.

To put it another way, there is a crucial difference between a statistically significant result and a *practically significant* result. While knowledge of statistics is an invaluable asset to the educator, it is his proper responsibility to be *guided* by statistical results; he should not, however, be *led* by them.

SELECTED READINGS

Guilford, J. P., *Fundamental Statistics in Psychology and Education*. New York: McGraw-Hill, 1965, chap. 1.

Huntsberger, David V., *Elements of Statistical Inference*. Boston: Allyn and Bacon, 1962, chap. 1.

Johnson, Palmer O., and Robert W. B. Jackson, *Modern Statistical Methods: Descriptive and Inductive*. Chicago: Rand McNally, 1959, chap. 1.

Tukey, John W., "The Future of Data Analysis," *Ann. Math. Statist.* **33**, no. 1 (March, 1962): 1.

Van Dalen, Deobold B., *Understanding Educational Research*. New York: McGraw-Hill, 1962, chap. 11.

Walker, H. M., *Studies in the History of Statistical Method*. Baltimore: Williams & Wilkins, 1929.

Wallis, W. Allen, and Harry V. Roberts, *The Nature of Statistics*. New York: Collier, 1962.

2
Descriptive Statistics

One of the most common uses of statistical methods in education is providing a technique through which education data, such as test scores, ratings, and grades, can be sensibly communicated. Teachers, counselors, and administrators are constantly faced with the necessity of succinctly describing these sets of data.

The description of data, such as a group of test scores, can be handled in several ways. Suppose one teacher wishes to tell another how a particular class performed on an examination. One way would be to recite each pupil's score, that is if he could ever hold the attention of his colleague for the necessary length of time. Alternatively, he could give someone his grade book and have him look at the class performance. But these descriptive procedures are highly uneconomical in terms of the teacher's time and the time of those whom he may wish to inform. Alternative methods are needed.

GRAPHICAL DESCRIPTIVE TECHNIQUES

One of the techniques many teachers employ to describe a set of test scores is to represent the data graphically as demonstrated with a set of test scores in Figure 2.1. The base line across the bottom of the figure represents the number of items each student in a class answered correctly on a ten-item true–false quiz. The crosses immediately above the numbers represent the students in the class. Five crosses are found above the score eight, and this means that five students answered eight of the ten true–false questions correctly. Similarly, there is only one cross above the number two, and so it can be concluded that one student answered only two questions correctly on the quiz.

Such a graphical method of describing the performance of a group is satisfactory for certain purposes and can be even more refined if one transforms the cross-marks into equivalent squares or rectangles, so that a type of upright bar graph can be built such as that depicted in Figure 2.2.

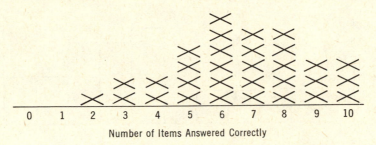

Figure 2.1 *A simple graphic method of describing a set of test scores for 31 pupils on a ten-item true–false quiz.*

In Figure 2.2 the test scores, originally seen in Figure 2.1, have been transformed into a graph where each student's score is represented by a small shaded rectangle. If the horizontal lines in the bar graph were erased, the figure would become a bar graph (sometimes called a histogram), such as that presented in Figure 2.3.

In each of these graphs one can easily see how a class of students performed on the quiz. Consequently, each of the graphs served its descriptive purpose satisfactorily. When referring to such graphs, the horizontal line is called the *abscissa* or *X* axis, and the vertical line is called the *ordinate* or *Y* axis. The nature of the abscissa and the ordinate must be clearly designated for the graph to be meaningfully interpreted. For example, in Figure 2.3, the abscissa represents the number of items answered correctly, and the ordinate represents the frequency or number of students who attained a given score.

Another method of portraying a set of scores graphically is to use a *frequancy polygon* which is simply a modification of the bar graph previously described. By connecting the midpoints of the highest point in each bar, one can develop a figure like that seen in Figure 2.4. If the reader will contrast the frequency polygon in Figure 2.4 with the bar graph in Figure 2.3, it will be seen that the shaded *area* beneath the heavy line which forms the frequency

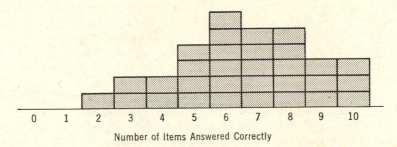

Figure 2.2 *A graphic method of describing a set of test scores with each rectangle depicting the performance of one of 31 pupils on a ten-item true–false quiz.*

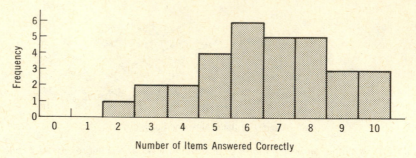

Figure 2.3 *Histogram representing scores of 31 pupils on a ten-item true–false quiz.*

polygon is actually equivalent to the shaded area originally contained below the outline of the bar graph.

The frequency polygon can be further modified by rounding the sharp corners and developing a curve something like that presented in Figure 2.5. All that has been done in Figure 2.5 is to smooth out the rough edges of the frequency polygon seen originally in Figure 2.4.

All of the preceding graphical methods are equivalent ways of portraying the *distribution* of test scores; that is, the way in which test scores of 31 pupils are distributed over all possible numbers of items answered correctly. Figures 2.1 through 2.5 are collectively referred to as frequency distributions. In particular, Figure 2.5 depicts a distribution *curve*. The distribution curve merely represents data of some kind, such as scores on the true–false quiz. The method of representation is area; the area beneath the curve between any two score values is proportional to the number of pupils obtaining scores between these two values. One might think of a distribution curve as a series of points (forming the curved line) which represent hypothetical frequencies, those that might be obtained for a test with a very large number of students. Note that the assumption of *continuous* score values is being made. In other words, scores such as 3.8, 9.107, 5.33, and so forth, are assumed to exist in theory,

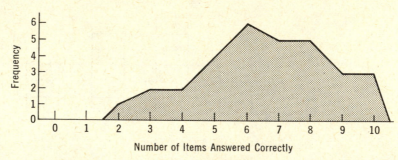

Figure 2.4 *Frequency polygon describing the performance of 31 pupils on a ten-item true–false quiz.*

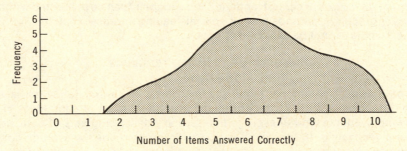

Figure 2.5 *A curve describing the performance of 31 pupils on a ten-item true–false quiz.*

even though only the *discrete* values 0, 1, 2, 3, and so forth, can actually be observed. This assumption is not only theoretically useful, but has immense practical value as well.

Each of the graphical methods discussed in the preceding paragraphs is suitable for describing data, if one wishes to employ visual techniques. However, there is another way of summarizing educational data through the use of statistical formulations. Such statistical methods offer an even more economical method of describing data.

DESCRIPTIVE STATISTICS

If an educator wished to describe a set of test scores to someone, he would probably want to convey at least two notions regarding their composition. In the first place, he would ordinarily like to indicate something about the *central tendency* of the scores, that is, where the scores appeared to center or group together on the scale used. Secondly, he would wish to give some notion of the *variability* of scores along that scale or, to phrase it another way, an idea of how far the scores spread out from the center of the score distribution.

Assume an instructor had given a hundred-item multiple-choice examination to a class of thirty students. He could summarize the performance of the class by indicating the typical score, or how many of the hundred questions most students had answered correctly. He could also describe how the scores spread out along the 100-point scale, or how students tended to differ from one another. The characteristics used by this instructor to describe his test scores represent the two major types of descriptive statistical measures: *measures of central tendency* and *measures of variability*. By employing statistical descriptions of a distribution's central tendency and variability, an accurate and economical representation of the data under consideration can usually be conveyed. This can be accomplished without being forced to employ graphical methods and, therefore, both time and effort can be conserved. A warning should be issued, however, that measures of central tendency and variability do not convey *all* the information of a distribution of scores. Two distributions could have very different shapes and yet have the same central tendency and variability measures. Measures of central tendency and variability can be presented without the aid of graphical methods only when a misleading impression of the distribution as a whole cannot be expected to occur.

MEASURES OF CENTRAL TENDENCY
The Mean

One of the most commonly employed measures of central tendency is the *mean*. The mean is actually the arithmetic average of a set of data. Most of us have employed this kind of average in informally describing sets of data since we were very young. If, for example, you wish to determine the average height of a group of students, you would simply find out the height of each individual, perhaps in inches, then add all the heights together and divide this total by the number of individuals in the group. This process would yield an average height which is called the mean.

As is commonly seen in descriptions of statistical quantities, the calculation of the mean may be depicted symbolically. This will provide an opportunity in the next few paragraphs to introduce the reader to some of the more common symbols used in statistics. Imagine that you are working with a set of test scores. The symbol X can be used to represent a single raw score on the test. For example, if a student had attained a score of 89 items correct on a 100-item test, his raw score would be 89 and would be represented in the following fashion: $X = 89$. Actually, any score is referred to as a raw score if it is untreated in any way. Thus, one's age, weight, years in school, and so forth could be considered raw scores.

In dealing with statistics one is frequently compelled to add together sets of scores or, employing a technical phrase, to *sum* them. The statistical symbol representing this summation operation is the capital Greek letter *sigma* (Σ). Whenever this symbol Σ is encountered in statistics, whatever quantity immediately follows it must be *summed*, that is, added together. For example, the notation ΣX indicates that the raw scores under consideration must be added together. In a class of 30 students, each student's score on an examination is represented by the symbol X; to signify that these 30 scores are to be added together, the expression ΣX is used.

Another symbol frequently used in statistics is the letter N, which represents the number of measurements in the group under consideration. To illustrate, if there were 30 students' scores to be described, then N in this instance equals 30. If there were 150 students, N would equal 150.

With these three symbols (X, Σ, N) a formula for the calculation of the mean can now be presented. The mean is represented in many statistical texts by the lowercase Greek letter *mu* (μ). Using this symbol, the formula for the mean would be

$$\mu = \frac{\Sigma X}{N}$$

(2.1)

which, when interpreted, would indicate that the mean is attained by summing all of the raw scores and dividing that summed quantity by the number of scores in the group.

A simple illustration of the use of this formula is presented below. With seven scores: 1, 2, 3, 4, 5, 6, 7; $\Sigma X = 28$

$$\mu = \frac{28}{7}$$
$$= 4$$

A mean for any set of data may be computed in this fashion. In educational and psychological research the mean is used as an index of central tendency more often than any other measure.

The Median

Another measure of central tendency employed in statistics is the *median*. By definition, the median is the midpoint in a set of ranked scores. Thus, if all scores of students who have taken a test were ranked (say highest to lowest) and a point were selected such that the same number of scores were both above and below it, that point would be the median. The median provides another kind of information about the central tendency of a distribution of scores and is of considerable value in describing data.

The calculation of the median is very simple in many instances. For example, examine the set of scores below.

7, 9, 11, 12, 13, 13, 15

In observing these seven scores the reader will see that the middle score is 12 and that both above and below this point there are three scores. The score 12, then, is the median for this set of scores. When working with an odd number of scores, it is often quite easy to determine the median point, particularly if there is only one score value in the center of the distribution.

A slightly different problem is presented when encountering an even number of scores, such as the eight scores presented below.

5, 6, 7, 9, 11, 12, 12, 14

In this instance it can be seen that the lower half of the distribution and the upper half of the distribution are easily discerned, but that no existing score can be used to divide them. Since, however, the uppermost score in the lower half (four scores) of the distribution is 9, and the lowermost score in the upper half (four scores) of the distribution is 11, an artificially inserted (*interpolated*) point of 10 is used as the median for the distribution, *even though in reality no such score was attained by anyone.*

In general, we find this interpolated value by computing the mean of the two observed scores (9 and 11 in the above example) on either side of the midpoint. This further serves to illustrate that the median is not a score but a *point* that divides a distribution into two equal halves. For instance, the median for a set of final exam papers might be 28.4, even though every student obtained whole number scores with no decimals. The median of these four scores: 10, 11, 12, 13 would be 11.5. Of course, the point dividing the distribution into two equal halves might be an actual score, as in this instance, 3, 4, 6, 8, 9, where the median is 6.

For more complicated situations in which the median must be determined, there are formulas which may be used to calculate the precise midpoint of a set of scores.[1] However, since exact computation of the median is not necessary for most practical purposes, these formulas will not be treated here.

The Mode

Another, less frequently used index of central tendency is called the *mode*. The mode is, simply, the most frequently occurring score in a distribution. For example, in Figure 2.2 the mode is 6. Usually the mode is located near the center of the distribution of scores, but this need not be the case. Sometimes one encounters distributions where two or more modes are present. In such instances we speak of bimodal or even trimodal distributions.

Which To Use — Mean, Median, or Mode?

When describing the central tendency of a set of data, an educator may be perplexed as to whether he should use the mean, the median, or the mode. Of these three only the mean uses all of the information available in a set of data; that is, every score in the distribution is used in computing the average, whereas much less information is required to compute the median or the mode. Ordinarily, then, use of the mean will provide a more sensitive index of central tendency. Statistically, the mean is also more stable than the median or mode, but sometimes there are disadvantages in using every score in the distribution.

Suppose a school superintendent wished to discover the "average" income of wage earners in his district, but knew that among the 5,000 families in the district, there were two men who literally earned over one million dollars per year. Would the mean (arithmetic average) provide him with his typical income? Of course not, for the two enormous incomes would inflate the mean income of his wage earners unrealistically. In such cases the median would be a better choice since it is not influenced by extreme scores.

The median is also a good index of central tendency when working with strangely shaped sets of data, for example, where there is an extremely high proportion of superior scores and a low proportion of extremely inferior scores. The median is similarly useful in describing sets of data which have been cut off or *truncated* on one or both ends as when the lower intelligence quotients for a group of youngsters are described as "65 and below."

The mode is an easily located measure of central tendency and, therefore, might be used if one were in a hurry and wished to describe roughly a set of scores. Also, in some cases, the mode is the only reasonable kind of central

[1]See, for example, Allen L. Edwards, *Statistical Methods for the Behavioral Sciences* (New York: Holt, Rinehart & Winston, 1954), p. 46.

tendency measure which should be used. If a shoe manufacturer is producing shoes of different sizes, his best bet for high sales is to emphasize shoe sizes near the modal value. He is primarily interested in what most of his customers will be able to wear; hence his concern is with the mode.

One should analyze the type of answers needed from the data, and then choose from the mean, the median, or the mode. As indicated earlier, most of the time the choice will be the mean.[2]

MEASURES OF VARIABILITY
The Range

In addition to measures of central tendency it is desirable to have some measures reflecting the way in which data are dispersed in either direction from the center of a distribution. Such statistical indices are called measures of variability.

The most easily calculated measure of variability is undoubtedly the *range*. This measure is obtained by subtracting the lowest score value from the highest as in Formula 2.2.

$$\text{Range} = X_h - X_l \qquad (2.2)$$

where

X_h = the highest score in the distribution
X_l = the lowest score in the distribution

For instance, one might have a distribution of scores such as 20, 25, 26, 27, 28, 29, 29, 30. The range for the distribution would be $X_h - X_l$ = range, or $30 - 20$ = 10. As can be seen, only two scores are involved in the calculation of this measure of variability. If these two scores are greatly divergent from the general variability of the distribution, the range may yield a misleading notion of the variability of the distribution. For example, if in a class of 32 pupils 30 test scores were located very close to the mean but there was one extremely high score and one extremely low score, the range for the class might reflect a much larger spread of scores than really existed.

The Standard Deviation

The most widely used statistical index of variability is known as the *standard deviation*. Typically, the standard deviation is used to describe variability when the mean is used to describe central tendency. Actually, the standard deviation is somewhat analogous to the mean. While the mean is an *average* of the scores in a set, the standard deviation is a sort of *average* of how distant the individual scores in a distribution are removed from the mean itself.

To obtain the standard deviation, statisticians make considerable use of the *distance of scores from the mean* along the baseline of a graphically represented distribution. In fact, we shall employ a new symbol, *x*, which is called a

[2]See D. Huff, *How to Lie with Statistics* (New York: Norton, 1954) for a good discussion of the misuses of measures of central tendency and other statistics in general.

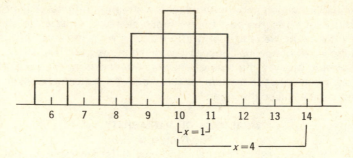

Figure 2.6 *Blocked-out bar graph representing 18 hypothetical test scores.*

deviation from the mean and is obtained by subtracting the mean from a raw score. Thus,

$$x = X - \mu \tag{2.3}$$

where

x = a deviation from the mean
X = the original raw score
μ = the mean

To illustrate the discussion of the standard deviation, a hypothetical distribution of test scores will be depicted (Figure 2.6) in a blocked-out bar graph where each rectangle represents a single raw score.

It is also possible to summarize these scores in a table (2.1) and to perform certain operations on the raw scores (column 1) such as deriving the x derivations (column 2) and squaring these derivations (column 3).

To obtain the deviations, the mean must be calculated, in this case $\mu =$ 180/18 = 10. The mean is then subtracted from each raw score to obtain the x scores in column 2. Column 3 is obtained by squaring each of the deviations. (Remember that a minus times a minus equals a plus.) We shall have need for column 4 later in this discussion. Now, having previously suggested that the standard deviation is analogous to an average of variability, the formula for the standard deviation should be examined to see how this measure is calculated.

$$\sigma = \sqrt{\frac{\Sigma x^2}{N}} \tag{2.4}$$

where

σ = the standard deviation of a set of scores, symbolized by the Greek lower-case letter *sigma*
Σx^2 = the sum of the squared deviations from the mean
N = the number of cases in the distribution

An inspection of the formula reveals that, aside from the number of cases, the critical quantity upon which the size of the standard deviation depends is Σx^2, frequently referred to as the "sum of squares." The sum of squares is a

Table 2.1
Eighteen Hypothetical Scores, Their Squares, Deviations, and Squared Deviations

(1) Scores X	(2) Deviations x	(3) Squared Deviations x^2	(4) (Raw Scores)^2 X^2
14	4	16	196
13	3	9	169
12	2	4	144
12	2	4	144
11	1	1	121
11	1	1	121
11	1	1	121
10	0	0	100
10	0	0	100
10	0	0	100
10	0	0	100
9	−1	1	81
9	−1	1	81
9	−1	1	81
8	−2	4	64
8	−2	4	64
7	−3	9	49
6	−4	16	36
$\Sigma X = 180$	$\Sigma(x-\mu) = 0$	$\Sigma(x-\mu)^2 = 72$	$\Sigma X^2 = 1,872$

quantity often encountered in statistical work, and one must be thoroughly familiar with the process by which it is obtained. First, the deviations from the mean are found by subtracting the mean from each raw score. Note from Figure 2.6 that the further the original score is removed from the mean, the greater will be the value of x. In the figure we can note that a score of 11 minus the mean would yield a deviation of only 1. Generalizing to scores on either side of the mean, a −4 has a greater *absolute* magnitude (disregarding the sign) than a −1 while a +4 would have a greater magnitude than a +1.

It would seem possible to sum all of these deviations and divide by the number of cases to provide an average of dispersion. However, as can be seen in Table 2.1, the sum of the deviations, Σx, is zero. To obviate the difficulty of a zero quantity, squaring the deviations will transform all negative deviations into positive quantities. By summing the squares and dividing this new total (Σx^2) by N, a measure of variability is obtained. Then, by taking the positive square root of this figure, we return to the original scale of measurement. As suggested, this process yields a sort of *average* of dispersion which, as can be seen from an analysis of the formula, becomes larger as the variability or dispersion of the distribution increases. Note the similarities of the formulas for the mean (2.1) and for the standard deviation (2.4). Both are basically averages.

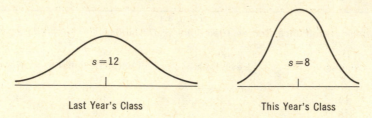

Figure 2.7   *Hypothetical class distributions with different standard deviations.*

If an educator reports that the standard deviation of his class on this year's final exam was 12 while the standard deviation for last year's class was only 8, we might form a mental image something like Figure 2.7.

As with most statistical concepts, the standard deviation becomes more meaningful when the student actually calculates a few, particularly if one attempts *to note the contributions made by the raw scores* to the statistical quantities involved. The standard deviation for the set of scores in Table 2.1 can be calculated as follows:

$$\sigma = \sqrt{\frac{72}{18}}$$
$$= \sqrt{4}$$
$$= 2$$

In computing this standard deviation, note how much difference the addition of new raw scores, for example, scores of 20 and 0, would have made in the size of σ. The deviation for these two new scores ($x = \pm 10$), when squared, actually exceeds the entire contribution of the eighteen scores already present, so we would have

$$\Sigma x^2 = 72 + 100 + 100 = 272, \qquad \sigma = \sqrt{\frac{272}{20}} = 3.7$$

Such is the sensitivity of the standard deviation.

Aside from its value in serving as a general indication of the dispersion in a set of measurements, the standard deviation can also be used as a unit of measurement along the baseline of a distribution of scores. For instance, in a normally distributed set of test scores, approximately 68 percent of the scores fall within an area plus and minus one standard deviation from the mean. This will be described in the next chapter.

If an educator must calculate a standard deviation for a set of scores, he can follow the procedure used previously; however, to save time, he may wish to employ a faster and easier method for obtaining Σx^2. It can be demonstrated that the sum of squares can be obtained without ever reducing the data to actual deviations by employing the following *raw-score formula for the sum of squares:*

$$\Sigma x^2 = \Sigma X^2 - \frac{(\Sigma X)^2}{N} \tag{2.5}$$

where

$$\Sigma x^2 = \text{the sum of squared deviations}$$
$$\Sigma X^2 = \text{the sum of squared raw scores}$$
$$\Sigma X = \text{the sum of raw scores}$$
$$N = \text{the number of cases}$$

Without delving into algebraic equivalencies, it can easily be shown that this raw-score formula (2.5) yields a quantity identical with that obtained from summing the individually squared derivations. This can be done by computing Σx^2 for the data in Table 2.1 in which the sum of squares equaled 72. For the raw-score formula ΣX^2 is obtained by adding together the squared raw scores in column 4. The sum of these squares is 1,872. Thus,

$$\Sigma x^2 = 1,872 - \frac{(180)^2}{18}$$
$$= 1,872 - \frac{32,400}{18}$$
$$= 1,872 - 1,800$$
$$= 72$$

The 72 obtained by the raw-score formula for the sum of squares is, of course, the same as the 72 obtained by the original method. This raw-score formula is particularly valuable when one has access to a desk calculator which can yield both ΣX and ΣX^2 by a relatively simple operation.

The Variance

If, in the calculation of the standard deviation, one had not completed the computation, that is, if the square root of

$$\frac{\Sigma x^2}{N}$$

had not been taken, another widely used but less easily understood measure of dispersion known as the *variance* would have been available. The formula for the variance is

$$\sigma^2 = \frac{\Sigma x^2}{N} \tag{2.6}$$

where

$$\sigma^2 = \text{the variance of a set of scores}$$
$$\Sigma x^2 = \text{the sum of the squared deviations from the mean}$$
$$N = \text{the number of cases}$$

Since the variance is merely the square of the standard deviation (or, conversely, the standard deviation is the square root of the variance), the same logic applies to this measure of variability as to the standard deviation. Again, it is a kind of average which reflects the distance of the individual scores from the mean of the distribution. The larger the variance, the greater the variability;

that is, the greater the distance of scores from the mean. The smaller the variance, the less the variability. Since variances are squared standard deviations, they are, of course, much larger than standard deviations (unless the standard deviation is less than one). For the data in Table 2.1, the variance would be 4. If the standard deviation were 12, however, the variance would rise to 144.

Thus, as noted, the standard deviation is a *linear* measure of variability, given in terms of the original units of measurement. The variance, however, is given in terms of *squared* units of measurement; as a measure of variability, the variance can be likened to the *area* of a surface, say a rectangle. Just as the area of a rectangle can be divided into two or more sections, so the variance can be partitioned into sources, each associated with some characteristic accounting for variability in the data. This ability to analyse the variance forms the basis of more advanced statistical techniques, as shall be subsequently seen.

DESCRIPTIVE STATISTICS AND THE TEACHER

Of what value are concepts such as the mean and standard deviation to the practicing educator? Perhaps the reader can see how the researcher has need of such descriptive tools but can not see how a classroom teacher could use these concepts. Imagine that a teacher has used the same final examination for several semesters. Perhaps he discovers that while the mean performance of his most recent groups exceeds that of earlier classes, the standard deviation is becoming smaller. What does this indicate? We might graphically represent the phenomenon as in Figure 2.8.

Apparently, student achievement is improving, as evidenced by the increased mean performance. Perhaps this is attributable to constantly improved instructional techniques. (Since the same exam has been used it is also possible that increasingly large numbers of students may have had access to a ''missing'' copy of the test.) What about the reduced variance of the groups, as evidenced by the increasingly smaller standard deviations? It may be that the teacher's methods are actually developing more homogeneous student achievement. Another explanation might be that, with improved mean performance, the upper limit of the test is acting as an inhibiting factor and artificially reduced the possible range of high scores, hence the smaller standard deviations.

Measures such as the mean, median, and standard deviation, in addition to economically describing data, can often sharpen teachers' perceptions of educational phenomena so that they can reach more insightful decisions regarding their instructional tasks.

A major value of understanding such statistics is that it permits the educator to correctly interpret test manuals for many commercially distributed tests. Such manuals are literally laden with the descriptive statistics described here.

REVIEW

In this chapter graphical and statistical methods of describing data were discussed. Various techniques for graphically portraying sets of data were examined. The distribution curves frequently employed in educational statistics

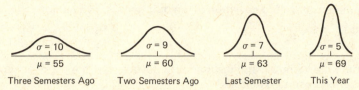

Figure 2.8 *Four hypothetical final-examination distributions.*

were seen to represent data through *area* wherein the area below the curve represented scores or some other type of numerical data.

Statistical descriptive techniques were then discussed. The mean, median, and mode were seen to be three commonly used measures of central tendency, with the mean or arithmetic average used most frequently.

Measures of variability often employed in education statistics are the range, standard deviation, and variance. The standard deviation is a sort of average of the distance of the raw scores from the mean of a distribution of scores. A large standard deviation reflects considerable dispersion or spread in a set of scores; a small standard deviation reflects a less variable set of scores.

EXERCISES

1. A class of 25 tenth-grade pupils obtained the following scores on a midterm examination. Determine the mean of the distribution.

49	42	40	38	34
48	41	39	37	30
48	40	39	36	29
47	40	38	36	28
42	40	38	35	26

2. What is the mean IQ of the following set of intelligence quotients?

120	118	114	110	100
119	115	112	106	94

3. Find the median for each of the following samples. Locate the median by counting and, if necessary, interpolating.

   (a) 106, 104, 100, 99, 96, 95
   (b) 14, 13, 11, 9, 8, 7, 6, 2, 2
   (c) 28, 27, 27, 26, 26, 25, 24, 22, 22, 20

4. Determine the mean for each of the following distributions.

   (a) 10, 10, 9, 9, 9, 8, 8, 7, 7, 7, 6, 6, 5, 4, 2, 2
   (b) 29, 28, 28, 27, 27, 27, 27, 21
   (c) 49, 48, 48, 48, 48, 47, 46, 43

5. Find the range and the mode of the following set of intelligence quotients.

   120, 119, 118, 118, 118, 117, 117, 115, 114, 111, 98, 92

6. Compute the standard deviation of ten quiz scores given below.

20	18	17	15	14
19	18	16	14	10

7. Compute the variance and the standard deviation of the set of achievement test scores presented below.

78	73	71	68	62
76	73	70	68	60
74	72	69	66	58
74	72	69	65	57

8. Two first-grade classes are given reading aptitude tests. Their scores are presented below.

Group A			Group B		
62	56	50	69	64	56
60	55	50	68	63	56
60	55	48	68	62	54
59	54	47	67	61	54
58	53	40	65	60	51
57	52	37	64	58	50
57	51	32	64	58	48

(a) Find the mean, median, standard deviation, and range for each group.
(b) Which group could you predict would perform better in first-grade reading assignments?
(c) Which group has the more variable or heterogeneous scores on the reading aptitude test?
(d) If other factors are equal, which group would you expect to perform most homogeneously in first-grade reading tasks?

9. Should the mean or the median be used as an index of central tendency for the set of scores listed below?

Score	Frequency
10 and above	4
9	6
8	14
7	10
6	7
5 and below	4

10. When someone refers to the "average income of the American man," is he referring to "mean man," "median man," or "modal man"?

11. A teacher describes the final examination performance of two of her history classes as follows: "Period two class had a mean of 76.4 and a standard

deviation of 6.3, while period four class had a mean of 69.8 and a standard deviation of 11.6.''

(a) Which class achieved a better overall performance in the final examination?
(b) Which class performed more homogeneously?
(c) If you had access to no additional information, in which class would you guess that the highest and lowest scores were made?

SELECTED READINGS

Cornell, Francis G., *The Essentials of Educational Statistics.* New York: Wiley, 1965, chaps. 4 and 5.

Edwards, Allen L., *Statistical Analysis.* New York: Holt, Rinehart & Winston, 1958, chaps. 3, 4, 5.

Guilford, J. P., *Fundamental Statistics in Psychology and Education.* New York: McGraw-Hill, 1965, chaps. 4 and 5.

Van Dalen, Deobold B., *Understanding Educational Research.* New York: McGraw-Hill, 1962, chap. 13.

3
The
Normal
Curve

Central to much of statistics is a theoretical distribution called the normal curve. The normal distribution curve is a symmetrical bell-shaped curve with most of the measurements located in the center and very few at the extremes. The curve presented in Figure 3.1 is an example of a normal distribution. Behavioral scientists have found that many of the traits as studied and measured by educators, such as intellectual ability, are distributed among people in an approximately normal fashion.

If, for instance, the intellectual abilities of a large number of individuals were graphically represented by a curve, most people would be located approximately near the mean. In addition, there would be a decreasing number of individuals whose scores would fall at the extremes of the curve, that is, those who possessed considerable or very little intelligence. In other words, the graphic portrayal of this particular attribute would look much like the curve in Figure 3.1. It should be added that while many variables in education are believed to be normally distributed, relatively large samples are often required in order to obtain a curve which accurately reflects this normality.

The normal distribution curve has several unique properties which make it valuable to the statistician. For example, the mean, median, and mode are identical in a normal curve, as an examination of Figure 3.1 will confirm. The normal curve is also extremely useful with respect to the question of *probability*, which will be discussed later. One of the most interesting features of the normal curve is that when its baseline is considered *in terms of standard deviation units*, certain proportions of the distribution can be isolated by ordinates (vertical lines) erected at the baseline.

The phrase "in terms of standard deviation units" is the key to understanding an extremely important aspect of the use of the normal curve. As seen earlier, the baseline of a distribution of scores represents the scale on which the measurements in the distribution have been taken, for example, IQ scores, cor-

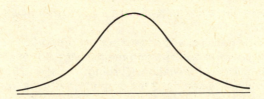

Figure 3.1 A normal distribution curve.

rect answers on a test, age, and so forth. Each distribution of such measurements has a mean and a standard deviation. The standard deviation, usually thought of as an index of variability, can also be employed as a *unit of measurement* which can be used along the baseline scale. This standard deviation unit is employed in much the same way that a foot ruler is used to measure distances. If the standard deviation of a distribution is 6.25, for example, the standard deviation "foot ruler" for that set of scores is 6.25. When such standard deviation units of measurement are applied to a normal curve, it is possible to identify the size of certain areas of the distribution as shown in Figure 3.2.

By erecting ordinates at the mean and +1 standard deviation in a normal distribution, one isolates 34.13 percent of the area in the curve. If, in a normally distributed set of IQ scores, for example, the mean were 100 and the standard deviation 16, 34.13 percent of the measurements would fall between IQ scores of 100 and 116.

Similarly, between the mean and minus one standard deviation unit, 34.13 percent of the scores are found in a normal distribution. In the IQ example ($\mu = 100$; $\sigma = 16$), 34.13 percent of the measurements would also fall between IQ scores of 84 and 100. Therefore, as noted in Figure 3.2, over two-thirds or 68.26 percent of a normal curve is contained within an area plus and minus one standard deviation from the mean. Since many variables with which the educator deals are distributed in an *approximately* normal fashion, the normal curve is of considerable value in describing data, particularly in terms of standard deviation units.

Table C in the Appendix offers some useful quantities associated with the normal curve, that is, the proportions of the normal curve bounded by ordinates erected at points along the baseline. These points include both whole and

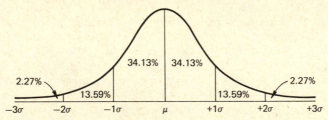

Figure 3.2 *Percentages of the normal distribution enclosed by ordinates erected at standard deviation points.*

fractional standard deviation units. A practical illustration will assist the reader in the use of Table C.

Later, it will be necessary to ascertain what proportion of the normal curve is found between various points along the baseline, for example, between the mean and +1.15 standard deviation. Turning to page 375, 1.15 in column 1 should first be located. In column 2 the proportion of area from the mean to the standard deviation point is found. In this case 0.3749 of the total area under the distribution curve is contained between the mean and +1.15 standard deviation units.

In column 3 the area in the larger portion of the total distribution when an ordinate has been erected at +1.15σ is cited. This larger portion of area, of course is obtained by adding 50 percent to our 37.49 percent for a total of 87.49 percent. In column 4 the area in the smaller portion of the distribution is given. In this instance 12.51 percent is found in the small area of the curve above +1.15σ. Column 5 gives the proportional height of the ordinate (vertical line) at various points along the baseline. The height of this ordinate is useful in the calculations of a few statistical techniques which will be described later.

NONNORMAL DISTRIBUTIONS

Many sets of data which will be encountered in educational situations are not normally distributed, nor even symmetrically distributed. Certain descriptive names have been given to such distributions. For example, a *skewed* distribution is one that has a disproportionately large number of scores at one end of the distribution, so that a sort of "tail" is formed at the other end of the distribution.

A distribution in which the tail extends toward the left or lower scores of the distribution is called a *negatively skewed distribution*. In Figure 3.3 an example is presented of a negatively skewed distribution, including the relative positions of the mean and median. Such a distribution might result from the administration of a very simple test to a class, where most pupils score well and only those few who did not pay any attention scored poorly.

A *positively skewed* distribution is one in which the tail extends toward the right or higher scores in the distribution. In Figure 3.4 an example of a positively skewed distribution is presented, including the relative position of the mean and median. A positively skewed curve might result if an extremely difficult test were given to a class, so that very few students attained high scores and most of the class received low scores.

From the illustrations of skewed curves it can be noted that the type of skew, positive or negative, depends upon the direction of the *tail* of the curve. Those skewed curves in which the tail goes toward the right, or positive direction, are positively skewed; those with tails in the left, or negative direction, are negatively skewed. Note that in relationship to the median, the mean is closer to the tail or direction of the "skew" in the distribution.

Comparing the normal distribution with such skewed distributions, the reader can see that the *area* notions associated with the use of the normal curve and standard deviation units do not apply if a distribution is markedly skewed

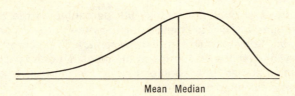

Mean Median

Figure 3.3 *A negatively skewed distribution showing relative positions of mean and median.*

or, in fact, if the distribution departs greatly from normality in any fashion. Only when a curve is *perfectly* normal can we assert that *precisely* 34.13 percent of the distribution falls between the mean and $+1.0\sigma$. *Approximately* normal distributions make possible the designation of *approximate* proportions of the distribution in terms of standard deviation units. If one wishes to employ normal curve notions with nonnormal distributions, the data must be treated in such a fashion as to artificially "normalize" the scores. This technique will be discussed later in the chapter.

PERCENTILES

Educators are not only interested in describing entire groups of scores, but also in describing the scores of particular group members in relation to the other scores in the group. For example, a teacher might wish to describe one student's score in relationship to scores of his classmates on the same exam. If one merely asserts that a student obtained a score of 76 on an achievement examination, relatively little information has been given; for a raw score of 76, without some type of reference base, could be good or bad, high or low.

One helpful method of describing individual scores is to employ *percentiles* or, as they are sometimes called, *centiles*. A percentile indicates a particular measurement's position in a group in terms of the percentage of measurements falling *below* it. For example, a student who scored at the 25th percentile on a nationally standardized test would have exceeded the performance of 25 percent of the students included in the national standardization group. Someone scoring at the 95th percentile would have exceeded the scores of 95 percent of the standardization group, or conversely, would have scored below only five percent of the group. The 50th percentile, then, is equivalent to the median since it divides the group into two equal segments. Sometimes the 25th percentile is

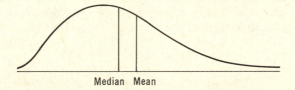

Median Mean

Figure 3.4 *A positively skewed distribution showing relative positions of mean and median.*

referred to as the *first quartile* and the 75th percentile as the *third quartile*. Remember that quartiles, like the median, are *points* — not areas or proportions of the distribution. Some people erroneously remark, "He scored *in* the fourth quartile." As was seen in the discussion of the median, points such as quartiles need not be actual scores, only positions along the baseline of a distribution which divide it into specified proportions.

It is important to note that percentiles may vary depending upon the reference group being used. Many times, for example, local school norms have been developed over a period of years for examinations used in other parts of the country. These norms typically do not coincide with national norm figures so that a raw score of 111 on an intelligence test might be equivalent to a percentile of 65 of local norms but, according to national normative figures, equals a percentile of only 57. Therefore, the comparison group used should always be specified when employing percentiles.

One difficulty in using percentiles as a technique for describing relative position can be illustrated in distributions that are fairly normal. A great many scores are centered near the mean of the group, so that a difference between the 40th and 60th percentiles, for example, may take up only a few points along the baseline. The same *distance* in score points along the baseline, if it occurs toward the extremes of the distribution, might involve only a trivial proportion of the cases in the group. The *distance* along the baseline between the 50th and 55th percentiles, for example, is much smaller than the distance between the 90th and 95th percentiles. In other words, one must be alert to the fact that percentiles, based as they are upon a cumulative percentage scheme, usually do not yield comparable distances in terms of score points on our baseline measurement scale.

Percentiles are, however, easily communicated measures of an individual's position in a group. Teachers will find that they often can use percentiles in interpreting student performances on standardized tests.

STANDARD SCORES

Another method for expressing relative positions of scores uses a score's distance from the mean *in terms of standard deviation units.* This descriptive technique involves measures known as *standard scores.*

Though percentiles are frequently used in describing pupils' test performances, standard scores are used more often in research work. Standard scores yield a very useful method of describing a raw score's position in a distribution expressing the score's *distance above or below the mean.* The first kind of standard score to be described is usually referred to as *z*, defined by the formula:

$$z = \frac{X - \mu}{\sigma} \qquad (3.1)$$

By examining Formula 3.1 it may be noted that in order to determine the standard score for an individual measurement, one must first calculate the mean

Table 3.1

A Comparison of Two Student's X Scores and z Scores on Four Quizzes

Quiz	μ	σ	Joan's X	Mary's X	Joan's z	Mary's z
1	130	22	152	141	1.00	0.50
2	75	10	70	60	−0.50	−1.50
3	38	7	59	38	3.00	0
4	200	60	140	320	−1.00	2.00
Mean			105.25	139.75	2.50	1.00

and the standard deviation of the group. Then, by subtracting the group mean from the raw score and dividing the difference by the standard deviation, z is obtained. For example, assume that a pupil had obtained a score of 45 on a test in which the mean was 38 and the standard deviation was 3.0. Then z would be calculated as follows:

$$z = \frac{45 - 38}{3.0} = 2.33$$

What does this z tell us? It reveals that the pupil obtained a raw score that was 2.33 *standard deviation units* (along the baseline) above the mean of the group.

Consider another example. Suppose a student's weight is 110 pounds when the national mean weight for his age group is 125 pounds and the standard deviation is 10 pounds. This student's standard score for weight would be calculated as follows:

$$z = \frac{110 - 125}{10} = -1.5$$

One can tell from a z of −1.5 that the underweight student is one and one-half *standard deviation units* below (note the minus sign) the mean weight for his age group.

If all raw scores of any distribution were transformed into z scores, one would find a resulting distribution of z scores with a mean of zero and a standard deviation of one.

Such z scores can be used to *average* students' scores on different tests since they have a common mean and standard deviation. This is done in order to obtain a more representative estimate of a student's total relative position than we could gain merely by summing raw score points. The advantage of standard scores is illustrated in Table 3.1, where two girls' scores on four quizzes have been compared in terms of raw scores and standard scores.

Whereas Mary has obtained more total points from the four tests, Joan has the higher z-score total. This disparity results from the greater contribution of points on examination number 4 to Mary's total score. Joan, in the other three tests, exceeds Mary's scores by marked differences in terms of standard deviation units, that is, in terms of the quality of their respective performances on three individual tests. Many educators have found that using average standard score estimates of performance yields a more representative picture of student attainment than is available by using total points.

It is also possible when adding together several examination performances to ascribe varying degrees of importance to different examinations by simply multiplying (weighting) the standard score for a given exam by two, three, and so forth.

COMPARISON OF PERCENTILES AND STANDARD SCORES

Although percentiles and z scores describe the position of a score in a distribution, they convey very different kinds of information. For example, it is easy to construct two distributions where a given score is at the same percentile in both distributions but has different z scores in each distribution. Consider the distributions 0, 10, 11 with a mean of 7, and 9, 10, 14 with a mean of 13. In both distributions the score 10 is the median or the 50th percentile. But in the first distribution 10 is above the mean and thus has a positive z score; in the second distribution, 10 is below the mean and thus has a negative z score. Neither measure of location, then, tells the whole story. Only when we know the mathematical nature of the distribution curve, can we infer a percentile location from a z-score location (or vice versa). For example, if the distribution curve is normal, then Table C tells us the exact relationship between percentiles and standard scores.

STANDARD SCORES, PERCENTILES, AND THE NORMAL DISTRIBUTION

As explained, only when the distribution of scores is completely defined can we determine the relationship between z scores and percentiles. Refer to Figure 3.2. Here we see that there is a "one-to-one" correspondence between the distance of a score from the mean (in standard deviation units) and the percentage of area under the normal curve between the mean and the score. The z score is, in fact, the distance away from the mean in standard deviation units. Thus, knowing a z score is knowing how many standard deviations the score is from the mean. *If the scores are normally distributed* and the z score for some raw score X is 1.5, then score X is 1.5 standard deviations away from the mean and there is approximately 43 percent of the area between it and the mean. Percentage of area under a distribution curve is directly interpretable as a percentage of scores. Thus, we can say that 43 percent of all scores in the distribution occur between the mean and the X score with a z score of 1.5.

Furthermore, since 50 percent of the scores fall below the mean in a normal distribution, the sum of 50 percent and 43 percent or 93 percent of all the scores fall below the X score with a z score of 1.5. That is, the raw score with a z score of 1.5 is at the 93rd percentile or has a *percentile rank* of 93. Thus, *knowing that the original raw score distribution was normal*, we are able to find the percentile rank for any score X by computing its z score and using Table C.

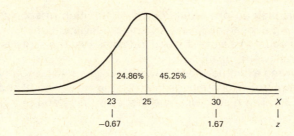

Figure 3.5 *Typical diagram for relating percentages of area under the normal curve to raw scores and corresponding z scores.*

As an example to further illustrate these points, consider a normal distribution with a mean of 25 and a standard deviation of 3. What is the percentile rank of a raw score of 30? First, the z score corresponding to $X = 30$ is computed using Formula 3.1; that is, $z = (30 - 25)/3 = 1.67$. Entering $z = 1.67$ into Table C we find that approximately 45 percent of the area lies between a score of 30 and the mean and thus the score of 30 has a percentile rank of $50 + 45$ or 95. If $X = 23$, then $z = -0.67$ and the approximate proportion of area between 23 and the mean would be 0.25 Thus the raw score of 23 would be at the 50 minus 25 or 25th percentile. In working problems of this nature, you will find it extremely advantageous to draw a simple diagram of a normal curve, keeping track of the particular proportion of area at each stage of the computations. For example, Figure 3.5 illustrates the diagram for the preceding problems.

PROBABILITY AND THE NORMAL CURVE

Although the concept of probability will be treated more extensively in the following chapter, it is sufficient to state here that the proportion of area under a distribution curve is also directly interpretable as a *probability*. For example, referring to the previous problem, we could ask "What is the *probability* of obtaining a score of 30 or less?" In fact, this question has already been answered since the probability is equal to the proportion of area below the score of 30. Thus, the probability of obtaining a score of 30 or less is 0.95. Likewise, the probability of obtaining a score of 23 or less is 0.25. The probability of obtaining a score of 23 *or more* is $0.25 + 0.50$ or 0.75. The probability of obtaining a score *between* 25 and 30 is 0.45.

TRANSFORMED STANDARD SCORES

Because of the manner of computation, z standard scores result in decimals and negative numbers, for example, $z = 2.14$, $z = -1.38$, and so forth. To avoid decimals and negatives a modified standard score has been developed which is used to alter the obtained values. These so-called *transformed standard scores* are referred to as Z scores and are obtained by multiplying z by 10 and adding 50.

$$Z = 10z + 50 = \frac{10(X - \mu)}{\sigma} + 50 \qquad (3.2)$$

Using this method one would find a distribution of scores expressed in terms of Z having a mean of 50 and a standard deviation of 10. A Z score of 40, for example, is equal to a z of -1.0 and indicates that the score is one standard deviation unit below the mean.

The following example shows how a Z score would be computed for a raw score of 56 drawn from a distribution in which the mean was 48 and the standard deviation was 6.0. The reader will note that as a first step the z value of 1.33 is calculated.

$$Z = \frac{10(56 - 48)}{6} + 50$$

$$= 10(1.33) + 50$$

$$= 63.3$$

Whereas large numbers of subjects in a distribution of scores might result in a z distribution ranging approximately six standard deviation units from -3.00 to $+3.00$, the Z score distribution for the same set of scores would range from 20 to 80.

It should be added that the transformed standard Z is sometimes referred to as T in other textbooks. However, T scores are given a considerably different kind of meaning in this volume.

Certain widely used tests employ different sorts of transformation schemes to eliminate decimals and negative numbers. The *College Entrance Examination Board* (CEEB) converts small z scores so that a mean of 500 and a standard deviation of 100 result. To experienced counselors and testers a college board exam score of 650 will be interpreted as "one and a half standard deviation units (150 points) above the mean (500 points) on the C.E.E.B. norms." Similarly, scores on the *Army General Classification Test* (AGCT) are converted to yield a standard score mean of 100 and standard deviation of 20.

NORMALIZED STANDARD SCORES

Sometimes a researcher is faced with a set of data which are not normally distributed but which he would like to artificially normalize. He can do this by transforming all of the scores to quantities called normalized standard scores (T).

Although it takes a certain amount of calculation effort to compute them, normalized standard scores are nothing more than a score (comparable in appearance to a Z score) that would be equivalent to the raw score, *if the distribution had been normal.* To calculate normalized standard scores, the raw scores are first considered as percentiles so as to determine which percentile the raw score is equivalent to. And second, it is determined what Z score would be equivalent to this percentile *in a perfectly normal distribution.*

An example of how the process works should clarify this notion. Suppose one of the higher scores in a distribution is taken and the proportion of scores actually falling below it is determined to be 0.89. One would then turn to the table of the normal curve and select the z score which represents the 89th percentile. In Table C this is found on page 375 when the area in the larger portion is 0.8907. Note that the z score corresponding to the percentage is 1.23. This z of 1.23 is then transformed to a T score by the same process used in deriving Z scores, that is, multiplying by 10 and adding 50. This process yields a T score of 62.3.

For an additional example, suppose a student scores at the 16th percentile in a group. What is his T score? By using Table C it can be seen that, when 16 percent is in the smaller part of the distribution, the z value is −1.0. Transforming this z (multiplying by 10 and adding 50), a T score of 40 is obtained.

If one were to follow the procedure for all the scores in a distribution, the scores would have been artificially regrouped into a normal shape—*on the basis of their centile equivalence to Z scores in a normal distribution.*

As in the case of Z scores, a T score distribution has a mean of 50 and a standard deviation of 10. While changing raw scores into z and Z scores does not alter the shape of the original distribution, the process for converting raw scores into T scores does, of course, distort the shape of the original distribution.

REVIEW

In this chapter several properties of the normal curve were examined, principally the proportions of the curve bounded by ordinates erected at given points along its baseline. It was noted, for example, that approximately two-thirds of a normal distribution is contained within an area plus and minus the standard deviation unit from the mean. The use of Table C in the Appendix was discussed.

Nonnormal distributions such as positively and negatively skewed curves were described, with the admonition that the foregoing notions about normal curve distribution proportions do not apply to such nonnormal distributions.

Percentiles and standard scores provide techniques for describing an individual's relative position in a group. While percentiles are based exclusively on the percentage of scores falling below a given score, standard scores are based on an individual score's distance above or below the mean in terms of standard deviation units. The relationship between z scores and percentile ranks in the normal distribution was considered in detail. The interpretation of the proportion of area under a curve as a probability statement was briefly discussed. A distribution of z standard scores has a mean of zero and a standard deviation of 1.0, whereas a distribution of Z scores has a mean of 50 and a standard deviation of 10. Normalized standard scores, or T scores, can be used to artificially transform a nonnormal set of data into a normalized distribution.

EXERCISES

1. If scores on a final examination are distributed in an approximately normal fashion, what percentage of classmates scored below a student whose examination score was one standard deviation below the mean?

2. If a distribution of scores departs from normality in such a way that there are a great many low scores and a few extremely high scores, how could we describe the distribution?

3. Assuming that a set of scores is distributed in the shape of a normal curve, match the following percentiles and z scores.

Percentiles	z scores (to be matched)
84th	−1.0
50th	2.0
16th	−2.0
98th	0.0
2nd	1.0

4. In a distribution with a mean of 80 and a standard deviation of 3.5, find the z scores for the following raw scores:

   (a) 87.0   (b) 76.5   (c) 83.5   (d) 73.0

5. In a distribution with a mean of 71.8 and a standard deviation of 6.4, find the z scores for the following raw scores:

   (a) 62.9   (c) 64.9   (e) 79.0
   (b) 71.9   (d) 78.6   (f) 74.1

6. Scores on the first exam in an educational statistics course were normally distributed with a mean of 12 and a variance of 4. The professor decides to grade "on a curve" such that the following z score intervals get the following grades:

Above 1.5	A
0.5 to 1.5	B
−0.5 to 0.5	C
−1.5 to −0.5	D
Below −1.5	F

   (a) Of the 30 students in the class, how many will receive each of the 5 letter grades?
   (b) What are the 4 test score cutoff points for the grading system?

7. For each of the raw scores in exercise 5, compute the Z scores.

8. If scores are distributed normally in a sample, what will the approximate percentiles be for the following Z scores?

   (a) 50   (b) 60   (c) 73   (d) 40

9. If a researcher wishes to match pairs of high-school sophomores according to intelligence, but finds that his potential subjects have one of three different types of intelligence scores, each with a different mean and standard deviation, what could he do in order to match the students?

10. If a distribution of scores is not approximately normal, what can we say regarding the percentage of scores exceeded by a Z score of 60?

11. Using the table of the normal curve, convert the following *T* scores into percentiles.

(a) 54.4   (b) 58.4   (c) 68.8   (d) 39.2

12. Convert the following raw scores (with the percentiles for each already indicated) into *T* scores.

(a) 62.3 (70th percentile)   (c) 41.4 (31st percentile)
(b) 74.0 (97th percentile)   (d) 52.2 (50th percentile)

SELECTED READINGS

Blalock, Hubert M., Jr., *Social Statistics*. New York: McGraw-Hill, 1960, chap. 7.

Blommers, Paul, and E. F. Lindquist, *Elementary Statistical Methods*. Boston: Houghton Mifflin, 1960, chap. 8.

Edwards, Allen L., *Statistical Methods for the Behavioral Sciences*. New York: Holt, Rinehart & Winston, 1957, chap. 12.

Guilford, J. P., *Fundamental Statistics in Psychology and Education*. New York: McGraw-Hill, 1965, chap. 7.

Walker, Helen M., and Joseph Lev, *Elementary Statistical Methods*. New York: Holt, Rinehart & Winston, 1958, chap. 12.

4

Inferential Statistics: Hypothesis Testing and Estimation

In addition to the descriptive statistical methods discussed in the last chapter, there are a number of techniques which are usually designated as *inferential statistics.* When an individual uses descriptive statistics, he talks about the data he has; but with inferential statistics, he talks about data that he does not have. Inferential techniques are customarily more complex than descriptive methods and, in most instances, make use of descriptive statistics such as the mean, median, and standard deviation. An educational research worker ordinarily has more occasion to use inferential statistical methods than a typical classroom teacher, but since educators will be using the results of such research investigations, they should be familiar with the more basic inferential procedures which will be discussed here.

Briefly, inferential techniques allow us to draw from sample data inferences which have wider generalizability. But this use should be considered in light of the purpose of educational research itself. The goal of educational research is to develop a science of behavior for educational situations. This science of behavior should consist of systematically organized statements of verified relationships between educational variables. When the nature of relationships between educational variables is discovered, meaningful predictions regarding educational phenomena can be made—indeed, we can truly become educational scientists.

How many times, for example, has a teacher faced the problem of which instructional technique will work best with a given group of students? Suppose the teacher must choose between Method *X* and Method *Y* for his class of below-average readers. He may have to make a guess as to which is superior and hope for the best. However, he discovers that several researchers have shown, each in relatively small experiments, that Method *Y* is clearly superior with slow readers. The teacher now can base his decision on the *inference* that the discoveries of the earlier researchers will also apply to his class. Essentially, then, inferential statistics permit one to determine the degree of confidence in the generality of findings from particular studies.

At the same time, however, we must not deemphasize the usefulness of descriptive statistics and their place in educational research. It is perfectly legitimate and often a necessary first step in theory building to investigate phenomena on a descriptive basis. Unfortunately, a certain aura of scientific authenticity has been developed around the *"significant* difference" resulting in many applications of inferential procedures where they are not warranted by the nature of the data. Strictly speaking, inferential procedures are only valid where (1) there is a target population to which the inferences can be made and (2) appropriate random sampling and/or assignment procedures have been employed. Many times the researcher has available only a "handy" sample—that is, a nonrandom sample from some target population which is "like" the population in terms of certain important variables. In this case, the researcher can employ inferential techniques so long as it is clear that any inferences made are "extra-statistical" in nature—that is, inferences which are not statistically valid in a strict sense, but which can serve for heuristically useful purposes.

EDUCATIONAL VARIABLES

Before turning to several problems encountered when searching for relationships between educational variables, some attention should be given to the term *variable.* Since the quest for knowledge regarding relationships between variables is at the very heart of educational research, educators should have a complete understanding of the meaning of this key term. Properly speaking, *a variable can be defined as an attribute in which individuals differ among themselves.* For example, individuals such as people, animals, or objects, may possess such attributes as weight, size, age, color, and so forth. These attributes or characteristics, if they are such that the individuals possess them differently, are termed variables. Variables may be attributes which are quite concrete, such as height, amount of hair, or money. Variables may also be extremely nebulous attributes such as "social sensitivity" or amount of "tact."

A distinction should also be drawn between variables which are *quantitative* and those which are *qualitative.* A quantitative variable denotes differences in amount, degree, or frequency. Examples of a quantitative variable would be the numbers of pupils in a school, scores on an examination, and frequency of absences. Quantitative variables such as these can be ordered as a consequence of the successively larger numerical designations given to individuals who possess greater quantities, or frequencies of the attribute. For example, with the quantitative variable "number of students entering college" there is a natural ordering of categories commencing with 0, 1, 2, 3, 4, and so forth. Order is essentially present when the variable is quantitative in nature.

On the other hand, *qualitative* variables are those for which individuals differ in kind or sort and, therefore, these variables possess no inherent ordering system such as with quantitative variables. For example, consider "major in college" which is a qualitative variable including categories such as "history,"

"English," or "mathematics." These categories are not intrinsically ordered. In fact, any order imposed on such variables is strictly arbitrary. Other examples of qualitative variables are make of automobile, nationality, religion, and type of books read. The degree of intrinsic order which is present in particular variables has, in part, led to a classification of measuring scales according to their mathematical properties. Different kinds of scales commonly used in educational research will be described in a later chapter.

It should be noted that an attribute which is a variable for one group of individuals may be an invariable or *constant* property for another. To illustrate, some individuals are living (plants, animals), whereas other individuals (minerals) are not. For *all* such individuals the attribute of life is a variable. However, since all human beings possess the attribute of life, this property is a constant rather than a variable for them. Similarly, intelligence is considered a variable for individuals considered as a whole, but if one were to measure intelligence by a particular test, then for those individuals who obtain a score of 111, intelligence should be considered a constant, not a variable.

The reader must remember that such elusive attributes as intelligence or achievement are often assessed with different measuring instruments or examinations. These measures are used as an index of the sought-for variable. Frequently the researcher *operationally defines* the variable as performance on a particular measure. For example, intelligence may be operationally defined as the pupil's score on Test X.

Further consideration of the nature of variables and how they can be treated is beyond the scope of this text, but the interested reader will find this intriguing topic treated extensively in introductory and advanced measurement books.

POPULATIONS AND SAMPLES

Unfortunately, in his attempts to establish the precise nature of the relationship between educational variables, the educator is usually forced to conduct his research with relatively small samples of an educational population. For example, he may wish to study the relationship between students' secondary school programs and their subsequent achievement in college. To investigate this relationship he could select a *sample* of college students and then collect data regarding their college performance and certain aspects of their secondary education program. He is not interested only in this sample of students, however. The researcher wishes to discover the nature of relationship between variables so that the relationship may be generalized to an entire *population* or *universe* from which his sample was drawn.

Educational researchers write a great deal about samples and populations. Since it has just been asserted that the purpose of inferential statistics is to permit one to draw better inferences regarding population phenomena, perhaps the kinds of samples which the researcher in education frequently studies should be discussed. It is not difficult to see how a group of kindergarten children, perhaps several thousand, drawn from various classes throughout the

United States would constitute a sample of the population of U.S. kindergarten pupils. But, imagine another situation in which a totally new method of teaching physics is being employed with a group of 200 senior high-school physics students. What population does this sample of 200 pupils represent? Although less obvious than the preceding example, the sample of physics students represents a population of similar physics students *who would be taught by the new instructional method*, even though no such group exists at the moment. Thus, samples may be studied with a view to generalizing notions about variable relationships in populations that may not even be extant at the time. More commonly, the educational researcher works with small samples of subjects, for example, school children who have been exposed to differential treatment conditions such as modified instructional techniques.

Actually, it is possible to consider any sample as representing an infinity of populations. For instance, a sample of 100 high-school juniors in a large city might be used to represent all similar pupils in the city, the county, the state, the nation, or the world. With some kinds of data, it is hazardous to draw inferences about populations which are considerably removed from the sample. Although one might confidently generalize about the latency of eye blink reactions from a sample of students in Indiana to similar students throughout the nation, it would be unwise to consider the attitudes of Indiana parents toward high-school basketball as representative of parents in other parts of the country.

Behavioral scientists encounter similar problems when they attempt to generalize to human behavior from the behavior of animals in the laboratory. The degree to which inferences drawn from sample data hold true is in large measure a function of the equivalence between the sample and the particular population to which the inference is to be applied.

One technical definition of the word *statistic* is "a measure based on a sample." For example, a standard deviation computed from sample data is called a statistic. Measures based on populations, rather than samples, are called *parameters.* If one could determine, for example, the standard deviation of IQ scores for all sixth-grade pupils in the world, that standard deviation would be called a parameter. Another way of thinking of inferential statistics, then, is to think of these techniques as ways of making *estimates* based on sample statistics about the nature of the parameters or "real values" in populations.

Greek letters are usually used to represent parameters whereas Roman letters are usually used to represent statistics. Table 4.1 presents the several parameters discussed in the previous chapter and the corresponding sample statistics used to estimate these parameters. The previous chapter treated the data as constituting a "population" since inferences were not being made and the data were being summarized for descriptive purposes only.

Of course, one rarely has access to parameters in educational situations, for it is far too difficult to obtain data from an entire population. Furthermore, in most cases it would be extremely wasteful of time and energy to obtain parameters directly, particularly when with large samples the parameters can be estimated quite accurately.

Table 4.1

Differences in Symbols Used with Sample and Population Data Measures

Sample Statistic Symbol	Measure	Population Parameter Symbol
$\overline{X}$	Mean	μ
s	Standard deviation	σ
s^2	Variance	σ^2

REPRESENTATIVENESS OF THE SAMPLE

To draw legitimate inferences about populations from samples, then, clearly, one must be certain that the sample really represents the population. If a sample is drawn from a population in a *biased* fashion so that the sample is not typical of the population, it would be impossible to generalize from the sample. For instance, if a study were to be conducted regarding new teaching materials in which only very bright children were involved, one could say little about the effectiveness of the teaching materials with youngsters of lesser ability. One method of avoiding biased selection is to *randomly* assign members of the population to the sample. Again, inferential statistics procedures theoretically *demand* that the samples be constituted by a random sampling method for valid inferences to be drawn. Although random sampling is required in theory, the researcher can probably draw meaningful inferences from sample data which have not been randomly drawn. To do this, however, he should try to take precautions so that no undue factors have biased his sample selection.

The Table of Random Numbers

A simple but time-consuming method of drawing a sample randomly is to assign numbers to the entire population, then enter the numbers on discs and place all discs in a container, to be drawn out one at a time. When the desired proportion of discs has been drawn from the container, the subjects whose numbers coincide with these discs can be considered a randomly selected sample.

A more efficient method of randomly sampling from a population is to employ a table of random numbers, such as Table B in the Appendix. Tables of random numbers consist of rows and columns of numbers arranged at random so that they can be entered at any point and used by reading in any direction, right or left, up or down. To illustrate the use of Table B, imagine that we wished to select five students at random from a group of ten students. First, we must assign numbers to the ten subjects as follows: 01, 02, 03, 04, 05, 06, 07, 08, 09, 10. The necessity of inserting the zero before all of the single digit numbers arises from the fact that 10 is a two-digit number and the number of digits for all subjects must be the same when using a random numbers table. Now turn to page 368 (any point in the table would be acceptable), where we shall arbitrarily enter the table in the upper right-hand corner and read *left* by using the upper

---

Table 4.2

Excerpt from a Table of Random Numbers

9 5 0 4 5	9 5 9 4 7
0 7 3 4 8	2 3 3 2 8
. . . .	. . . .

---

two rows, as seen in Table 4.2.

The first two-digit number encountered is 78, then 42, then 93, 53, 92, 58, 44, and finally 03. Since the first seven two-digit numbers were all larger than the numbers of the ten subjects, they were simply skipped over. However, 03 is a number for one of the subjects, so this is the first number of the sample of five. Continue reading to the left and it will be seen that no more of the ten numbers are found in the upper two rows all the way to the left side of the table. One might drop down two rows and read now to the right so that the first number is 76 and the second is 10, which should also be drawn for the sample. In a similar fashion proceed until five of the ten numbers have been selected. If the same numbers are encountered twice before five subjects have been selected, simply pass over those numbers which have already been selected.

Other Sampling Methods

In addition to random sampling methods, there are other ways of securing a representative sample of the population. If the population is composed of certain subgroups which may respond differently to the experimental variables, the researcher can better represent the population by drawing a *stratified* sample which represents such subgroups proportionately. For instance, if "school neighborhood" is related to performance on a personality test, the research worker would want to be sure to include subjects from different neighborhoods in the same proportions that exist in the total population. Or, again, if sex is a relevant variable in an educational experiment, then a proportionate number of boys and girls should be included in the sample matching the proportion of boys and girls in the population under consideration.

Having determined the proportions of subgroups to be represented in the sample, the researcher then may randomly draw each subgroup sample which makes the total sample a *stratified random sample*. Stratified random samples are particularly good representatives of the population. Other, more complicated, sampling techniques are described in advanced texts dealing with problems of research design.

HYPOTHESIS TESTING

Once he has satisfied himself as to the representativeness of his sample, the researcher is then in a position to test a particular *hypothesis* concerning the relationship between variables. Hypotheses are suppositions, presumed to be true for the sake of subsequent testing. In educational research, hypotheses concern the existence of relationships between variables.

When research workers test hypotheses regarding such relationships, they can discover valuable information, even if they fail to establish any relationship between certain variables. For example, suppose a researcher hypothesized that there was a relationship between student "overachievement" and degree of personal anxiety. If, in testing the hypothesis, he discovered that he cannot accept the hypothesis that there is such a relationship—he simultaneously cannot reject the notion that these two variables are *not* related. An educational science of behavior must also encompass notions regarding those variables which are *unrelated;* hence, the tested hypothesis yields important information regardless of the outcome of the test.

So far the treatment of hypothesis testing may have suggested that one only tests for relationships, never differences. Yet most readers can probably think of situations in which the researcher wants to find out if the performance of two groups is *different*, not related. Perhaps this apparent contradiction can be clarified by pointing out that *when different groups are used in research situations*, *these groups usually represent a research variable.* When a researcher tests for group differences on a particular measure, he is in reality assessing the nature of the *relationship* between (*a*) the variable represented by the measure and (*b*) the variable represented by the groups.

To illustrate, suppose a researcher tests the hypothesis that boys will outperform girls on certain tests of geometrical aptitude. He might divide his sample into a group of boys and a group of girls, administer a geometry aptitude test, and see if the two groups perform differently on the test. Now, although it may appear that he is looking for a difference between the groups, deeper consideration will reveal that the researcher is really attempting to see if there is a *relationship* between the *variable* of sex, on the one hand, and the variable of geometry aptitude, on the other. Ultimately, almost all hypotheses in educational research are suppositions about relationships between variables.

Even though this is true, it is often helpful to think of inferential statistical techniques in terms of whether they test for differences, as in testing differences between means of two or more groups, or whether they test for the existence of relationships (as in correlation, which will be treated in the next chapter). Since a number of different types of inferential statistics are described in the pages to follow, the reader may find it valuable to view each in light of the question, "Is it a *difference-testing* technique or a *relationship-testing* technique?"

STATISTICAL SIGNIFICANCE

Investigations which test well-conceived hypotheses can yield evidence of considerable importance to educational decision-makers. Therefore, it is crucial to accept as tenable those hypotheses that are true and to reject those that are false. But how does the researcher really decide which hypotheses to accept and which to reject? Is the decision so obvious that anyone could merely "inspect" the data and reach a proper conclusion? Answers to these questions penetrate to the very core of inferential statistics.

Probability

Central in the rationale underlying inferential statistics is the notion of probability. Since the researcher wishes to generalize from sample phenomena to population phenomena, he would like to be fairly sure that what is observed in the sample is not a function of mere chance alone. It is possible to determine statistically with considerable precision if a sample phenomenon is attributable to chance. This can be illustrated by probability statements associated with sets of coin tosses. As we know, the chance of a coin landing heads-up when tossed is one out of two. However, the likelihood that a tossed coin will come up heads two times in a row is only one out of four. Similarly, the chance of obtaining three heads out of three coin tosses is only one out of eight. The probability of getting ten heads out of ten coin tosses is only one in 1,024. All of these probabilities can be determined from a distribution of statistical events used in a fashion similar to the way in which the normal curve can be used. In the case of coin tosses, we use a statistical probability distribution based on two events (heads or tails). By using such curves we can determine what the probability is that an observed set of events or a more extreme set of such events can be attributed to chance alone.

In a coin tossing example, one might visualize a situation in which two people were betting for cups of coffee, with the loser buying the beverage. Imagine that one of the individuals does all the coin flipping. Perhaps the other decides to call tails every time, figuring to win approximately half of the wagers. If the coin turned up heads ten times in a row, the person who called tails would obviously have to buy more than his expected share of coffee. Further, since we have just seen that the probability of getting ten consecutive heads is 1/1024, the loser might begin to suspect that there was something suspicious about the coin—or the person flipping it!

In a similar fashion, the statistician determines the probability that an observed research phenomenon or one more extreme is attributable to chance alone. If the probability is rare, for example only 1 in 100, then the phenomenon is usually attributed to something *other* than chance—ordinarily the experimental conditions under investigation. It is the experimenter, incidentally, who decides what is a "rare" event in any given investigation.

When a statistical test reveals that the probability is rare that a set of observed sample data is attributable to chance alone, this result is labeled as *statistically significant.* For example, if two group means are so different that only one time in 1000 would we find such a difference *by chance alone*, the difference would be statistically significant. *By statistically significant, we mean that the observed phenomenon represents a significant departure from what might be expected by chance alone.*

An example involving the use of the normal curve may help clarify the notion of statistical significance. Certain statistical tests yield a value, the chance probability of which is interpreted from the baseline and area of the normal distribution. For example, certain statistical models for testing mean

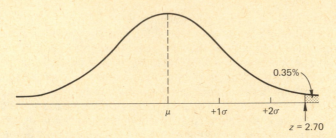

Figure 4.1 *A z value of + 2.70 represented on a normal distribution.*

differences yield *z* values. Suppose one such formula produces a *z* value of
+ 2.70. Recall the section on probability and the normal curve in the previous
chapter. From a table of the normal curve one can determine that such a *z*
value will occur *by chance alone* in a normal distribution less than one percent
of the time. This is illustrated in Figure 4.1 where only 0.35 percent of the distribution is cut off in the tail at the right of the curve by an ordinate erected at
+ 2.70 standard deviation units. Such a *z* value is statistically significant, that is,
a significant departure from what might be expected by chance alone. Under
such circumstances, therefore, the observed mean difference would be attributed to something other than chance, usually the experimental conditions.

Other probability distributions, in addition to the normal curve, are used to
interpret the results of statistical significance tests. For example, it shall be
seen later that certain distributions called the *t*, *F*, and χ^2 distributions are used
as often as the normal curve for such purposes. However, the same general
approach is used with these other probability distributions as was employed in
the previous example dealing with the normal curve. A value yielded by the
significance test is interpreted along the baseline of the distribution to determine what the probability is that the data under study (or more extreme data)
could have been produced by chance alone.

NULL HYPOTHESIS

A commonly used method of stating hypotheses in research is known as the
null hypothesis, often symbolized as H_0. This way of phrasing hypotheses
postulates that there is *no* (null) relationship between the variables under analysis. For example, a null hypothesis applied to a test of mean differences between
two groups of pupils would be: "There is *no* difference between the mean performance of the two groups." If it is found, on the basis of a statistical test, that
there *is* a significant mean difference, the null hypothesis is *rejected*. If, on the
other hand, it is found that whatever mean difference exists may occur frequently *because of mere chance*, the null hypothesis cannot be rejected.

Sometimes statisticians refer to a *research hypothesis* (H_1) which is, in
essence, a positive statement of the null hypothesis. The researcher is really
interested in the substantive question of the research hypothesis, but gets at it
statistically through the null hypothesis. This apparently unnecessary step in

phrasing hypotheses stems from the way statistical tests are set up. All inferential tests yield quantities which are interpreted along the baseline of some kind of statistical probability distribution. Depending on its position, the less likelihood there is of this value's chance occurrence, the greater probability there is of its statistical significance. To illustrate, when using the normal curve it has been seen that obtaining a z of +2.70 is, on the basis of mere chance, an improbable event. Now, if we always employ null hypotheses, our statistical results such as the z value will make perfect sense, for they will indicate that the null hypothesis is an *improbable* event and, accordingly, should be *rejected*. It would not be very consistent to find a really *improbable* difference between means, obtain an *improbable* z value, and then say that the research hypothesis (stated positively) is *probable*. It is important to remember that decisions as to whether to accept or reject such hypotheses always are related to the general notion of probability.

The experimenter can, of course, state his hypotheses in a positive fashion and make a mental transition to null hypothesis terms. This, in fact, is seen frequently in reports of research studies. There is some danger when the beginner employs this approach, since, if he finds his observed relationship will occur by chance only 5 times in 100, he may conclude that his research hypothesis (stated positively) will be confirmed 95 percent of the time if he were to replicate his research. This is simply not true. If the observed phenomenon would occur by chance only 5 times in 100, then the null hypothesis can be rejected with a high probability that the *rejection* is warranted. Converse notions about the probability of supporting the research hypothesis cannot be made legitimately. For that matter, if a really strong relationship has been detected by an initial research study, it would probably recur in *all* future replications of the research.

By employing statistical tests we attempt to determine the probability that chance alone underlines an observed relationship. If it is discovered that there is only one chance in 100 that the relationship is a mere "fluke," then the null hypothesis (of no relationship) can be rejected with a very high probability of being correct.

But we may be wrong! There is still *one* chance in 100 that what has been observed is attributable to chance. Therefore, we consider the null hypothesis tenable or untenable, rather than "true" or "false." Researchers can accept or reject these hypotheses, although never considering them *absolutely verified, for there will always be one chance in 100, or even one chance in 10,000, that the observed phenomenon actually occurred because of chance alone.* Conversely, one cannot *prove* that the null hypothesis is true, even if a particular set of data appear to strongly support it.

Levels of Significance

When the chance probability of an event's occurrence (or a more extreme event) is 5 in 100, we say that the event is statistically significant at the 0.05, or 5 percent, level. The same reasoning is true with 0.10, 0.01, 0.001 probability levels and, in fact, for any probability level. Sometimes the symbol p is used as follows: $p < 0.05$, to indicate the probability of the event's occurrence (by chance) is less than (<) 0.05. Conversely, a symbol scheme of $p > 0.05$ would indicate that the probability was greater than 0.05. The probability of obtaining a z value of $+2.70$ in the example described earlier is less than 1 in 100; thus the probability level is $p < 0.01$, and the z value is significant beyond the 0.01 level.

What significance levels should be used in rejecting null hypotheses? There are several schools of thought regarding this question. It has been conventional in behavioral science research work to use the 0.05 and 0.01 levels of significance. (Of course, if a statistical test yields a result which is significant at the 0.01 level, it is also significant at the 0.05 level.) These are the significance levels usually reported in research literature. Some researchers contend that these arbitrary levels should be maintained, for otherwise researchers might be inclined to reject null hypotheses with 0.06, 0.09, 0.10, 0.12 or similarly varied significance levels. Such a practice, they contend, would lead to chaotic interpretations of hypotheses where a researcher might "stretch" a probability level in order to support a favored research hypothesis. However, others argue that the level of significance should be a function of the hypothesis tested. They claim that in certain instances a very stringent level of significance, such as 0.001, should be employed while in other situations lower levels of significance, perhaps 0.25, for example, are acceptable.

Proponents of the latter view offer illustrations such as a situation at the preschool level where a method of separating children into reading ability groups is being tested with an experimental group versus a control group. Perhaps the experimental group, diagnosed and separated by the new method, attains a mean performance in reading at the end of the first grade that is better than that of the control youngsters, but only at the 0.30 level of in order to support a favored research hypothesis. However, others argue that this level of significance would be totally acceptable, if there were no other method available for separating the prereaders. In other words, they contend that using a relationship based on 70 to 30 odds is better than guessing blindly.

In other situations, their argument continues, the level of significance might be set as low as 0.0001. For example, if a great sum of money is to be spent on new educational equipment, the equipment should demonstrate its efficacy so there is even less than one chance in 10,000 that the results are accidental.

Both of these schools of thought, however, agree that the level of significance should be set by the researcher *prior* to gathering and testing the data. *Post facto* decisions regarding significance levels offer too much opportunity for the researcher, perhaps unknowingly, to let his biases color his judgment. It is distressing that even though this maxim is widely endorsed, few researchers actually practice it.

TWO TYPES OF ERROR

Related to the discussion of significance levels is the problem of making an error in judging the tenability of the null hypothesis. If the null hypothesis is true (that is, there is no real relationship between the variables under study) but because of the significance test the hypothesis was rejected, what is known as a *Type I error* has been committed. If the null hypothesis is false but after the significance test it has not been rejected, a *Type II error* has been made.

The probability of making a Type 1 error, that is, rejecting a true null hypothesis, can be decreased merely by lowering the level of significance. For example, a true null hypothesis is less likely to be rejected (and a Type I error committed) at the 0.01 level than at the 0.05 level. Unfortunately, as the probability of making a Type I error decreases, the probability of making a Type II error *increases*. If the significance level is moved from 0.01 to 0.05, certainly fewer null hypotheses will be accepted. If a more stringent significance level is set, however, it becomes increasingly difficult to reject certain null hypotheses which *should* be rejected. For instance, if the significance level is moved from 0.05 to 0.01, then research data which yield a 0.03 probability would not allow one to reject the null hypothesis. It is extremely important, therefore, that the researcher decide (in view of the educational decisions that might be made on the basis of his particular research) which type of error would be most serious, and set his significance level accordingly.

Power of a Test

Not only will the significance level affect the rejection of null hypotheses that should be rejected, but also the selection of the statistical test itself is related to this question. Some inferential tests are more apt to reject a false null hypothesis than others which are designed to serve the same general statistical function. Tests which are more likely to reject false null hypotheses are called more powerful tests. The exact *power of a test* can be determined with some accuracy, but it is a rather technical process. It will suffice at this time merely to point out that statistical tests which are designed to serve the same purpose may not prove equally effective in rejecting null hypotheses.[1] Less powerful statistical tests are often used in research studies where large samples are available, since it can be mathematically demonstrated that any deficiencies in a statistical test's power can be remedied by adequately increasing the number of cases treated.

The concepts of Type I and Type II errors and the power of a statistical test can be clarified by inspecting the four combinations possible when either rejecting or not rejecting an either true or false null hypothesis. These possibilities are presented in Table 4.3. The probability of committing a Type I error is denoted by the Greek letter *alpha* (α); the probability of committing a Type II error is denoted by the Greek letter beta (β). Many researchers refer to the Type I error as an α error, the size of the significance level being equal to α. For example, the researcher working at the 5 percent or 1 percent significance

[1]For a more thorough discussion of the power of a test see Allen L. Edwards, *Statistical Methods for the Behavioral Sciences* (New York: Holt, Rinehart & Winston, 1954), pp. 261–271; Wilfred J. Dixon and Frank J. Massey, Jr., *Introduction to Statistical Analysis* (New York: McGraw-Hill, 1957), chap. 14; Sidney Siegel, *Nonparametric Statistics* (New York: McGraw-Hill, 1956), pp. 20–21.

Table 4.3

Consequences of Statistical Decisions Regarding the Null Hypothesis When It Is Either True or False

| | | Null Hypothesis H_o | |
		H_o true	H_o false
	No Rejection	OK	Type II error Probability $= \beta$
Statistical Decision			
	Rejection	Type I error Probability $= \alpha$	OK Power $= 1 - \beta$

---

levels would set $\alpha = 0.05$ or $\alpha = 0.01$, respectively. Since the probability of not rejecting a false H_o is β, $1 - \beta$ is the probability of rejecting a false H_o (doing the correct thing) which is the power of the test of significance. Thus, power is dependent on the size of the Type II error which is dependent on the size of the Type I error as well as other experimental considerations.

ONE- AND TWO-TAILED TESTS

A final point about hypothesis testing must be made regarding the distinction between so-called *one-tailed* and *two-tailed* tests of significance. The one and two tails refer to the tails of the probability curves from which the value yielded by the statistical test is interpreted. The reader will recall that we interpreted a *z* value of $+2.70$ as significant beyond the 0.01 level. A value of $+2.70$ falls in the right tail of the normal curve distribution. What should be done with a *z* of -2.70? This value, too, is significant beyond the 0.01 level even though it falls in the left rather than the right tail of the curve.

In a well-conceived research investigation, the experimenter can often make a prediction as to the precise type of a relationship which will be observed. These predictions are usually based on prior research related to the hypothesis under analysis, or upon some type of theoretical rationale. For example, an investigator contrasting the performance of two groups might test the research hypothesis (H_1) that Group A's performance will be *superior* to that of Group B. Stated in the form of a null hypothesis, H_0, the phrasing would be that Group A's performance will be equal to/or less than that of Group B. Symbolically, using mean performance as the statistic, this null hypothesis would be expressed as $\mu_a \leq \mu_b$.

When the researcher does not make a prediction, he allows for the possibility of a statistical result which may be either positive or negative, that is, $-z$ or $+z$. Hence, he must use a two-tailed test to interpret his result as in Figure 4.2.

If the researcher makes a directional prediction regarding the outcome of his investigation, he is permitted to use a one-tailed test of significance such as those depicted in Figure 4.3.

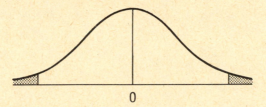

Figure 4.2 *Two-tailed test of significance where the value yielded by the significance test must fall in either of the shaded areas in order to reject the null hypothesis.*

By using one-tailed tests a null hypothesis will be rejected more often if the direction of the difference or relationship is the same as that predicted by the researcher. Since all of the rejection area is in one tail, the value yielded by the significance test need not be as large, that is, as far from the mean, in order to be statistically significant.

For example, in the case of the normal curve, a z value must be at least as large as ± 1.96 to be significant at the 0.05 level using a two-tailed test. If the researcher makes a directional hypothesis, that is, predicts a *positive z* value, then the z need only be $+1.65$ in order to reject the null hypothesis when $p < 0.05$. This difference is illustrated in Figure 4.4.

It should be pointed out that one-tailed tests do not have, strictly speaking, a logical statistical basis. Only specific null hypotheses such as those of "no difference" or "x amount of difference" can be strictly tested; nonspecific hypotheses involving "less than" or "greater than" cannot be strictly tested. Again, however, it is possible to perform statistical tests which are not mathematically valid in the strict sense, so long as it leads to empirically useful results. Thus, one-tailed tests can be employed *when thoroughly justified* on some empirical evidence or theoretical rationale.

However, it takes more than a mere "hunch" to justify the use of one-tailed tests. To take an extreme case, once the directional hypothesis is posited, even if the significance test yields a fantastically improbable result *in the opposite direction*, the researcher cannot ethically reject the null hypothesis. Such an unusual occurrence would certainly offer grounds for replicating the research study—this time using a two-tailed significance test.

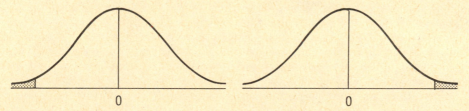

Figure 4.3 *One-tailed tests of significance where the value yielded by the significance test must fall in the shaded area in order to reject the null hypothesis.*

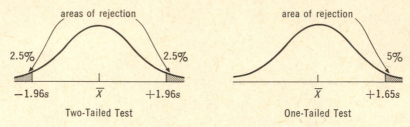

Figure 4.4 *Areas of null hypothesis rejection on a normal curve contrasted for a two-tailed test and a positive direction one-tailed test at the 0.05 level.*

ESTIMATION

Thus far inferential statistical procedures have been treated exclusively in the context of testing hypotheses. The results of such tests provide techniques for treating the question of whether the observed phenomenon is likely to be attributable to chance or whether there is considerable probability that non-chance factors are operating. In other words, it is determined whether the results of statistical tests are "significant." Yet, is the answer to this question sufficient for the educational researcher?

Most educational decisions, if they are predicted upon assumed relationships between variables, such as whether Method A or Method B yields greater achievement, require notions of *how strong* the variable relationship actually is. It is not enough to know if Method A is better than Method B, even in terms of statistical significance. Educational decision-makers need to have an idea of *how much better* Method A really is.

Certainly, a consideration of the complexities inherent in studying behavioral science relationships will suggest that precise answers to such questions will not be readily forthcoming. However, techniques are available to research workers for *estimating* such things as the population mean or the magnitude of differences between two population means. The next section of the chapter will be devoted to a consideration of *estimation* approaches in statistical methodology.

Many consider the testing of null hypotheses to represent a relatively primitive level of inference, whereas estimation approaches reflect research sophistication of a markedly higher order. Proponents of this viewpoint argue that little knowledge is really produced by merely locating statistical "significance." They contend that statistical significance is often only a function of the number of subjects used in the research sample. For example, a seemingly trivial mean difference between two groups often turns out to be statistically significant if the samples involved are large enough. Savage[2] makes this point well, asserting, "Null hypotheses of no difference are usually known to be false before the data are collected; when they are, their rejection or acceptance

[2]Richard J. Savage, "Nonparametric Statistics," *J. Am. Statist. Assoc.* **52** (1957), 332–333.

simply reflects the size of the sample and the power of the test, and is not a contribution to science."

Some authors have shown that the researcher's emphasis on null hypothesis tests of significance has actually led him to overlook the important question of estimation. From the practicing educator's point of view these arguments make considerable sense, for educators are far more frequently concerned with questions of the *magnitude* of relationships between variables than with the mere existence of such relationships.

Basically, hypothesis-testing procedures and estimation procedures are designed to answer two different questions. Tests of hypotheses allow us only to answer the question of whether or not there is a relationship (difference). On the other hand, estimation procedures can be used to answer the questions, "How great is the difference?" or "How strong is the relationship?" Answers to *both* types of questions are needed by the educational decision-maker.

This discussion should not be interpreted as an attempt to disparage hypothesis-testing in educational research. Quite the contrary, sound hypothesis-testing is one of the fundamental operations in developing an educational science of behavior. But it is only *one* of the fundamental operations; another at least equally important step is estimation.

Point Estimation of the Population Mean

There are procedures available for determining the "best" estimate of a population parameter using a sample statistic. This technique, known as *point estimation*, allows one to use a statistic based on a sample to supply the best estimate of such population values as means and standard deviations. Statisticians have an explicit set of criteria in mind when they refer to an estimate as being "best," the most important being the criterion of *unbiasedness*. Before discussing the nature of an unbiased estimate, let it first be stated that the sample mean $\bar{X}$ (see Table 4.1) is an unbiased estimate of the population mean μ. The formula for the sample mean is just like Formula 2.1 in Chapter 2, except that n is used denoting the size of the sample drawn from the population of size N:

$$\bar{X} = \frac{\Sigma X}{n} \tag{4.1}$$

Here, ΣX refers to the sum of the scores in the *sample* rather than in the population.

Now suppose we have a large population of scores with a mean of 50. Next, we draw a random sample of 30 scores from the population and use these scores to compute an estimate of the population mean using Formula 4.1. Suppose we replace the 30 scores in the population and again draw a random sample of 30 scores and compute a new estimate of the population mean. We now have two estimates of μ. If we repeated the process 1000 times we would have 1000 estimates of μ. These estimates are merely numbers, and we can construct the distribution curve representing the 1,000 estimates. This curve is called the *sampling distribution of the mean.* It turns out that the more samples we draw, the closer the sampling distribution of the mean is approximated by the normal curve, such that the mean of the sampling distribution equals the mean of the population. That is, if we computed the mean of the 1,000 estimates, we would get a value very close to 50. This property, known as the *central limit theorem for the mean*, forms the basis of the statistical inference procedures discussed previously. It is the property which enabled us to portray Figures 4.1 through 4.4 using the normal curve. When the mean of the sampling distribution of a statistic equals the population parameter the statistic is estimating, we say that the estimate is *unbiased*. Thus, because of the central limit theorem, the sample mean is an unbiased estimate of μ.

Point Estimation of the Population Variance and Standard Deviation

It is *not* the case that a variance computed for a sample using Formula 2.6 in Chapter 2 would be an unbiased estimate of the population variance σ^2. We can, however, obtain an unbiased estimate of σ^2 if we divide the sum of squared deviations by one less than the number of cases in the sample, namely $n-1$. Denoting the variance estimate computed on sample data as s^2, the formula would be

$$s^2 = \frac{\Sigma(X - \bar{X})^2}{n-1} = \frac{\Sigma x^2}{n-1} \tag{4.2}$$

where the sum of squared deviations, Σx^2, is computed in exactly the same manner as indicated in Chapter 2. If we wish to obtain an estimate of the population standard deviation σ, we simply take the square root of the variance estimate:

$$s = \sqrt{\frac{\Sigma(X - \bar{X})^2}{n-1}} = \sqrt{\frac{\Sigma x^2}{n-1}} \tag{4.3}$$

The reason for dividing by $n-1$ is based on the concept of *degrees of freedom*, abbreviated *df*. The notion of degrees of freedom is one of the more difficult concepts to grasp in beginning statistical inference. Although we will deal with the use of *df* in subsequent chapters, the role of *df* in estimation will be briefly introduced in the following section.

Degrees of Freedom

Whenever population parameters have to be estimated, a sample of data is taken from that population. For example, in estimating μ, sample data is used to compute $\bar{X}$. All the information about the population is contained in the sample. The total number of independent "pieces of information" are, loosely speaking, the degrees of freedom. Suppose we have the following sample of five scores: 1, 2, 3, 4, 5. We thus have 5 independent pieces of information or 5 *df*. In general, if we have a sample of n scores, we have n *df* to start with. When we estimate the mean, we use up one of these degrees of freedom. This is because knowing the sample mean $\bar{X}$, we automatically know the value of any score in the sample, given the values of the remaining $n-1$ scores. (Recall from Chapter 2 that the sum of deviations about the mean must always equal zero.) In the above example, knowing that $\overline{X} = 3$, we can deduce the value of the remaining score, given, say, the scores 1, 2, 3, and 5. To take a meaningful (unbiased) arithmetic average, one must divide by the number of df present in the quantities being averaged. In Formula 4.2 for the estimated population variance, the quantities being averaged are deviations about the sample mean. Since these deviations are based on $n-1$ df, the average sum of squared deviations must be obtained by dividing by $n-1$.

Interval Estimation of the Mean

Although point estimation is a first step in hypothesis testing, point estimates have little intrinsic utility in practical situations unless some notion is given of possible error limits. This leads to a second, more important form of estimation known as *interval estimation*.

By using an interval estimation procedure it is possible to determine a range or interval such that, if the procedure were repeated, the parameter in question would be included a specified proportion of the time. For example, from sample data it is possible to determine a 95 percent confidence interval for the population mean. Only 5 percent of the time by use of this process would confidence intervals be obtained which did not include that parameter, that is, the population mean.

It is tempting to assert with a certain probability interval, such as 99 percent, that one is 99 percent certain that the population mean is included in the interval. Actually, once an interval has been calculated from sample data the parameter either falls inside or outside the interval, so the probability is either 1 or 0. All we can say is that the *process* by which the interval is obtained will yield intervals which will contain the parameter 99 times in 100.

In order to construct a confidence interval for the population mean, we must first obtain some notion of the *sampling error* that results from using the sample statistic $\overline{X}$ as an estimate of μ. Recall the section on estimating the mean, where the 1,000 sample estimates and the resulting sampling distribution of the mean were discussed. The fact that these estimates are not all equal, that is, the sampling distribution has *variability*, is indicative of the fact that there exists error in estimation. In fact, an estimate of this sampling error is obtained by computing the *standard deviation of the sampling distribution*. Thus, for the 1,000 scores (which happen to be sample means) we compute the standard deviation using Formula 4.3. This standard deviation is often referred to as the *standard error of the mean* (symbolized $s_{\overline{x}}$). The term "error" (instead of "deviation") is used only insofar as a deviation from the mean in this case is a "mistake" due to sampling.

Clearly, the researcher would have a problem if he had to compute 1,000 Xs every time he wanted to estimate $s_{\overline{x}}$ for some population of interest. Fortunately, the central limit theorem for the mean tells us that the standard error can be estimated by dividing the sample standard deviation by the square root of the sample size. That is,

$$s_{\bar{x}} = \frac{s}{\sqrt{n}} \qquad\qquad (4.4)$$

For example, in the above sample of 5 scores, $s = 1.6$; the standard error of the mean, $s_{\bar{x}}$, is then equal to $1.6/\sqrt{5}$ or 0.73.

Now since the sampling distribution of the mean is normally distributed, we can make use of Table C to determine the z score cutoff points which would include, say, 99 percent of the area in the sampling distribution. These z values tell us how many standard errors (deviations) of the mean it takes to construct intervals expected to contain the population mean 99 times out of 100. For example, the z values for the 99 percent confidence interval are -2.57 and $+2.57$, often denoted ± 2.57 for notational simplicity. For this sample data, $s_{\bar{x}} = 0.32$; thus 99 percent of the area in the sampling distribution of the mean lies between the score points -2.57 (0.73) and $+2.57$ (0.73). Since the sample mean $\bar{X} = 3$ is our best guess of the population mean, our best guess of these boundary points is $3 - 2.57$ (0.73) or 1.12 and $3 + 2.57$ (0.73) or 4.88. In general the boundary points for any 99 percent confidence interval can be given by $\bar{X} \pm 2.57(s_{\bar{x}})$.

Likewise, the 95 percent confidence interval can be constructed; consulting Table C we find z values of ± 1.96 leaving 2.5 percent of the area in either tail of the normal distribution. The formula $\bar{X} \pm 1.96(s_{\bar{x}})$ would then give us the boundary points for the 95 percent confidence interval. A final example should serve to illustrate the process. Consider a sample of 100 achievement test scores which have a mean of 50.20 and a standard deviation of 6.0. In this case 6.0 would be divided by 10, the square root of 100, to obtain a standard error of 0.6. This 0.6 is then multiplied by the plus and minus normal curve z values associated with the probability figures desired for the interval. Since the present example used a 95 percent interval, the z values which limit 95 percent of the normal curve are used, that is, -1.96 and $+1.96$. Thus $(0.6)(-1.96) = -1.18$, and $(0.6)(1.96) = 1.18$. These values are both added to the sample mean of 50.20 to obtain the confidence limits of 49.02 and 51.38. If the process were repeated, 95 percent of the time the population mean would fall between such confidence limits.

Confidence intervals apply not only to individual statistics, but also to difference or relationship statistics. For example, from a given difference between two sample means, a confidence interval can be calculated for the difference between the two population means. Clearly, such estimates can be of great assistance to the educational decision-maker who must choose whether or not to adopt new instructional techniques for his students.

Usually a 95 percent or 99 percent confidence interval is used in this type of estimation, and sometimes both. Intervals having greater or lesser probabilities can also be determined. The arguments in favor of more or less stringent probability levels for confidence intervals are much the same as those for setting significance levels in testing null hypotheses.

Although more frequent use of interval estimation is urged by most writers, one unfortunately sees relatively infrequent instances of it in the research literature of the behavioral sciences. A reasonable sequence of activities for educational researchers could well be: (1) description, (2) tests of hypotheses, (3) interval estimation, and (4) evaluation. By short-circuiting the interval estimation operation, researchers make the final evaluative operation far more difficult.

Procedures used for developing confidence intervals for the more commonly used statistical operations will be described in subsequent chapters.

REVIEW

The central task of educational research is to discover the nature of relationships between educational variables. Inferential statistical procedures aid the researcher by allowing him to determine the mathematical probability that relationships discovered in a sample actually exist in the total population.

Typically, the researcher tests an hypothesis, often stated in negative terms as the null hypothesis, regarding the nature of a relationship between at least two variables. Data reflecting these variables are then gathered from a sample which represents a broader population. On the basis of the sample data, the hypothesis under consideration is either accepted or rejected and, if possible, results are generalized to the population.

When an event occurs which cannot be readily attributed to mere chance, the event is termed statistically significant, meaning that it departs significantly from what might be expected by chance alone. Often his research design permits the investigator to identify the relationships between variables that are not likely to be a function of chance. Inferential statistical techniques allow research hypotheses to be accepted or rejected with precise probability notions.

The conventionally accepted levels of probability used in rejecting null hypotheses are 0.05 and 0.01. Researchers can use different significance levels, however, and can employ them with either one-tailed or two-tailed significance tests, with the latter being the more stringent.

A population parameter can be estimated in two ways: in terms of its probable value (point estimation) or in terms of the probable numerical boundaries containing its value (interval estimation). When the point estimation process is conceptualized to occur over a great number of times, a distribution (called the sampling distribution) of the resulting estimates is created. The standard deviation (called the standard error) of this distribution is an index of the error made in the estimation process. The central limit theorem states that the sampling distribution of $\overline{X}$ (the estimate of μ) is normally distributed; a formula is available to compute the standard error ($s_{\overline{x}}$) of this distribution, which can then be used to construct confidence intervals for the estimation of μ.

The importance of estimation procedures is increasing in the opinion of statisticians. Interval estimation operations are considered to answer different kinds of questions than those allowed by hypothesis-testing operations. Hypothesis tests tell whether a relationship exists; interval estimation procedures indicate how strong the relationship is. A recommended procedure is to report confidence intervals, which indicate, at particular levels of probability, the magnitude of the relationship under investigation.

EXERCISES

1. If, in testing a null hypothesis regarding the relationship between two variables, we discover that the relationship observed in our sample is so strong that it or a stronger relationship would have occurred by chance alone only one time in 10,000, should we accept or reject the null hypothesis?

2. If we test for differences between the means of two samples and find, through the statistical model, that the mean difference is so small that it would occur by chance alone 90 percent of the time, what should our action be regarding the null hypothesis of mean difference?

3. If we find that the means of two experimental groups are so divergent that the difference is significant at the 0.05 level, does this mean that if we repeated the study a number of times we would get the same kind of mean difference?

4. A researcher sets the level of significance for rejecting the null hypothesis at 0.05. His statistical test yields a z value of 6.83. What should his action be regarding the null hypothesis?

5. If the level of significance for the null hypothesis is set at 0.05, what should the researcher's decision be in each of the following situations?

    (a) if $p < 0.05$ (c) if $p < 0.01$ (e) if $z = 0.19$
    (b) if $p > 0.05$ (d) if $p > 0.01$ (f) if $z = -3.92$

6. When a researcher, on the basis of past experimentation, makes a prediction regarding the direction of mean differences between an experimental and control group, is he permitted to use a one-tailed test?

7. Is a one-tailed test or a two-tailed test more likely to reject the null hypothesis?

8. If a z value of 1.65 is needed to reject a 0.05-level null hypothesis for a one-tailed test, what is the probability level of a z value of 1.65 for a two-tailed test?

9. When a researcher rejects the null hypothesis at the 0.01 level he is in essence saying, "There is only one chance in 100 that what I have observed in the sample is due to the fluctuations of probability alone." Suppose this rare instance is the case, and the null hypothesis is rejected erroneously. Would the researcher have committed a Type I or a Type II error?

10. A school psychologist discovers that a researcher has demonstrated that one method of counseling yields significantly higher mean achievement with

underachievers than does a second method of counseling. The psychologist consults the research article in the literature and learns that a significant mean grade point difference of 1.32 was produced over a semester by the differential counseling methods. At this point, the psychologist is weighing the merits of introducing the superior method. Is he more interested in questions of hypothesis-testing or estimation?

11. A college dean wishes to estimate the average number of hours spent watching television by his freshmen students. A random sample of 100 freshmen students are asked to record their number of TV hours daily for a period of two weeks. The mean number of hours reported by the students is 20.6 and the standard deviation is 6.0.
    (a) Construct the 95 percent and 99 percent confidence intervals which the dean could use in estimating mean TV hours for his population of freshmen students.
    (b) Suppose that only 50 students were sampled with the mean and standard deviation remaining unchanged. Repeat (a) with these data and discuss the change in confidence interval size.

SELECTED READINGS

Blalock, Hubert M., Jr., *Social Statistics*. New York: McGraw-Hill, 1960, chaps. 8, 9, and 12.

Blommers, Paul, and E. F. Lindquist, *Elementary Statistical Methods*. Boston: Houghton Mifflin, 1960, chaps. 10 and 11.

Dixon, Wilfred J., and Frank J. Massey, *Introduction to Statistical Analysis*. New York: McGraw-Hill, 1957.

Edwards, Allen L., *Statistical Methods for the Behavioral Sciences*. New York: Holt, Rinehart & Winston, 1954.

Hoel, Paul G., *Elementary Statistics*. New York: Wiley, 1960, chaps. 5, 6, and 7.

Husek, T. R., *Measurement Implications for Educational Statistics*. Los Angeles: Baker Press, 1959.

Kish, Leslie, "Some Statistical Problems in Research Design," *Am. Sociol. Rev.* **24**, no. 3 (June, 1959): 328–338.

Siegel, Sidney, *Nonparametric Statistics for the Behavioral Sciences*. New York: McGraw-Hill, 1956, chap. 2.

Van Dalen, Deobold B., *Understanding Educational Research*. New York: McGraw-Hill, 1962, chap. 14.

5
Correlation

Since the ultimate goal of a science of behavior for education is to isolate and understand more fully the nature of relationships among educational variables, one should not be surprised to learn that techniques which analyze these relationships receive primary attention in statistics volumes. For example, the types of relationships that interest educators would include the following: (1) the relationship between pupils' intelligence and their achievement in learning situations; (2) the relationship between student reading ability and subsequent performance in school work; (3) the relationship between certain home—family conditions and the occurrence of delinquent behavior in juveniles. These are but a few of the many relationships which educators must adequately understand if they are to attain their instructional objectives more effectively.

Although we are treating correlational techniques in chapters separate from the chapter on descriptive statistics, it should be emphasized that indexes of correlation are every bit as descriptive as indexes of central tendency and variability. When appropriate, all such indexes (statistics), whether they be means, variances, or coefficients of correlations, can be tested for statistical significance as well.

STATISTICAL CORRELATION

In popular usage the term *correlation* refers to any type of relationship between events or objects. Phrases such as "correlated subject matter" and "the correlation between theory and practice" refer to general kinds of relationships. In statistical analysis, however, *correlation* refers exclusively to a quantifiable relationship between two variables.

In statistical correlations, there must be two measures for each subject (person) in a group. If this condition is satisfied, the data can be inserted into a statistical formulation which will reveal the type and strength of the relationship under study. The most widely employed measure of statistical correlation is the product–moment correlation coefficient devised by Pearson. Many other techniques used to describe relationships are analogous to the Pearson product–moment correlational approach.

THE MEANING OF STATISTICAL CORRELATION

Consider the problem when one tries to describe the nature of a relationship between two educational variables. For instance, suppose we study the size of elementary school children's vocabularies with reference to their performance on group intelligence tests. We would like to know how vocabulary comprehension is related, if at all, to the way in which youngsters score on group IQ examinations. It may be that we suspect group IQ tests are based very largely on vocabulary comprehension.

In order to discover the nature of this relationship, we might administer a suitable vocabulary examination, along with a group intelligence test, to a number of elementary school youngsters. Now we could gather a rough notion of the way in which these two measures were related by visually inspecting the scores of the children on the two tests. We might observe, for example, that many of the students who obtained high scores on the intelligence test also scored well on the vocabulary quiz, and those who scored low on one measure also tended to perform poorly on the other test. What does this visual inspection tell us? First, it suggests that there is probably a degree of relationship between the two variables under study. Second, it is also likely that the relationship is *positive*, rather than *negative*, in nature. In positive relationships we shall see that individuals who score high (or low) on one measure tend to score similarly on the other measure as well. In negative relationships, an individual who scores high on one measure tends to score low on the other.

Although one can gain some insights regarding the nature of the relationship under investigation by merely inspecting the scores, this is usually possible only when the relationship is rather clear-cut. If the relationship does not have great strength and is therefore nor readily apparent, the visual inspection technique may actually yield erroneous conclusions. This frequently occurs because of selective perception on the part of the person scanning the data.

A preferable inspection method used for studying relationships requires that the data be plotted in a frequency table such as that depicted in Figure 5.1. Note that in the table the measurement scales representing the variables of vocabulary size and intelligence have been classified into five-point intervals for economy of tabulation. Note also that each tally mark represents the *dual* performance of an individual on measures X and Y. For example, a student who obtained an intelligence test score of 146 and a vocabulary quiz score of 97 would be represented by the single tally mark in the cell at the upper right-hand corner of the table. Similarly, every other tally mark represents *two* scores of the 67 individuals represented in the table.

By examining a chart such as Figure 5.1, called a scattergram or correlation chart, one can gain an even more precise notion of the nature of the relationship under investigation. One can see with more certainty that there is a

$X =$ Score on Group Intelligence Test

$Y =$ Score on Vocabulary Quiz	90-94	95-99	100-104	105-109	110-114	115-119	120-124	125-129	130-134	135-139	140-144	145-149
95-99									/	/	//	/
90-94			/				/	/		/		
85-89				/			⊪⊪		//			
80-84					//	/	/			/	/	
75-79					//	//	//	/				
70-74			//		/	///	//	//				
65-69				⊪⊪ /	/	//	/	/				
60-64			/		//	/	/					
55-59		/										
50-54	//	//	/			/						
45-49	/	/										

Figure 5.1   *Frequency table.*

relationship, positive in nature, and fairly strong. Yet, we are still unable to attach any precisely quantified label regarding the strength of the relationship. At this point, we can see the need for an accurate numerical index of the strength and direction of such relationships. The product–moment correlation coefficient provides us with that index.

RATIONALE OF THE PRODUCT–MOMENT COEFFICIENT

One of the first things an individual usually learns about product–moment correlation is that its coefficient (symbolized as r) ranges between 1.00 and −1.00 with a perfect postive relationship reflected by an r of 1.00, a perfect negative relationship reflected by an r of −1.00, and a lack of any relationship reflected by an r of zero. Yet, though many students have dutifully committed such notions to memory, it is surprising to learn how few really understand what sorts of data relationships yield various types of correlation coefficients.

When r = 1.00

Consider a very simple situation where we have only five subjects. Each subject has two scores; one score on variable X and one score on variable Y. Hypothetical scores for this situation are shown in Table 5.1. Looking at these scores, we would tend to state that there existed a positive relationship between

Table 5.1
Hypothetical Set of Data for a Perfect, Positive Linear Relationship: r = +1.0.

Subject	X	Y	z_x	z_y	$z_x z_y$
A	1	7	−1.4	−1.4	2.0
B	2	9	−0.7	−0.7	0.5
C	3	11	0.0	0.0	0.0
D	4	13	0.7	0.7	0.5
E	5	15	1.4	1.4	2.0
				Sum	5.0
				Mean	1.0

variables *X* and *Y*. But what specific quantitative properties lead us to this belief? First, we note that the rank order of *every* subject's score on *X* is the same as that of his score on *Y*. For example, subject D obtains the second highest score on *X* and also has the second highest score on *Y*. Second, we note that the distance between the scores of *any* two subjects on *Y* is always twice that between the scores of the same two subjects on *X*. Thus, the distance between the scores of subjects B and E on variable *Y* is 11 − 5, or 6, and the distance between the scores of these same two subjects on *X* is 5 − 2, or 3. These two criteria define what we mean by a *linear* relationship; we see in Figure 5.2 that when the relationships between the scores on variables *X* and *Y* are graphically plotted, the five pairs of points all lie on the same straight line.

Another, more compact, way of defining the linear relationship is the statement that every individual's score is exactly the same *relative* distance above or below the mean for variable *X* as it is for variable *Y*. By the term "relative distance" we mean distance in terms of standard deviation units. Since *z* scores tell us how many standard deviations above or below the mean a given raw score is, we can revise the above definition as follows: A perfect linear relationship between two variables *X* and *Y* exists whenever every individual's *z* score for variable *X* is the same as that for variable *Y*. Consider again the data in Table 5.1. The means for variables *X* and *Y* are 3 and 11 respectively; the standard deviations are 1.41 and 2.82 respectively. The *z* scores for each subject can be computed and these are also shown in the table. Note that both the value and sign of the *z* scores for each individual on both variables is the same. The value (or magnitude) of the *z* score tells us the relative distance of a score from the mean; the sign (or direction) of the *z* score tells us whether the score is above (+) or below (−) the mean.

Finally, we wish to establish a single index of the relationship such that (1) the index will increase to the extent that the relationship becomes more linear, that is, comes closer and closer to the above definition and (2) the index indicates the direction of the relationship, that is, whether the relationship is positive or negative. Looking again at Table 5.1, we note that the *product* of the *z* scores for any subject must always be positive, since his *z* scores will always

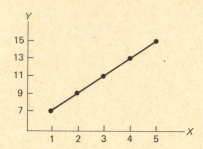

Figure 5.2 *Scatterplot for the data in Table 5.1.*

have the same sign. For example, the product of the z scores for individual A is (−1.42)(−1.42) or 2.02. Furthermore, we note that the *sum* of these z score products is exactly equal to the number of subjects. Thus, the mean of these z-score products must be 5/5 or 1.00.

It is always the case that when the data conform to the above definition of a perfect, positive, linear relationship, the mean z-score product will equal 1.00. Thus we have a possible candidate for an index of relationship (denoted *r*), namely

$$r = \frac{\Sigma z_x z_y}{n} \tag{5.1}$$

where z_x is the z score for an individual on variable X, z_y is the z score for the same individual on variable Y, and *n* is the number of cases or individuals in our sample.

What remains to be demonstrated is that $r = -1.00$ when the data conform to the definition of a perfect, *negative*, linear relationship, that $r = 0$ when there is no relationship in the data, and that *r* can attain all values between −1 and +1 for less than perfect (but nonzero) types of relationships in the data.

When r = −1.00

Consider, for example, what happens when we take the data in Table 5.1 and completely reverse the relative standings of the subjects in terms of their scores on variable Y. This situation is shown in Table 5.2 where, although we have retained the same relative distance between any two individuals' scores for variables X and Y, we have reversed the rank ordering of the individuals' scores for variables X and Y. Thus, for any individual, his z scores on variables X and Y are *equal but opposite in sign.* This is exactly the definition of a perfect, negative (or inverse), linear relationship between two variables. We see in Figure 5.3 that when this relationship between the scores on variables X and Y are plotted graphically, the five pairs of points again all lie on the same straight line — but this time the line slopes downward. This property of the slope of the line and the direction of the relationship is consistent; that is, whenever the relationship is positive, the line will slope upwards (as in Figure 5.2) and whenever it is negative, the line will slope downwards (as in Figure 5.3).

Table 5.2
Hypothetical Set of Data for a Perfect, Negative Linear Relationship: r = −1.0

Subject	X	Y	z_x	z_y	$z_x z_y$
A	1	15	−1.4	1.4	−2.0
B	2	13	−0.7	0.7	−0.5
C	3	11	0.0	0.0	0.0
D	4	9	0.7	−0.7	−0.5
E	5	7	1.4	−1.4	−2.0
				Sum	−5.0
				Mean	−1.0

Now since the z scores for any subject are always opposite in sign, the product of the z scores will always be *negative.* The sum of the products, then, will always be negative and in this case, the sum is equal to minus the number of subjects. Thus, the mean of these z-score products must be −5/5 or −1.00. Again, this is always the case for a perfect, negative, linear relationship.

When r = 0

Consider another rearrangement of the scores on variable Y for the five subjects in our example. This time (see Table 5.3) there is no apparent consistency in relative standing for the five individuals across both variables. One individual may score relatively high on both X and Y (for example, subject D) whereas another individual may score relatively high on X but low on Y (for example, subject E). Reverse patterns are seen for subjects B and A; subject C retains the same standing on both variables. Thus, the patterns of positive and negative relationships within the data should "cancel" out one another leaving no relationship whatsoever. This is, in fact, the situation when we consider the z-score products; for every nonzero, positive z-score product, there is a nonzero, negative z-score product having the same magnitude. Thus the sum of these products will be zero and their mean must be zero.

Inspecting the graph (see Figure 5.4) of this relationship, we see that no

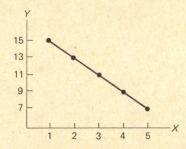

Figure 5.3 *Scatterplot for the data in Table 5.2.*

Table 5.3
Hypothetical Set of Data for a Perfect, Zero Linear Relationship: r = 0

Subject	X	Y	z_x	z_y	$z_x z_y$
A	1	13	−1.4	0.7	−1.0
B	2	7	−0.7	−1.4	1.0
C	3	11	0.0	0.0	0.0
D	4	15	0.7	1.4	1.0
E	5	9	1.4	−0.7	−1.0
				Sum	0.0
				Mean	0.0

one straight line can be drawn through all five pairs of points. In fact, the one straight line which comes closest to all the points (the dotted line) is perfectly horizontal, having no slope whatsoever.

Other Values of r Between +1 and −1

Ordinarily, no set of data yields an *r* which is exactly equal to +1, −1, or 0. We have considered these special cases because they provide a certain insight into the nature of Formula 5.1. Typically, the index of relationship given by Formula 5.1 (the Pearson product–moment *correlation coefficient*) is some decimal value between +1 and −1 indicating a greater or lesser degree of positive or negative linear relationship. For example, if subject A received a score of 9 on variable *Y* in Table 5.1, the relationship, although still positive, would not be as strong; A's new *z* score on *Y* would be −0.71, the new *z* score product would be (−1.42)(−0.71) or 1.01, and Formula 5.1 would yield a new *r* of 4/5 or 0.8.

Perhaps the easiest way of appreciating the possible values that the correlation coefficient can assume is to investigate the scattergram depicting the given relationship. The scattergrams in Figures 5.2 through 5.4 are fairly simplistic in that they are based on only five cases and represent very special values of *r*. Consider, for example, a large number of people obtaining scores on two tests *X* and *Y*. The score pairs can be graphically plotted and usually repre-

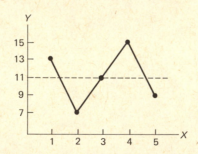

Figure 5.4 *Scatterplot for the data in Table 5.3.*

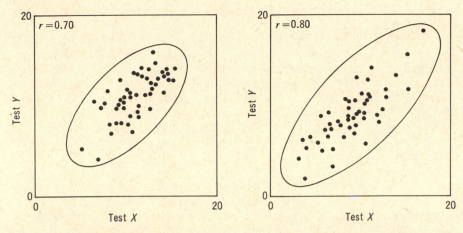

Figure 5.5 *Correlation chart with r = 0.70.*   **Figure 5.6** *Correlation chart with r = 0.80.*

sented by an elliptical ring as in Figures 5.5 through 5.8. Note that if the direction of the closed oval curve is from lower left to upper right, the *r* is positive. On the other hand, if the oval extends from upper left to lower right, a negative *r* is present. A careful examination of the points in the charts may give the reader further insight into the meaning of positive and negative relationships.

For example, inspect the shape of the oval itself. If the oval is a fairly narrow one, perhaps "cigar-like" in shape, the relationship is a rather strong one. The more closely the oval resembles a straight line, the closer *r* approaches a perfect relationship of ±1.00. At the other extreme, the total absence of relationship

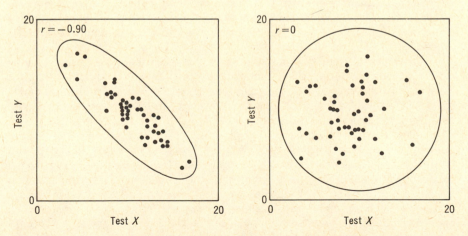

Figure 5.7 *Correlation chart with r = −0.90.*   **Figure 5.8** *Correlation chart with r = 0.0.*

would be reflected in a perfect circle enclosing the points on a correlation chart as in Figure 5.8.

It should be reiterated that, even in the case of a perfect correlation, individual scores on two measures do not have to be *identical*. Rather, in terms of deviation scores or standard scores the *distance* of both an individual's scores from the means of their respective groups must be the same. For example, the very small sample of scores, in Table 5.1, would yield an *r* of 1.00 even though the scores for any individual on the two tests are not the same. Some students, encountering correlation for the first time, incorrectly assume that an individual need score precisely the same on both measures in order for a perfect correlation to be produced.

THE STRENGTH OF THE CORRELATION COEFFICIENT

How large must *r* be in order for us to say that the relationship between two variables is a strong one? Or, conversely, how small can a correlation coefficient be in order for us to reject it because it represents a trivial relationship? In general, there are no precise answers to such questions. One valuable guide which we do have depends upon the notions of probability and statistical significance discussed in Chapter 4. But, leaving the question of statistical significance for a moment, it should be noted that for certain purposes an *r* of 0.50 might be considered satisfactory whereas in other situations an *r* of 0.90 or higher would be required. An illustration of this can be drawn from the educational measurement field where a test constructor must frequently demonstrate the equivalence of two different forms of the same test. Typically, a group of students is required to complete both forms of the test, and their scores on the two measures are then correlated. If the two test forms are to be considered equivalent, we would expect a very high positive correlation between scores on the two forms, a correlation somewhere in the neighborhood of 0.90. Yet in other educational situations, for example, in relating academic achievement to a predictor test of achievement, such as an IQ test, we are often satisfied with an *r* of between 0.40 and 0.50. An *r* of 0.70 in such a situation would be exceptional indeed.

When statisticians refer to ''high'' and ''low'' correlation coefficients, they are usually using the absolute scale of 1.00 to 0.0 as their guide. ''High'' or ''strong'' correlation coefficients, therefore, should not necessarily be thought of as ''important,'' nor should ''low'' or ''weak'' correlation coefficients necessarily be considered ''unimportant.''

It should be added that notions of causality are not inherent in product–moment correlation. Because two variables are strongly correlated does not imply that one ''caused'' the other. Though it *may* indeed be true that variable *X* is causally related to variable *Y*, one cannot impute causal relationships to such variables on the basis of the correlation coefficient alone. In fact, variables *X* and *Y* may both be ''caused'' by variable *W*, which is thus indirectly responsible for the relationship between *X* and *Y*. Correlation is a necessary but not sufficient condition for the popular meaning of the word ''cause.''

Finally, it must be emphasized that the coefficient we have been discussing is a measure of *linear* correlation only. Meaningful relationships between two variables do not necessarily have to be linear. When the correlation coefficient *r* is low, little *linear* relationship exists between the two variables; that is not to say, however, that no relationship whatsoever exists—in fact, a strong, *curvilinear* relationship may exist in the data. The scatterplot in Figure 5.9 would yield a very low value of *r* but a very high value for any index sensitive to a curvilinear (in this case, quadratic) relationship.

THE SIGNIFICANCE OF THE CORRELATION COEFFICIENT

If one wishes to generalize findings regarding a sample relationship to the population represented by that sample, it is important to ascertain the probability that the observed relationship could be attributed to chance alone. In other words, to generalize to a population regarding relationships between variables, we should determine the statistical significance of the sample relationship.

We use the phrase "statistical significance of the sample relationship" to mean the statistical significance of the sample statistic *r*. Statistical significance is only meaningful in terms of a specifically stated null hypothesis about the *population* correlation coefficient, denoted by the Greek letter *rho* (ρ). In general, we can test any hypothesis regarding the value of the parameter ρ. Most often, however, we are concerned whether or not the linear relationship in the population is something other than zero. Thus, the null hypothesis most often tested is $H_0 : \rho = 0$. Following the rationale of hypothesis testing discussed in the previous chapter, if the sample value *r* represents a sufficiently rare event for sampling from a population with $\rho = 0$, then we reject the assumption that $\rho = 0$; we conclude that there is, in fact, a significant relationship in the population and that *r* is an estimate of the magnitude and direction of this relationship.

Determining the statistical significance of *r* is relatively simple since tables of values that must equal or exceed *r* at given levels of significance have been prepared. These tables are usually designed for two-tailed hypothesis tests, that is, where *r* may be either positive or negative. Table D in the Appendix contains these values. Table D is easily used by entering the table with the number of pairs minus two and determining the level of significance for the value of *r*.

An example of the use of Table D will assist the reader. Suppose that a researcher is testing a hypothesis regarding the relationship between 30 students' scores on an aptitude test and their subsequent scores on a performance test. The significance level he has set in advance of gathering the data is 0.05. Having satisfied all requisite assumptions for the product–moment *r*, he calculates a coefficient of 0.41. The significance of this coefficient with an *n* of 30 is determined by entering Table D where the number 28 ($n-2$) appears under the column "degrees of freedom." Reading across the four columns to the right, it can be seen that an *r* of 0.41 is large enough to be significant at the 0.05 level, but not at the 0.02 level. Since the previously established significance level has

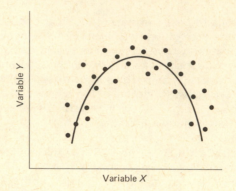

Figure 5.9 *A nonlinear (curvilinear) relationship between variables X and Y.*

been achieved, the researcher can now reject the null hypothesis, accepting the alternative hypothesis that the two variables under study are indeed probably related.

It can be seen that the notion of statistical significance for *r* is, sensibly enough, tied to the size of the sample. Since a larger sample will provide a more representative index of the nature of a relationship, smaller values of *r* become statistically significant as the size of *n* increases.

Again, some writers place correlation under the heading of descriptive statistics, for its function is to describe the existing state of relationship between two sets of scores. Yet, research workers are usually anxious to generalize to a population their findings about a relationship present in a sample. Thus, it is not so important to classify a statistical technique (such as measuring a relationship) as it is to understand the purpose for which the technique is being employed.

A CONFIDENCE INTERVAL FOR *r*

The reader will recall from the discussion of estimation procedures in the previous chapter that techniques are available for computing a confidence interval for a given *r*. By determining a confidence interval of 95 percent for a particular *r* based on sample data, an interval can be established, so that in 95 percent of similar computations the interval will contain the population correlation coefficient. This is of value to an educator who must have a relatively precise notion of the limits of the actual population relationship between two variables.

In order to compute confidence limits for a given sample *r*, it is necessary to transform the *r* to a special z_r value by using a logarithmic transformation. Tables are available which give the value of z_r for different values of *r*. In this text Table O in the Appendix is used for this purpose. The z_r value is then inserted in a formula which yields the confidence limits for *r*. The use of Table O and the subsequent computation procedures for determining the confidence interval will be discussed in the next chapter.

ASSUMPTIONS UNDERLYING PRODUCT–MOMENT CORRELATION

As is the case with many of the more complex statistical procedures, there are certain assumptions underlying the proper interpretation of the product–moment r. As may be seen in the next chapter, there are several simple formulas which may be applied to data in order to obtain the correlation coefficient. These formulas will yield an r regardless of the kind of data used, as long as there are two numerical scores for each subject. This correctly suggests that a correlation coefficient can be *calculated* with little consideration of the nature of the data. If we wish to use inferential procedures, however, we must satisfy certain assumptions about our data.

The distinction between calculation and validity of the test of significance is an important one in all phases of statistics and can be illustrated in the case of correlation. In order to draw proper inferences regarding the calculated r, the data must fulfill two important assumptions: For all values of one measure (all X scores, for example) the distribution of the other measure's values (Y scores) must be approximately normal and equal in variability. This assumption of equality in variance is known technically as the assumption of homoscedasticity (*homo* means equal, *scedasticity* means scattering). The concept can be more readily understood through an examination of Figure 5.10 where for each value of X a curve has been drawn which depicts the associated Y values. If the variances or standard deviations of these curves are fairly similar, the assumption of homoscedasticity has been satisfied. Furthermore, each of the distributions should be normal in shape. These notions must apply not only to values of Y for X, but also to X values for Y. Ordinarily, the data in a correlation analysis are distributed in normal and homoscedastic fashion when the relationship is linear in nature and sufficient data has been sampled.

MULTIPLE CORRELATION

Sometimes a researcher is interested in the relationship between one variable and a combination of two or more other variables considered simultaneously. It is possible to determine the extent of such a relationship through a procedure known as *multiple correlation*. By this technique a coefficient (R) is computed which is interpreted in approximately the same way as was a simple r. The multiple correlation coefficient, however, is not merely a sum of the relationships between one variable and several others. Rather, R is based on intercorrelations between variables, so that the highest possible relationship, as in the case of r, is 1.00. Really, multiple correlation provides an index of the relationship between *two* variables, one and a weighted *combination* of more than one.

An example of the type of situation in which an educator might want to compute a multiple R would arise if he wished to know the relationship between a dependent (criterion) variable, such as student performance on a senior high-school mathematics test, and two independent (predictor) variables considered together, such as: (1) student intellectual aptitude, and (2) student performance on a mathematical achievement test taken in junior high school. He might be

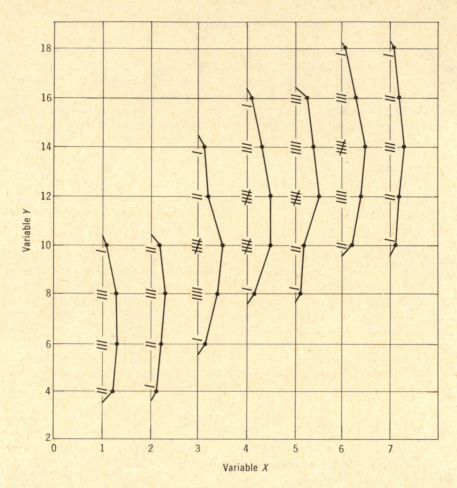

Figure 5.10 *A correlation chart with Y distributions represented for values of X where the assumption of homoscedasticity has been satisfied.*

interested in this relationship between combined independent variables and a dependent variable to see if the resulting *R* was much stronger than the simple *r* between the dependent variable and either criterion variable. Often one can increase the strength of the relationship between a criterion and several predictor variables by computing a multiple *R*.

This phenomenon is illustrated in Table 5.4 where simple *r* coefficients have been computed between 275 college students' one-semester grade point ratios (the dependent variable) and their scores on two predictor measures: (1) *American Council on Education Psychological Examination* (ACE) which provides an index of intellectual aptitude, and (2) the *Survey of Study Habits and*

Table 5.4.

Intercorrelations among 275 College Students' SSHA Scores, ACE Scores, and One-Semester Grade Point Ratios Plus a Multiple Correlation Coefficient between: (1) Grade Point Ratio, and (2) SSHA. and ACE. Scores Considered Simultaneously

Relationship	Coefficient
Grades versus ACE	$r = 0.45$
Grades versus SSHA.	$r = 0.48$
SSHA versus ACE.	$r = 0.22$
Grades versus ACE and SSHA.	$R = 0.60$

SOURCE: W. J. Popham and M. R. Moore, "A Validity Check on the Brown Holtzman Survey of Study Habits and Attitudes and the Borow College Inventory of Academic Adjustment," Personnel Guidance J., **38**, no. 7 (March 1960): 552–554.

Attitudes (SSHA) which is designed to measure factors associated with student academic success other than intellectual aptitude. Note from Table 5.4 that when ACE scores are related to grades an *r* of only 0.45 is produced. Similarly, when SSHA scores are related to grades an *r* of 0.48 is yielded. But when grades are related by multiple correlation to ACE and SSHA scores *considered simultaneously*, and *R* of 0.60 is produced.

Observe that the separate *r* coefficients for grades versus ACE and grades versus SSHA have not been simply added to obtain *R*, for the correlation between the two predictors of 0.22 has been taken into consideration. Once the product–moment correlations between the several variables involved in a multiple correlation problem have been computed, the calculation of *R* is relatively simple. The computation procedures for multiple correlation will be discussed in the next chapter.

PARTIAL CORRELATION

In a different type of research situation involving more than two variables the statisticians make use of a technique called *partial correlation*. This technique is used to assess the relationships between two variables when another variable's relationship with the initial two has been held constant or "partialed out."

It is recognized that the relationship between two variables is often unclear because of their mutual relationship with a third variable. For example, if one were to compute an *r* between mental age and weight for a group of youngsters ranging in age from one to ten years a substantially high and positive coefficient would result. Does this mean that intelligence is related to a person's weight? Obviously, the third variable, chronological age, to which both mental age and weight are related, must be considered in this analysis, for it is the *mutual* relationship of mental age and weight to chronological age which superficially makes it appear that the heavier individuals are brighter.

To use another commonly cited example, it is sometimes found that the relationship between school grade point average and students' hours of study is negative. If one were to accept this relationship as it stands, it would appear that students who wished to make high grades should be urged to study less. Yet, when the effect of intelligence is held constant through partial correlation, the relationship between grades and study hours becomes positive and usually significant. The fact that the two variables originally under investigation were mutually related to a third confused the picture. The "missing" variable, of course, is intellectual ability, which allows extremely bright students to attain high marks by studying less.

Ideally, researchers could avoid this problem by selecting only subjects who were alike with respect to the third variable. For example, in the preceding illustration only students of the same intellectual ability would have been selected. The effect of the third variable upon the relationship between the two variables being studied would thereby be controlled through the research design. Unfortunately, such approaches often reduce the sample size to trivial proportions. In addition, the researcher frequently wishes to conduct his investigations within an actual school environment, thereby necessitating the inclusion of intact, heterogeneous groups.

For these reasons partial correlation offers a convenient method for dealing with such problems, particularly in preliminary phases of an investigation when the researcher is reluctant to expend too much time on rigorously controlling the relevant variables through experimental design. The symbolic representation of a partial correlation coefficient is $r_{12.3}$ which signifies the relationship between variables one and two after their mutual relationship to variable three has been removed or partialed out. It is also possible to hold constant additional variables in which case the partial correlation coefficient becomes $r_{12.34}$, $r_{12.345}$, and so forth. The important thing to remember is that the subscript numbers to the right of the decimal point indicate the controlled variables, while the subscript numbers to the left of the decimal point indicate the two correlated variables. For example, if $r_{12.3} = 0.62$, this means that the correlation between variables one and two, when the influence of variable three has been controlled, is 0.62. Similarly, if $r_{23.14} = 0.34$, then we know that, when the influence of variables one and four has been controlled, the relationship between variables two and three is 0.34. In other words, *if* all subjects in the study had been alike with respect to variables one and four, the relationship between variables two and three would have been 0.34. A partial r with only one variable held constant is frequently referred to as a *first-order partial*, while a partial r with two variables held constant is called a *second-order partial*, and so on.

The computational operations described in the next chapter will provide additional insight into the meaning of partial correlation.

SPECIAL MEASURES OF RELATIONSHIP

There are occasions when the researcher wishes to assess the degree of relationship between two variables, but certain features of his data make it impossible to employ the normal product—moment correlation procedure. For some of these situations, special correlation procedures have been developed. For instance, suppose the researcher wishes to assess the degree of relationship between a variable which is continuously distributed over a range of score values, such as college-entrance-examination scores, and a second variable which is dichotomous, such as: (1) boarding on campus, or (2) boarding off campus. Here is a situation which does not lend itself to standard product—moment correlation procedures, yet there is a special statistical relationship technique designated for precisely this type of problem.

Before turning to some of these special correlation methods, it is necessary to draw a distinction between variables which are *dichotomous* and those which have been *dichotomized*. Generally speaking, variables are represented by two or more points on a scale of measurement. Most variables in educational research are represented by many points on a measurement scale. For example, almost all test scores fall into this category. Such variables are usually called *continuous* variables. There are some variables, however, which are represented by *only* two points on a scale. These are *dichotomous* or two-category variables. Examples of dichotomous variables are sex (male *or* female), marital state (married *or* unmarried), and residence (living on *or* off campus).[1]

Sometimes researchers encounter continuous variables which, for analysis purposes, must be artificially dichotomized. Thus, a continuous variable such as students' scores on a final exam might be considered as either scores below the median *or* scores at the median and above. This would not be an actual dichotomous variable, but would be an artificially *dichotomized* variable.

Four statistical techniques exist which are suitable for describing the degree of relationship between various combinations of two dichotomous, dichotomized, and continuous variables. The four special correlation methods are the *point biserial coefficient* (r_{pb}), the *biserial coefficient* (r_b), the *phi coefficient* (ϕ), and the *tetrachoric coefficient* (r_t). Although these specialized techniques are not widely used, it may be helpful to the reader to examine Table 5.5 which presents the particular type of variable relationship each method is designed to assess.

In the case of the product—moment correlation coefficient it has been stressed that the relationship between the variables must be capable of being expressed by a straight line. If the relationships depart from linearity in a marked fashion, an alternative technique must be used. For the product—moment coefficient, when a nonlinear relationship is present, the *correlation ratio*, η (*eta*), can be employed.

A typical example of a nonlinear relationship is found when performance scores are correlated with chronological age. By plotting the values for such a relationship, the researcher will usually discover a noticeable curvature in the

---

[1]It should be pointed out that there are also variables which are discontinuous but have more than two categories. One could consider marital status, for example, as a trichotomous variable, that is, (1) married, (2) never married, (3) formerly married but now single.

Table 5.5

Four Special Correlation Methods and the Variable Relationships They Are Designed to Assess

Method	Variable Relationship to Be Assessed
Point biserial coefficient (r_{pb})	Continuous versus dichotomous
Biserial coefficient (r_b)	Continuous versus dichotomized
Phi coefficient (ϕ)	Dichotomous versus dichotomous
Tetrachoric coefficient (r_t)	Dichotomized versus dichotomized

array of the paired values. Incidentally, the algebraic sign of η is always positive; hence most statisticians urge that it be considered only as an index of the closeness of the relationship between two variables, not the direction of the relationship.

An extensive examination of these procedures is beyond the scope of this book; the selected readings cited at the close of the chapter contain further treatment of these measures.

REVIEW

Correlation techniques provide the statistician with a procedure for quantifying the nature of relationships between two or more variables. In the case of the most common correlational procedure, the product–moment correlation coefficient of linear relationship, the strength and direction of a relationship between two variables is described by the value of r which ranges from a perfect relationship of ± 1.00 to a nonexistent relationship of zero.

The strength of the correlation coefficient is usually interpreted according to the nearness of r to the perfect correlations of ± 1.00. As with many other statistics, the probabilistic significance of r can be readily determined, so that an observed relationship can be attributed either to chance or nonchance factors.

Multiple correlation and partial correlation are relationship techniques designed to deal with more than two variables. Multiple correlation describes the degree of relationship between a variable and two or more variables considered simultaneously. A multiple R is interpreted in essentially the same way as a product–moment r. Partial correlation allows the statistician to describe the relationship between two variables after controlling or "partialing out" the confounding relationship of another variable(s).

Point coefficient relationship measures and the correlation ratio were briefly discussed at the close of the chapter.

EXERCISES

1. Which of the following correlation coefficients represents the *strongest* relationship between two variables?

(a) $r = 0.59$ (b) $r = 0.05$ (c) $r = -0.71$

2. Presented below are three simple correlation charts indicating the nature of the relationship between two variables. In each instance, decide whether or not the product–moment correlation coefficient should be used to assess the degree of relationship.

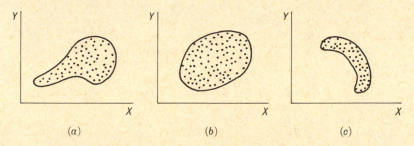

(a)   (b)   (c)

3. If a null hypothesis of relationship between two measures is to be tested by the calculation of r and its subsequent interpretation at the 0.01 level of significance, what action regarding the null hypothesis should be taken in each of the following situations?

   (a) $r = 0.65$ $n = 24$ (c) $r = -0.40$ $n = 45$ (e) $r = -0.75$ $n = 9$
   (b) $r = $ 0.85 $n = 7$ (d) $r = 0.14$ $n = 590$

4. If a researcher wishes to assess the strength and direction of a possible relationship between two continuously distributed variables and can demonstrate that the assumptions of homoscedasticity and linearity are satisfied, which statistical relationship technique should he employ?

5. Suppose an educator wishes to test for a relationship between scores on an intelligence test and whether or not a group of individuals are foreign-born. Which relationship technique should he employ?

6. In running a standard product–moment correlation computation between achievement scores and scores on a newly devised personality test, a classroom teacher plots the data to determine if the assumption of homoscedasticity and normality can be satisfied. To her surprise, the data are curvilinearly rather than linearly arranged. Which relationship technique is called for in this instance?

7. If a researcher wishes to assess the degree of relationship between (1) achievement, and (2) intelligence and interest considered simultaneously, which relationship technique should be employed?

8. If a school counselor wishes to assess the degree of relationship between achievement and intelligence, while holding constant the variable of reading ability which is related to both achievement and intelligence, which correlational procedure should he select?

9. A county district school psychologist has just completed a correlational analysis in which sixth graders' scores on the *California Test of Mental Maturity* were correlated with seventh grade language arts achievement, *r* equaling 0.53. The psychologist, realizing that the *r* of 0.53 is only based on a single sample, wants to supply the school personnel in the district with some guidelines for the possible relationship between CTMM scores and language arts achievement they can expect in the future. He would like to supply them with a high and a low boundary of the correlation coefficient between these measures which will cover this relationship 95 percent of the time. What statistical technique should be used in this situation?

SELECTED READINGS

Blalock, Hubert M., Jr., *Social Statistics*. New York: McGraw-Hill, 1960, chaps. 17 and 19.

Edwards, Allen L., *Statistical Methods for the Behavioral Sciences*. New York: Holt, Rinehart & Winston, 1957, chaps. 8 and 10.

Guilford, J. P., *Fundamental Statistics in Psychology and Education*. New York: McGraw-Hill, 1965, chaps. 6, 14, and 16.

McNemar, Quinn, *Psychological Statistics*. New York: Wiley, 1962, chaps. 10, 11, and 12.

Tate, Merle W., *Statistics in Education*. New York: Macmillan, 1955, pp. 229–266.

Walker, Helen M., and Joseph Lev, *Statistical Inference*. New York: Holt, Rinehart & Winston, 1953, chap. 11.

Weinberg, George H., and John A. Schumaker, *Statistics: An Intuitive Approach*. Belmont, Calif.: Wadsworth, 1962, chap. 17.

6

Correlation— Computation Procedures

There are many methods by which the product–moment correlation coefficient may be computed. Most of these methods are simply variations of a basic formula for r. One method involves the use of a correlation table similar to Figure 5.1 in the previous chapter. Although most statistics texts give considerable attention to the computation of r through the use of a correlation table, we believe that such computation methods which involve great quantities of hand calculation will rarely be used by educators since they are too time-consuming. If someone has many correlation coefficients to compute, he will either gain access to a desk calculator or send his data to a computer center for analysis. Few people today have time to compute many correlation coefficients by the laborious hand-calculation techniques required in the correlation table method.

However, there is one advantage to the correlation table method of computing r that should not be overlooked, namely, the possibility of visually inspecting the plotted data to see whether the selection of a linear index of correlation is reasonable. The same result can be achieved, however, by plotting a sample of the data on a graph prior to the final calculation of r.

FORMULAS FOR THE PRODUCT–MOMENT COEFFICIENT

One basic formula (algebraically equivalent to equation 5.1 in the previous chapter) used in the calculation of the product–moment correlation coefficient is

$$r_{xy} = \frac{\Sigma xy}{n s_x s_y} \qquad (6.1)$$

where

r_{xy} = correlation coefficient between X and Y
Σxy = sum of cross products of deviation scores for X and Y
s_x and s_y = standard deviations of X and Y scores
n = number of pairs

The basic formula can be manipulated algebraically to result in the following *raw-score correlation formula* (6.2) which uses original measurements. It is this formula which the reader should master, for it is the easiest to compute on an automatic calculator.

$$r = \frac{\Sigma XY - \dfrac{(\Sigma X)(\Sigma Y)}{n}}{\sqrt{\left(\Sigma X^2 - \dfrac{(\Sigma X)^2}{n}\right)\left(\Sigma Y^2 - \dfrac{(\Sigma Y)^2}{n}\right)}} \qquad (6.2)$$

The reader will recognize a number of familiar quantities in this raw-score correlation formula. Actually, in addition to n (the number of *pairs*), the five quantities needed in order to calculate r by this method, are, ΣX, ΣX^2, ΣY, ΣY^2, and ΣXY which can be obtained in a relatively simple fashion with most desk calculators.

With small samples it is reasonable to compute Formula 6.2 by hand. For purposes of illustration, r for the relationship between the two hypothetical sets of test data in Table 6.1 can now be calculated. The appropriate values are substituted and the raw-score correlation formula is used as follows:

$$r_{xy} = \frac{618 - \dfrac{(78)(61)}{10}}{\sqrt{\left(760 - \dfrac{(78)^2}{10}\right)\left(533 - \dfrac{(61)^2}{10}\right)}}$$

$$= \frac{618 - 475.8}{\sqrt{(760 - 608.4)(533 - 372.1)}}$$

$$= \frac{142.2}{\sqrt{(151.6)(160.9)}}$$

$$= \frac{142.2}{\sqrt{24392.44}}$$

$$= \frac{142.2}{156.2}$$

$$= 0.91$$

A correlation of 0.91 is, of course, an index of a strong relationship between the two variables under study. By entering Table D with eight degrees of freedom (number of pairs minus two), one finds that an r of 0.91 is significant beyond the 0.01 level.

Even if hand calculated, the raw-score formula (6.1) can be used effectively with small samples. With larger samples, some of the quantities necessary for its computation may already be available as a result of prior calculation of

Table 6.1

Hypothetical Scores for Ten Subjects on Two Tests, as well as the Totals Needed for the Calculation of r by the Raw-Score Formula

Subject	Test 1 X	Test 2 Y	X^2	Y^2	XY
a	8	3	64	9	24
b	2	1	4	1	2
c	8	6	64	36	48
d	5	3	25	9	15
e	15	14	225	196	210
f	11	12	121	144	132
g	13	9	169	81	117
h	6	4	36	16	24
i	4	4	16	16	16
j	6	5	36	25	30
Σ	78	61	760	533	618

descriptive statistics. It might be noted that the raw-score formula (6.2) is equivalent to the following formula in terms of deviation scores:

$$r_{xy} = \frac{\Sigma xy}{\sqrt{(\Sigma x^2)(\Sigma y^2)}} \tag{6.3}$$

The sums of squares for the *x* and *y* variables are typically at hand from the computation of standard deviations. (See Chapter 8, p. 114 for an example illustrating the use of Formula 6.3.)

   With larger samples, however, use of an automatic calculator is encouraged. These mechanical devices may appear formidable, but can be mastered quite easily. Anyone who must compute many statistics should attempt to develop a reasonable degree of competence with such calculators as soon as possible. They can tremendously expedite the computation of most statistical tests. In recent years, high-speed computers have, fortunately, become increasingly available to those who must make such computations.

   A second computation example using the raw-score formula, but which results in negative *r*, will now be included for the hypothetical data in Table 6.2.

   The appropriate quantities are substituted in Formula 6.2 and *r* is obtained as follows:

$$r_{xy} = \frac{78 - \dfrac{(35)(21)}{5}}{\sqrt{\left(345 - \dfrac{(35)^2}{5}\right)\left(151 - \dfrac{(21)^2}{5}\right)}}$$

$$= \frac{78 - 147}{\sqrt{(345 - 245)(151 - 88.2)}}$$

Table 6.2

Hypothetical Scores for Five Subjects on Two Measures, as well as the Totals Needed for the Calculation of r by the Raw-Score Formula

Subject	Measure 1 X	Measure 2 Y	X^2	Y^2	XY
1	6	2	36	4	12
2	10	1	100	1	10
3	3	8	9	64	24
4	14	1	196	1	14
5	2	9	4	81	18
Σ	35	21	345	151	78

$$= \frac{-69}{\sqrt{(100)(62.8)}}$$

$$= \frac{-69}{\sqrt{6280}}$$

$$= \frac{-69}{\sqrt{79.25}}$$

$$= -0.87$$

By consulting Table D one finds that an r of -0.87 ($df = 3$) is not significant beyond the 0.05 level. The lack of significance, of course, is due to the extremely small sample. If a relationship of such magnitude persisted with larger samples, the result would certainly be significant at a much lower probability level.

Confidence Interval

As indicated in the previous chapter, to compute a confidence interval of a given probability level for r, the coefficient must be transformed into a special z_r value through the use of Table O. For example, if the correlation between 52 pupils' scores on two tests was 0.60, the first step would be to consult Table O and find that for an r of 0.60, a z_r value of 0.69 should be used.

The next step is to determine the *standard error* of the particular z_r which is $1/\sqrt{n-3}$. In this instance, the standard error $= 1/\sqrt{52-3} = 0.14$.

Then the probability level desired for the confidence interval is decided upon and the normal curve $\pm z$ values are selected which enclose that proportion, for example, 95 percent of the normal curve. In the case of a 95 percent confidence interval the z values would be ± 1.96.

The next step is to multiply the ± 1.96 by the standard error of 0.14 and combine the result with the z_r value of 0.69. Thus, $0.69 \pm (1.96)(0.14)$ yields z_r

values of 0.96 and 0.42. These quantities are then transformed, through the use of Table O, back into correlation coefficients to form the boundaries of the 95 percent confidence interval. In this example the confidence limits for r would be 0.40 and 0.75.

　　If confidence intervals at a different probability level are to be determined, the same procedure is followed except different normal curve z values are employed. For example, a 99 percent confidence interval for these data would be generated as follows: $0.69 \pm (2.58)(0.14) = z_r$ values of 1.05 and 0.33, which yields 99 percent confidence limits for r of 0.32 and 0.78.

　　The reader should be aware that this procedure for constructing a confidence interval for estimating a *population* correlation coefficient is based on exactly the same logic used in Chapter 4 for the construction of a confidence interval in the estimation of a population mean.

MULTIPLE CORRELATION

Although there are other methods of computing a multiple R which indicates the relationship between one variable (Y) and two or more other variables (e.g., X_1 and X_2) considered simultaneously, a straightforward computation procedure makes use of the individually computed r's between the variables involved in the problem. These product–moment correlation coefficients are then substituted in the following formula designed for three variables:

$$R_{y \cdot x_1 x_2} = \sqrt{\frac{r_{yx_1}^2 + r_{yx_2}^2 - 2r_{yx_1}r_{yx_2}r_{x_1 x_2}}{1 - r_{x_1 x_2}^2}} \qquad (6.4)$$

where

　$R_{y \cdot x_1 x_2}$ = coefficient of multiple correlation between Y and a combination of X_1 and X_2

　r_{yx_1} = the product-moment correlation coefficient between Y and X_1

　r_{yx_2} = the product-moment correlation coefficient between Y and X_2

　$r_{x_1 x_2}$ = the product-moment correlation coefficient between X_1 and X_2

　　Using the correlation coefficients reported in Table 5.4 on page 77 to illustrate the use of Formula 6.4 we substitute as follows:

$$R_{y \cdot x_1 x_2} = \sqrt{\frac{(0.45)^2 + (0.48)^2 - 2(0.45)(0.48)(0.22)}{1 - (0.22)^2}}$$

$$= \sqrt{\frac{0.2025 + 0.2304 - 0.0950}{1 - 0.048}}$$

$$= \sqrt{\frac{0.3379}{0.952}}$$

$$= \sqrt{0.3549}$$

$$= 0.5957$$

The *R* of 0.60 (rounding) is, of course, considerably greater than the individual correlations between the criterion variable and either predictor variable.

It is also possible to compute a multiple correlation coefficient between a criterion variable and more than two predictor variables. The interpretation of the resulting *R* is precisely the same as in the case of two predictors. The formula for such problems is a logical extension of Formula 6.4, but can be simplified by using previously computed multiple correlation coefficients. Discussions of such extensions are found in most advanced statistical texts.

PARTIAL CORRELATION

When a researcher wishes to study the relationship between two variables which presumably may be wholly or partly due to the effect of a third variable, the technique known as partial correlation allows him to control the effects of the third variable. With only one variable to be held constant, the formula for a first-order partial *r* is given in Formula 6.5.

$$r_{xy \cdot z} = \frac{r_{xy} - r_{xz} r_{yz}}{\sqrt{1 - r_{xz}^2} \, \sqrt{1 - r_{yz}^2}} \tag{6.5}$$

In the above formula, $r_{xy \cdot z}$ represents the amount of relationship between variable *X* and variable *Y* after the influence of variable *Z* has been controlled.

If it is necessary to control the influence of two or more variables, that is, to compute second- or higher-order partials, the formulas are logical extensions of Formula 6.5. For example, a second-order partial requires the use of Formula 6.6.

$$r_{vx \cdot yz} = \frac{r_{vx \cdot y} - (r_{vz \cdot y})(r_{xz \cdot y})}{\sqrt{1 - r_{vz \cdot y}^2} \, \sqrt{1 - r_{xz \cdot y}^2}} \tag{6.6}$$

In calculating second- or higher-order partials, it is requisite to first compute the lower-order partials required for the formula. For instance, note that, in formula 6.6, several first-order partials would initially have to be computed through Formula 6.5, in order that they could be substituted in the formula for the second-order *r*.

The use of formula 6.5 can be illustrated with correlations between (1) scores on a standardized intelligence test, (2) high-school grade point averages, and (3) hours of study per week. The following correlations indicate the strength of the three relationships for 100 high-school seniors:

Relationship	Coefficient
(1) Intelligence versus (2) grades	$r_{12} = 0.58$
(2) Grades versus (3) study time	$r_{23} = 0.10$
(1) Intelligence versus (3) study time	$r_{13} = -0.40$

If we wish to study each of the possible relationships between these three variables, considered two at a time, while holding the third constant through partial correlation, we simply insert the appropriate coefficients into Formula 6.5. For example, if it is wished to obtain $r_{12.3}$, that is, the relationship between (1) intelligence, and (2) grades, while partialing out the influence of (3) study time, then Formula 6.7 is set up and solved as follows:

$$r_{12.3} = \frac{0.58 - (-0.40)(0.10)}{\sqrt{1 - (-0.40)^2} \sqrt{1 - (0.10)^2}}$$

$$= \frac{0.62}{(0.917)(0.995)}$$

$$= 0.68$$

Note that $r_{12} = 0.58$, whereas $r_{12.3} = 0.68$, which indicates that, if study time is held constant, that is, if every subject in the sample studied the same number of hours per week, then the relationship between grades and intelligence is even stronger than when subjects are heterogeneous with respect to study hours.

The other partial correlations in this sample would be computed as follows:

$$r_{13.2} = \frac{-0.40 - (0.58)(0.10)}{\sqrt{1 - (0.58)^2} \sqrt{1 - (0.10)^2}}$$

$$= \frac{-0.458}{(0.815)(0.995)}$$

$$= -0.56$$

$$r_{23.1} = \frac{0.10 - (0.58)(-0.40)}{\sqrt{1 - (0.58)^2} \sqrt{1 - (-0.40)^2}}$$

$$= \frac{0.332}{(0.815)(0.917)}$$

$$= 0.44$$

The partial coefficient $r_{13.2} = -0.56$, in contrast to the original r_{13} of -0.40, indicates that, if grades are held constant, the negative relationship between intelligence and study hours is even stronger. This indicates that brighter students in this sample spend fewer hours in study than their less gifted classmates.

The relationship between grades and study time, when intelligence is held constant, rises from the original r_{23} of 0.10 to a more reasonable relationship where $r_{23.1} = 0.44$. This indicates, as one might expect, that if intelligence is comparable, more time devoted to study is positively related to higher grades.

Second- and third-order partials are computed using Formula 6.6 in a similar fashion, having initially calculated the first-order partial r's.

REVIEW

In this chapter procedures were described for computing product—moment correlation coefficients, multiple correlation coefficients, and partial correlation coefficients. Although the computations necessary for these coefficients can be hand-calculated, the use of a desk calculator or other mechanical computation device was strongly advocated.

The technique for determining a confidence interval for the product—moment coefficient was outlined involving the use of Table O in the Appendix. It was seen that the computation of such confidence intervals is quite simple.

EXERCISES

1. Compute the product—moment correlation coefficient for the 20 pairs of scores given below.

Subject	Measure 1	Measure 2	Subject	Measure 1	Measure 2
a	40	20	k	33	13
b	40	16	l	33	15
c	39	17	m	32	14
d	37	18	n	32	11
e	37	18	o	30	12
f	36	20	p	30	11
g	35	14	q	30	10
h	35	14	r	29	12
i	34	15	s	28	9
j	34	12	t	26	10

2. Is the coefficient obtained in problem 1 statistically significant? If so, at what level?

3. Compute the product—moment correlation coefficient between the X and Y measures given below:

X	Y	X	Y
49	42	40	38
46	42	38	39
44	44	38	40
44	40	36	29
42	43	34	37

4. Is the r obtained in exercise 3 statistically significant at the 0.01 level?

5. An experimenter carefully matched 50 pairs of subjects on the basis of age, sex, intelligence, and previous achievement. He then randomly assigned one sex of the matched pairs to an experimental condition (E) and the other set to a control condition (C). The criterion measure used in the research was performance on an achievement test. The experimenter was

interested in the relationship of the dependent variable scores for the two groups. Calculate the product–moment *r* for the following set of data:

E	C	E	C	E	C	E	C	E	C
25	18	22	25	20	16	17	14	12	12
25	19	22	20	20	12	17	18	12	9
25	20	22	20	20	24	17	12	12	9
25	21	22	19	19	24	16	11	11	14
24	20	21	19	19	16	16	9	11	18
24	16	21	18	19	16	14	20	11	21
24	15	21	21	18	19	14	21	10	11
24	15	21	21	18	19	13	18	10	9
23	21	20	14	17	21	13	16	9	13
23	25	20	12	17	23	13	13	9	12

6. Is the correlation coefficient in the foregoing problem significant at the 0.01 level?

7. A class in educational research was given a 25-question quiz on educational statistics early in the term. At the conclusion of the course a 100-question final exam was administered. Compute the *r* between these two measures. Is the coefficient significant beyond the 0.05 level?

Statistics Quiz	Final Examination	Statistics Quiz	Final Examination
23	82	15	54
20	90	20	95
15	78	21	81
20	74	20	69
21	84	19	84
22	78	17	69
20	82	21	77
12	80	19	78
15	84	18	85
		23	90

8. In the table below are 52 prospective secondary teachers' scores on three tests. Compute multiple correlation coefficients: (a) for the relationship between (1) X and (2) Y and Z considered simultaneously, that is, $R_{x \cdot yz}$; (b) for the relationship between (1) Y and (2) X and Z considered simultaneously, that is, $R_{y \cdot xz}$; and (c) for the relationship between (1) Z and (2) X and Y considered simultaneously, that is, $R_{z \cdot xy}$.

Subject	Test X	Y	Z	Subject	Test X	Y	Z
1	7	23	83	27	4	21	40
2	5	30	87	28	9	20	82
3	10	27	62	29	2	24	160
4	6	18	105	30	6	25	63
5	9	22	55	31	12	29	66
6	10	27	73	32	11	24	92
7	12	26	105	33	10	26	106
8	11	18	71	34	12	31	61
9	10	23	107	35	11	37	96
10	14	22	136	36	12	32	109
11	10	27	110	37	12	29	84
12	14	22	94	38	13	33	38
13	7	29	131	39	5	27	84
14	12	23	108	40	11	35	84
15	4	16	72	41	12	35	76
16	9	22	86	42	11	35	103
17	9	22	106	43	4	33	160
18	2	27	97	44	13	30	80
19	12	24	83	45	13	37	52
20	6	27	109	46	6	34	98
21	7	23	69	47	9	36	77
22	8	24	69	48	8	37	93
23	14	24	67	49	10	36	148
24	11	23	138	50	8	19	48
25	14	27	69	51	2	31	70
26	8	30	136	52	9	30	89

9. For the data in the previous example compute (a) the partial correlation coefficient for variables X and Y when Z is held constant, $r_{xy \cdot z}$; (b) the partial correlation coefficient for variables Y and Z when X is held constant, $r_{yz \cdot x}$; and (c) the partial correlation coefficint for variables X and Z when Y is held constant, $r_{xz \cdot y}$.

10. Compute a 95 percent confidence interval for a correlation coefficient of 0.80 when $n = 403$.

11. Compute a 99 percent confidence interval for a correlation coefficient of 0.65 when $n = 28$.

SELECTED READINGS

Blalock, Hubert M., Jr., *Social Statistics*. New York: McGraw-Hill, 1960, chaps. 17 and 19.

Edwards, Allen L., *Statistical Methods for the Behavioral Sciences*. New York: Holt, Rinehart & Winston, 1957, chaps 8 and 10.

Guilford, J. P., *Fundamental Statistics in Psychology and Education*. New York: McGraw-Hill, 1965, chaps. 6, 14, and 16.

McNemar, Quinn, *Psychological Statistics*. New York: Wiley, 1962, chaps. 10, 11, and 12.

Tate, Merle W., *Statistics in Education*. New York: Macmillan, 1955, pp. 229–266.

Walker, Helen M., and Joseph Lev, *Statistical Inference*. New York: Holt, Rinehart & Winston, 1953, chap. 11.

Weinberg, George H., and John A. Schumaker, *Statistics: An Intuitive Approach*. Belmont, Calif.: Wadsworth, 1962, chap. 17.

7
Regression

Correlational methods such as those described in the two previous chapters enable the statistician to determine the strength and direction of the relationship between two variables. Often, to our surprise, correlation techniques reveal that there is no appreciable relationship between variables which we would have guessed were very strongly related. Frequently, however, the researcher does discover a strong relationship existing between two variables. For example, a series of research investigations may indicate that student anxiety, with the *r* between achievement scores and scores on an anxiety test equaling − 0.43. Or again, the researcher may discover a correlation coefficient of 0.52 between the scores of master's degree candidates on a verbal analogies test and their subsequent performance on an objective examination taken at the end of the master's program. Of what value are such relationships? How may the educator profitably employ such relationships once they have been uncovered?

It should be apparent that *any* increase in the educator's fund of knowledge regarding the variables with which he works will be of some value. Even if there is but an awareness of the *general* nature of relationships between variables, such an awareness should help the educator to reach wiser decisions. For instance, since research indicates that a student's secondary-school grade point average is related to his college achievement, the college counselor can roughly identify a number of freshmen who may need academic assistance during their initial year in college. Similarly, a teacher who knows that general mental ability is positively related to student classroom performance can, if he has access to IQ data for his students, better understand why certain students have difficulty with their lessons.

In addition to understanding such general types of relationships, the educator often wishes to make reasonable *predictions* for one student at a time. For instance, high-school counselors are frequently concerned with the likelihood of a particular student's academic success in college. While we know that a relationship exists between intellectual ability and academic performance, is it possible to particularize this relationship in order to make a prediction of success or failure for an individual student? There is a statistical technique designed to do precisely this; that is, allow one to make predictions regarding a person's performance on one variable (e.g., academic success), given his performance on another variable (e.g., intellectual ability). This statistical technique is called *regression*. It is closely related to the product–moment correlation technique.

It will be recalled that the correlation coefficient discussed in the previous chapters was an index of *linear* relationship. Likewise, the prediction model to be discussed in this and the following chapter will be restricted to linear relationships, and the statistical technique can be more explicitly referred to as linear regression. In Chapter 5 we noted that important relationships between variables may not be linear in form and other indexes of relationship were needed. Likewise, the methods of linear regression can be generalized to include *nonlinear* regression. The procedures of nonlinear regression are sufficiently complicated so as not to be included in the present text; they are treated in more advanced statistical textbooks.

In making predictions regarding an individual's theoretical score on one measure from his score on an initial measure, we usually refer to the variable *from* which we are making the prediction as the *independent* variable or *predictor* variable. The variable that is predicted is called the *dependent* variable or the *criterion* variable. Thus, in predicting a student's score on a history examination from his earlier performance on the *Henmon–Nelson Test of Mental Ability*, the *Henmon–Nelson* score is the predictor or independent variable while the history exam score is the criterion or dependent variable.

RATIONALE

Briefly, the use of regression involves the following steps through which one can make a prediction of an individual's performance on a criterion variable, referred to as *Y*, from the individual's performance on a predictor variable, referred to as *X*. First, a sample of subjects is selected which is similar to those for whom predictions ultimately will be made. We can call this set of subjects the *regression sample*. For example, for predictions regarding eighth-grade youngsters's success in a ninth-grade algebra course, a sample of eighth graders must be secured. If the predictor variable (*X*) is to be performance on a group intelligence test, then the test must be administered to the sample. (However, if intelligence scores are already available, then ninth-grade pupils could be used.) Upon completion of the ninth-grade algebra class, students' scores on a comprehensive final examination (*Y*) must also be secured. Now if variables *X* and *Y* are correlated, as revealed by a product-moment *r*, it is possible to develop a *regression equation* which can be used to predict *future* eighth grader's scores on the ninth-grade algebra examination from previously administered intelligence tests scores. Predictions are not made for the regression sample, of course, for the criterion data are already known. The regression equation, which also can be plotted on a graph, takes this form:[1]

$$\tilde{Y} = a + bX \tag{7.1}$$

where $\tilde{Y}$ ($\sim$ = "*tilde*") is the *predicted* criterion variable score for a student who obtains score X on the predictor variable. In Formula 7.1 a and b are quantities which are yielded by an analysis of the X and Y data from the regression sample. The size and algebraic sign of b will depend upon the strength and direction of the relationship between X and Y observed in the student sample originally studied. For instance, in the present example the value of a might be 5.5 and the value of b might be 0.92. Hence our regression equation would be $\tilde{Y} = 5.5 + 0.92X$. Thus, to predict a student's expected score ($\tilde{Y}$) on the ninth-grade algebra exam, we insert his actual score on the eighth-grade intelligence test and solve the equation. To illustrate, if John Doe obtained a score of 110 on the intelligence test we would solve as follows: $Y = 5.5 + 0.92(110)$ which reduces to $\tilde{Y} = 106.7$. A score of 106.7 would be the prediction ($\tilde{Y}$) for John's performance on the Y variable, the algebra examination.

In essence, the statistician makes regression predictions for individuals based on data tendencies revealed in the previous study of samples of similar individuals. In the regression sample a certain relationship exists between the predictor variable and the criterion variable, such that an individual with a given score on the predictor is likely to achieve a certain score on the criterion. The regression equation of $\tilde{Y} = a + bX$ simply reflects the nature of the data relationship in the regression sample.

It should be noted that in order to make reasonably meaningful predictions for individuals from relationships demonstrated to exist in a sample, the individual must be relatively similar to the others in the regression sample. For example, a regression equation based upon the performance of eighth graders on an intelligence test could not appropriately be used to predict the ninth-grade algebra success of a fifth-grade pupil.

It is also important that factors affecting performance on the predictor and criterion variables remain relatively constant. Consequently, if a new summer algebra enrichment class has been formed between the eighth and ninth grades for all pupils, our regression scheme will probably prove ineffective. A new student sample composed of those who had taken the summer course will have to be studied to build a revised regression scheme. Similarly, any factors which may significantly alter performance on either predictor or criterion variable will usually necessitate the development of a new regression equation.

THE MEANING OF *a* AND *b*

As indicated in the preceding discussion, the values of a and b, the basic components of the regression equation, are determined from a set of sample data where scores for both X and Y are available. Both a and b are best under-

---

[1]The reader might recall from elementary algebra that this is the general equation for a straight line.

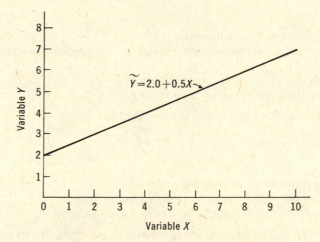

Figure 7.1   *Plot of regression line for Y = 2.0 + 0.5X.*

stood by referring to the *regression line* formed when the regression equation is plotted on graph. In Figure 7.1 a regression line for $\tilde{Y}$ is plotted for the regression equation $\tilde{Y} = 2.0 + 0.5X$. This regression line is formed by a technique called the method of least squares. Briefly, the regression line is placed in a representative position, where the sum of the squared distances between it and the points formed by the X and Y scores of the regression sample is at a minimum.

In the regression equation *a* is known as the *intercept* of the regression line, that is, the value of $\tilde{Y}$ when X is 0. Thus, *a* is the value of Y where the regression line *intercepts* or crosses the ordinate of the Y variable. The value of *a* in the present regression equation example is 2.0. Note in Figure 7.1 that the regression line *intercepts* the Y axis at 2.0.

The value of *b* is determined by the angle between the X axis and the regression line; hence *b* is called the *slope* of the regression line. (Technically *b* is the tangent of the angle formed by the regression line and the X axis.) Another way to view *b* is to think of it as the rate of change or increased value of Y with each unit increase of X. In the present example *b* is 0.5. Note in Figure 7.1 that as X becomes one unit larger, $\tilde{Y}$ becomes 0.5 units larger. For example, if X is 2.0 then $\tilde{Y}$ is 3.0, while as X increases to 3.0 then $\tilde{Y}$ becomes 3.5. The increase of 0.5 in the value of Y is, of course, the value of *b*, the slope of the regression line. Quite frequently *b* is also called the *regression coefficient*.

Although the computation of *a* and *b* will be considered in much greater detail in the chapter to follow, the reader can gain insight into their meaning by considering the following computational forms for these quantities:

$$b = r \frac{s_y}{s_x} \tag{7.2}$$

where

> b = the regression coefficient
> r = the product–moment coefficient of correlation between variables X and Y
> s_x = the standard deviation of variable X
> s_y = the standard deviation of variable Y.

Having determined the value of b, a is computed as follows:

$$a = \overline{Y} - b\overline{X} \tag{7.3}$$

where

> a = the intercept of the regression line
> $\overline{Y}$ = the mean of the Y values in the regression sample
> $\overline{X}$ = the mean of the X values in the regression sample.

Note that b is a function of the correlation coefficient. Given the variances for X and Y, when the magnitude of the relationship (size of r) between X and Y increases (or decreases), the regression coefficient b increases (or decreases). When the direction of the relationship (sign of r) is positive (or negative), b is positive (or negative) and the slope of the prediction line is in an upward (or downward) direction.

When the X and Y raw scores are first converted to standard z-score form, the regression line plotted in terms of z scores passes exactly through the origin (zero intercept) and has a regression coefficient exactly equal to the correlation coefficient ($b = r$). These properties can be ascertained from Formulas 7.2 and 7.3 by recalling that the mean and standard deviation of any distribution of z scores are always 0 and 1, respectively.

ACCURACY OF REGRESSION PREDICTIONS

Just how accurate will the predicted $\tilde{Y}$ value be for any given value of X? This question must be answered before an educator can make proper use of the predicted success of any student. In general, the question can be answered as follows: If the assumptions underlying the use of regression have been satisfactorily met, the greater the absolute value of r, the more accurate the predictions will be. In other words, as the observed relationship between the X and Y variables in the regression sample approach $+1.00$ or -1.00, one can be certain of more accurate predictions. If the relationship were absolutely perfect (and it never is in educational research!), one could predict with complete accuracy.

Requisite Assumptions

As in the case of the product–moment correlation, there are two assumptions which must be satisfied, in order to legitimately make inferences using the described regression scheme. Both refer to data in the regression sample on which the regression equation is based. First, the requirement of homoscedasticity must be satisfied. That is, when plotted on a table similar to a correlation chart, the variances in *Y* values for any given values of *X* should be comparable. To phrase it another way, the spread of *Y* scores for individually considered values of *X* must be about the same.

Second, it must be assumed that the values of *Y* for given values of *X* are distributed (in each column of a correlation table) in an approximately normal fashion.

When the assumptions of homoscedasticity and normality of criterion scores have been met, a measure called the *standard error of estimate* may be used to gauge the accuracy of the predicted criterion scores. Before discussing this index, however, it would be well to illustrate in greater detail what we mean by using the line of regression to make predictions and what we mean by an error in prediction.

Using the regression line to make predictions

Table 7.1 presents the scores obtained by 5 subjects on the predictor variable *X* and the criterion variable *Y*; means, standard deviations, the correlation coefficient, the regression equation, and predicted *Y* scores are also indicated. Figure 7.2 shows the scattergram for these data and also indicates the line of regression used to predict values of *Y* given values of *X*. The solid lines represent the correspondence between the *observed* (raw) scores on the *X* and *Y* variables. The dotted lines represent the paths for the *predicted Y* (the $\tilde{Y}$) scores given the observed *X* values. Solid points are used to represent observed values; crossed points are used to represent predicted values. For example, subject D obtained an *X* score of 8 and a *Y* score of 13; the predicted *Y* score for subject D is 17.8. We can obtain this prediction either by substituting $X = 8$ into the regression equation and solving algebraically or by employing the graph in Figure 7.2, using the dotted lines and reading off the *Y* value corresponding to the *X* value of 8. Thus, in predicting the *Y* score for subject D, we make an error of −4.8 points. These *errors of prediction* are given for all 5 subjects in Table 7.1 and represented in Figure 7.2 by the wavy line segments.

The regression line is often referred to as the line of "best fit" to the points in the scattergram. As mentioned, the mathematical criterion for finding this line is to minimize the sum of the squared errors of prediction; that is, we find that line in the scattergram such that the sum of the squared lengths of the wavy line segments is at a minimum. It turns out that this line has the equation given above. Furthermore, it is always the case that one point on the line of best fit is that point corresponding to the means of the two variables. Intuitively it should make sense that the best prediction for the mean of variable *X* is the mean of variable *Y*. Thus, it is relatively easy to construct the regression line: Locate the points corresponding to the intercept and the pair of means and draw the line through these two points.

The Standard Error of Estimate

The standard error of estimate ($s_{y \cdot x}$) reflects the accuracy of the relationship between predictor and criterion. It is used to estimate the agreement of a

---

Table 7.1
Hypothetical Data for Illustrating the Use of the Linear Regression Model

Subject	a	b	c	d	e
X	2	4	6	8	10
Y	7	1	19	13	25
$\tilde{Y}$	3.4	8.2	13.0	17.8	22.6
Errors $(Y - \tilde{Y})$	3.6	−7.2	7.0	−4.8	2.4

$$\bar{X} = 6 \qquad \bar{Y} = 13$$
$$s_x = 2.8 \qquad s_y = 8.4$$
$$r = 0.80$$
$$\tilde{Y} = 2.4X - 1.4$$

---

predicted $\tilde{Y}$ score with the "real" Y score. The standard error of estimate is used in the same manner as a standard deviation is used as a unit of measurement along the baseline of a normal distribution. In fact, the standard deviation of the errors of prediction is what is referred to as the standard error of estimate.

For example, if the standard error of estimate is 5.0 and the predicted $\tilde{Y}$ score is 100, then, as in a normal curve with a mean of 100 and a standard deviation of 5.0, the actual criterion score will fall within an area plus or minus 5.0 of the predicted Y score 68 times out of 100. Moving plus or minus two standard errors of estimate from the predicted score, one can assert that the actual criterion score will fall within ± 10 points of the predicted Y score 95 per-

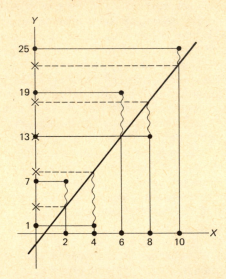

Figure 7.2 *Scattergram and regression line for the data in Table 7.1.*

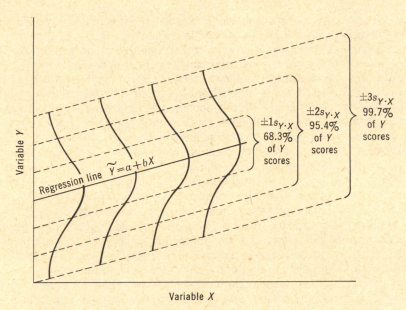

Figure 7.3 *A plotted regression line with disparity between predicted Y and actual Y scores depicted as a function of the size of the standard error of estimate.*

cent of the time. If one moves ±15, that is, three standard errors of estimate in either direction from the predicted Y score, then the prediction, with these margins of error, will be accurate almost 100 percent of the time.

Using this example, one can see then that a prediction could be described more accurately as follows: For a given X score, the actual Y score ($Y = 100$) will be between 95 and 105, 68.3 percent of the time; between 85 and 115, 99.7 percent of the time.

A similar explanation of the use of the standard error of estimate can be supplied graphically as in Figure 7.3 where, for any value of X, the predicted criterion score Y would fall on the regression line itself, but the *actual Y* score would range within the superimposed normal curves according to the size of $s_{y \cdot x}$.

Again, additional insight into the nature of the standard error of estimate can be obtained by considering one form of its computational formula:

$$s_{y \cdot x} = s_y \sqrt{1 - r^2} \tag{7.4}$$

First, note in Figure 7.2 that the spread (variance) of the predicted Y scores is less than that of the original, observed Y scores. This is always the case when any degree of linear relationship exists between the two variables. Thus, the variance of the predicted Y scores is a certain proportion of the variance of the observed Y scores. *It can be shown that this proportion is always equal to r^2, the square of the correlation coefficient.* For the data in Table 7.1, the variance of the $\tilde{Y}$s is $(0.80)^2$ or 0.64 of the variance of the Ys. The remaining proportion of the observed Y-score variance $(1-r^2)$ is due to the errors of prediction. So in our example, $1-0.64$ or 36 percent of the observed Y-score variance is *not* predictable. The *amount* of unpredictable Y-score variance is then $(1-r^2)s_y^2$. The amount of unpredictable variance for the above data is $(0.36)(8.4)^2$ or 25.9. By taking the square root of this quantity, we obtain a measure in standard deviation units. The reader should see that the square root of the quantity $(1-r^2)s_y^2$ is exactly the quantity given by Formula 7.4. Thus, the standard deviation of the errors in Table 7.1, otherwise known as the standard error of estimate, is equal to $\sqrt{25.9}$ or 5.1. We can obtain this value directly by using Formula 7.4: $s_{y \cdot x} = 8.4\sqrt{0.36}$ or 5.1 within rounding error.

The proportion (or percentage) of predictable variance r^2 often serves as an index of the *strength* of the correlation between two variables. Many researchers use the phrase "percentage of variance shared in common" by the two variables when using the index r^2. The reader should not be confused by this terminology once he realizes that the "percentage of shared common variance" refers to the percentage of predictable variance and this percentage remains the same whether we predict Y from X or X from Y (see following section).

At this point, the student should become acutely aware of the distinction between statistical significance and statistical meaningfulness. It is possible that an r of 0.20 can be statistically significant ($p < 0.05$) so long as we have data on 100 subjects or more. This means, of course, that we have a sample of data from a population which in all probability has a nonzero linear relationship between variables X and Y, and our best guess as to the magnitude of the relationship is 0.20. But how meaningful is this relationship? We can say that we are accounting for 4 percent of the predictable variance; that is, we are *not* able to predict 96 percent of the observed Y-score variance given the X-score data. In order to account for at least half the predictable variance, we need a correlation of 0.71.

This notion of predictable variance is a troublesome one for most beginning students of statistics. As a final example, consider the regression lines and data for Figure 7.2 versus Figure 5.2 in Chapter 5. We have already seen that in Figure 7.2, we are not predicting with perfect accuracy. That is, we "give up" some of the original Y-score variance to variability in error due to prediction, as evidenced by the smaller spread of predicted Y scores (crossed points) relative to the larger spread of original Y scores (solid points). Now look at Figure 5.2; imagine constructing the dotted lines for predicting the Y scores for each of the five X scores. These dotted lines would, in fact, be the solid lines as well, since we have a perfect relationship; in other words, the observed and predicted Y scores are one and the same. Thus, the variability of the predicted Y scores is equal to that of the observed Y scores and *all* Y-score variance is perfectly predictable. Usually, however, the relationship is not perfect and we can predict only r^2 of the Y-score variance.

The foregoing discussion should make it clear that, even with a statistical prediction scheme such as linear regression, the statistician is not able to make errorless predictions. He is, however, able to define and quantify the amount of error involved. This could not be done on the basis of a simple correlation co-efficient between a predictor variable and a criterion variable. Such predictions can be invaluable in various educational situations, particularly those which deal with vocational and academic counseling. Another use of linear regression is often seen in efforts to predict various types of school district and class enrollments for purposes of staffing or housing.

PREDICTING X FROM Y

Thus far only predictions of Y values from given values of X have been discussed. If the reader considers the logic underlying regression prediction, he should see that two variables are involved, one the predictor and the other the predicted. It would be easy to reverse the roles of the variables so that the predictor now becomes the predicted and vice versa. In this case, the percentage of predictable variance remains the same since r remains unchanged. Furthermore, the regression line still passes through the point corresponding to the means of the two variables since $\bar{X}$ and $\bar{Y}$ remain unchanged. But the slope b will always change unless both variables have the same variance; the intercept a will always change unless both variables have the same means and variances. Inspection of Formulas 7.2 and 7.3 will verify these observations. It is merely a matter of convention that the criterion or predicted variable is usually called Y and the predictor called X. In other words, by redesignating the variables, it is also possible to predict X from Y.

RELIABILITY OF THE CRITERION

It should be noted that one must have a reliable criterion variable, that is, one which can be measured with some degree of consistency, to make any kind of accurate prediction. The most elaborate prediction scheme, employing several different and highly sensitive predictor variables, is destined for failure if the criterion variable to be predicted is measured in such a way as to yield erratic, unreliable data. The question of reliability, of course, is discussed in greater detail in most measurement texts.

MULTIPLE-REGRESSION PREDICTION

It is possible to increase the accuracy of predictions by using more than one predictor variable in a regression scheme. This technique, known as *multiple-regression* prediction, uses two or more predictor variables, both of which are related to the criterion variable, by incorporating them into a more complex prediction scheme. Although more involved than simple regression with a single-predictor variable, multiple regression employs the same rationale in making predictions.

The formula for a multiple-regression equation is not too different from the simple single-predictor variable equation. For two predictors, the formula takes the following form:

$$\tilde{Y} = a + b_1X_1 + b_2X_2 \tag{7.5}$$

where

$\tilde{Y}$ = the predicted criterion score
a = a constant
b_1 = the regression coefficient for the first predictor variable
X_1 = the first predictor variable
b_2 = the regression coefficient for the second predictor variable
X_2 = the second predictor variable

Multiple-regression equations involving more than two predictor variables are simply logical extensions of formula 7.5.

Several comments regarding multiple-regression prediction should be made in passing. First, it is possible to reduce the standard error of estimate in a given single-predictor scheme by adding a second predictor variable which is related to the criterion variable. Second, the most advantageous additional predictor to add will usually be one which, while related to the criterion, is not too strongly related to the predictor variable already being used. To illustrate this last point, one might think of a situation in which academic achievement is the criterion variable and performance on a group IQ test is the predictor. If we add a second group IQ test to form a multiple-regression scheme we shall have added relatively little to the power and accuracy of the prediction formula, since both predictor variables are doing essentially the same job. One could more effectively augment the accuracy of the prediction scheme by selecting a second predictor which was strongly related to the criterion but *not* strongly related to the first predictor. In such a case, a student's performance on the *Brown–Holtzman Survey of Study Habits and Attitudes* might be a suitable second predictor, for it purportedly measures *nonintellectual* factors which are associated with academic achievement.

Bloom and Peters[1] observe that school grades, achievement test scores, or aptitude test scores will ordinarily correlate with college grades from 0.40 to 0.60. However, multiple correlations using two or more of these in combination will usually range from 0.55 to 0.65. Similarly, the accuracy of regression predictions can be increased by combining different predictors. It is possible to have three, four, or even more predictors in a multiple-regression scheme, but one soon reaches a point at which the slightly increased prediction precision provided by each new predictor variable does not justify the additional effort and expense of including more predictors. In most educational situations, little is gained by using more than four or five predictor variables because of the intercorrleation between these predictors.

With today's greatly increased availability of electronic computers, most multiple-regression equations are calculated by such high-speed equipment. Using an electronic computer, a researcher can solve in a few seconds multiple-regression problems which might take him many hours if computed by hand or desk calculator.

[1]Benjamin S. Bloom and Frank A. Peters, *The Use of Academic Prediction Scales for Counseling and Selecting College Entrants.* New York: Free Press, 1961, p. 25.

REVIEW

Whereas correlation methods provide one with a picture of the general relationship between two variables, through regression a prediction may be made regarding a particular individual's score on a criterion variable, given his score on a predictor variable. A typical example of the use of regression arises in predicting a student's academic success in one or more school programs based on his scores on aptitude tests.

The data necessary to set up a prediction equation are gathered from a group of subjects similar to those from whom predictions are to be made. From these subjects, known as the regression sample, measures are taken on both the predictor and criterion variables. If the relationship between predictor and criterion is strong, relatively precise predictions can be made for subsequent individuals. Through the use of the standard error of estimate, margins of error for prediction accuracy can be computed.

It is possible to increase the accuracy of predictions through the use of a multiple-regression procedure which incorporates more than one predictor variable and, accordingly, yields smaller or more precise standard errors of estimate.

EXERCISES

1. If a school counselor wishes to devise a scheme for predicting subsequent achievement performance of sophomore students, will he ultimately be more interested in product–moment correlation or in regression?

2. Is it possible to designate certain variables as criterion variables and others as predictor variables by the very nature of the variables? For instance, would it be safe to say that academic achievement was always a criterion variable?

3. Why is it important to have the individual for whom predictions are to be made resemble the individuals constituting the regression sample?

4. Two regression equations have been developed for different predictions, based on different regression samples of equal size. In situation A the r between predictor and criterion variable was 0.69; in situation B the r between predictor and criterion was 0.58. In which situation will the most accurate predictions be made?

5. If a sixth-grade youngster achieves a score of 30 on a predictor test, when the following regression equation has been set up for him and his class-mates, what will be his predicted score on the criterion test?

$$\tilde{Y} = 28.5 + 0.50X$$

6. Which of the following standard errors of estimates would allow the most accurate predictions?

$$s_{y \cdot x} = 12.0, \qquad s_{y \cdot x} = 8.4$$

7. Is a single-predictor regression scheme or a multiple-predictor regression scheme apt to result in more precise predictions with reduced error estimates?

SELECTED READINGS

Edwards, Allen L., *Statistical Methods for the Behavioral Sciences*. New York: Holt, Rinehart & Winston, 1957, chap. 7.

Ferguson, George A., *Statistical Analysis in Psychology and Education*. New York: McGraw-Hill, 1959, chap. 8.

McNemar, Quinn, *Psychological Statistics*. New York: Wiley, 1962, chap. 8.

Tate, Merle W., *Statistics in Education*. New York: Macmillan, 1955, pp. 267–320.

Walker, Helen M., and Joseph Lev, *Elementary Statistical Methods*. New York: Holt, Rinehart & Winston, 1958, chap. 9.

Weinberg, George H., and John A. Schumaker, *Statistics: An Intuitive Approach*. Belmont, Calif.: Wadsworth, 1962, chaps. 16 and 18.

Wert, James E., Charles O. Neidt, and Stanley J. Ahmann, *Statistical Methods in Educational and Psychological Research*. New York: Appleton-Century-Crofts, 1954, chap. 13.

8
Regression—Computation Procedures

Most of the formulas needed in the computation of linear regression problems were supplied in the previous chapter to demonstrate the relatively simple calculations involved in regression prediction. In this chapter the use of these and other algebraically equivalent formulas will be explained along with a number of computational examples. In most of these operations the use of some type of mechanical calculator is extremely desirable.

One's purpose in computing a regression problem is to develop the regression equation (Formula 7.1)

$$\tilde{Y} = a + bX$$

with which values of Y can be predicted from known values of X. We should also compute the standard error of estimate for Y ($s_{y \cdot x}$), so that we will have an idea of how accurate the prediction will be.

The first step in developing the regression equation is to select an appropriate regression sample, that is, a sample of subjects similar to the individuals for whom we wish to make predictions. Data must then be gathered from this sample regarding both the predictor variable (X) and the criterion variable (Y).

A COMPUTATIONAL EXAMPLE

Let us use a hypothetical example to illustrate the total regression operation. Suppose a counselor wished to predict the success of a certain college's M.Ed. degree candidates on a comprehensive final examination, which must be passed prior to the granting of the degree. If he could make such predictions with a reasonable degree of accuracy, the advising of potential master's degree candidates could be much more effective. He must now determine if there are any measures which will assist him in this prediction. To simplify matters, suppose that, at the college in this example, all potential M.Ed. candidates must take a nationally standardized entrance examination designed to assess their verbal skills. This measure can probably serve as a predictor. The counselor now has a criterion variable (Y) which is performance on the comprehensive final examination. He also has a potential predictor (X) in the preliminary verbal skills test, which is administered at the beginning of the M.Ed. program.

In such situations data for past student performance are usually available, so assume that the counselor can obtain the scores of all of the last three year's M.Ed. candidates on both measures, that is, the final comprehensive examination and the preliminary verbal examination. The regression sample is 200 subjects. The counselor is willing to defend the proposition that these 200 subjects are similar to the students for whom he ultimately wishes to make predictions.

To determine the regression equation, we must compute the values of a and b. Formulas for both these quantities were given in the previous chapter. The formula for b,

$$b = r\frac{s_y}{s_x}$$

is a "definitional" formula in the sense that it permitted a certain amount of insight into the nature of b. If one has already computed the standard deviations and the correlation coefficient, then this formula is the easiest one to use. As was the case with the standard deviation and correlation formulas, algebraically equivalent, computational formulas also exist in terms of the raw scores X and Y (or deviation scores x and y) so that b can be calculated directly from the data. In terms of deviation scores, b can be computed using the following formula:

$$b = \frac{\Sigma xy}{\Sigma x^2} \tag{8.1}$$

where the deviation sums of crossproducts and squares can be obtained from the following formulas:

$$\Sigma x^2 = \Sigma X^2 - \frac{(\Sigma X^2)}{n}$$

$$\Sigma y^2 = \Sigma Y^2 - \frac{(\Sigma Y^2)}{n}$$

$$\Sigma xy = \Sigma XY - \frac{(\Sigma X)(\Sigma Y)}{n}$$

Now, suppose we have the following data for the 200 subjects in the regression sample:

$$\Sigma xy = 3{,}200 \qquad \Sigma x^2 = 8{,}000 \qquad \Sigma y^2 = 7{,}000$$

Substituting the appropriate values into Formula 8.1 and solving,

$$b = \frac{3{,}200}{8{,}000} = 0.400$$

Thus b, the regression coefficient for Y on X, is 0.400.

In order to compute a for the prediction equation, one must use Formula 7.3 from the previous chapter

$$a = \bar{Y} - b\bar{X}$$

Although the means for Y and X have not yet been given, let us assume they are the following: $\bar{Y} = 85.0$, $\bar{X} = 100.0$. Solving for a, we find

$$a = 85.0 - (0.40)(100.0)$$

$$= 45.0$$

The regression equation can now be set up as follows:

$$\tilde{Y} = 45.0 + 0.40X$$

Now if the counselor were predicting the performance of an M.Ed. candidate on the final comprehensive exam, he would simply insert the candidate's score on the preliminary verbal skills exam (X) into the prediction formula. For example, an individual with an X score of 92.0 would have a predicted $\tilde{Y}$ of 81.8, since

$$\tilde{Y} = 45.0 + 0.40 (92.0)$$

$$= 81.8$$

The Standard Error of Estimate

The standard error of estimate can then be computed from formula 8.2 (algebraically equivalent to 7.4 in the previous chapter) as follows

$$s_{y \cdot x} = \sqrt{\frac{\Sigma y^2 - \frac{(\Sigma xy)^2}{\Sigma x^2}}{n - 2}} \tag{8.2}$$

$$= \sqrt{\frac{7,000 - \frac{(3,200)^2}{8,000}}{200 - 2}}$$

$$= 5.37$$

When applied to the predicted Y score of 81.8, the $s_{y \cdot x}$ can be interpreted as meaning that 68.3 percent of the time the individual's actual Y score will fall at least within a range of ± 5.37 points from the predicted 81.8, that is, within the interval 76.43–87.17.

A SECOND COMPUTATIONAL EXAMPLE

Let us carry out a second computational example from an actual set of scores obtained by eighteen students on the *Wonderlic Personnel Test*, a briefly administered group intelligence test, and a 100-question final examination in a professional educational course. A regression equation can be developed using the intelligence test, administered at the beginning of the course, as the

---

Table 8.1

Performance of 18 Students on an Intelligence Test Administered at the Beginning of a Course in Professional Education and a Final Examination Administered at the End of the Course

Student	Intelligence Test X	Final Exam Y	X^2	Y^2	XY
1	21	71	441	5,041	1,491
2	21	57	441	3,249	1,197
3	23	78	529	6,084	1,794
4	23	72	529	5,184	1,656
5	26	72	676	5,184	1,872
6	26	67	676	4,489	1,742
7	26	75	676	5,625	1,950
8	30	67	900	4,489	2,010
9	31	80	961	6,400	2,480
10	31	78	961	6,084	2,418
11	32	71	1,024	5,041	2,272
12	32	77	1,024	5,929	2,464
13	32	74	1,024	5,476	2,368
14	33	84	1,089	7,056	2,772
15	34	75	1,156	5,625	2,550
16	35	70	1,225	4,900	2,450
17	37	91	1,369	8,281	3,367
18	39	86	1,521	7,396	3,354
Σ	532	1,345	16,222	101,533	40,207

---

predictor variable (X) and the final examination as the criterion variable (Y). The scores in Table 8.1 were drawn from one of the authors' college classes. A regression scheme derived from them might be of value to the instructor in grouping students for teaching purposes or for working with individual students.

The necessary quantities for the various formulas to be used must first be computed. They are Σx^2, Σy^2, Σxy, $\bar{X}$, and $\bar{Y}$. Thus,

$$\Sigma x^2 = \Sigma X^2 - \frac{(\Sigma X)^2}{n} \quad = 16,222 - \frac{(532)^2}{18} = 498.45$$

$$\Sigma y^2 = \Sigma Y^2 - \frac{(\Sigma Y)^2}{n} \quad = 101,533 - \frac{(1345)^2}{18} = 1,031.61$$

$$\Sigma xy = \Sigma XY - \frac{(\Sigma X)(\Sigma Y)}{n} = 40,207 - \frac{(532)(1,345)}{18} = 454.78$$

$$\bar{X} = \frac{\Sigma X}{n} = \frac{532}{18} \quad = 29.55$$

$$\bar{Y} = \frac{\Sigma Y}{n} = \frac{1,345}{18} \quad = 74.72$$

The correlation coefficient representing the relationship between these two variables can then be computed according to Formula 6.3.

$$r = \frac{\Sigma xy}{\sqrt{(\Sigma x^2)(\Sigma y^2)}}$$

$$= 0.63$$

This computation is not really necessary in setting up the prediction equation but it is so simply done that many researchers compute r somewhere along the line in a regression operation.

Now b may be computed from Formula 8.1.

$$b = \frac{\Sigma xy}{\Sigma x^2}$$

$$= \frac{454.78}{498.45}$$

$$= 0.912$$

Having found b, a is then computed from Formula 7.3.

$$a = \bar{Y} - b\bar{X}$$

$$= 74.72 - 0.912(29.55)$$

$$= 47.77$$

The regression equation for predicting final-exam scores in the professional education course from scores on the intelligence test is

$$\tilde{Y} = 47.77 + 0.912X$$

The standard error of estimate is then found by using Formula 8.2.

$$s_{y \cdot x} = \sqrt{\frac{\Sigma y^2 - \frac{(\Sigma xy)^2}{\Sigma x^2}}{n - 2}}$$

$$= \sqrt{\frac{1{,}031.61 - \frac{(454.78)^2}{498.45}}{16}}$$

$$= 6.21$$

With the regression equation of $\tilde{Y} = 47.77 + 0.912X$, and the standard error of estimate of 6.21, fairly accurate predictions can now be made for the success of future students in the professional education class in question. For example, if a student gets a score of thirty on the intelligence test, his final-exam score could be predicted as follows: $\tilde{Y} = 47.77 + 0.912 \, (30)$, or 75.13. Using the standard error of estimate we could then associate the probability of accuracy in predicting the final examination score within given ranges. For example:

Given an X score of 30, the actual Y score will fall between

$$
\begin{array}{lll}
\pm 1 s_{y \cdot x} \text{ of } \tilde{Y} & (68.92 - 81.34) & 68.3\% \text{ of the time} \\
\pm 2 s_{y \cdot x} \text{ of } \tilde{Y} & (62.71 - 87.55) & 95.4\% \text{ of the time} \\
\pm 3 s_{y \cdot x} \text{ of } \tilde{Y} & (56.50 - 93.76) & 99.7\% \text{ of the time}
\end{array}
$$

MULTIPLE-REGRESSION PREDICTION
Two Predictor Variables

When using more than one predictor variable in a regression scheme, the prediction equation is simply a logical extension of the one-variable prediction formula. For example, with two predictors we employ Formula 7.5.

$$\tilde{Y} = a + b_1 X_1 + b_2 X_2$$

The reader will recall from the previous chapter that X_1 and X_2 represent the two predictor variables, and b_1 and b_2 represent their respective regression coefficients.

The computation necessary to set up a multiple-regression equation involving the simultaneous solution of linear equations, is more complicated than for a single predictor. Although a computational example of this process will be given in the chapter, the reader wishing to read further regarding linear equation solutions should consult any of the standard college algebra texts.

What is needed for the prediction equation are the values of a, b_1, and b_2. As in the case of single-predictor regression, these values are based upon the performance of subjects in the regression sample which has been chosen. The computation of a multiple-regression equation can be illustrated with the hypothetical scores of ten students contained in Table 8.2 where the criterion variable (Y) is performance on a comprehensive high-school physical science examination administered at the close of the senior year. One predictor variable (X_1) is student final exam score in freshman science, and the second predictor variable (X_2) is student IQ, as measured by a standard group intelligence test. Although this small sample can be used to illustrate the computation procedure for multiple-regression prediction, a much larger regression sample would actually be required for any sort of reliable prediction.

In order to set up the appropriate linear equations, the following values must be calculated from the data in Table 8.2:

$$
\begin{array}{ll}
n = 10 & \Sigma X_1{}^2 = 30,322 \\
\Sigma Y = 757 & \Sigma X_2{}^2 = 122,657 \\
\Sigma X_1 = 548 & \Sigma X_1 Y = 41,919 \\
\Sigma X_2 = 1,105 & \Sigma X_2 Y = 83,949 \\
\Sigma Y^2 = 58,041 & \Sigma X_1 X_2 = 60,683
\end{array}
$$

Table 8.2

Comprehensive Physical Science Examination Scores, Freshman Science Final Examination Scores, and Intelligence Quotients of 10 High-School Students

Student	Physical Science Examination Y	Freshman Science Final Examination X_1	Intelligence Quotient X_2
1	91	62	118
2	89	63	109
3	79	58	110
4	78	57	112
5	78	59	120
6	72	52	110
7	70	51	104
8	69	47	122
9	67	49	102
10	64	50	98

For a two-predictor regression equation these values are then substituted in the following three equations:

$$\Sigma X_1 Y = b_1 \Sigma X_1{}^2 + b_2 \Sigma X_1 X_2 + a \Sigma X_1$$

$$\Sigma X_2 Y = b_1 \Sigma X_1 X_2 + b_2 \Sigma X_2{}^2 + a \Sigma X_2$$

$$\Sigma Y = b_1 \Sigma X_1 + b_2 \Sigma X_2 + an$$

Substituting, we then have

(1) $\qquad 41{,}919 = b_1\, 30{,}322 + b_2\, 60{,}683 + a\, 548$

(2) $\qquad 83{,}949 = b_1\, 60{,}683 + b_2\, 122{,}657 + a\, 1{,}105$

(3) $\qquad 757 = b_1\, 548 + b_2\, 1{,}105 + a\, 10$

In solving linear equations simultaneously there are several slightly different approaches, but the step-by-step process outlined here may be used with all such problems.

First, divide equations (1), (2), and (3) by their respective coefficients of *a*, carrying as many digits beyond the decimal as the desk calculator will allow:

(4) $\qquad 76.4945255 = b_1\, 55.3321167 + b_2\, 110.7354014 + a$

(5) $\qquad 75.9719457 = b_1\, 54.9167421 + b_2\, 111.0018099 + a$

(6) $\qquad 75.7 \quad = b_1\, 54.8 + b_2\, 110.5 + a$

Next, to remove the *a* subtract (or add if the signs of *a* are unlike) (6) from (4) and (5) successively:

(7) $\qquad 0.7945255 = b_1\, 0.5321167 + b_2\, 0.2354014$

(8) $\qquad 0.2719457 = b_1\, 0.1167421 + b_2\, 0.5018099$

Then divide equations (7) and (8) by their respective coefficients of b_2:

(9) $$3.3751945 = b_1\, 2.2604653 + b_2$$
(10) $$0.5419297 = b_1\, 0.2326421 + b_2$$

Next, to remove the b_2 subtract (or add if the signs of b_2 are unlike) (10) from (9):

(11) $$2.8332648 = b_1\, 2.0278232$$

Now solve for b_1 by dividing the quantity at the left of the equal sign by the coefficient of b_1:

$$b_1 = 1.3971952$$

Then substitute the value of b_1 in equation (9) [or (10)] and solve for b_2:

$$3.3751945 = (1.3971952)\,(2.2604653) + b_2$$
$$b_2 = 3.3751945 - 3.1583113$$
$$b_2 = 0.2168832$$

Next, substitute the values of b_1 and b_2 in equation (4) [or either (5) or (6)] and solve for a:

$$76.4945255 = (1.3971952)\,(55.3321167) + (0.2168832)\,(110.7354014) + a$$
$$a = 76.4945255 - (77.3097679 - 24.0166482)$$
$$a = 76.4945255 - 101.3264161$$
$$a = -24.8318906$$

We have now solved the values necessary for substitution in the multiple-regression equation. Before setting up the equation, however, one should check the accuracy of a, b_1 and b_2 by substituting our computed values for these quantities in one of the original linear equations [(1), (2), or (3)]. Substituting in (3) we check as follows:

$$757 = (1.3971952)\,(548) + (0.2168832)\,(1,105) + (-24.8318906)\,(10)$$

$$757 = 765.662969 + 239.655936 - 248.318906$$

$$757 = 756.999999 \text{ (checks)}$$

It is now possible to set up the multiple-regression equation to predict student scores on the comprehensive physical science examination scores as follows:

$$\tilde{Y} = 24.8318906 + 1.3971952X_1 + 0.2168832X_2$$

To illustrate the use of this prediction scheme, suppose a student has achieved a score of 61 on the final examination (X_1) of his freshman science course and has an IQ of 111 on the particular intelligence test (X_2) used in developing the regression formula. His predicted score on the criterion examination ($\tilde{Y}$) would be computed as follows:

$$\tilde{Y} = -24.8318906 + (1.3971952)(61) + (0.2168832)(111)$$
$$\tilde{Y} = -24.8318906 + 85.2289072 + 24.0740352$$
$$\tilde{Y} = 84.471$$

Standard Error of Estimate

In order to gauge the accuracy of the predicted $\tilde{Y}$, once more the standard error of estimate must be employed in the same way that it was used with a single-predictor regression scheme. The standard error of multiple estimate is yielded by the following formula that employs the coefficient of multiple correlation between the variables involved in the regression problem. (The analogy between this and Formula 7.4 should be quite clear.)

$$s_{y \cdot x_1 x_2} = s_y \sqrt{1 - R^2_{y \cdot x_1 x_2}} \tag{8.3}$$

To use Formula 8.3 we must first compute R for the variables involved in our problem. This is done by computing the separate product–moment correlation coefficients and then substituting them in the formula 6.4 as follows:

$$r_{yx_1} = \frac{41,919 - \dfrac{(757)(548)}{10}}{\sqrt{\left(58,041 - \dfrac{(757)^2}{10}\right)\left(30,322 - \dfrac{(548)^2}{10}\right)}}$$

$$= 0.838$$

$$r_{yx_2} = \frac{83,949 - \dfrac{(757)(1,105)}{10}}{\sqrt{\left(58,041 - \dfrac{(757)^2}{10}\right)\left(122,657 - \dfrac{(1,105)^2}{10}\right)}}$$

$$= 0.470$$

$$r_{x_1 x_2} = \frac{60,683 - \dfrac{(548)(1,105)}{10}}{\sqrt{\left(30,322 - \dfrac{(548)^2}{10}\right)\left(122,657 - \dfrac{(1,105)^2}{10}\right)}}$$

$$= 0.321$$

$$R_{y \cdot x_1 x_2} = \sqrt{\frac{(0.838)^2 - (0.470)^2 - 2(0.838)(0.470)(0.321)}{1 - (0.321)}}$$

$$= 0.864$$

The standard deviation of the criterion variable for the regression sample must also be inserted in Formula 8.3. The value of s_y in this example is 9.04. Now it is possible to compute the standard error of multiple estimate from Formula 8.3.

$$s_{y \cdot x_1 x_2} = 9.04 \sqrt{1 - (0.864)^2}$$
$$= 9.04(0.504)$$
$$= 4.56$$

With this standard error of multiple estimate we can be confident that roughly two-thirds of the time the predicted $\tilde{Y}$ score from the multiple-regression equation will be no more than ± 4.56 from the actual Y score the subject will attain.

More than Two Predictor Variables

If more than two predictor variables are used in the multiple-regression problem, the necessary formulas are always logical extensions of the two-predictor formulas. For example, with three predictors the regression equation would take the following form:

$$\tilde{Y} = a + b_1 X_1 + b_2 X_2 + b_3 X_3 \tag{8.4}$$

The linear equations needed for the determination of a, b_1, b_2, and b_3 would be set up as follows:

$$\Sigma X_1 Y = b_1 \Sigma X_1{}^2 + b_2 \Sigma X_1 X_2 + b_3 \Sigma X_1 X_3 + a \Sigma X_1$$

$$\Sigma X_2 Y = b_1 \Sigma X_1 X_2 + b_2 \Sigma X_2{}^2 + b_3 \Sigma X_2 X_3 + a \Sigma X_2$$

$$\Sigma X_3 Y = b_1 \Sigma X_1 X_3 + b_2 \Sigma X_2 X_3 + b_3 \Sigma X_3{}^2 + a \Sigma X_3$$

$$\Sigma Y = b_1 \Sigma X_1 + b_2 \Sigma X_2 + b_3 \Sigma X_3 + an$$

These linear equations are solved simultaneously in the same fashion described previously for the two-predictor regression problems.

Meeting Assumptions

The same assumptions associated with single-predictor regression models must be satisfied in the case of multiple-regression problems, that is, given the use of a *linear* regression model, the assumptions of homoscedasticity and normality of criterion scores must be met. Statistical tests of these assumptions are available and can be found in most advanced statistical texts.

REVIEW

The computational operations necessary for single-predictor and multiple-predictor linear regression were described in the chapter. Although the calculations appear formidable at first glance, a step-by-step analysis of the operations involved reveals that most of the mathematical operations are quite simple. In solving regression problems, however, the use of some type of mechanical calculator is almost a necessity.

The only added complexity involved in multiple-regression computation is the simultaneous solution of linear equations. A detailed example of how this is done was presented in the chapter, but the reader was urged to consult a standard algebra text if the example and discussion were insufficient.

In the case of both single-predictor and multiple-predictor models, the determination of the standard error of estimate is important. Procedures for its calculation and use were described in the chapter.

EXERCISES

1. Determine the value of a and b in the prediction equation $\tilde{Y} = a + bX$ on the basis of the data for the ten subjects given below.

X	Y	X	Y
50	20	37	11
40	10	36	10
39	15	36	13
38	16	35	11
37	12	34	10

2. Using the values of a and b from the preceding problem, determine the predicted $\tilde{Y}$ score for each of the following values of X:

(a) 48   (c) 40   (e) 31
(b) 42   (d) 38   (f) 28

3. A regression sample of 50 subjects has been selected in order to develop a prediction scheme to forecast the probable achievement of students in an advanced trigonometry course, based upon a specially devised predictor test (X). The predictor test was given to the 50 subjects prior to taking a trigonometry course and, one academic year later, a comprehensive examination (Y) was given to measure their performance in the course. Develop the prediction equation $\tilde{Y} = a + bX$ on the basis of the scores of these 50 subjects.

X	Y	X	Y	X	Y	X	Y	X	Y
62	150	57	111	54	110	51	119	47	125
61	151	57	110	53	119	51	119	46	109
61	143	56	121	53	118	51	114	45	111
61	146	56	120	53	116	51	110	45	107
59	145	56	119	53	110	50	111	44	106
59	140	56	104	52	138	50	111	43	106
58	139	55	143	52	132	49	109	42	104
58	141	55	142	52	130	49	107	42	103
57	142	54	146	52	111	48	124	41	101
57	138	54	111	52	110	47	126	40	101

4. Using the prediction scheme developed in the foregoing problem, determine the value of $\tilde{Y}$ for each of the following X scores.

(a) 60   (c) 55   (e) 42
(b) 59   (d) 48   (f) 40

5. Compute the value of the standard error of estimate for the prediction equation in exercise 3.

6. On the basis of the foregoing standard error of estimate, approximately how many times in 100 would an individual with a predicted ($\tilde{Y}$) score of 120 on the trigonometry final examination actually score more than 10.78 above or below the predicted score?

7. Set up the prediction equation $\tilde{Y} = a + bX$ for the following regression sample:

X	Y	X	Y	X	Y	X	Y
20	43	17	38	15	32	12	30
20	43	17	38	14	30	12	29
19	40	16	40	14	30	11	28
19	41	16	36	13	41	11	28
18	40	15	35	13	39	10	27

8. For the following multiple-regression scheme, determine the $\tilde{Y}$ values for the five individuals whose predictor scores are cited: $\tilde{Y} = 12.30 + 0.684X_1 + 0.230X_2$

Individual	Y	Predictor I X_1	Predictor II X_2
a	———	61	37
b	———	62	39
c	———	64	42
d	———	59	31
e	———	28	29

9. For this practice exercise the data represents a sample far too small to satisfy the requisite assumptions of the technique. However, to illustrate the procedure, set up a multiple-regression prediction equation so that the values

of *X* may be predicted from values of *Y* and *Z* for the following regression sample.

Subject	*X*	*Y*	*Z*
a	6	3	2
b	7	3	2
c	8	5	4
d	6	4	3
e	5	2	1

SELECTED READINGS

Edwards, Allen L., *Statistical Methods for the Behavioral Sciences*. New York: Holt, Rinehart & Winston, 1957, chap. 7.

Ferguson, George A., *Statistical Analysis in Psychology and Education*. New York: McGraw-Hill, 1959, chap. 8.

McNemar, Quinn, *Psychological Statistics*. New York: Wiley, 1962, chap. 8.

Tate, Merle W., *Statistics in Education*. New York: Macmillan, 1955, pp. 267–320.

Walker, Helen M., and Joseph Lev, *Elementary Statistical Methods*. New York: Holt, Rinehart & Winston, 1958, chap. 9.

Weinberg, George H., and John A. Schumaker, *Statistics: An Intuitive Approach*. Belmont, Calif.: Wadsworth, 1962, chaps. 16 and 18.

Wert, James E., Charles O. Neidt, and J. Stanley Ahmann, *Statistical Methods in Educational and Psychological Research*. New York: Appleton-Century-Croft, 1954, chap. 13.

9
The
t
Test

In educational situations one encounters numerous problems wherein it is important to determine whether the mean performances of two groups are significantly different. For example, educators often examine a new method of instruction on an experimental group of students and employ a conventional method with a comparable control group. If the mean performance of the experimental group on a criterion test is considerably better than that of the control group, one might conclude that the new method of teaching is so effective that it should be employed in other classes of a similar nature. But just *how* great does the difference between the two group means have to be in favor of the experimental method?

If, for example, on a 100-item spelling test the experimental group (taught by a new spelling technique) attained a mean of 95 correctly spelled words, while the control group's mean of correctly spelled words was only 30, one could readily judge in favor of the experimental method. Yet, mean differences in educational research are rarely so clear-cut. For instance, if there was only a small mean difference in favor of the experimental group—perhaps a mean of 89 for the experimental students and a mean of 82 for the control group—one could not be as certain. Is a seven-point differential merely the result of chance instead of a real difference produced by the experimental method? If we were to administer the posttest to two randomly selected groups which had *not* been exposed to the new spelling method, would we find a seven-point difference between such groups *by mere chance*?

The *t* test is used to determine just how great the difference between two means must be for it to be judged significant, that is, a significant departure from differences, which might be expected by chance alone. Another way of stating the function of the *t* test is to assert that, through its use, we test the null hypothesis that two group means are not significantly different, that is, the means are so similar that the sample groups can be considered to have been drawn from the same population. Putting it in symbols, we test the statistical hypothesis H_0: $\mu_1 = \mu_2$ where μ_1 and μ_2 are the two hypoth cal population means. The null hypothesis then states that the two population means are really one and the same. We wish to reject this hypothesis (that is accept the alternative H_1: $\mu_1 \neq \mu_2$) at some level of statistical significance. In other words, we wish to state with some degree of confidence that our obtained *sample difference* $\bar{X}_1 - \bar{X}_2$ is too great to be a chance event under the assumption of our null hypothesis.

The reader is reminded that, because a mean difference is "significant," it is not necessarily a meaningful or important mean difference. Other factors, such as how useful in terms of decision-making the mean difference is, must be used to judge the importance of any statistically significant event.

A standard formula for the *t* test is presented as follows:

$$t = \frac{\bar{X}_1 - \bar{X}_2}{\sqrt{\dfrac{s_1^2}{n_1} + \dfrac{s_2^2}{n_2}}} \tag{9.1}$$

where

$t =$ the value by which the statistical significance
of the mean difference will be judged
$\bar{X}_1 =$ the mean of group 1
$\bar{X}_2 =$ the mean of group 2
$s_1^2 =$ the variance of group 1
$s_2^2 =$ the variance of group 2
$n_1 =$ the number of subjects in group 1
$n_2 =$ the number of subjects in group 2

From a statistical standpoint, any procedure for testing statistical significance must be based on at least three aspects: (1) a statistic which reflects (or is sensitive to) the difference or relationship of interest in the population, (2) a well-defined sampling distribution for this statistic and (3) the standard deviation (standard error) of this sampling distribution. (The notions of sampling distribution and standard error were introduced in Chapter 4; the reader is advised to review that material.) In the case at hand, the sample statistic is a *difference* between means $(\bar{X}_1 - \bar{X}_2)$, the well-defined sampling distribution is the *t* distribution, and the standard error of the distribution of mean differences is $\sqrt{s_1^2/n_1 + s_2^2/n_2}$. The *t* value given by Formula 9.1 can now be viewed as a kind of "*z* score," not for a single $\bar{X}$, but for a difference between two $\bar{X}$s. That is, under the null hypothesis of *zero* difference between population means, the *t* in Formula 9.1 is simply the ratio of the difference between a sample statistic and its corresponding population parameter to the standard error of the sample statistic. Thus, the *t* value is an index of where an observed sample mean difference is in the distribution of all possible sample mean differences that might have occurred. Since the shape of the *t* distribution is symmetrical and bell-shaped much like the normal curve, the larger the *t* value, the smaller the probability of obtaining a sample difference equal to (or greater than) the difference actually observed. When this probability reaches the desired critical level (e.g., 0.05), we have a significant mean difference.

These statistical notions are admittedly abstract; the reader may well profit from coordinating this discussion with that in Chapter 4 regarding the sampling distribution of the sample mean. From a more intuitive standpoint, however, we can set statistical notions aside and reason from a common sense point of view that there are three separate factors to be considered before the experimenter pronounces a mean difference between two groups to be significant: (1) the magnitude of the difference between the two means; (2) the degree of "overlap" between the two groups as revealed by the variability of each group; and (3) the number of subjects in the two samples. These three factors will be examined more thoroughly in the following sections.

MEAN DIFFERENCES

Other things being equal, the larger the value of t, the greater the probability that a statistically significant mean difference exists between the two groups under consideration. An examination of the t-test model supplied in Formula 9.1 will reveal that if the two group means were absolutely identical, there would be no difference between them. Hence, a zero in the numerator of the formula would yield a zero t value. Generally speaking, the larger the difference between the two means, the greater the value of t will be (greater in the absolute sense, i.e., regardless of algebraic sign). Thus, we may ordinarily conclude that the larger the t value, the less the probability is that the difference between the two means is a function of mere chance.

Although the size of t necessary for statistical significance varies with the sizes of the samples involved, it may assist the reader to see how large t must be in order to be significant at the 0.05 level when the sample size varies. Observe in Table 9.1, as the number of degrees of freedom becomes larger, a smaller t value is sufficient to reject the null hypothesis. (Degrees of freedom were discussed in Chapter 4 regarding the estimation of the variance. In the t-test situation, two variances must be estimated; thus, we have $n_1 - 1$ and $n_2 - 1$ degrees of freedom for groups 1 and 2 respectively, or $n_1 + n_2 - 2$ degrees of freedom in all.)

However, this "larger the t, greater the significance" notion is complicated by the denominator of the t formula. This is as it should be, since the mere fact that two means differ tells one very little, until something is known about the variability of the two groups under consideration. Obviously, there must be *some* mean difference present, or it would be immediately concluded that there is no significant difference between the identical means of the two groups.

GROUP VARIABILITY

In addition to the actual mean difference, a factor of considerable import in determining whether to accept or reject the null hypothesis is the variability

Table 9.1
Selected t Values for the 0.05 Level of Significance with Varying Size Samples, as Reflected by Degrees of Freedom (Two-Tailed Test)

Degrees of Freedom	t at 0.05 Level
1	12.709
2	4.303
3	3.182
5	2.571
10	2.228
30	2.042
50	2.008
500	1.965

of the groups involved. If the variances of the two groups are particularly great, that is, there is much spread in the distributions, relatively small mean differences between two groups will result in considerable overlap between the two distributions, such as in Figure 9.1. With so much overlap between the groups, one might be reluctant to conclude that the means of the two distributions were *really* different.

However, with smaller standard deviations in the samples concerned, the identical mean difference might be judged to reflect a real-population mean difference. For example, consider the situation depicted in Figure 9.2.

In Figure 9.2 small standard deviations exist for the two groups under consideration, whereas in Figure 9.1 very large standard deviations were present. In both cases an equivalent mean difference (10 units) occurred, but in the second instance one would be willing to place much more confidence in the assertion that the two samples were *not* drawn from the same population, since the groups are so clearly distinct.

This notion generalizes to the principle that, other factors being equal, the smaller the variances of the two groups under consideration, the greater the likelihood that a statistically significant mean difference exists.

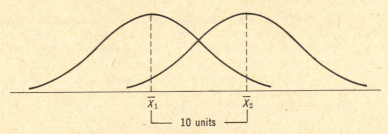

Figure 9.1 *Mean difference of ten units between two groups with relatively large standard deviations.*

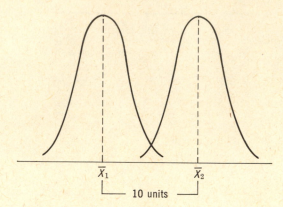

Figure 9.2 *Mean difference of ten units between two groups with relatively small standard deviations.*

SAMPLE SIZE

The third factor to be considered in testing for a significant mean difference is the size of the samples involved. To illustrate the necessity of taking sample size into account, we will suppose that the efficacy of a novel teaching method is being tested by using the new method with only two individuals. A conventional method might also be employed with only two control students. Even if the means of the two student "groups" differed by as much as 100 points, one would probably be unwilling to state with much confidence that the new method was greatly superior to the conventional method.

The size of the sample, of course, is an extremely important determinant of the significance of the difference between means, for with increased sample size, means tend to become more stable representations of group performance. The larger the sample, the greater confidence one can place in a relatively minor difference between the means. However, with an extremely small sample, one should be reluctant to place much confidence in even large difference between two means. Furthermore, the larger the sample sizes, the greater the degrees of freedom and the smaller the critical t value needed for significance (see Table 9.1).

To reiterate, common sense suggests that three factors are important when considering the significance of differences between the means of two groups: (1) the magnitude of the difference between the two means; (2) the size of the samples involved; and (3) the variability of the two groups. Now by reexamining the model for the t test presented in Figure 9.3, the reader will see that this common-sense viewpoint is actually incorporated in the formula. We will briefly discuss how these three factors are included in the t formula.

Mean Difference

As indicated earlier, the difference between the two means must be considerably larger than zero, or t will be very small. Thus, mean difference as

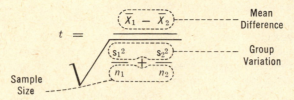

Figure 9.3 *Three factors incorporated in the t-test for mean differences.*

represented in the numerator of the formula is a crucial element in determining the size of *t*.

Sample Size

Note that in the denominator, as the sample size involved in the study becomes larger, the value of the fractions under the square root sign become smaller. For example, assume that the variance for Group One is only 2.0. Now if the number of subjects in Group One is only 4, then the left fraction in the denominator would be only 2/4 or 1/2. However, if there are 20 subjects in Group One and the variance is still 2.0, then the fraction becomes merely 1/10. When 1/10 is divided into *whatever* mean difference exists in the numerator of the fraction, the *t* value will be considerably greater than if 1/2 is divided into the same mean difference. In essence, then, it can be seen that increased sample size yields a larger *t* value, as long as other factors (i.e., mean difference and group variances) remain constant. As seen in Table 9.1, the *t* table by which one judges the significance of the obtained *t* value, also takes sample size into account so that a given *t* value is more likely to be significant if the number of subjects is large.

Group Variability

In a similar fashion, the sizes of the group variances affect the size of the *t* value, because they are incorporated in the denominator of the *t* ratio. Assuming that the sample size is 10 for each group, it can be seen that a variance of 5.0 for Group One would result in a denominator contribution of 5/10 (or 1/2), to be divided along with the denominator contribution from Group Two into the mean difference. If the variance of Group One were doubled, or 10.0, the mean difference would be divided by 10/10 (or 1), plus the denominator contribution from Group Two. Clearly, a smaller quantity divided into the same mean difference yields a larger *t* value. Hence, the *t* model takes into consideration previously discussed notions about variance size and amount of overlap between groups, that is, smaller variances are more likely to result in significant mean differences, other factors being equal.

THE TABLE OF *t*

Once the value of *t* has been determined from a *t*-model formula, one can ascertain whether it is statistically significant by comparing it with a table of *t* values. The *t* values presented in Table F of the Appendix are those which an obtained *t* value must equal or exceed, in order for the probability of the mean difference under consideration to be as rare (or more rare) as the probability proportions given at the top row of the table. In order to use Table F, it must be known how many *degrees of freedom* are involved so that the column can be entered at the left of the table under the *df* heading.

Now, suppose a researcher is testing a null hypothesis of no difference between means of two samples with 16 subjects in each group. If he were using the 0.05 level to test the null hypothesis, then Table F would be entered with 30 degrees of freedom and a *p* (probability level) of 0.05. The point of intersection yields a *t* value of 2.042. This indicates that the obtained *t* value, derived from the actual data for the two samples, must equal or exceed (positively or negatively) 2.042, in order to reject the null hypothesis at the 0.05 level.

Had the obtained *t* been 2.75, for example, the researcher would have rejected the null hypothesis and concluded that the two samples were not drawn from the same population. If the obtained *t* had been only 1.56, he would have considered the null hypothesis tenable and concluded, based on these samples, that there was insufficient evidence to consider the mean difference attributable to any factor other than chance.

t MODELS

Although the *t* test has been dealt with as though there were but one *t* formula, there are actually several slightly different formulas which are used depending upon: (1) the number of subjects in the groups; (2) the presence of correlation between group data; and (3) the similarity, or homogeneity, of population variances. When $n_1 = n_2$ and $\sigma_1^2 = \sigma_2^2$, for example, the *t* formula used is slightly different than when $n_1 \neq n_2$ and $\sigma_1^2 \neq c_2^2$. Different degrees of freedom are also involved, depending upon the research design and appropriate *t* formula. A simple scheme employed to select the appropriate *t* formula and the accompanying degrees of freedom for different types of research situations is given in the following chapter.

Presence of Correlation

A consideration of the problems of testing for mean differences when a positive correlation is present between data in the two groups will indicate why this factor must be taken into consideration in analyzing data. Suppose one tests the significance of differences between mean criterion performances of two groups of matched pairs. If the matching has been done carefully, one would suspect that scores of the two members of a pair would tend to be more similar than if no matching had taken place and the groups had been selected at random. Since the scores would tend to be more similar, there is *less* likelihood that the means of the two groups will be different. Hence, this factor is taken into consideration by determining the correlation between the scores of pairs in the groups and adjusting the *t* value upward to some extent. A special *t* model which is designed for correlated data should be used whenever a relationship between data in the two groups of scores exists. Such correlation between data in the groups is usually present in situations involving matched pairs or when two measures have been taken for the same person, as in pre- and posttest mean comparisons.

Homogeneity of Variances

As noted earlier, it is theoretically important to ascertain whether the variances of two populations from which sample groups are drawn can be considered equal, or homogeneous, before one selects a particular *t* model. The homogeneity of two population variances can be checked quickly by a simple statistical technique known as the *F* ratio in which the larger sample variance is divided by the smaller one. The resulting quantity is known as *F* and is interpreted for statistical significance from a table much like the *t* table. Table G in the Appendix contains the values for the *F* distribution. The use of Table G will be explained in the next chapter.

As in the interpretation of *t*, when the value of *F* becomes larger, there is generally a greater likelihood that we have a statistically significant difference between the two variances. If statistically significant, the null hypotheses of no difference between the population variances is rejected, and it is concluded that the variances in the two populations are nonhomogeneous. This simple *F* test must be conducted to assist us in selecting one of several different *t* formulas. All of these factors will be explained further in the computational procedures for the *t* test in the following chapter.

In actual practice few researchers check the assumption of variance homogeneity, for with large enough sample sizes one need not worry about the influence of even markedly divergent variances.

CONFIDENCE INTERVALS

In much the same manner that confidence intervals were described earlier for the mean and the correlation coefficient, such estimates can be computed for the difference between means. This type of estimation is often of considerable value to the educator who must decide whether a new instructional approach should be adopted in preference to conventional procedures. It is helpful to know just how large or how small the true population mean difference is apt to be. For example, it might aid an administrator's decision to purchase a set of programmed instructional materials if a 95 percent mean difference confidence interval of 4.5 to 10.6 points favoring the programmed materials had been found. This would indicate that if a similar statistical process were carried out, similar confidence intervals would be yielded which would contain the true population mean difference 95 percent of the time. The computation procedures to be followed in setting up confidence intervals for mean differences will be described in the next chapter.

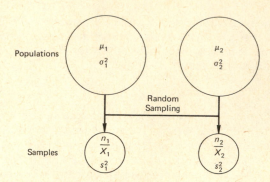

Figure 9.4 *Conceptualization of the t-test situation.*

ASSUMPTIONS UNDERLYING THE *t* TEST

Research situations appropriate to the use of the *t* test can be conceptualized as indicated in Figure 9.4. When the two groups are based on a pre-existing variable (e.g., sex, political affiliation, brain damage, etc.), this conceptualization is quite straight-forward. For example, if we wished to compare males and females on some measure, say IQ, we can conceptualize a population of males and a population of females, each with their own means and variances (population parameters) on the IQ measure. We then take a sample of males and a sample of females from their respective populations and compute sample estimates (statistics) for the population parameters. For the sake of "statistical argument" we assume that the population means (μ_1 and μ_2) are equal, that is there is no difference between males and females on the measure of IQ. Then, if the observed difference between our sample estimates ($\bar{X}_1$ and $\bar{X}_2$) is expected to occur by chance only a small percentage of the time (e.g., 5 percent), we conclude that what we had assumed for the sake of "statistical argument" was in fact an error—that is, within a certain level of probability (e.g., 0.05), we were wrong to assume $\mu_1 = \mu_2$ and are right in accepting that $\mu_1 \neq \mu_2$ or that there exists a difference in IQ between our populations of males and females.

When the two groups are based on an experimental variable, for example, a treatment group versus a control group, this conceptualization is a bit more abstract. For example, in the treatment–no treatment design, we conceptualize the treated and untreated subjects as having been sampled from a population, hypothetically split into two, treated and untreated subpopulations respectively. We then have an analogous situation. (See Chapter 17 for a more complete discussion of these distinctions.)

With this conceptualization in mind, there are three assumptions necessary for the validity of the *t* test: (1) the samples must be *randomly* drawn from their respective populations, (2) the scores must be *normally distributed* in the populations, and (3) the scores must have the same variance in the populations ($\sigma_1^2 = \sigma_2^2$). The assumption of random sampling allows us to use the notion of a sampling distribution and to compare our obtained sample difference to all those sample differences that might have occurred. The assumptions of normality and homogeneity of variance allow us to use the *t*-distribution to make our probability decisions.

With respect to the assumptions of normality and homogeneity of variance, one can depart quite markedly from them and still obtain a *t*-value which can be correctly interpreted. This property of being able to violate statistical assumptions while still retaining a valid statistical test is known as *robustness*. The *t* test can be shown to be a *robust* statistical test. Also, certain statistical adjustments are possible when the assumption of equal variances is violated. The assumption of random sampling is a *logical* assumption, that is the logic of the inference procedure rests on the notion of randomness. Thus, the student is urged to employ only random selection techniques in selecting his samples. As is often the case, however, one often has difficulty in drawing pure random samples in educational situations. One can still make *reasonable* use of inferential procedures like the *t*-test so long as he is able to demonstrate that the samples are not a biased representation of the population under study, that is, that they are not unlike those samples that would have been obtained had the sampling been carried out in strictly a random fashion.

A Journal Example of the t Test

Prior to concluding this chapter, it may assist the reader to examine a typical example of the manner in which *t* tests are reported in the professional journals. In Table 9.2 results of a *t* test analysis are presented in which the performance of two groups of teachers on the *Minnesota Teacher Attitude Inventory* (MTAI) is contrasted. The two teacher samples were designated as "superior" or "inferior" on the basis of raters' judgments and were assumed to be representative of the populations of superior and inferior teachers.

The researcher almost always reports the means, the number in each sample, and the *t* value yielded by the analysis. The standard deviation or variance for each group should also be presented. The significance of the obtained *t*, if it is statistically significant, is usually given below the table. In the example in Table 9.2, one can see that the research analysis yielded a statistically significant *t*; thus the researchers were warranted in rejecting the null hypothesis at the 0.01 level. In other words, the data support the hypothesis that there is a difference in teacher attitude between "superior" and "inferior" teachers, with the "superior" teachers tending towards the more favorable end of the attitude continuum.

REVIEW

The *t* test was described as a statistical model designed to determine whether two groups, as represented by their means, are significantly different. In yielding an index of the significance of mean differences, *t* formulas take into account the following factors: (1) mean difference, (2) population variability, (3) sample size, and where applicable, the presence of correlated data.

Table 9.2
A Comparison of M.T.A.I. Scores for "Superior" and "Inferior" Teachers

Group	Number	Standard Deviation	Mean M.T.A.I. Score	t
Superior	72	40.66	23.60	
				2.81[a]
Inferior	72	38.83	5.30	

SOURCE: W. J. Popham and R. R. Trimble, "The Minnesota Teacher Attitude Inventory as an Index of General Teaching Competence," Educ. Psychol. Measurement, **20**, *no. 3 (Autumn, 1960), pp. 509–512.*
[a]*Significant beyond the 0.01 level.*

The *t* test, as is the case with most other significance tests, is computed by analyzing sample data in such a way that a statistic, in this case *t*, is generated. The statistic is subsequently interpreted for statistical significance from a probability table that indicates the probability that an observed mean difference or more extreme difference could be attributed to chance alone. If the *t* value is sufficiently large, the null hypothesis is rejected and the researcher concludes that the two samples under investigation are not drawn from the same population, that is, they are different.

Slightly different *t* formulas are used depending on the particular sample data under analysis. Typically the data are first treated by an *F* ratio to determine whether the variances of the two population groups are significantly different. *F*.values, like *t* values, are interpreted for significance from a probability table in the Appendix. Confidence intervals may be developed for differences between sample means.

Underlying use of the *t* test are the assumptions that (1) the sample data have been drawn randomly from the population; (2) the population from which each sample is drawn is normally distributed; and (3) the populations have the same variance.

EXERCISES

1. Assume two researchers are individually testing a null hypothesis which involves a *t*-test comparison of the means of two groups. Researcher A uses 50 subjects in each group while Researcher B uses 100 subjects in each group. Other factors being equal, which researcher is more likely to reject the null hypothesis?

2. Assuming that both researchers had used identical numbers of subjects in their two samples, suppose that Researcher A has samples which have much smaller standard deviations than those involved in Researcher B's *t* test. If all other factors are equal, which researcher is more likely to reject the null hypothesis?

3. Suppose Researcher A has carefully matched pairs of subjects in his two groups, and Researcher B has drawn his two groups at random. Will Researcher A or B be more apt to have the greatest mean difference between his two samples?

4. If you *wished* to reject a null hypothesis of mean difference between two samples, would you be happier with a *t* value of 6.8 with one degree of freedom or a *t* value of 2.25 with 30 degrees of freedom?

5. Assume that two *t* tests from different experiments are about to be calculated. In one instance the mean difference is 13.05, and in the other case the mean difference is only 6.20. Is it true that the *t* test with the larger mean difference will always yield the largest *t* value?

6. If one *t* test yields a *t* value of -2.42 and a second yields a *t* value of 1.99, which *t* value is least probable and therefore more apt to be statistically significant?

7. From Table F in the Appendix determine whether: (1) a one-tailed *t* test with $t = 1.90$ and $df = 9$; or (2) a two-tailed *t* test with $t = 2.10$ and $df = 9$ would entitle a school psychologist to reject a null hypothesis of mean difference between two experimental groups at the 0.05 level.

SELECTED READINGS

Blalock, Hubert M., Jr., *Social Statistics*. New York: McGraw-Hill, 1960, chap. 13.

Blommers, Paul, and E. F. Lindquist, *Elementary Statistical Methods*. Boston: Houghton Mifflin, 1960, chap. 12.

Boneau, C. A., "The Effects of Violations of Assumptions Underlying the *t* Test," *Psychol. Bull.* **57** (1960): 49–64.

Edwards, Allen L., *Statistical Methods for the Behavioral Sciences*. New York: Holt, Rinehart & Winston, 1957, chaps. 13 and 14.

Hays, William L., *Statistics for Psychologists*. New York: Holt, Rinehart & Winston, 1963, chap. 10.

Johnson, Palmer O., and Robert W. B. Jackson, *Modern Statistical Methods: Descriptive and Inductive*. Chicago: Rand McNally, 1959, chap. 6.

Wert, James E., Charles O. Neidt, and J. Stanley Ahmann, *Statistical Methods in Educational and Psychological Research*. New York: Appleton-Century-Crofts, 1954, chap. 8.

10

The t Test— Computation Procedures

Once a researcher has determined to his satisfaction that a *t* test should be used to treat his data, he is, figuratively, only halfway home. To be sure, he has decided that, when testing the null hypothesis that two group means are not significantly different, a *t* test is appropriate. But he is still faced with several decisions which must be made prior to calculating and interpreting the value of *t* by which he can test the null hypothesis. For one thing, there are several slightly different models of the *t* test which, although they yield approximately the same value of *t*, do indeed differ to some extent. Which should he choose? Then too, there is the matter of degrees of freedom. How many degrees of freedom should be used to interpret an obtained value of *t*? Finally, what adjustments should be made if there is some relationship between scores in the two groups?

These questions must be resolved before testing the hypothesis under consideration. The following discussion should enable the reader, when facing different research situations, to quickly select the appropriate *t* model and to correctly interpret the significance of *t* after it has been calculated.

Basically, the researcher must ask three questions regarding his data. Answers to these questions will allow him to select and interpret the appropriate statistical model:

1. Is there a positive correlation of any considerable magnitude between data in the two populations under consideration?
2. Are the variances of the two populations significantly different or can the two population variances be considered homogeneous?
3. Is there an equal number of subjects in each sample?

The first question to be considered relates to the existence of any appreciable positive correlation between data for the two populations. Such correlation may exist in two situations:

1. When the *t* test involves a comparison between two groups which are composed of matched pairs.
2. When the *t* test compares two measures taken on the same subjects, as in the case of testing significance of pre- and posttest gains for the same pupils.

In other educational research situations there is no way of discovering whether any correlation exists between the data in our two groups. Therefore, we can use *t* models that do not need to take the presence of relationship into account. However, this matter should be resolved by the researcher prior to selecting his *t* model.

Let us assume for the moment that there is no correlation present between data for the two groups. We must then determine if the variances of the two populations are homogeneous. First, we estimate the population variances using the sample variances. Then we use an *F*-ratio test in which the lesser sample variance is divided into the greater sample variance. The computation procedure for the calculation and interpretation of *F* will be explained shortly.

Finally, the number of subjects in each sample group may or may not be equal. This too must be noted in selecting the proper formula, as well as the appropriate number of degrees of freedom.

UNCORRELATED DATA

If a researcher is not dealing with matched pairs or with two measures for the same individuals, he cannot compute a correlation coefficient, so he assumes no relationship between data in the two groups. If there is no positive relationship between the group data, two *t* models can be used. The selection depends upon whether the variances are homogeneous and whether the *n*s are equal. The two models given are the *separate variance formula* on the left (seen before in Chapter 9) and the *pooled variance formula* on the right.

In some instances there is no difference in the *t* values which are yielded if these two different formulas are applied to the same data.

$$t = \frac{\bar{X}_1 - \bar{X}_2}{\sqrt{\dfrac{s_1^2}{n_1} + \dfrac{s_2^2}{n_2}}} \quad (9.1)$$

$$t = \frac{\bar{X}_1 - \bar{X}_2}{\sqrt{\left(\dfrac{(n_1 - 1)s_1^2 + (n_2 - 1)s_2^2}{n_1 + n_2 - 2}\right)\left(\dfrac{1}{n_1} + \dfrac{1}{n_2}\right)}} \quad (10.1)$$

Separate Variance *t* Model   Pooled Variance *t* Model

In other situations, there is a considerable difference in the *t* yielded from identical data. Use of the pooled variance model, however, will result in a *t* value which may usually be interpreted with more degrees of freedom than could be used with the separate variance model. Since a smaller *t* value is needed to reject a given null hypothesis when a greater number of degrees of freedom are present, this indicates that the same *t* value, when computed by the pooled variance formula, will be more likely to be significant than if it had been obtained by the separate variance formula. It follows that the pooled variance formula is the more powerful test, that is, more apt to reject a null hypothesis.

In selecting one of the two t models, we need to know whether the number of subjects in the two groups is identical. This, of course, is easily determined. We must also determine whether the variances of the two populations are homogeneous.

Homogeneity of Variances

We are concerned about the homogeneity of the two *population* variances, that is, the likelihood that $\sigma_1^2 = \sigma_2^2$. We use the sample variances s_1^2 and s_2^2 to estimate these population parameters, assuming that if we cannot reject the null hypothesis of homogeneous population variability with the sample statistics, the population parameters can be considered equal for the purpose of conducting the t test.

To test the hypothesis that $\sigma_1^2 = \sigma_2^2$, a simple statistical test, the F ratio, is employed. The formula for F is as follows:

$$F = \frac{s_g^2}{s_l^2} \qquad (10.2)$$

where

$F =$ the value by which variance homogeneity will be tested
$s_g^2 =$ the greater (larger) sample variance
$s_l^2 =$ the lesser (smaller) sample variance

In computing F, we simply divide the smaller variance into the larger variance. The resulting quotient, (F), is interpreted for statistical significance from the table of F (Table G). In using the table of the F distribution we must employ the degrees of freedom for such variance, or, as variances are sometimes called, each *mean square*. Degrees of freedom for this test are equal to the number in the group minus one.

A practical example will assist the reader in using the F table. Suppose a statistician is testing the null hypothesis of variance homogeneity for two populations where for sample One $s_1^2 = 10.5$, $n_1 = 25$ and for sample Two $s_2^2 = 3.5$, $n_2 = 29$. He computes F as follows, placing the larger variance in the numerator of the F ratio:

$$F_{24,28} = \frac{10.5}{3.5}$$

$$= 3.0$$

Note that the degrees of freedom $(n-1)$ for each of the variances have been listed as subscripts to the F (the degrees of freedom for the larger variance on the left). When interpreting the F for statistical significance, these degrees of freedom are used to locate the tabled values which the obtained F must equal or exceed if it is to be judged significant.

Turn to the F table on page 384, and you will note that the row of degrees of freedom across the top of the table is used for the greater mean square. The degrees of freedom for the lesser mean square are at the left of the table. In the present example, enter the top of the table with the degrees of freedom for the group with the larger variance, that is, 24. Enter the left side of the table with the degrees of freedom for the group with the smaller variance, 28. These two entries intersect at a point where the tabled roman-type value is 1.91 and the boldface value is 2.52. If the computed value of F equals or exceeds the tabled values, then the null hypothesis should be rejected and the hypothesis of variance homogeneity considered untenable. If, on the other hand, the tabled values exceed the computed F value one may consider the variance to be homogeneous. In this example, the computed F value of 3.0 exceeds both of the tabled values, so one should reject the null hypothesis of variance homogeneity.

A few words should be devoted to the probability levels represented by the roman type and boldface values in Table G. The F table is designed for use with one-tailed tests of significance. For such one-tailed tests, the roman type represents the 5 percent point, and the boldface represents the 1 percent point. As we shall later see when using the analysis of variance statistical technique, an F is yielded which should be interpreted according to a one-tailed test. It is with the F value yielded by analysis of variance that the F table is usually employed. In the F-ratio test of variance homogeneity, observe that it is not known in advance of the data collection which group's variance will be greater. Hence, it is not certain which variance will eventually be placed in the numerator of the ratio. Since it might be either of the two variances, a *two-tailed* test is used to interpret the F ratio. When interpreting the computed F value from a homogeneity of variance test one must, therefore, use the tabled roman type values to represent the 10 percent level and the boldface values to represent the 2 percent level. To compute the 1 and 5 percent levels of significance for two-tailed F-ratio tests is an intricate and laborious process, so researchers typically employ a one-tailed F table and merely double the probability levels.

Selecting the t Model and Degrees of Freedom

Remembering that we are still discussing uncorrelated data, the factors have now been treated which are necessary for the selection of the correct t model and degrees of freedom. Since the equivalence of n_1 and n_2, as well as the homogeneity of σ_1^2 and σ_2^2, will serve as guides, a fourfold scheme can be devised to determine which formula and degrees of freedom to employ:

When $n_1 = n_2$ and $\sigma_1^2 = \sigma_2^2$:[1]
Use separate or *pooled variance formula* with degrees of freedom equal to $n_1 + n_2 - 2$. (Both formulas are algebraically equivalent when $n_1 = n_2$).

When $n_1 \neq n_2$ and $\sigma_1^2 = \sigma_2^2$:
Use *pooled variance formula* with degrees of freedom equal to $n_1 + n_2 - 2$.

[1]That is, the null hypothesis of variance homogeneity cannot be rejected with the F-ratio test.

When $n_1 = n_2$ and $\sigma_1^2 \neq \sigma_2^2$:

Use *pooled variance formula* or *separate variance formula* with degrees of freedom in each instance equal to $n_1 - 1$ or $n_2 - 1$. (Do not use $df = n_1 + n_2 - 2$.)

When $n_1 \neq n_2$ and $\sigma_1^2 \neq \sigma_2^2$:

Use *separate variance formula* with tabled t value for a given level of significance determined by averaging t values for (a) degrees of freedom equal to $n_1 - 1$ and (b) degrees of freedom equal to $n_2 - 1$.

Calculation of the t value for different levels of significance in the last instance should be clarified. To illustrate, if the researcher wishes to use the 0.01 level in such a situation with $n_1 = 25$ and $n_2 = 13$, he finds that table t at the 0.01 level for $df = 24$ is 2.797, and t at the 0.01 level for $df = 12$ is 3.055. He now calculates the average of these two t values by dividing the difference between the two values by two and adding this quantity to the smaller value as follows: $3.055 - 2.797 = 0.258$; $0.258 \div 2 = 0.129$; $2.797 + 0.129 = 2.926$. This value, 2.926, is the value which the computed t must equal or exceed in order to be significant at the 0.01 level.

If the calculated t had been 2.80, it would not be sufficiently large to reject the null hypothesis at the 0.01 level. Such a t would, however, be large enough to reject the null hypothesis at 0.05 level.[2]

Computational Examples

It may assist the reader to work a sample problem, making the necessary decisions and conclusion regarding the tenability of the null hypothesis. We shall assume that the researcher has developed an experimental design in which it is requisite to test the null hypothesis that the examination means of two groups do not differ significantly.

Initially, the researcher determines whether the data in the two groups are related, as might be the case in a study involving matched pairs in the two groups. Let us assume he is working with two independent groups, so he does not need correlated t models and can choose from either the separate variance or pooled variance models.

Now, turn to the sample data before reaching further decisions on the selection of a t model. Preliminary calculations yield the following set of values for Group A and Group B, the two samples under investigation:

Group A	Group B
$n = 11$	$n = 25$
$s^2 = 9$	$s^2 = 12$
$\bar{X} = 13.85$	$\bar{X} = 11.20$

The first check on the data is to see whether the variances of the two popu-

[2]Another frequently used method for determining the t value to use as desired probability level in this situation has been supplied by W. G. Cochran and Gertrude M. Cox, *Experimental Designs*, New York: Wiley, 1950.

lation groups are homogeneous. This is accomplished by computing an *F* ratio and dividing the larger variance, in this case that of Group B, by the smaller variance as follows:

$$F_{24,10} = \frac{12}{9}$$

$$= 1.33$$

From Table G we find that with 24 degrees of freedom for the greater mean square (variance) and 10 degrees of freedom for the lesser mean square, an *F* value equal to or exceeding 2.74 is required to reject the null hypothesis of variance homogeneity at the 0.10 level. Similarly, the 0.02 level would demand an *F* of at least 4.33. With an *F* of 1.33, the hypothesis of variance homogeneity cannot be rejected, so it is concluded that the population variances represented by the two samples are, for statistical purposes, equal.

Also note that the number of subjects in the two groups is not the same, with 25 subjects in Group B and only 11 subjects in Group A.

The researcher is now in a position to select a *t* model as well as the degrees of freedom with which to interpret the *t*. Referring back to the fourfold selection scheme outlined on pages 141–142, it can be seen that when $n_1 \neq n_2$ and $\sigma_1^2 = \sigma_2^2$, the pooled variance formula (10.1) is used. As this is the case in this example, Formula 10.1 is selected, noting that the degrees of freedom for interpreting the significance of *t* are $n_1 + n_2 - 2$. Substituting the necessary data in the pooled variance formula, we find that

$$t = \frac{13.85 - 11.20}{\sqrt{\left(\frac{(10)(9) + (24)(12)}{11 + 25 - 2}\right)\left(\frac{1}{11} + \frac{1}{25}\right)}}$$

$$= \frac{2.65}{\sqrt{\frac{378}{34}(0.091 + 0.040)}}$$

$$= \frac{2.65}{\sqrt{(11.118)(0.131)}}$$

$$= \frac{2.65}{\sqrt{1.456}}$$

$$= \frac{2.65}{1.207}$$

$$= 2.196$$

With a *t* of 2.196, the *t* table is now entered to determine whether the null hypothesis can be rejected. Using $n_1 + n_2 - 2$ degrees of freedom, in this case $11 + 25 - 2 = 34$ *df*, we find that *t* at the 0.05 level must be at least 2.032, and at the 0.01 level t must be 2.728. Since the calculated t of 2.196 exceeds the 0.05 level t (2.032) but not the 0.01 level t (2.728), the null hypothesis can be rejected at the 0.05 level, but not at the 0.01 level of significance. This is true, of course, for a two-tailed test such as we are using.

It can be concluded that the observed mean difference would occur *by chance alone* less than 5 times in 100. Therefore, our researcher can determine, with odds considerably in his favor, that the observed difference can be attributed to the independent variable under study. To rephrase this statement, there exists a relationship between the *dependent* variable represented by the test performance and the *independent* variable represented by the two treatment groups.

The reader will find that by following the general scheme outlined in this computational example, t tests can be easily selected and properly interpreted. Of course, with different data, the t model selected, as well as the degrees of freedom, may vary.

To cite another example, if a t test were to be computed with the following data it would be found that the population variances were not homogeneous ($F_{99,99} = 200.74/85.63 = 2.42$, $p < 0.02$). Thus, the separate variance formula (9.1) is used with $n_1 - 1$ degrees of freedom. (The pooled variance formula could also be used with the same degrees of freedom.)

Group 1	*Group 2*
$n_1 = 100$	$n_2 = 100$
$\overline{X}_1 = 82.6$	$\overline{X}_2 = 68.4$
$s_1^2 = 200.74$	$s_2^2 = 85.63$

Substituting in Formula 9.1, the value of t is found.

$$t = \frac{82.6 - 68.4}{\sqrt{\dfrac{200.74}{100} + \dfrac{85.63}{100}}}$$

$$= \frac{14.2}{\sqrt{2.01 + 0.86}}$$

$$= \frac{14.2}{\sqrt{2.87}}$$

$$= \frac{14.2}{1.69}$$

$$= 8.4$$

With a t value of 8.4 and 99 degrees of freedom, we find from Table F that the mean difference is significant beyond the 0.01 level.

CORRELATED DATA

When one tests the mean differences of two groups in which subjects have been matched, or in which two measures for the same subjects compose the data as in the pre- and post test comparisons, it is likely that the measurements composing the two groups are positively correlated. The presence of correlation, of course, can be checked by computing the usual product–moment correlation coefficient.

If there is a relationship between the scores composing the two groups, as indicated by *r*, a special *t* model designed specifically for this purpose must be used. As mentioned in the previous chapter, the reason for using a special model stems from the tendency of the two group means to be more similar if correlation exists. If a positive correlation is present, scores in the one group will be related to or somewhat like scores in the other. This tendency of correlated scores to be somewhat more similar than data drawn from uncorrelated groups results in means which are also *less* likely to be significantly different than means drawn from independent groups. The correlated *t* model embodies an adjustment expression which is subtracted from the denominator of the separate variance *t* model, thereby increasing the magnitude of *t*. The value of *t* is adjusted upward to compensate for the tendency of the means to be similar. The extent of the adjustment is a function of the magnitude of *r*, as seen in the correlated *t* formula presented below:

$$t = \frac{\bar{X}_1 - \bar{X}_2}{\sqrt{\dfrac{s_1^2}{n_1} + \dfrac{s_2^2}{n_2} - 2r\left(\dfrac{s_1}{\sqrt{n_1}}\right)\left(\dfrac{s_2}{\sqrt{n_2}}\right)}} \tag{10.3}$$

The value of *t* derived from this correlated model is interpreted for significance according to degrees of freedom equaling the number of *pairs* minus one.

Computational Example

If an educator wishes to determine whether any significant gain in knowledge of biology has occurred for a group of 100 pupils following a special summer outdoor program, he could administer a pretest and a posttest covering the subject matter to the pupils before and after the summer program. Since the same individuals take both tests, he might anticipate the existence of a positive correlation between their scores on these two measures. If he wishes to test for significant mean differences between posttest and pretest by use of a *t* model, he must ascertain whether such a correlation actually exists.

Suppose he finds that an *r* of 0.41 is present between pupils' scores on the two tests. He should then use the *t* model presented in Formula 10.3 to test the null hypothesis. The following values will be needed for the computation:

Posttest	Pretest
$n = 100$	$n = 100$
$s^2 = 64.0$	$s^2 = 49.0$
$\bar{X} = 46.4$	$X = 42.5$

These values would then be substituted in the formula as follows:

$$t = \frac{46.4 - 42.5}{\sqrt{\dfrac{64.0}{100} + \dfrac{49.0}{100} - 2(0.41)\left(\dfrac{8}{10}\right)\left(\dfrac{7}{10}\right)}}$$

$$= 4.76$$

By consulting the t table with 99 degrees of freedom, it can be seen that a t of 4.76 is significant beyond the 0.01 level. Thus, the educator may reject the null hypothesis of pretest and posttest mean equivalence, concluding that a significant gain in biology knowledge was made by the 100 pupils. To be certain this gain was produced by the special summer program, an educational researcher would have to contrast the growth of these 100 pupils with a comparable group of youngsters who did not take part in the summer program.

CONFIDENCE INTERVALS

In computing confidence intervals for differences between means, essentially the same procedure is followed as in determining any confidence interval. First, compute *the standard error of mean difference*. In each of the previously described t models, the standard error of mean difference is the denominator of the t ratio. The particular denominator to be used will depend upon the t model used in the analysis. For example, if the separate variance t model was used, then the standard error of mean difference is the denominator of Formula 9.1:

$$\sqrt{\frac{s_1^2}{n_1} + \frac{s_2^2}{n_2}}$$

This standard error is then multiplied by plus and minus the t value associated with the desired confidence interval (for example the 95 percent level) and the degrees of freedom involved. The resulting value is then added to and subtracted from the mean difference observed in the sample, thus yielding the appropriate confidence limits.

Calculating a confidence interval can be illustrated by using the data in an earlier example in the chapter on page 144. In that example the mean difference was 14.2, the standard error of mean difference, that is, the lower part of the t model was 5.35, and the degrees of freedom were 99.

The 99 percent confidence interval for this mean difference would be computed by multiplying 5.35 by the appropriate 99 percent t values of ± 2.64 and adding the results to the mean difference of 14.2 points. The result yields 99 percent mean difference confidence limits of 0.40 and 28.0 points. The 95 percent confidence points would be computed as follows: $14.2 \pm (1.99)(5.35) = 3.7$ and 24.7.

REVIEW

The principal problem in the use of a t test is to select the appropriate t model and correct number of degrees of freedom. Selection of the correct t

test hinges on the presence of correlated data, the homogeneity of the variances of the two populations, and the equality of the number of subjects in the two groups.

With uncorrelated data the researcher chooses between the separate variance *t* model or the pooled variance *t* model. A special *t* model exists for correlated data. Computation procedures for all of these *t* models were described in the chapter.

The number of degrees of freedom varies with the different *t* models, so one must be attentive to the *df* available in particular situations.

The procedure for testing homogeneity of variances through the *F* ratio was outlined in the chapter. A description of the operations for setting up mean difference confidence intervals was also given.

EXERCISES

1. Decide whether to use the separate variance *t* model or the pooled variance *t* model for each of the following situations, as well as the degrees of freedom which should be used in each instance.

(a)   *Group 1*   *Group 2*

           $n = 25$ $n = 14$
           $s^2 = 100.0$ $s^2 = 92.3$
           $\overline{X} = 62.80$ $\overline{X} = 73.42$

(b)   *Group 1*   *Group 2*

           $n = 14$ $n = 14$
           $s^2 = 102.0$ $s^2 = 20.0$
           $\overline{X} = 43.71$ $\overline{X} = 36.28$

(c)   *Group 1*   *Group 2*

           $n = 18$ $n = 18$
           $s^2 = 161.8$ $s^2 = 154.9$
           $\overline{X} = 72.41$ $\overline{X} = 67.82$

(d)   *Group 1*   *Group 2*

           $n = 24$ $n = 16$
           $s^2 = 26.9$ $s^2 = 107.1$
           $\overline{X} = 106.12$ $\overline{X} = 100.22$

2. Compute the value of *t* for each of the four sets of data above. Using the 0.05 level of significance (two-tailed), determine whether the null hypothesis of mean difference should be accepted or rejected.

3. Since it is necessary to check for homogeneity of population variances prior to selecting the appropriate t model for independent groups, the F ratio must be employed. Compute F for the five pairs of variances below, indicating whether the parameters they estimate should be considered homogeneous or heterogeneous. Use the 0.10 level of significance for rejecting the null hypothesis of variance homogeneity.

(a) $s_1^2 = 480.42, n_1 = 14; s_2^2 = 682.49, n_2 = 15$
(b) $s_1^2 = 286.31, n_1 = 62; s_2^2 = 494.37, n_2 = 51$
(c) $s_1^2 = 127.42, n_1 = 10; s_2^2 = 197.43, n_2 = 10$
(d) $s_1^2 = 142.81, n_1 = 100; s_2^2 = 42.64, n_2 = 51$
(e) $s_1^2 = 1{,}000.67, n_1 = 41; s_2^2 = 2{,}527.00, n_2 = 61$

4. Select the appropriate t model and degrees of freedom for the two independent samples given below. Compute the value of t and, using the 0.01 level, make a decision regarding the acceptance or rejection of the null hypothesis.

Group A	Group B
42	41
69	38
48	46
37	49
42	37
18	36
64	42
71	18

5. Treat the following data in the same fashion as in the foregoing problem.

Group X	Group Y
104	100
102	100
100	97
100	94
98	93
97	92
94	92
90	90
87	86
80	74

6. Using the t model for correlated observations, compute the value of t and reach a decision regarding the null hypothesis ($p < 0.01$) when for matched pair Group 1, $\bar{X} = 62.70$, $s^2 = 64.00$, $n = 16$; for Group 2, $\bar{X} = 42.70$, $s^2 = 49.00$, $n = 25$; and the correlation between scores of the two sets of matched pairs is 0.49.

7. A random sample of twenty high-school seniors have been exposed to two experimental treatments designed to produce anxiety. After each treatment the students completed a test designed to measure degree of anxiety. Compute the correlation coefficient between the two anxiety scores of the twenty pupils, determine the value of *t*, and reach a decision regarding the null hypothesis of mean difference between anxiety level after Treatments A and B. Use the 0.01 level of significance.

Subject	Score After Treatment A	Score After Treatment B	Subject	Score After Treatment A	Score After Treatment B
1	94	62	11	86	60
2	92	60	12	80	55
3	91	63	13	80	56
4	90	68	14	80	52
5	90	71	15	78	48
6	89	60	16	77	45
7	89	54	17	76	45
8	87	54	18	75	43
9	87	52	19	74	49
10	86	59	20	74	42

8. Using a one-tailed test, on the basis of the prediction that the experimental group will achieve a higher mean than the control group, a researcher concludes a *t* analysis which yields a *t* of 1.80 in the predicted direction. Using the 0.05 level of significance with 15 degrees of freedom, should the null hypothesis be accepted or rejected?

9. A researcher, on the basis of his theoretical position and previous empirical studies, predicts that boys will outperform girls on a test of mechanical aptitude. He therefore adopts a one-tailed *t* test, using the 0.05 level of significance. What should his action be regarding the null hypothesis if, contrary to his expectations, the girls perform so much better than the boys that a *t* value significant at the 0.001 level is yielded?

SELECTED READINGS

Blalock, Hubert M., Jr., *Social Statistics*. New York: McGraw-Hill, 1960, chap. 13.

Blommers, Paul, and E. F. Lindquist, *Elementary Statistical Methods*. Boston: Houghton Mifflin, 1960, chap. 12.

Edwards, Allen L., *Statistical Methods for the Behavioral Sciences*. New York: Holt, Rinehart & Winston, 1957, chaps. 13 and 14.

Johnson, Palmer O., and Robert W. B. Jackson, *Modern Statistical Methods: Descriptive and Inductive*. Chicago: Rand McNally, 1959, chap. 6.

Wert, James E., Charles O. Neidt, and J. Stanley Ahmann, *Statistical Methods in Educational and Psychological Research*. New York: Appleton-Century-Crofts, 1954, chap. 8.

11

Single-Classification Analysis of Variance

With increasing frequency a statistical technique known as the *analysis of variance* is encountered in the research literature of education and psychology. As shall be seen, the analysis of variance has several properties which make it particularly suitable for a variety of research tasks. Yet many educators who lack statistical training undoubtedly regard the analysis of variance as a particularly baffling example of statistical symbol juggling. To try to remove the confusion surrounding this useful technique, it should be stated at the very outset that analysis of variance, in its most basic form, is nothing more than a clever statistical method of *testing for significant differences between means of two or more groups.* Typically, the performance of these groups can be considered to represent results of the treatment by an independent variable whose possible relationship to a dependent variable is being studied.

It is important to note that analysis of variance may be used to test the significance of mean differences between more than two groups simultaneously, for as shown previously, a *t* test is usually employed in testing mean differences between only two groups. Actually, the *t* test is merely a special case of the more general *F* test for two groups or more. Exactly the same logic underlying Figure 9.4 is used here in the general case. We now conceptualize any number of populations, sampling from each, and drawing inferences about the populations from analysing the sample data.

Suppose a researcher working with three samples wishes to determine whether the mean performance of any two of his three groups is significantly different. He could, of course, compute three separate *t* tests rather than use analysis of variance. For example, with Groups A, B, and C, a *t* test could be employed to assess the significance of mean differences first between Groups A and B, then Groups B and C, and finally Groups A and C. The number of *t* test calculations in this case is not prohibitive. However, with a large number of groups the task of computing individual *t* tests becomes more onerous. With ten groups, for instance, the number of separate t tests necessary in order to determine if there were significant mean differences between any of the groups would rise to 45! Obviously a statistical procedure using a single operation that can tell the researcher whether any significant differences exist between the means of many groups has far more merit.

Besides the convenience associated with using analysis of variance procedures instead of a series of t tests, it should be pointed out that there are some dangers associated with computing many individual t tests. To mention but one of these dangers, by chance alone a few t test results should appear to be statistically significant when many such tests have been computed. One should, of course, beware of ascribing too much import to such results.

Early in this discussion we should clarify one important point. When a researcher uses the analysis of variance statistical model he is primarily interested in *mean* differences rather than *variance* differences. He is able to draw conclusions about means through the process of analyzing variance in a particular way, hence the name of the procedure, analysis of variance. This point cannot be stated too strongly, for far too many students flounder in attempting to comprehend analysis of variance because they perceive the technique as a method of yielding some critical notions regarding the variances of groups. The ingenious method by which the statistician is able to draw conclusions about *mean* differences through the process of analyzing *variances* will be discussed in subsequent paragraphs.

Before proceeding to a discussion of the rationale underlying analysis of variance, it should be noted that this very powerful statistical test can be modified for a number of more complex analysis of variance models. These will be described in Chapters 13 and 14. But in order to understand how more complex models function, it will be instructive to examine first the most basic form of the technique, that is, single-classification analysis of variance.

By "single classification" we mean that the researcher has organized his data in such a fashion as to test for differences in a dependent or criterion variable among groups as they relate to a single independent variable. For example, a college administrator might wish to discover if there were any significant differences in intelligence among students majoring in English, history, philosophy, and mathematics. In this instance the independent variable would be the college major and the dependent variable would be student intelligence. The independent variable is often referred to as a *factor* in the analysis of variance design. In this example, the factor is college major and it has four *levels* corresponding to the four majors under study. Single-classification designs are often referred to as *one-way* or single-factor designs.

The students involved in the analysis could be regrouped in order to study intelligence in terms of other independent variables, such as year in college, age, sex, and so forth. In other words, additional factors could be added to the design creating a multiple classification or factorial analysis of variance design having more than one factor. However, in a single-classification analysis of variance model, the researcher is concerned with only one independent variable at a time. With this brief introduction to single-classification analysis of variance, the general method employed in analysis of variance designs will now be considered.

BASIC RATIONALE OF ANALYSIS OF VARIANCE
A Brief Outlook

At first glance it might appear unlikely to analyze variances in such a way that we can learn anything of consequence about means. After all, variances are measures of variability, and means are measures of central tendency; hence learning about central tendency by examining variability may appear to be a highly circuitous process. It is important to recall from our earlier discussion of a variance and its square root, the standard deviation, that these variability measures are comparable to an average of the distance of the raw scores in a distribution *from the mean* of that distribution. There is, then, a definite relationship between variances and means. It is this functional relationship which is used in determining the significance of mean differences by analyzing variances in a particular fashion.

In essence, the method employed in the analysis of variance is to compute the variances of the separate groups being tested for mean differences. The scores of all subjects in the subgroups are then artificially combined into one total group. This is done by regrouping, for analysis purposes, all of the scores in the several groups as though they were one, and then computing the variance of the total group. If the variance of the combined total group is approximately the same as the *average* variance of the separate subgroups, then there exists no significant difference between the means of the separate groups. If, on the other hand, the variance of the combined total group is considerably larger than the average variance of the separate subgroups, then a significant mean difference exists between two or more of the subgroups.

A Graphic Illustration

This explanation of the basic rationale of analysis of variance may seem rather obscure, but a pictorial illustration will be of assistance. We shall examine two hypothetical examples of analysis of variance situations. The first illustration will depict data for which the null hypothesis is tenable, that is, there exists no significant difference between two or more of the subgroup means. The second will depict data for which the null hypothesis is untenable, that is there exists a significant mean difference between two or more of the subgroups.

Four distributions are presented in Figure 11.1. The upper three represent groups which the researcher is interested in testing for significance of mean differences. The distribution depicted at the bottom of the figure represents a regrouped pooling of the upper three samples. This is accomplished by combining all scores as though they formed one total group. Note the similarities and differences in the four distributions. The means of all four groups ($\bar{X} = 50$) are identical, as are the variances ($s^2 = 100$). The number of subjects in

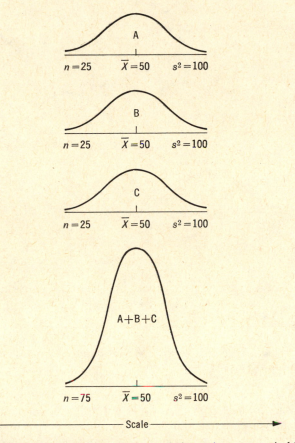

Figure 11.1 *Three separate samples and one pooled sample composed of the three subgroups considered as a total group.*

the upper three groups is 25 per group, and in the pooled group, of course, there are 75 subjects. The pooled group can be thought of as having three equivalently shaped groups of 25 subjects added on top of one another to form a new group of 75 subjects which, although more dense, has exactly the same range as the three subgroups. Since this is the case, we should not be surprised that the variance of the pooled or total group is the same as the *average* variance of the three sample groups. This situation represents data in which absolutely no mean differences exist between any of the three groups and in which, therefore, the null hypothesis is certainly tenable.

Contrast the situation presented in Figure 11.1 with the four distributions depicted in Figure 11.2. Figure 11.2 represents a situation in which sizable mean differences exist between the separate groups so that the null hypothesis is

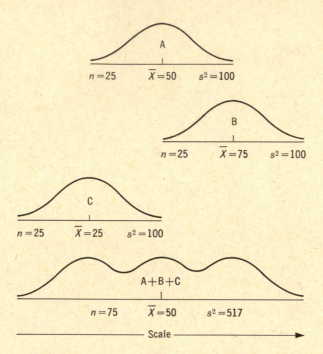

Figure 11.2 *Three separate samples and one pooled sample composed of the three sub-groups considered as a total group.*

quite untenable. As in Figure 11.1, we find that the upper three distributions are those which we are testing for mean differences. Once more, the lower distribution represents a pooled group composed of all 75 scores of the upper three groups. As before, the variances of the three upper groups are equal, $s^2 = 100$. In Figure 11.2, however, three subgroups are presented in which mean differences are rather large. Observe that for the pooled group the variation of the scores is radically different from that observed in Figure 11.1, where the pooled group variance was equal to the average of the separate group variances. Although the average of the separate group variances is still 100 in Figure 11.2, the variance of the pooled group is 517. This situation exists because many scores from the three upper groups when incorporated in the total group are farther away from the total group's mean. The shape of the pooled distribution is more spread out and, of vital significance, *the variance of the pooled group is considerably larger than the average variance of the three separate groups.* Comprehension of this relationship between separate group mean differences and pooled group variance is indeed the key to understanding how analysis of variance, by treating a measure of variability, can reveal important facts about mean differences. If the relationship is not clear, it is suggested that the illustrations presented in Figure 11.1 and Figure 11.2, as well as the accompanying discussion, be reexamined carefully before proceeding.[1]

In cases where the null hypothesis is tenable, relatively little difference between means will exist and, consequently, the average variance of the separate subgroups involved will be about the same size as the variance of the pooled group. In cases where the null hypothesis is untenable, differences between the means of the separate groups will be of a greater magnitude, so that the variance of the pooled group will be considerably larger than the average variance of the separate groups. Statisticians have merely devised a precise way of determining how great the difference between the variance of the pooled group and the average variance of the separate subgroups needs to be in order to reject the null hypothesis. This process is called the analysis of variance.

With this general explanation of the method underlying analysis of variance, consider an extremely brief discussion of the actual technique used by the statistician in arriving at a decision regarding the null hypothesis. A more detailed step-by-step explanation, complete with a computational example, will be found in the next chapter.

First, the sums of squares (Σx^2) for each of the separate groups are computed individually. The reader will recall from the discussion of the standard deviation how a sum of squares is computed. These sums of squares are then added together to form a quantity referred to as the *within groups* sum of squares (SS) or the within sum of squares.

1. Compute within SS by totaling sums of squares of each subgroup.

Then the sum of the squares for the pooled group is calculated in the usual manner. This quantity is referred to as the *total group* sum of squares or the total sum of squares.

2. Compute total SS for pooled group.

The within groups sum of squares is then subtracted from the total sum of squares. The resulting difference is called the *between groups* sum of squares or the between sum of squares.[2]

3. Determine between SS by subtracting within SS from total SS.

[1]The astute reader may have recognized our rather nonrigorous use of Figures 11.1 and 11.2 and the phrase "significant differences between group means." These distributions depict *samples*, randomly drawn from populations with characteristics similar to those depicted for the samples. When we speak of significant mean differences, we are speaking about *population means*. Differences between sample means are, of course, evident merely upon their inspection. Statistically speaking, then, we are testing the null hypothesis $H_0: \mu_1 = \mu_2 = \mu_3$. If this hypothesis is rejected, then we are accepting the alternative hypothesis $H_1: \mu_1 \neq \mu_2$ and/or $\mu_1 \neq \mu_3$ and/or $\mu_2 \neq \mu_3$.

[2]Computationally, it is often easier to calculate the between SS directly, subtracting it from the total SS to obtain the within SS.

The between groups sum of squares, since it represents that amount of variability in the pooled group which was not present already in the separate groups, is attributable to the differences in means of the subgroups. The larger the between groups SS, therefore, the greater is the difference between the subgroup means. Conversely, the smaller the between groups SS, the less divergent are the subgroup means.

The next step in the analysis is to divide the within and between sums of squares by the degrees of freedom associated with them. The reader may recall from our earlier discussion of variance that, when a sum of squares is divided by the degrees of freedom associated with it, the result is referred to as a variance estimate or, as it is sometimes called, a *mean square.* In analysis of variance the term mean square is used to describe the quantities yielded when the within groups and between groups sums of squares are divided by their respective degrees of freedom. When the within groups sum of squares is divided by its degrees of freedom (the number of subjects less the number of groups) the *within mean square* is obtained. When the between groups sum of squares is divided by its degrees of freedom (the number of groups less one) the *between mean square* is obtained.

4. Divide within SS and between SS by appropriate degrees of freedom to obtain within and between mean squares.

The next step in the analysis is to divide the between mean square by the within mean square (often called the "error term"). The result of this division operation yields a value referred to as *F*.

5. Obtain *F* by dividing within mean square into between mean square.

An inspection of step 5 will reveal that the size of the *F* value hinges upon the relative magnitude of the two mean squares involved. It has already been noted that the between groups sum of squares becomes larger as the differences between group means increase. This is also true of the between groups mean square, that is, the greater the magnitude of the differences between subgroup means, the greater the magnitude of the between mean square.

Hence, the magnitude of F tends to increase as the differences among the group means increase. This assumes, of course, that the within mean square remains relatively constant. You may wish to reexamine the graphic illustrations presented in Figures 11.1 and 11.2 to see that the within mean squares in the two situations represented would remain the same in both cases.

Once the value of *F* has been obtained, the statistician may check its significance through the use of a special table of the sampling distribution of *F* (Table G in the Appendix). If the obtained *F* value is sufficiently large to be statistically significant, the null hypothesis is considered untenable and the researcher concludes that significant differences between the means of two or more of his populations exist.

6. Interpret significance of F from the Table of F.

It must be pointed out that if the null hypothesis has been shown to be untenable, that is, the existence of significant mean differences between two or more groups has been demonstrated, the researcher is not yet able to determine which means are significantly different from which other means. Fortunately, methods for carrying out further analysis to determine the exact location of mean differences have been developed. Two commonly used techniques of this type are those described by Tukey[3] and Duncan.[4]

INTERPRETING F AS A RATIO OF SYSTEMATIC VARIANCE
TO ERROR VARIANCE

The between mean square is often said to reflect *systematic* variability whereas the within mean square reflects *error* variability. There is no "mistake" about the presence of variance within each group. The term "error" arises insofar as the researcher has made no attempt to control for individual differences (variance) within each group, as with the addition of other independent variables to the design. For example, we can imagine the three groups in Figure 11.2 to represent subjects treated under three different programmed instruction sequences for the same course content. If we were to expect that the only reason for variability in achievement test scores (dependent variable) was the differing instructional programs, then we would expect all the subjects of Group A to receive a score of 50, those of Group B a score of 75, and those of Group C a score of 25 — that is, no variability whatsoever within treatment groups. The fact that this does not occur may be due to any number of reasons; prior achievement level, intellectual aptitude, sex, social economic status, attitude towards programmed instruction, unreliability in measuring achievement, attention levels, health, and so forth. All these kinds of variance sources are *confounded* in the within source of variance. Since the researcher does not (or cannot) control these extraneous (but not necessarily irrelevant) sources of variance, he labels the within-variability error variance or unsystematic variance.

To review, then, the systematic or between source of variance reflects the variability due to the independent variable, or, in this example, the differences between the three methods of programmed instruction. The unsystematic, error, or within source of variance reflects the variability due to all the remaining, uncontrolled factors. To the extent that the systematic variance is less than or equal to the unsystematic or error variance, the researcher would be hard put to claim any real differences due to his treatment conditions. The ratio of the between mean square to the within mean square is exactly a reflection of this comparison. When this F ratio is 1.0, we have no more controlled variability than uncontrolled variability; F ratios of 1.0 (or less) can never, in practice, be significant. When the F ratio is sufficiently greater than 1.0 for a given amount of

[3]J. W. Tukey, "Comparing Individual Means in the Analysis of Variance," *Biometrics* **5** (1949): 99–114.

[4]D. B. Duncan, "Multiple Range and Multiple F Tests," *Biometrics* **11** (1955): 1–42.

data (degrees of freedom), the researcher can begin to make a meaningful claim that the results of his experimental treatments made a real difference.

RESEARCH SITUATIONS SUITABLE FOR ANALYSIS OF VARIANCE

We should not end the discussion of single-classification analysis of variance without discussing the types of educational situations in which this technique is most appropriate.

As suggested by the previous discussion, a common use of analysis of variance is to test for mean differences between more than two groups of subjects exposed to different experimental treatments. For example, a researcher might contrast the achievement of three groups of college students who were instructed in three essentially distinct ways. The first group may have employed conventional lecture-discussion techniques; the second a project method of teaching could have been employed; and for the third a nondirective approach could have been utilized. If it can be demonstrated that the three groups were relatively comparable with respect to variables considered relevant to achievement (e.g., intelligence), a terminal achievement examination could be administered to determine whether the performances of the three groups were significantly different. This hypothesis and many similar hypotheses could be tested appropriately by analysis of variance.

Another common educational use of analysis of variance is seen in test development procedures where the measurement specialist has designed a new test instrument and administered it to a large normative sample of students. He often categorizes the students into subgroups on the basis of some variable which is possibly related to performance on the test, that is, years of education. Analysis of variance can then be employed to test for mean differences in the performance of the subgroups on the new test. If the analysis of variance, through the magnitude of the F value, reveals that there are no significant mean differences in performance on the instrument by the several groups involved, the test developer may then conclude that the variable represented, although considered by him as potentially relevant to test performance, appears to have no relationship to performance on the test. If, however, the subgroups perform in a significantly different fashion on the instrument, he would probably conclude that the variable was indeed related to test performance and that separate norms taking the variable into consideration should be prepared.[5]

Another example of a situation in which analysis of variance is appropriate, is seen in the case of a school administrator who wishes to determine whether students coming from several relatively distinct socioeconomic areas in his school district are different in any important fashion with respect to intellectual

[5]For example, if the normative sample is classified into subgroups according to college major, it may be discovered that the group majoring in English scores higher on the test than students majoring in industrial arts. The test developer therefore should establish separate norms where, for instance, a raw score of 78 might fall at the 35th percentile for English majors and at the 51st percentile for industrial arts majors. Such norms, of course, would allow more meaningful interpretations of scores.

Table 11.1

A Simple Analysis of Variance of Final Achievement Performance of Five Groups of Ten Students Taught by Different Instructional Methods

Source of Variation	Degrees of Freedom	Sum of Squares	Mean Square	F
Between groups	4	19.72	4.93	0.873
Within groups	45	254.30	5.65	
Total	49	274.02		

aptitude. Such information could be important in a number of curricular decisions made in the district. Specifically, the administrator could have a standardized group intelligence examination administered to his students and subsequently categorize scores into the appropriate number of socioeconomic groups. (Socioeconomic status could have been determined by any of several sociological techniques.) By applying analysis of variance to the groups' performance on the intelligence test, it would be possible to discern if there were actually any significant differences between the socioeconomic categories represented by the several groups.

Although the foregoing illustrations do not exhaust the types of educational situations in which analysis of variance is appropriate, the reader may see similarities between the examples presented and other research situations where analysis of variance can be suitably employed.

TYPICAL REPORT OF AN ANALYSIS OF VARIANCE

The treatment of this technique will be concluded by examining a typical report of an analysis of variance as it might be described in educational research literature. In Table 11.1 a hypothetical analysis of variance summary is presented, similar to what might be encountered in any educational journal reporting research results. While the form of the table may vary slightly from journal to journal, most elements will be comparable to the sample in Table 11.1.

In examining an analysis of variance table such as that presented in Table 11.1, the reader would probably first turn to the *F* value since this quantity, the end result of the entire analysis, indicates whether the null hypothesis is tenable. In the example under consideration the *F* value is only 0.873 and is not statistically significant. When it is significant, an asterisk is usually placed near the *F* value and the level of significance is indicated below the table. Actually, *F* values of less than one are never significant, so in this example the researcher would not even find it necessary to consult the *F* table in order to conclude that the null hypothesis could not be rejected.

In analysis of variance tables the phrase "source of variation" is employed to identify the three ways of viewing variation which we have already discussed, that is, *between groups* or the amount of variation resulting from mean differences between the separate groups, *within groups* or the amount of variation between subjects within the separate groups, and *total* or the amount of variation present when the separate groups are considered as one pooled group. Remember that the within group variation is essentially the variance that is left over when the between variation is subtracted from the total variation.

The mean squares, it will be recalled, are obtained by dividing the sums of squares for the three sources of variation by their respective degrees of freedom. Though it is possible to divide the total sum of squares by the total degrees of freedom in order to obtain a total mean square, this is rarely done since the total mean square is not used to derive the value of *F*. The *F* value, of course, is the quotient yielded by dividing the within mean square into the between mean square. This value is subsequently interpreted for statistical significance from the Table of *F*. The reader is again reminded that statistical significance might not mean practical significance in terms of daily operations.

Additional insights into the nature of single-classification analysis of variance are found in the next chapter which includes the actual computation of the analysis of variance as well as certain assumptions associated with the use of this technique. For more extensive discussions of this important technique see the section of selected readings.

REVIEW

Single-classification analysis of variance provides the researcher with a technique for simultaneously testing whether means of two or more population groups are significantly different. This statistical model capitalizes on the integral relationship between the mean and the variance so that, by analyzing variances of several groups, conclusions can be drawn regarding the similarity of the means of those groups.

A graphic example illustrating the logic underlying this important technique was presented in Figures 11.1 and 11.2 of the chapter. The reader was urged to study the illustration noting that when the null hypothesis is tenable the average dispersion present in the subgroups under analysis will be about the same as the dispersion present in a pooled group representing all scores. When the null hypothesis is untenable, the dispersion in the pooled group will markedly exceed the average dispersion of the subgroups.

Analysis of variance has the advantage of comparing means of many groups in a single statistical test. The *F* value yielded by this test is interpreted for its level of probability in Table G of the Appendix.

Several common situations in which single-classification analysis of variance would be applicable were presented in the chapter, along with an example of analysis of variance as it might be reported in a professional journal.

EXERCISES

1. If a statistician makes a few preliminary calculations in a single-classification analysis of variance problem and discovers that the average variances of the five subgroups involved is almost identical to the pooled group variance formed by artificially combining all five sets of data, will the null hypothesis be accepted or rejected?

2. If a researcher wishes to test for mean differences between four groups, would he probably find it more economical to use a series of *t* tests or an analysis of variance?

3. Two single-classification analyses of variance have just been computed by an educational research worker. In Analysis A the between groups mean square is relatively large; in Analysis B the between groups mean square is close to zero. In which analysis is the null hypothesis more likely to be rejected, that is, in which analysis are there apt to be significant mean differences?

4. Once a significant *F* value has been yielded from a single-classification analysis of variance involving eight subgroups, can the researcher then identify by inspection the particular groups means that are significantly different?

5. If the within groups mean square is markedly larger than the between groups mean square, are there significant differences between the group means in an analysis of variance?

SELECTED READINGS

Edwards, Allen L., *Experimental Design in Psychological Research*. New York: Holt, Rinehart & Winston, 1960, chap. 10.

Edwards, Allen L., *Statistical Methods for the Behavioral Sciences*. New York: Holt, Rinehart & Winston, 1957, chap. 16.

Guilford, J. P., *Fundamental Statistics in Psychology and Education*. New York: McGraw-Hill, 1965, chap. 13.

Walker, Helen M., and Joseph Lev, *Statistical Inference*. New York: Holt, Rinehart & Winston, 1953, chap. 9.

Wert, James E., Charles O. Neidt, and J. Stanley Ahmann, *Statistical Methods in Educational and Psychological Research*. New York: Appleton-Century-Crofts, 1954, chap. 10.

12

Single-
Classification
Analysis
of
Variance—
Computation
Procedures

Before reaching a decision regarding the appropriateness of analysis of variance for a given research task one must first consider the actual research design and the purpose of the intended statistical analysis, for example, determining the significance of mean differences between several groups. As we have seen, once a suitable technique has been selected, there are usually certain assumptions underlying the use of the technique which must be satisfied. Prior to the final selection of any statistical method, these assumptions must be considered. Several assumptions peculiar to analysis of variance should be heeded before the researcher decides to use this technique.

From a theoretical viewpoint the assumptions underlying analysis of variance must be rigorously fulfilled so the technique yields information which is accurately interpretable. There is increasing evidence, however, that even though fairly significant departures from strict theoretical assumptions may exist, analysis of variance is sufficiently "robust" that it will still yield results which may be meaningfully interpreted.

One assumption of analysis of variance is that the measures within each level or classification must represent random samples. Though it is often difficult in the behavioral sciences to rigorously satisfy this condition, it is usually possible to approximate random sampling, or at least to rule out the possibility that an obviously biased subgroup is representing a population. For example, in a school where students have been assigned to experimental classes on an alphabetical basis, there is less probability of bias than if students chose their own teachers or were assigned to classes in terms of their previous grades.

Another major assumption of analysis of variance is that the variances within the populations from which the subgroups are sampled are homogeneous, that is, not significantly different among themselves. Though this is usually true when experimental data are gathered from subjects which have been randomly assigned to subgroups, the assumption of subgroup homo-

---

Table 12.1

Raw Scores (X) and Squared Raw Scores (X²) on a Terminal Achievement Test for Subjects Taught by Three Different Instructional Methods

Method A		Method B		Method C	
X	X^2	X	X^2	X	X^2
7	49	4	16	2	4
10	100	6	36	2	4
10	100	7	49	3	9
11	121	9	81	7	49
12	144	9	81	6	36
Σ50	514	35	263	20	102

---

geneity of variance can be tested by several techniques. One of the most widely used is Bartlett's test.[1] A simple, but less rigorous test of homogeneity of variance has also been described by Edwards.[2] This latter technique will be explained shortly. In addition to homogeneity of variance, it is also assumed that the population data from which the subgroup samples are drawn is normally distributed.

As indicated previously, these assumptions must be considered before finally choosing this technique. But, if the departures of his data from the two specified conditions are not drastic, it is likely that the researcher may employ analysis of variance without fear of spurious interpretations.

COMPUTATION PROCEDURE

The computation of analysis of variance is a fairly time-consuming process, yet quite simple and straightforward. In order to obtain the *F* value by which the tenability of the null hypothesis is assessed, the following quantities are needed: (1) the sums of squares for the total group, between groups, and within groups; (2) the degrees of freedom for the within groups and between groups; and (3) the mean squares for the between groups and within groups. In showing how each of these quantities is calculated, it will be helpful to illustrate each operation by referring to sample data presented in Table 12.1. The data in the table represent the achievement test scores of three groups of students taught by different instructional methods. Though there are equal numbers of subjects in the group this need not be the case.

A Homogeneity of Variance Check

Since it must be assumed that the variances within the populations of the analysis are not significantly different, it is a good practice to check variance

[1]M. S. Bartlett, "Some Examples of Statistical Methods of Research in Agriculture and Applied Biology," *J. Roy Statis. Soc. Suppl.* **4** (1937): 137–170.

[2]Allen L. Edwards, *Statistical Methods for the Behavioral Sciences* (New York: Holt, Rinehart & Winston, 1954) pp. 327–328.

homogeneity at the outset of the analysis. A simple first test of homogeneity of variance may be made by calculating the individual variances of the subgroups (using these as estimates of the corresponding population variances) and dividing the smallest s^2 into the largest s^2. The quotient of this division is an F value which is interpreted for statistical significance by the Table of F (Table G in the Appendix).

If the F yielded by dividing the smallest group variance into the largest group variance is not statistically significant, it is concluded that the population variances can be considered homogeneous. If the F is significant, one should apply Bartlett's test to the data, for in some instances the extreme variances will appear heterogeneous but the total set of variances when tested will prove to be homogeneous.

In the present computational example the variances of the three methods groups are $s_a^2 = 3.5$, $s_b^2 = 4.5$ and $s_c^2 = 5.5$. Dividing the smallest into the largest we find that $F = 5.5/3.5 = 1.57$ which is not statistically significant. Hence, the assumption of variance homogeneity is considered tenable.

SUMS OF SQUARES
Total

In order to calculate the total SS, the scores in all of the subgroups must be viewed as representing a single set of measurements. The total sum of squares can be computed by the standard raw-score formula used in such instances.

$$\text{Total SS} = \Sigma X^2 - \frac{(\Sigma X)^2}{n}$$

Substituting the data from Table 12.1, the total sum of squares would be

$$\text{Total SS} = 879 - \frac{(105)^2}{15}$$

$$= 144$$

Between

To find the between SS, the following formula may be used

$$\text{Between SS} = \Sigma \frac{(\Sigma X)^2}{n_g} - \frac{(\Sigma X)^2}{n} \qquad (12.1)$$

where

$$\Sigma \frac{(\Sigma X)^2}{n_g}$$

represents the total of each group's sum of raw scores squared and then divided by the number of subjects in the group (n_g); $(\Sigma X)^2/n$ represents the sum of all raw scores squared and divided by the total number of subjects (n).

For the data in Table 12.1, the between groups sum of squares is thus computed

$$\text{Between SS} = \frac{(50)^2}{5} + \frac{(35)^2}{5} + \frac{(20)^2}{5} - \frac{(105)^2}{15}$$

$$= 90$$

Within

Having obtained the total SS and the between groups SS, we can readily find the within groups SS by subtracting the between SS from the total SS. Because of the possibility of making a computational error in calculating the former two sums of squares, it is often desirable to actually compute the within groups sum of squares by the following formula

$$\text{Within SS} = \sum \Sigma X^2 - \frac{(\Sigma X)^2}{n} \qquad (12.2)$$

in which the raw score sum of squares formula is applied individually to the several subgroups yielding quantities which are then summed. Thus, identifying each group in the example by a differentiating subscript, we have

$$\Sigma x_a^2 = 514 - \frac{(50)^2}{5} = 14$$

and

$$\Sigma x_b^2 = 263 - \frac{(35)^2}{5} = 18$$

and

$$\Sigma x_c^2 = 102 - \frac{(20)^2}{5} = 22$$

By adding these three sums of squares together, $14 + 18 + 22 = 54$, we arrive at the within groups sum of squares.

This value is the same as would have been obtained by subtracting the between SS from the total SS, $144 - 90 = 54$ since

$$\text{Total SS} = \text{Between SS} + \text{Within SS}$$

DEGREES OF FREEDOM

The degrees of freedom for between groups and within groups are needed to obtain the between and within mean squares. Though the total group sum of squares is not absolutely necessary, it can be conveniently employed. The reader will recall that the *total degrees of freedom* are equal to the number of subjects less one $(n-1)$. The *between groups degrees of freedom*, similarly, are equal to the number of *groups* less one $(k-1)$. A simple method of obtaining the *within groups degrees of freedom* is to subtract the number of groups from the number of subjects $(n-k)$. In the present example the total degrees of freedom would be $15 - 1 = 14$; the between degrees of freedom would be $3 - 1 = 2$; and the within degrees of freedom would be $15 - 3 = 12$.

MEAN SQUARES

To compute the between groups mean square, divide the between sum of squares by the between degrees of freedom. Thus

$$\text{Between mean square} = \frac{90}{2} = 45.0$$

Similarly, the within groups mean square is computed by dividing the within sum of squares by the within degrees of freedom. Hence,

$$\text{Within mean square} = \frac{54}{12} = 4.5$$

COMPUTATION AND INTERPRETATION OF F

The value of F is obtained by dividing the between mean square by the within mean square.

$$F = \frac{\text{Between groups mean square}}{\text{Within groups mean square}} \qquad (12.3)$$

Hence, we find that

$$F = \frac{45.0}{4.5} = 10.0$$

Having obtained the F value for our example, it may now be interpreted for statistical significance in order to reject or not reject the null hypothesis. By using the Table of F (Table G in the Appendix) we can learn whether the obtained F value is sufficiently large to be significant at the 0.05 or 0.01 levels. The 0.05 and 0.01 F values in the table are located by employing the between and within degrees of freedom which have been used to obtain the F value. If the obtained F is equal to or larger than the tabled values of F, then the obtained F is considered to be statistically significant and, accordingly, the null hypothesis is rejected.

The reader will note in Table G the column of degrees of freedom appearing at the extreme left of the table. In this column the degrees of freedom corresponding with the *within* degrees of freedom are located. Using the *between* degrees of freedom, we then locate the appropriate degrees of freedom in the horizontal row across the top of the F Table and determine where the row and column intersect. The lightface type at the point of intersection is the value of F significant at the 0.05 level, and the boldface type is the value of F significant at the 0.01 level. In this example, looking at the left-hand column we locate the row of the within degrees of freedom (12) and then in the row at the top of the table locate the column of the between degrees of freedom (2). At the point of inter-section of this row and column a lightface value of 3.88 and a boldface value of 6.93 is found. Since the obtained F of 10.0 exceeds the boldface figure, it may be concluded that the value of F is significant beyond the 0.01 level and the null hypothesis, that is, there exists no significant difference between the achievement performance of the three groups, should be rejected.

If the obtained F value had been as large or larger than the lightface value but not as large as the boldface value, then the F would have been significant at the 0.05 level but not at the 0.01 level. If the obtained F is smaller than both tabled values, then the researcher typically accepts the null hypothesis. F values which approach, but do not reach, the necessary magnitude of the tabled values may suggest the advisability of further research on the problem.

The calculation technique is basically the same when more groups than those in our example are involved, only more subgroup sums of squares must be calculated in order to obtain the within SS. For a further discussion of the computation of single-classification analysis of variance, see the references cited in the selected readings.

REVIEW

The basic assumptions of single-classification analysis of variance are that the subgroup scores be randomly drawn, that the population variances associated with these subgroups be homogeneous, and that the dependent variable be normally distributed in the populations. The homogeneity of variance assumption can be checked by the simple test of dividing the smallest subgroup variance into the largest subgroup variance and interpreting the quotient F value for statistical significance from the Table of F.

To compute the F value by which the null hypothesis of subgroup mean differences is tested, the following quantities must be calculated: (1) the total, between, and within sums of squares, (2) the between and within degrees of freedom, and (3) the between and within mean squares. F is yielded by dividing the within mean square into the between mean square.

Computation procedures associated with each of these quantities were described as well as the interpretation of the statistical significance of F through the use of Table G in the Appendix.

EXERCISES

1. With a between groups SS of 1,000 ($df = 100$) and a total SS of 2,500 ($df = 105$), determine the F value for a test of mean difference between six groups and decide whether the null hypothesis should be rejected at the 0.01 level.

2. Decide by using Table G whether the following F value would be significant beyond the 0.05 level:

    (a) $F_{7,24} = 3.46$ (b) $F_{6,200} = 2.49$ (c) $F_{7,514} = 1.12$

3. Decide by using Table G whether the following F values would be significant beyond the 0.01 level of

   (a) $F_{14,100} = 2.34$ (b) $F_{2,40} = 84.37$ (c) $F_{9,30} = 5.42$

4. For the following three groups of scores find the total sum of squares, the within groups sum of squares, and the between groups sum of squares.

Group X	Group Y	Group Z
62	60	59
60	60	49
50	58	49
48	53	47
47	49	42

5. Decide whether the variances of the populations from which the above three groups were sampled can be considered homogeneous by using the simple homogeneity of variance test described in the chapter.

6. Compute a single classification analysis of variance on the following data, determining the within groups mean square, the between groups mean square, and the value of F.

A	B	C	D
14	17	14	8
12	15	12	6
10	12	12	5
10	9	11	4
9	9	11	2
6	7	10	2
6	7	10	2

7. A group of 30 high-school sophomores have been randomly assigned to three groups. Each group has participated in a series of meetings designed to modify their attitudes toward professional prize fighting. In each of the three groups a different attitude modification approach was employed. Below are the scores of the 30 students on an attitude scale administered at the close of the series of meetings. Applying single-classification analysis of variance, compute the value of F.

Method 1	Method 2	Method 3
38	35	32
37	34	32
37	33	30
36	33	29
36	31	28
34	30	24

34	29	24
30	26	23
30	25	21
27	25	21

8. Find the value of the mean square between groups, the mean square within groups, and *F* for the following data.

A			B			C		
29	24	17	22	18	10	32	24	19
28	24	16	20	17	10	30	21	16
28	20	15	20	16	9	28	20	16
26	18	10	20	14	9	27	20	15
25	18	10	19	11	6	26	19	15

SELECTED READINGS

Edwards, Allen L., *Experimental Design in Psychological Research*. New York: Holt, Rinehart & Winston, 1960, chap. 10.

Edwards, Allen L., *Statistical Methods for the Behavioral Sciences*. New York: Holt, Rinehart & Winston, 1957, chap. 16.

Guilford, J. P., *Fundamental Statistics in Psychology and Education*. New York: McGraw-Hill, 1965, chap. 13.

Walker, Helen M., and Joseph Lev, *Statistical Inference*. New York: Holt, Rinehart & Winston, 1953, chap. 9.

Wert, James E., Charles O. Neidt, and J. Stanley Ahmann, *Statistical Methods in Educational and Psychological Research*. New York: Appleton-Century-Crofts, 1954, chap. 10.

13
Multiple-
Classification
Analysis
of
Variance

In Chapter 11 it was pointed out that the most basic form of the analysis of variance statistical technique permits the researcher to determine whether there are significant differences between means of two or more populations. In such analyses the researcher is basically attempting to discover whether there is a relationship between a dependent variable (such as test performance) and an independent variable (such as method of instruction) represented by several levels of classification. In a more complex form of this model, known as *multiple-classification analysis of variance*, the relationship between one dependent variable and two or more independent variables or factors can be tested. Further, one can test for relationships between the dependent variable and various interactions of the factors in the design.

To illustrate the increased utility of multiple-classification analysis of variance over single-classification analysis of variance a fairly common educational research example can be employed. Suppose an experiment is designed which tests a null hypothesis regarding the relationship between student achievement and several varieties of an instructional method which feature an increasingly "nondirective" role for the teacher. The dependent variable in this instance would be student achievement measured by a standardized achievement test. The independent variable, or factor, instructional method, would have three levels represented by three classes of thirty students, each taught by the same instructor who deliberately modified his degree of "directiveness" while teaching. In the "directive" group the teacher employs a strict instructor-controlled lecture method; in the "nondirective" group the teacher allows students to completely control structure, content, and procedures; in the "combination" group an attempt is made to combine both methods.

Now a one-way or single-classification analysis of variance design could be used to test the null hypothesis, indicating whether there were any significant mean differences among the mean performance of the three groups. If no significant mean differences were found, the null hypothesis would be considered tenable, that is, the existence of a relationship between the dependent variable and independent variable would not have been demonstrated by this particular experiment.

It is possible, however, that the experiment was not designed with sufficient sensitivity to yield significant results. There may be other independent variables which, because of their relationship to the criterion variable under consideration, are confounding the results. For instance, there may be reason to suspect that students' intellectual aptitudes in some way relate to the success of nondirective teaching methods. It is possible to redesign a similar study so that there are *two* independent variables, such as (1) instructional method, and (2) ability level. The student sample can be divided so that each of the three instructional methods groups is partitioned into two comparable ability groups (e.g., those judged "bright" and "average or below" by their teachers). It is now possible to test the relationship between the dependent variable (achievement test scores) and both of the two independent variables. This kind of research design is often referred to as a *factorial* analysis of variance design with two factors, instructional method and intellectual aptitude, having three and two levels respectively. Other common terminology designates this situation as a 3×2 (a three-by-two) factorial design, indicating the number of factors, the number of levels in each factor, and, indirectly, the total number of *treatment combinations* ($3 \times 2 = 6$). Remember that the presence of a relationship in this instance is indicated by significant achievement test mean differences among groups or levels representing an independent variable or factor. More importantly, it is also possible to test a relationship between the dependent variable and an *interaction* of the two independent variables. (The concept of interaction will be discussed more extensively later in this chapter.)

As in the case of single-classification analysis of variance, all three of these hypotheses are tested by the size of individual F values, which, when yielded by the statistical analysis, are interpreted for significance from the table of F (Table G) as described in Chapter 11. In the present example there would be an F value for instructional method, which would indicate whether the achievement test means of the methods groups were significantly different. There would also be an F value for ability level, which would indicate whether the achievement test means of the two ability level groups differed significantly from each other. Finally, there would be an F value for interaction indicating whether the performance of the students on the achievement test is related to particular combinations of instructional methods and ability levels.

Continuing with the same example, suppose the experiment originally described is repeated. With the new multiple-classification analysis of variance design the independent variables are: (1) instructional method, represented by the "directive," "combination," and "nondirective" student groups; and (2) ability level, represented by the same students who have now been classified for analysis purposes as those judged "bright" and those judged "average and below." The dependent variable is still student performance on the achievement

Table 13.1

Mean Achievement Test Performance of 90 Hypothetical Students, Classified According to Instructional Method and Ability Level

		Instructional Method		Total Ability Level
	Directive	Combination	Nondirective	
Ability level				
"Bright"	$\bar{X} = 55.4$	$\bar{X} = 59.6$	$\bar{X} = 63.0$	$\bar{X} = 59.3$
"Average or below"	$\bar{X} = 45.2$	$\bar{X} = 41.3$	$\bar{X} = 38.3$	$\bar{X} = 41.6$
Total instructional method	$\bar{X} = 50.3$	$\bar{X} = 50.5$	$\bar{X} = 50.7$	

test. We shall also test for the significance of a relationship of the dependent variable and an *interaction* of the two independent variables.

After an appropriate experimental period, the criterion achievement test would be administered to obtain results, such as those presented in Table 13.1. Notice that there is relatively little difference among the performance of the three instructional method groups, but that a marked disparity exists between the mean performance of the ability level groups. Observe also that the brighter students evidence increasingly superior performance as the instructional method becomes less directive, and the less able students perform better in the more directive teaching situation. Data such as these would probably yield a set of *F* values similar to those presented in Table 13.2. In this table note that the *F* for method is nonsignificant, as could be expected from the close similarity of the methods group means. Also observe a significant *F* reflecting the considerable difference between the means of the ability level groups. Finally, the *F* for interaction is also significant. Inspection of the means in Table 13.1 reveals the source of this significant interaction, namely, that the "bright" subjects tended to achieve better in less directive teaching situations with the reverse being the case for "average or below" subjects.

It should be stressed that all other foregoing discussion was based on hypothetical examples, used purely for purposes of exposition. The fictitious data presented in Table 13.1, of course, should not be used as fuel to stoke the sometimes heated controversies of nondirective and directive teaching method enthusiasts.

BASIC RATIONALE

In order to understand how multiple-classification analysis of variance can perform so many functions it may be necessary to review the discussion in Chapter 11 (pp. 154–157) of the rationale of single-classification analysis of variance. The basic technique employed by the statistician in all analysis of variance approaches is to use variance, that is, the amount of variation of the

---

Table 13.2

Analysis of Variance F Values for Student Performance under Three Different Teaching Methods When Students Were Classified by Ability Levels

Source of Variation	F	Significance Level
Method	0.13	Not significant
Ability	10.78	0.01
Interaction	9.42	0.01

---

scores of a sample from their group mean, in order to learn something about means. By referring back to Figures 11.1 and 11.2, which depict data situations where the null hypothesis is considered tenable and untenable, the reader will recall the essentials of simple analysis of variance. Briefly, when the variation in a pooled group (formed by considering the scores in separate groups as though they were only one group) is approximately the same as the average variation of the separate groups, then there is no significant difference between the separate group means and the null hypothesis is tenable. On the other hand, if the pooled group variation is much larger than the average variation of the separate groups, then a significant difference between at least two of the group means exists and the null hypothesis is untenable.

It is not too difficult to apply the more extensive discussion of Chapter 11 to any independent variable in a multiple-classification analysis of variance problem. The same basic logic of the simple analysis of variance case is maintained, with only slight modifications.

Two-Way Classification

The sources of variance associated with the independent variables or factors of the design are often designated as *main effects*, distinguishing them from the interaction sources of variance. In multiple classification analysis of variance, we determine the amount of variation which is attributed to *each* main effect, or independent variable, by calculating what is essentially a *between sum of squares* for the subgroups representing each independent variable. If there are two independent variables, we view the scores first in the groups representing one variable and compute a between sum of squares for the first main-effect variable; we then view the scores in the groups which correspond to the second independent variable and compute a between sum of squares for the second main-effect variable. This process is continued until a between sum of squares has been computed for all independent variables.

Each of these "between" sums of squares can be thought of as representing the amount of variation caused by the differences between the means of the subgroups representing that variable. For example, if instructional method is one of the independent variables, a sum of squares for method must be computed. The larger this sum of squares, the greater the difference existing between the means of the methods subgroups.

Having computed a sum of squares for each independent variable, it must then be determined how much variation can be attributed to the interaction between the independent variables. To do this, a sum of squares for interaction needs to be calculated. The larger the interaction sum of squares, the greater the relationship between the dependent variable and the interaction of the independent variables. To find the interaction sum of squares, when there are two independent variables, a special sum of squares must be computed. From this quantity, often called the *subgroup sum of squares*, the total sums of squares for the two main-effect variables are subtracted. The remainder will be the interaction sum of squares which reflects the amount of variation attributable to the interaction of the main-effect variables when related to the dependent variable. In other words, if we conceptualize all the treatment combinations or subgroups of the two-way design laid out as a single factor or one-way design, the between sum of squares for this "expanded" factor would reflect all three sources of variation: the main effects of the independent variables and the effect due to their interaction. It is the sum of squares for all these subgroups taken as one factor that we designate as the subgroup sum of squares.

As in the case of single-classification analysis of variance, we must find the *within sum of squares* needed to form the "error term" used in the denominator of the several F tests to be conducted. The within sum of squares is computed exactly as it was in the one-way design in the previous chapter, conceptualizing the present two-way design in its expanded, single-factor form. From a computational standpoint, however, the error sum of squares is easily found by subtracting all of the main effect and interaction sum of squares from the total.

The main effect, interaction, and within sums of squares are then divided by their appropriate degrees of freedom (discussed in Chapter 14) to obtain mean squares. These mean squares are then used to form F ratios with the within mean square always placed in the denominator of the ratio. For example, in a two-way classification (two independent variables) analysis of variance the following F ratios would be formed:

$$\frac{\text{Mean square for main-effect variable number one}}{\text{Within mean square}} = F \text{ for main-effect variable number one}$$

$$\frac{\text{Mean square for main-effect variable number two}}{\text{Within mean square}} = F \text{ for main-effect variable number two}$$

$$\frac{\text{Interaction mean square}}{\text{Within mean square}} = F \text{ for interaction}$$

These F ratios are then interpreted for statistical significance from the table of F, entering the table with the degrees of freedom for the mean squares involved. If the F is sufficiently large to be statistically significant, we reject the particular null hypothesis associated with the ratio which yielded the F.

A Further Word about Interaction

The meaning of an interaction effect in multiple-classification analysis of variance designs is rather difficult to explain. A few more illustrations involving interaction effects may assist the reader.

The general principle involved in interaction effects is the same as in all analysis of variance models, namely, the researcher is testing for the existence of a relationship between the dependent variable and another variable. Ordinarily, one sets up subgroups representing an independent variable, so that differences between the groups will indicate the existence of such a relationship. In the case of an interaction effect, the potential relationship under analysis is between the dependent variable and the *combined* interacting of the two (or more) independent variables. It is possible, then, in the case of a two-way classification model to obtain nonsignificant F values representing both independent or main-effect variables but a highly significant F for interaction.

An example of this situation can be drawn from a practical elementary school situation. A colleague once reported results of a pilot investigation in which the dependent variable was children's reading improvement and two independent variables were sex of teacher and sex of pupil. Nonsignificant F values were obtained in the analysis of variance for both independent variables, that is, there was no relationship in this study between reading improvement and whether the teacher was male/female or whether the pupil was boy/girl. However, a significant F for interaction was produced. An inspection of the means revealed that girl pupils made much greater reading gains with female teachers than did boy pupils with female teachers. Conversely, the boys performed somewhat better with male teachers than did girls with male teachers. The differences were of a sufficient magnitude to result in a significant interaction effect.

This example permits the graphic illustration of how interaction effects would or would not be produced. Figure 13.1 presents a graph of the mean reading improvement scores for each of the four possible subgroups.

The situation in (*a*) of Figure 13.1 existed in the actual example just described concerning reading improvement. Note the marked crossing of the lines representing boys and girls.

Suppose there had been no significant interaction effects nor main-effect differences associated with sex of pupil (main-effect *X*), but a significant difference associated with sex of teacher (main-effect *Y*). In other words, what if there was a difference in reading improvement scores of pupils taught by male and female teachers, but no differences associated with the other independent variable. Then the situation would appear something like (*b*) of Figure 13.1.

If there were no significant interaction effects and no differences associated with sex of teacher (main-effect *Y*), but only a significant difference associated with sex of pupils (main-effect *X*), then the situation would be represented in a fashion similar to that in (*c*) of Figure 13.1.

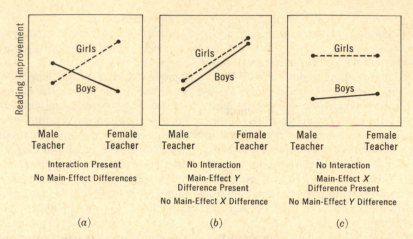

Figure 13.1 *Three graphic representations of data reflecting the presence and absence of interaction and main effects when Boys/Girls = main-effect X and Male Teachers/Female Teachers = main-effect Y.*

Three-Way and Higher Classifications

The same approach to multiple-classification analysis of variance problems is used when there are two, three, or more independent variables that we use to classify the dependent variable data. The underlying logic of the approach is unchanged. We are still attempting to discover the relationship between a dependent variable and certain independent variables which are represented by two or more subgroups.

With three independent variables (*A*, *B*, and *C*) however, the interaction situation becomes much more complex. Not only do we have an interaction between independent variables *A* and *B*, *B* and *C*, *A* and *C*, but we also have a combined interaction of all three independent variables, that is, $A \times B \times C$. (In multiple-classification analysis of variance parlance the designation "factor $A \times$ factor *B*" may be expressed as "factor *A* by factor *B*" and indicates the interaction between *A* and *B*.)

With two main-effect variables the notion of interaction is not difficult to understand. With three or more independent variables, it becomes increasingly more difficult. Certainly, what is learned from such complex interactions is that no simple interpretations can be made of single effects. If the reader can recall the fairly obvious example of two-way interaction depicted in Table 13.1, and mentally add another dimension for each additional independent variable in the analysis, this will probably serve him as well as more detailed mathematical expositions of the meaning of complex interactions.

ADVANTAGES OF MULTIPLE CLASSIFICATION

As suggested, multiple-classification analysis of variance approaches offer the researcher an extremely important tool in his statistical repertoire. In educational research particularly, the importance of multiple-classification analysis of variance cannot be overemphasized. Since education is one of the most complex behavioral fields, investigations must employ data-analysis techniques that take into consideration not only more than one variable but also extremely subtle interactions between variables. Multiple-classification analysis of variance procedures provide such analytic techniques.

Furthermore, because it is possible to isolate variation attributable to several main effects and to their interaction, it is possible to sensitize the various F tests of significance. Increased sensitivity occurs since the size of the within mean square, the error term in the denominator of the F ratio is reduced with the identification of each new source of variation. A smaller error term results in larger, hence more significant, F values. (More will be said about these, as well as other design aspects, in Chapter 17.)

A word of caution however, for since analysis of variance is such a powerful and sensitive statistical tool one must be doubly careful that the data subjected to this type of statistical analysis truly represent the variables under study. There is an old research adage warning investigators not to "gather data with a rake and study them with a microscope." Figuratively, multiple-classification analysis of variance provides us with the microscope; one must guard against collecting data grossly.

Requisite Assumptions

The same assumptions applied to single-classification analysis of variance and discussed at the beginning of Chapter 12 also pertain to the multiple-classification models. To reiterate briefly these assumptions: (1) the subjects in each subgroup are random samples from their corresponding populations; (2) the measures must be normally distributed in the subgroup populations; and (3) the variances within the subgroup populations must be homogeneous.

As indicated in the previous chapter, there is increasing evidence attesting to the "robustness" of analysis of variance models, that is, their ability to withstand fairly serious departures from the normality and homogeneity of variance assumptions without disturbing the validity of the final statistical analysis, namely, the F tests.

AN EXAMPLE OF TWO-WAY ANALYSIS OF VARIANCE
FROM THE RESEARCH LITERATURE

It will prove helpful to the reader to study an example of the way in which multiple-classification analysis of variance operations are reported in the literature of educational research. The following appeared in an issue of the *Journal of Educational Research*.[1]

In this experiment the researcher wished to establish: (1) whether incidental learning takes place in a foreign-language learning situation; and (2)

---

[1]Paul Pimsleur, "Incidental Learning in Foreign Language Learning," *J. Educ. Res.* **54**, no. 3 (November, 1960): 111–114. Reported with the permission of author and publisher.

if there is such incidental learning, is it related to a student's over-all performance in learning the foreign language?

An experiment was set up in which two comparable French classes of eighteen students, taught by the same teacher, were exposed to two different types of drills. The experimental group was given a drill task focusing on the position of pronouns in sentences which included a number of new past participle forms. The control group was given an unrelated task, a pronunciation exercise. The experimenter was actually interested in the experimental group's mastery of the past participles used in the pronoun positioning drill. If the experimental subjects learned the past participles significantly better than the controls, the result was ascribed to the influence of the pronoun drill and was therefore described as "incidental learning." At the conclusion of the drill, both groups were given several examinations, including an oral recognition test on the past participles.

Students received grades in the French class based on their total performance, irrespective of the experiment. Grades of A, B, C, and D were assigned to students in the experimental and control groups.

The researcher was now able to answer the following questions by employing a multiple-classification analysis of variance treatment: (1) Did the experimental subjects who were incidentally exposed to new past participles perform significantly better on the oral recognition test than the control subjects who were not exposed to the past participles? (2) Do A, B, C, and D students (considered irrespective of membership in the experimental or control group) differ in their performance on the oral recognition test? (3) Does the combination of membership in the experimental or control group interacting with level of grade earned make a difference; more specifically, did the higher-level students (A and B) in the experimental group evidence more incidental learning than their lower-level (C and D) classmates?

Data were subjected to a multiple-classification analysis of variance treatment in which the first independent variable (exposure to the incidental learning task) was represented by the experimental and control groups, and the second independent variable (grade level) was represented by the four grade groups, those who earned A, B, C, or D in the French course. The interaction between these two variables was also tested.

The analysis as reported, with slight editorial modification, is presented in Table 13.3. As can be seen in the table there was a significant F ($p < 0.05$) resulting from the performance difference of the experimental and control groups. Inspection of the means for the two groups revealed that the experimental group outperformed their control counterparts, thereby evidencing incidental learning of the past participles. There was also a significant F ($p < 0.01$) resulting from the differential in performance of the A, B, C, and D students on the oral recognition test. As expected, those earning higher grades in the course scored better on the test. The F for interaction was not significant, indicating no appreciable relationship between performance on the test and the combination of the two independent variables.

Table 13.3
Analysis of Variance on Oral Recognition Scores

Source	Sum of Squares	Degrees of Freedom	Mean Square	F
Exposure to material (experimental versus control)	22	1	22.00	5.23[a]
Grade in course (A, B, C, D groups)	86	3	28.67	6.81[b]
Interaction	10	3	3.33	0.79
Within	118	28	4.21	
Total	236	35		

[a]Significant 0.05.
[b]Significant 0.01.

Thus, the researcher concluded that students do learn incidentally in a foreign language learning situation, that A, B, C, and D students differ, but that better students (as indexed by their grades) do not appear to learn incidentally more effectively than poorer students.

Other researchers tend to report their analysis of variance results using a similar format, although the labels used in tables and texts may vary. For example, independent variables may be referred to as rows or columns, rather than by the name which describes the variable. If the reader will recall that rows and columns merely describe subgroups which represent a variable, this terminology will not prove confusing.

Of course, greater insight into the nature of multiple-classification analysis of variance may be gained by reading the following chapter on computation procedures for this statistical technique.

REVIEW

Multiple-classification analysis of variance presents the educational researcher with a powerful analytic tool which is well adapted to dealing with the complexities of inquiry in the behavioral sciences. Multiple-classification analysis of variance is designed to test realtionships between a dependent variable and several independent variables or factors in the design. Furthermore, relationships between the dependent variable and interactions of the independent variables can also be tested. In each case the independent variables are represented by two or more classifications of the data, such as when data are divided into groups according to intellectual ability. The dependent variable is some type of numerical data such as student scores on a test.

The rationale underlying the technique is essentially the same as that seen in single-classification analysis of variance, namely, variances of groups are analyzed so as to reveal any significant mean differences between the groups.

As with all analysis of variance models, the multiple-classification test yields *F* values which are interpreted for levels of probability from the table of *F*. In a two-way classification, that is, when there are two sets of subgroups representing two independent variables, *F* values would be yielded for both independent variables as well as an *F* value for interaction. A discussion of the meaning of interaction was given in the chapter. A typical journal example of multiple-classification analysis of variance concluded the chapter.

EXERCISES

1. If a secondary-school principal wishes to test for differences in reading achievement between five groups of high-school freshmen who are graduates of five different elementary schools, should he use single- or multiple-classification analysis of variance?

2. If a school psychologist wishes to discover whether there are significant mean differences in personality test scores between three groups of seventh-grade students representing different religious affiliations and at the same time wishes to classify his subjects according to intellectual ability and see if there are differences between the ability groups on the personality measure, should he use single- or multiple-classification analysis of variance?

3. In a two-way multiple-classification analysis of variance problem three *F* values will be yielded, two for differences in main effects on independent variable groups and one for interaction. Is it possible for the interaction *F* to be statistically significant if the two main-effect *F* values are not significant?

4. A single-classification analysis of variance has been computed on a set of data divided into three independent variable subgroups. The *F* yielded by this analysis is almost, but not quite, significant at the 0.05 level. If a second independent variable had been identified and a multiple-classification analysis of variance been computed on the same data, is it possible that the *F* value associated with the initial three groups independent variable would be significant? Why?

5. If the mean squares for every source of variation, that is, independent variables and interactions, are less than the within groups mean square, will all the null hypotheses be considered tenable or untenable?

SELECTED READINGS

Edwards, Allen L., *Statistical Methods for the Behavioral Sciences*. New York: Holt, Rinehart & Winston, 1957, chap. 17.

Ferguson, George A., *Statistical Analysis in Psychology and Education*. New York: McGraw-Hill, 1959, chap. 16.

Guilford, J. P., *Fundamental Statistics in Psychology and Education*. New York: McGraw-Hill, 1965, chap. 13.

McNemar, Quinn, *Psychological Statistics*. New York: Wiley, 1962, chap. 16.

Wert, James E., Charles O. Neidt, and J. Stanley Ahmann, *Statistical Methods in Educational and Psychological Research*. New York: Appleton-Century-Crofts, 1954, chaps. 11 and 12.

14

Multiple-
Classification
Analysis
of
Variance—
Computation
Procedures

The computation of multiple-classification analysis of variance becomes increasingly complex as the number of independent variables is increased, for with each additional main-effect variable there are additional interaction analyses to compute. Actually, if it were not for the calculation of the values necessary to compute these interaction F values, the computation of multiple-classification analysis of variance would be almost identical to that seen in single-classification analysis of variance problems.

TWO-WAY CLASSIFICATION

The first computational example to be described will involve the most simple multiple-classification design, that is, one with only two independent variables. Suppose a school system curriculum committee has agreed to employ a unique approach to the teaching of mathematics. Imagine further that members of the curriculum committee believe that the quality of student performance under the new system may be related to students' prior achievement in conventional mathematics and also to their tendency to persevere in past study patterns. A district research consultant designs a one-semester study in which the dependent variable is achievement in mathematics, as measured by a specially designed mathematics problem-solving test.

The first independent variable is designated as level of achievement previously attained by the student in mathematics. According to their performance on an achievement examination administered during the ninth grade, a random sample of the sophomores who will be using the new materials is classified into three groups: (1) high achievers, those who scored at least one-half standard deviation above the national mean on the ninth-grade mathematics achievement examination; (2) average achievers, those who scored within the range ± one-half standard deviation from the national mean on the ninth-grade mathematics achievement examination; and (3) low achievers, those who scored at least one-half standard deviation below the national mean on the ninth-grade mathematics achievement test.

The second independent variable is designated as students' tendency to perseverate in prior study routines, as measured by a "rigidity" test administered to all students in the experiment. Those who obtained high scores on the test reflected a greater tendency to persevere in stereotyped behavior on the test; those who scored low revealed a greater tendency to abandon previous behavior patterns on the test. According to their test scores students were divided into three equal groups designated as "high rigidity," "average rigidity," and "low rigidity."

Three null hypotheses can now be tested with a two-way classification multiple analysis of variance model:

H_{01} There will be no difference between the three achievement populations in their mean performance on the mathematics problem-solving test.

H_{02} There will be no difference between the three rigidity populations in their mean performance on the mathematics problem-solving test.

H_{03} There will be no interaction between student membership in both independent variable populations and their mean performance on the mathematics problem-solving test.

Though an actual experiment of this type would involve far more subjects, only the 27 scores presented in Table 14.1 will be used for ease of computation and exposition. These hypothetical scores represent student performance on the mathematics problem-solving test at the end of a semester during which the new teaching materials were used.

HOMOGENEITY OF VARIANCE

The homogeneity of variance assumption must be checked with respect to groups contributing directly to the within mean squares error term. In the one-way design, these groups are simply those under the levels of the factor or independent variable. When the design contains more than one factor, groups can be formed in different ways. For example, in the design shown in Table 14.1, we can form groups in three different ways: (1) three 9-member achievement groups, high, average, and low; (2) three 9-member rigidity groups, high, average, and low; or (3) nine 3-member combination rigidity–achievement groups, high–low, high–average, high–high, average–low, average–average, and so forth. It is these latter nine groups which we conceptualize as random samples from nine corresponding populations with normal distributions and equal variances. These nine combination groups or *subgroups* are referred to as the *cells* in a factorial analysis of variance design; they are usually ordered from left to right starting with the first row. In other words, we conceptualize

Table 14.1

Mathematics Problem-Solving Test. Scores of 27 Students Classified According to Prior Mathematics Achievement and Performance on a Test of Rigidity

Rigidity Tendency	Prior Mathematics Achievement							
	Low Achievers		Average Achievers		High Achievers		Total	
	X	X^2	X	X^2	X	X^2	X	X^2
High rigidity	38	(1,444)	51	(2,601)	59	(3,481)		
	40	(1,600)	43	(1,849)	49	(2,401)		
	35	(1,225)	48	(2,304)	56	(3,136)		
Subtotal	113	(4,269)	142	(6,754)	164	(9,018)	419	(20,041)
Average rigidity	44	(1,936)	50	(2,500)	56	(3,136)		
	43	(1,849)	51	(2,601)	58	(3,364)		
	45	(2,025)	50	(2,500)	55	(3,025)		
Subtotal	132	(5,810)	151	(7,601)	169	(9,525)	452	(22,936)
Low rigidity	50	(2,500)	52	(2,704)	62	(3,844)		
	51	(2,601)	54	(2,916)	62	(3,844)		
	48	(2,304)	57	(3,249)	65	(4,225)		
Subtotal	149	(7,405)	163	(8,869)	189	(11,913)	501	(28,187)
Total	394	(17,484)	456	(23,224)	522	(30,456)	1,372	(71,164)

the multiple-classification design as a single-classification design with nine groups and go on to test the homogeneity of variance assumption.

The variances for the nine cells, in the order explained, are computed in the usual fashion $[\Sigma x^2/(n-1)]$, and only two will be demonstrated here:

$$\text{High–Low:} \quad \frac{4{,}269 - \dfrac{(113)^2}{3}}{2} = 6.34$$

$$\text{High–Average:} \quad \frac{6{,}754 - \dfrac{(142)^2}{3}}{2} = 16.34$$

The remaining variances are 26.34, 0.99, 0.34, 2.34, 2.34, 6.34, and 3.00.

By dividing the smallest variance into the largest variance, the variance for the fifth cell or the average–average combination into that for the third cell or the high–high combination, we obtain $F_{2,2} = 26.34/0.34 = 77.47$. With 2 and 2 degrees of freedom we find from Table G that an F value as large as 99.00 would be required to reject the null hypothesis ($p < 0.02$) of equal population variances. Since the F is 77.47, the assumption of variance homogeneity cannot be rejected and we can proceed with our tests of main effects and interactions.

SUM OF SQUARES

Using the standard raw-score formulas for computing sums of squares, the sum of squares for total, and for all main-effect variables are now computed.

Total

Drawing upon the data in Table 14.1 the total sum of squares is computed as follows:

$$\text{Total SS} = 71,164 - \frac{(1.372)^2}{27} = 1,446.1$$

Columns

The notions of *columns* and *rows* can now be explained. By glancing at Table 14.1 the reader will see that when the scores are considered from the viewpoint of the independent variable of achievement level they are grouped in vertical columns. Note also that the scores, when viewed in terms of the variable of rigidity tendency, are grouped in horizontal rows. As the descriptive terms, rows and columns, are more generally applicable to all multiple classification analysis of variance problems (as well as to a number of other statistical operations), they are used here. In this example, remember that columns represent the achievement level groups. Thus, when the SS for *columns* is determined, the SS for achievement level is found. When the SS for *rows* is computed, the SS for rigidity tendency is determined.

The columns SS can be found by employing Formula 12.1.

$$\sum \frac{(\Sigma X)^2}{n_g} - \frac{(\Sigma X)^2}{n}$$

In this formula the scores are summed for each achieved group, then squared and divided by the number in the group $(\Sigma X)^2/n_g$. All of these quantities are then added together: $(\Sigma X)^2/n_g$. Finally, we subtract the standard correction term which is the sum of all scores, squared and divided by the total number in the sample $(\Sigma X)^2/n$. In the present example the columns SS would be computed as follows:

$$\text{Columns SS} = \frac{(394)^2}{9} + \frac{(456)^2}{9} + \frac{(522)^2}{9} - \frac{(1,372)^2}{27}$$

$$= 17,248.4 + 23,104.0 + 30,276.0 - 69,717.9$$

$$= 910.5$$

This quantity, just as the between SS in single-classification analysis of variance, represents the amount of the total sum of squares which is due to the differences between means of the three achievement groups.

Rows

We turn now to the rigidity groups, which are represented by the rows in the two-way classification design. The rows SS is computed in basically the same way (Formula 12.1) as the columns SS, that is, the raw scores for each rigidity group are summed, then squared, and divided by the number of subjects in the group. The quantities are then totaled. The usual correction term is subtracted from this total and the result is the rows SS. In this example the rows, or rigidity tendency, SS is computed as follows:

$$\text{Rows SS} = \frac{(419)^2}{9} + \frac{(452)^2}{9} + \frac{(501)^2}{9} - \frac{(1,372)^2}{27}$$

$$= 19,506.8 + 22,700.4 + 27,889.0 - 69,717.9$$

$$= 378.3$$

This value represents the amount of the total sum of squares which is due to the differences between means of the three rigidity groups.

Interaction

In order to compute the *interaction* SS a special sum of squares called the *subgroup* SS is needed and from it the sums of squares for the rows and columns are subtracted.

$$\text{Interaction SS} = \text{Subgroup SS} - (\text{Rows SS} + \text{Columns SS})$$

The sum of squares for subgroups is calculated by considering each of the sets of scores formed by combinations of the rows and columns as distinctive subgroups. As explained, there would be nine such cells or subgroups formed by the three achievement-level and three rigidity-tendency categories. For instance, in the upper left corner of Table 14.1 the three scores made by those who were low achievers and highly rigid ($X = 38$, $X = 30$, $X = 35$) form one subgroup. Again formula 12.1 is used to calculate the sum of squares, only now each subgroup is considered separately. That is, each set of subgroup raw scores is totaled, squared, and divided by the number of subjects in the subgroup. All of these values (nine in this example) are then added. From them the usual correction term is subtracted to get the subgroup SS. In this example the subgroup sums of squares is computed as follows:

$$\text{Subgroup SS} = \frac{(113)^2}{3} + \frac{(142)^2}{3} + \frac{(164)^2}{3} + \frac{(132)^2}{3} + \frac{(151)^2}{3}$$

$$+ \frac{(169)^2}{3} + \frac{(149)^2}{3} + \frac{(163)^2}{3} + \frac{(189)^2}{3} - \frac{(1,372)^2}{27}$$

$$= 4,256.3 + 6,721.3 + 8,965.3 + 5,808.0 + 7,600.3 +$$

$$+ 9,520.3 + 7,400.3 + 8,856.3 + 11,907.0 - 69,717.9$$

$$= 1,317.2$$

The interaction SS is now obtained by subtracting the rows and columns sums of squares from the above value:

$$\text{Interaction SS} = 1{,}317.2 - (910.5 + 398.3)$$

$$= 28.4$$

This quantity is that part of the total sum of squares which is due to a relationship between the dependent variable and the combined independent variables represented by the rows and columns.

Within

The within sum of squares is that portion of the total SS not already attributed to a given source.

$$\text{Within SS} = \text{Total SS} - (\text{Rows SS} + \text{Columns SS} + \text{Interaction SS})$$

In this example, the within SS is obtained as follows:

$$\text{Within SS} = 1{,}446.1 - (910.5 + 378.3 + 28.4)$$

$$= 128.9$$

The within SS, when divided by the appropriate number of degrees of freedom, will serve as the error term in the three F ratios.

DEGREES OF FREEDOM

The degrees of freedom associated with each sum of squares are easily determined in two-way classification analysis of variance designs by using the following scheme:

Source of Variation	Degrees of Freedom
Rows	number of rows $-1 = (r-1)$
Columns	number of columns $-1 = (c-1)$
Interaction	rows -1 times columns $-1 = (r-1)(c-1)$
Within	number in sample $-$ rows times columns $= (n-rc)$
Total	number in sample $-1 = (n-1)$

Thus, in the present example the following degrees of freedom are used:

Rows	$r-1 = 3-1 = 2$
Columns	$c-1 = 3-1 = 2$
Interaction	$(r-1)(c-1) = (2)(2) = 4$
Within	$n-rc = 27-(3)(3) = 18$
Total	$n-1 = 27-1 = 26$

MEAN SQUARES

Mean squares used in the final statistical operations of this analysis, the F ratios, are obtained by dividing the rows, columns, interaction, and within sums of squares by their respective degrees of freedom. Thus, the computational example yields the following mean squares:

$$\text{Rows MS} = \frac{378.3}{2} = 189.15$$

$$\text{Columns MS} = \frac{910.5}{2} = 455.25$$

$$\text{Interaction MS} = \frac{28.4}{4} = 7.10$$

$$\text{Within MS} = \frac{128.9}{18} = 7.16$$

COMPUTATION AND INTERPRETATION OF F VALUES

Having all the necessary mean squares, we are now in a position to test the three null hypotheses posed at the outset of the analysis. This is done by computing and interpreting the F value associated with each hypothesis. In each F ratio the within mean square is placed in the denominator. Thus, for testing the H_{01} that there is no difference between the mean performance of the three achievement groups (as represented by columns), the following F ratio is set up:

$$\text{For achievement, } F_{2,18} = \frac{455.25}{7.16} = 63.58$$

Consulting the Table of F we find that with two degrees of freedom for the numerator mean square and 18 degrees of freedom for the denominator mean square, an F of at least 6.01 is needed for the result to be significant at the 0.01 level. The achievement F value of 63.58 exceeds this figure and we therefore reject the null hypothesis under consideration.

To test the second null hypothesis (H_{02}) that there is no difference in the mean performance of the three rigidity groups, the following F ratio is set up:

$$\text{For rigidity tendency, } F_{2,18} = \frac{189.15}{7.16} = 26.41$$

Since the F for rigidity tendency is 26.41, the null hypothesis is again rejected at the 0.01 level.

In testing the final null hypothesis (H_{03}) of a relationship between the dependent variable and an interaction of the two independent variables, an F ratio with the interaction MS in the numerator is set up:

$$\text{For interaction, } F_{4,18} = \frac{7.10}{7.16} = 0.99$$

This very small F ratio is nonsignificant, as F must be greater than 1.00 to be significant; hence, H_{03}, the final null hypothesis, cannot be rejected.

Table 14.2

Analysis of Variance of the Performance of 29 Students, Classified by Prior Mathematics Achievement and Rigidity Tendency, on a Mathematical Problem-Solving Test

Source of Variation	SS	df	MS	F
Achievement level	910.5	2	455.25	63.58[a]
Rigidity tendency	378.3	2	189.15	26.41[a]
Achievement × rigidity	28.4	4	7.10	0.99
Within	128.9	18	7.16	
Total	1,446.1	26		

[a] $p < 0.01$.

The total analysis of variance described in this example would resemble Table 14.2, when reported in a research journal.

The abbreviations used in Table 14.2 may be altered slightly, but the reader should have little difficulty interpreting such modified analysis of variance presentations.

THREE-WAY CLASSIFICATION

In more complex research designs, the investigator may be concerned with the possible relationship between a dependent variable and three or more independent variables, as well as the presence of significant interactions among the independent variables and the dependent variable. In general, the computation procedure followed for such analyses parallels that described for a two-way classification problem. The total SS and the within SS are computed in the normal fashion.

Each main-effect SS is computed by summing the raw scores for each group representing the main-effect variable. These sums are then squared, divided by the number of measurements in each group, and totaled. From this total the standard correction term is subtracted to yield the particular main-effect SS.

For each interaction SS, a subgroup SS is computed by considering as a separate group each combination of the main-effect variables involved in the interaction and following a procedure similar to the computation of a main-effect SS. From the subgroup SS all sums of squares for main effects included in the interaction are then subtracted to yield the interaction SS.

This procedure can be illustrated in a three-way classification problem, where the dependent variable is a student's score on a school-adjustment scale, and the independent variables are sex, grade level, and intelligence level. The number of students in the study will be 120. The three grade levels involved will be 7th, 8th, and 9th, with 40 subjects in each group. Intelligence scores will be classified into four categories with 30 subjects in each group. Sex is represented by two categories, with 60 boys and 60 girls included. Sums of squares

Table 14.3
Analysis of Variance of the School-Adjustment Scores of 100 Studies Classified According to Sex, Grade Level, and Intelligence

Source of Variation	Degrees of Freedom	Sum of Squares	Mean Square	F
Sex	1			
Grade level	2			
Intelligence	3			
Sex × grade level	2			
Sex × intelligence	3			
Grade level × intelligence	6			
Sex × grade level × intelligence	6			
Within	95			
Total	119			

and mean squares must be computed for the sources of variation cited in Table 14.3. The degrees of freedom for each source of variation have been specified in the table.

Total. The total SS is found in the usual manner, that is, the sum of the squared raw scores for the total sample minus the standard correction term formed by squaring minus the standard correction term formed by squaring the sum of all raw scores and dividing by the number of scores. The number of degrees of freedom equals one less than the number of subjects, $120 - 1 = 119$.

Sex. The sex SS is computed by disregarding grade level and intelligence, then summing the 60 scores in each group, squaring these sums, and dividing each by 60. These two quantities are totaled, and from this the standard correction term is subtracted. The number of degrees of freedom is one less than the number of categories, $2 - 1 = 1$.

Grade Level. The grade level SS is found by disregarding sex and intelligence, then separately summing the 40 scores in each grade level, squaring these sums, and dividing each by 40. These three quantities are totaled and from this the standard correction term is subtracted. The number of degrees of freedom is one less than the number of categories, $3 - 1 = 2$.

Intelligence. The intelligence SS is obtained by disregarding sex and grade level, then separately summing the 30 scores in each intelligence level group, squaring these sums, and dividing each by 30. These four quantities are then summed, and from this the standard correction term is subtracted. The number of degrees of freedom is the number of categories less one, $4 - 1 = 3$.

Sex × Grade-Level Interaction. The SS for sex by grade-level interaction, since it is the interaction between two main-effect variables, is known as a *first-order interaction*. This SS is found by disregarding intelligence and summing the 20 scores of each sex at each grade level (there will be six such subgroups), squaring these sums, and dividing each by 20. These six quantities are then summed, and from this the standard correction term is subtracted. The result is the *subgroups* SS for sex and grade level. From this subgroups SS subtract the sex SS and the grade-level SS to obtain the sex by grade-level interaction SS. The number of degrees of freedom is the product of the number of degrees of freedom for sex and grade level, $(1)(2) = 2$.

Sex $\times$ Intelligence Interaction. The SS for sex by intelligence interaction, also a first-order interaction, is found by disregarding grade level and summing the 15 scores of each sex at each intelligence level (eight subgroups), squaring these sums, and dividing each by 15. These eight quantities are then summed and from this the standard correction term is subtracted. The result is the subgroups SS for sex and intelligence. From this subgroups SS we subtract the sex SS and the intelligence SS to find the sex by intelligence interaction SS. The number of degrees of freedom is the product of the number of degrees of freedom for sex and intelligence, $(1)(3) = 3$.

Grade Level $\times$ Intelligence Interaction. The SS for grade level by intelligence interaction, also a first-order interaction, is computed by disregarding sex and summing the ten scores of each grade level at each intelligence level (there will be 12 such subgroups), squaring these sums, and dividing each by ten. These 12 quantities are then summed, and from this the standard correction term is subtracted. The result is the *subgroups* SS for grade level and intelligence. From this subgroups SS we subtract the grade level SS and the intelligence level SS to obtain the grade level by intelligence interaction SS. The number of degrees of freedom is the product of the number of degrees of freedom for grade level and intelligence, $(2)(3) = 6$.

Sex $\times$ Grade Level $\times$ Intelligence Interaction. The SS for sex by grade level by intelligence interaction, since it is the interaction between three main effects, is known as a *second-order interaction*. This SS is found by summing the five scores of each sex at each grade level at each intelligence level (24 subgroups), squaring these sums, and dividing each by five. These 24 quantities are then summed, and from this the standard correction term is subtracted. The value obtained represents the sum of squares for sex $\times$ grade level $\times$ intelligence interaction *together* with the sums of squares for the three main effects *and* the three first-order interactions. The sex $\times$ grade level $\times$ intelligence interaction SS is obtained by subtracting the main-effect and first-order interaction sums of squares. The number of degrees of freedom is a product of the number of degrees of freedom for sex, grade level, and intelligence, $(1)(2)(3) = 6$.

Within. The within SS can be found by subtracting from the total SS, the sums of squares for the three main effects, the three first-order interactions, and the single second-order interaction. The number of degrees of freedom is found by subtracting from the total number of degrees of freedom the product of the number of *categories* in the three main-effect variables, $119 - (2)(3)(4) = 95$.

Mean Squares. As usual, the mean squares are found by dividing the sums of squares by their respective degrees of freedom.

F Values. As in previous examples, *F* values are found by dividing the within mean square into the several main effect and interaction mean squares. In this example there would be seven *F* values produced. These values are then interpreted from the table of *F*.

DISPROPORTIONALITY

Thus far the examples for multiple classification have contained proportional numbers of subjects in the various categories and subcategories. It is not necessary to have proportional numbers of measurements in each category, but when disproportionality exists, the researcher may either randomly discard some of his scores to make the data proportional, or apply special methods to allow for disproportionality. If the loss of data is not great, it is probably wiser to randomly delete scores in order to achieve proportional subclass representation. However, if the number is too great, the researcher may lose too much information. Hence, adjustment procedures such as those outlined by Wert, Neidt, and Ahmann[1] are recommended.

REVIEW

In this chapter, computation procedures for two-way and three-way classification analysis of variance models were described. In the case of two-way classification problems, it is often helpful to think of the subgroups representing the two main-effect variables as rows and columns. Two-way classification analysis of variance designs yield two main-effect *F* values and an *F* value for interaction between the two main-effect variables. Three-way classification analysis of variance designs yield three main-effect *F* values, three first-order interaction *F* values for interaction between two main effects, and a single second-order interaction *F* value for interaction between the three main effects.

The degrees of freedom associated with the different *F* values are readily determined from the tables and discussions presented in the chapter. Sums of squares and mean squares are calculated in essentially the same manner as the single-classification analysis of variance model.

[1]James E. Wert, Charles O. Neidt, and J. Stanley Ahmann, *Statistical Methods in Educational and Psychological Research*. New York: Appleton-Century-Crofts, 1954, pp. 211–225.

EXERCISES

1. For the following data compute the main effects and interaction mean squares, the three F values, and in each instance determine whether the null hypothesis should be rejected at the 0.05 level.

Methods					
A	B	C	A	B	C
Males			Females		
8	11	19	16	10	5
9	12	18	10	11	4
9	4	11	11	13	7
5	9	15	9	12	10
4	10	10	7	4	3
8	10	9	14	5	9
3	11	8	10	9	8
10	14	16	8	13	11
9	9	12	17	10	4
7	5	9	18	9	5

2. An experimenter has decided to test for significance of mean differences between achievement scores of three groups of subjects taught by different instructional methods and at the same time has classified his subjects according to intellectual ability. Find the F values for (a) instructional method, (b) ability level, and (c) interaction between instructional method and ability level. Determine whether any of these F values are significant beyond the 0.05 level. The data are as follows:

Ability Group	Instructional Method								
	I			II			III		
High	68	54	49	67	60	54	54	46	39
	60	54	48	63	59	53	50	42	32
	60	50	40	60	56	50	48	40	30
Average	53	49	41	52	50	43	43	40	34
	52	49	40	51	46	40	42	40	30
	50	44	33	50	44	38	42	36	30
Low	57	46	33	49	41	34	38	29	24
	53	40	30	49	40	32	36	29	23
	51	39	28	43	36	27	30	27	22

3. For the following three-way classification analysis of variance determine the F values (and interpret for statistical significance) for the three main

effects (*A*, *B*, *C*), the three first-order interactions (*A* × *B*, *A* × *C*, *B* × *C*), and the single second-order interaction (*A* × *B* × *C*).

		A_1		A_2		A_3	
		9	5	10	6	12	7
		9	5	10	6	12	7
	C_1	8	4	9	3	10	7
		7	4	8	3	9	6
		6	4	7	3	8	6
B_1							
		11	7	10	8	11	7
		10	6	10	7	11	7
	C_2	10	5	9	7	10	7
		8	5	9	6	9	6
		7	4	8	5	8	6
		10	6	10	7	12	10
		8	5	9	6	12	9
	C_1	7	4	8	6	12	9
		7	3	8	3	11	9
		6	3	7	3	10	8
B_2							
		9	5	9	6	10	7
		8	4	9	6	9	7
	C_2	7	4	8	6	9	7
		6	3	7	4	7	6
		6	3	7	5	8	6

SELECTED READINGS

Edwards, Allen L., *Statistical Methods for the Behavioral Sciences.* New York: Holt, Rinehart & Winston, 1957, chap. 17.

Ferguson, George A., *Statistical Analysis in Psychology and Education.* New York: McGraw-Hill, 1959, chap. 16.

Guilford, J. P., *Fundamental Statistics in Psychology and Education.* New York: McGraw-Hill, 1965, chap. 13.

McNemar, Quinn, *Psychological Statistics.* New York: Wiley, 1962, chap. 16.

Wert, James W., Charles O. Neidt, and J. Stanley Ahmann, *Statistical Methods in Educational and Psychological Research.* New York: Appleton-Century-Crofts, 1954, chaps. 11 and 12.

15
Analysis
of
Covariance

The researcher who begins to probe educational problems will soon encounter situations where he must employ a student sample in an actual school setting. More often than not, educational researchers find it necessary to work with pupils in a real school situation, where the pupils provide the research worker with most of the data necessary to attempt to develop an educational science of behavior. Disregarding the fact that often the only available source for the appropriate student sample will be found in school classrooms, there is a decided advantage in using realistic school situations to investigate relationships between educational variables. Typically, an investigator wishes to generalize research findings to real school situations, so his research is frequently (but not always) most generalizable when the investigation is conducted in the milieu of an authentic school environment.

Unfortunately, however, it is usually very difficult for school teachers and administrators to cater completely to the wishes to the researcher regarding the manipulation of students for experimental purposes. It is often impractical to move students from one teacher to another, or from one curriculum to another, in order to help the experimenter work out a "tight" research design. The researcher must, therefore, resign himself to the necessity of dealing with "pre-existing" student groups on many occasions. Even if he can match students on measures related to the criterion variable, the matching operation inevitably reduces the size of the sample, since many students cannot be properly matched and must be discarded from the analysis.

The use of pre-existing groups, of course, poses certain research design problems. For instance, suppose that a researcher wishes to study the relationship between the dependent variable of students' physical science achievement and an independent variable of their teachers' knowledge of the subject matter. He could ascertain how much a number of teachers knew about physics by having their subject-matter supervisors rate the teachers according to their knowledge of physics. Further, he could discover the extent of the students' physics achievement by giving them a postcourse physics test. By dividing the teachers into two or more groups according to knowledge of physics (to represent the variable), he could then see if the students of the more knowledgeable teachers performed better on the postcourse test than students who studied with teachers who knew less about physics.

But the sophisticated researcher will always try to determine if other variables are related, perhaps causally, to the dependent variable under study. In this case, for example, student intellectual ability is surely related to performance on the post-course test. Suppose the researcher administers a group intelligence test to his subjects and finds that those students studying with the more knowledgeable teachers also happen to be more intelligent than the other students. If the results of the study indicate that the students of the better informed physics teachers score higher than the other students on the criterion examination, how should this be interpreted? Is there indeed a positive relationship between student physics achievement and teachers' knowledge of the subject matter or is this merely another case of brighter students outperforming their less able counterparts? Unfortunately, the latter question cannot be answered by this study, for a variable (intelligence) which is relevant to the dependent variable (achievement) has been *confounded* with the dependent-independent variable (teachers' knowledge) relationship under investigation.

If the educational researcher had all the freedom he might wish in such a situation, he could simply manipulate the groups composing his samples by stratified random sampling procedures, so that all subgroups representing the independent variable were equivalent with respect to possible confounding relevant variables. In the foregoing example, for instance, the investigator would have to reassemble the groups so that they were equal in intellectual ability. For that matter, the groups should be comparable with respect to *any* relevant variable which might confound the relationship under investigation. As indicated previously, however, this is usually impossible to do in most school programs. What then, is the educational researcher to do in such situations?

Fortunately, a statistical tool of considerable value known as *analysis of covariance* can be employed in such instances as that just described. This technique, an extension of the analysis of variance model combined with certain features of regression analysis, provides a useful statistical device for educational investigators. In brief, analysis of covariance may be used when a relationship is being studied between a dependent variable and two or more groups representing an independent variable. This powerful technique allows the researcher to *statistically equate the independent variable groups with respect to one or more variables which are relevant to the dependent variable.* Thus, analysis of covariance allows the researcher to study the performance of several groups which are unequal with regard to an important variable *as though* they were equal in this respect. To illustrate, it would then be possible to equate statistically the intelligence levels of the groups taught by teachers with varying degrees of physics knowledge and view any mean differences that resulted as though the groups had been equivalent in intellectual ability.

Sometimes the possible confounding variables will be identified in advance of the data collection. In other cases the researcher discovers such confounding variables only after the data have been gathered. Both situations can be appropriately handled through the use of the analysis of covariance model. It should be emphasized, however, that *subjects (or, in general, experimental units) must be measured on the control variable before any experimental treatment is administered.* If this were not the case, measures on the control variable could, in fact, be affected by (correlated with) the treatments or independent variable; performing the analysis of covariance in these circumstances would, in effect, tend to equate the treatment groups after the treatments were administered!

Not only can group differences in one relevant variable be compensated for by analysis of covariance, but any number of variables relevant to the dependent variable can be statistically adjusted so that they do not confound the analysis of the independent-dependent relationship. Obviously, such a tool has important implications for educational researchers since it permits the use of pre-existing student groups while still controlling variables which might otherwise confound the results of the investigation. Although analysis of covariance should not be indiscriminately applied to educational research, it is distressing that the technique is not used more often in school research investigations. In many instances the relationships studied would have been much more clear had they been statistically treated with a technique controlling probable confounding variables.

It must be strongly emphasized, however, that analysis of covariance cannot completely overcome the dangers inherent in dealing with pre-existing groups. When the independent variable is experimental in nature, for example a treatment *versus* control group design, random assignment of subjects to the two groups is, strictly speaking, the only way to insure complete validity of the analysis of covariance statistical tests. If the treatment conditions are assigned to pre-existing groups, then the analysis of covariance results can be meaningfully interpreted *only* to the extent that the researcher can make a case for the pre-existing compositions of his groups being not unlike those which would have been obtained under pure randomization conditions. When the independent variable is not experimental, for example males *versus* females design, the pitfalls when interpreting analysis of covariance results are even greater. As an extreme example, consider what it would mean to adjust (equate) statistically male and female groups on the variable height in order to compare the groups on the dependent variable weight. Many less obvious problem situations could be illustrated concerning the potential for erroneous conclusions using analysis of covariance techniques on pre-existing groups.[1] The reader is warned against the indiscriminant use of analysis of covariance procedures as a "cure-all" device for the blind equation of pre-existing groups.

[1]See F. M. Lord. "A Paradox in the Interpretation of Group Comparisons," *Psychological Bulletin* **68** (1967): 304–305.

Like analysis of variance, the model from which it is derived, analysis of covariance can be used in both single-classification form when there is only one independent variable and multiple-classification form, when there are two or more independent variables. In the single-classification scheme the researcher is interested in the existence of mean differences between two or more groups (which represent the independent variables) with respect to the measure which represents the dependent variable. It is convenient in analysis of covariance problems to speak of the dependent variable as the *criterion variable* and the relevant variable(s), for which we wish to make adjustments, as the *control variable*(s).

An illustration of a single-classification analysis of covariance problem would be seen when a researcher tests the following null hypothesis: "There is no difference in the mean performance on an English achievement test of three, differently instructed student groups which have been statistically equated with respect to intelligence." In this case the independent variable is method of instruction and the criterion variable is student performance on the English achievement test. The control variable is student intelligence, probably measured by a group intelligence test.

Rationale

The rationale underlying analysis of covariance involves a combination of analysis of variance and regression concepts. In its most basic form, we can think of analysis of covariance as nothing more than an analysis of variance of *adjusted* criterion scores. To make the proper adjustment, a regression equation can be computed for each group using the methods of Chapters 7 and 8 to predict the criterion scores from the scores on the control variable. If we wish to "equate" the groups on the control variable, then we can pick any constant score value (usually the overall sample mean) and predict the criterion mean score for each group (using each group's regression line) for this constant control variable value. The resulting values are the *adjusted* group means. The adjusted scores for each group member are simply the *predicted* criterion scores using the group regression line. It is with these predicted scores that the analysis of variance is then performed, yielding the usual F ratio to test for amount of variation resulting from differences between the groups.

Perhaps this verbal explanation of the adjustment process can be more easily understood by looking at the situation graphically. Figure 15.1 presents the rather idealistic (but nevertheless illustrative) scattergrams for three equally sized hypothetical groups with control variable X predicting criterion variable Y. Clearly, the three groups are initially different on the control variable, having means 20, 30, and 70 respectively. They also differ on the criterion variable, having means of 25, 15, and 65 respectively. These values (solid points) can be read off the graph in the usual manner, following the solid lines between the X-axis and Y-axis. The regression lines for each group are also shown, each one intersecting the vertical line representing the overall control variable mean of 40. When these points of intersection are transferred to the Y-axis (dotted lines),

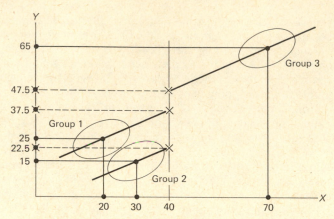

Figure 15.1 *Graphical presentation of the adjustment process in analysis of covariance (solid points = unadjusted values; crossed points = adjusted values).*

we can read off the *adjusted* mean scores for each group (crossed points), 37.5, 22.5, and 47.5 respectively. Note, for example, how the third group, initially much higher on the control variable, is also much higher (as would be expected) on the *unadjusted* criterion variable. But when the adjustment takes place, this disparity in mean difference between group 3 and groups 1 and 2 is reduced. The reader should attempt to explain why the unadjusted mean difference between groups 1 and 2 is less than the corresponding adjusted mean difference. (See exercise 6 for further insight into this adjustment process.)

A Research Example

An actual example of single-classification analysis of covariance may assist the reader in understanding this most useful technique. The research involved a study of the value of filmed science courses in public schools.[2] A sample of 247 high-school physics students was divided into two groups—experimental and control. The control students studied physics in a conventional lecture–discussion for a full academic year. At the same time the experimental students were using a series of thirty-minute filmed lecture–demonstrations on physics which constituted a full year's course in high-school physics. Although there was some teacher instruction in the experimental group, the bulk was provided through the use of the films.

At the end of the school year a standardized achievement examination was given to all students to measure the efficiency of the filmed and conventional instruction methods. This posttest served as the criterion variable. Measures were also taken of the students' precourse knowledge of physics, their

[2]W. J. Popham and J. M. Sadnavitch, "The Effectiveness of Filmed Science Courses in Public Secondary Schools," Kansas State College of Pittsburg, August, 1960, 66 pp.

Table 15.1

Analysis of Covariance of Experimental and Control Physics Students' Achievement Performance

| Source of Variation | Residuals | | | F |
	Degrees of Freedom	Sum of Squares	Mean Square	
Between	1	936.465	936.465	14.839[a]
Within	242	15,272.671	63.110	
Total	243	16,209.136		

[a]Significant beyond the 0.01 level.

intelligence, and their previous overall grade point averages. These latter three measures were used as control variables.

The data were subjected to a single-classification analysis of covariance to test the following null hypothesis: "There will be no significant difference in the postcourse physics achievement of the film-taught and conventionally-taught students, when initial differences between the two groups have been adjusted with respect to initial knowledge of physics (achievement pretest), intellectual aptitude (group intelligence test), and previous scholastic performance (grade-point average)." The mathematics involved in the computation of such an analysis of covariance, though lengthy, are relatively simple. At the end of the computation, the covariance analysis was presented as seen in Table 15.1. Most of the terms in the table are identical to those used in reporting analysis of variance results. The term "residuals" can be thought of as meaning "adjusted," referring to the fact that the degrees of freedom, sums of squares, and mean squares have been adjusted in terms of the control variables. It can be noted from the table that a significant F value was yielded. Therefore, the null hypothesis was rejected.

It is necessary to inspect the criterion means to be certain which group is significantly superior. Remember that the original criterion means for the group are adjusted to compensate for initial differences between the groups on the control variables. It is the adjusted means that one must inspect. Since the reader of the research report gets a better idea of the results of the study if unadjusted and adjusted criterion variable means, as well as control variable means, are reported, it is common to find a table such as Table 15.2 which supplies the criterion and control variable means for the present example.

Note in Table 15.2 that the adjustment of the criterion means is rather trivial in this instance, although in other cases the adjustment may be quite great. Observe that the control group's unadjusted original mean has been slightly increased, and the experimental group's original mean has been adjusted downward. The reason for these particular adjustments can be inferred from the differences between the experimental and control groups on the control variables. The experimental group's mean was adjusted downward, because of that group's

Table 15.2
Physics Students' Criterion and Control Variable Means

		Criterion		Control		
		Postachievement		Pretest		
	n	Adjusted	Unadjusted	Achievement	IQ	GPA
Experimental group	135	55.78	56.78	47.22	116.77	2.92
Control group	112	60.15	59.29	48.77	112.96	2.99

initial superiority over the control group in intelligence (116.77 to 112.96). This difference outweighed the differences on the other two control variables favoring the control group. The contribution to the mean adjustment made by each control variable is determined primarily by (1) the magnitude of the initial difference between the groups, and (2) the strength of the relationship between the criterion measure and the control measure. In this instance the correlation coefficients between the criterion variable and the control variables were (1) pretest achievement (0.68), (2) IQ (0.51), and (3) GPA (0.30).

By inspecting the adjusted means, the reader can see that the conventionally taught students performed significantly better than their film-taught counterparts. This research study, then, would not support the use of the particular film series, as it was employed during the study.

The Influence of Relevant Variables

This example of analysis of covariance illustrates how minor differences between groups with respect to relevant variables can be extremely influential. If the researcher analyzes only group differences with respect to the dependent variable, without taking into consideration the apparently trivial differences between groups on other measures, he often obtains a misleading picture of the true differences between groups. Often group criterion means, which appear to be highly significant when considered alone, will be adjusted to virtual equivalence through analysis of covariance because of the high-scoring group's superiority on relevant variables. Sometimes the reverse is also seen, that is, small unadjusted mean differences between groups may end up being extremely large adjusted differences after each group's performance on relevant variables is taken into account.

Nor do these initial differences between groups on the relevant variables have to be statistically significant. It is not sufficient merely to test for significant differences between groups on variables relevant to the dependent variable and, if no significant differences are found, to conclude that the groups are essentially equal. The reader should try to visualize a situation in which one group is superior to a second group on *all* of several relevant variables, none of the differences being significant, but all favoring the same group. The composite effect of these minor, but systematic, advantages of the favored group can be most important. This effect will be detected by analysis of covariance. Computing a number of individual *t* tests on the relevant variables at the outset, for example, would not reveal the important superiority of one group.

One of the advantages of analysis of covariance is that it reduces the size of the error term (the within mean square) used as the denominator of the *F* ratio, thus increasing the size and significance of the *F* values. It should be noted that if an effect is statistically significant *only* after numerous control variables have been employed to reduce the error term, then it may be impossible to see the effect at work in daily life. When a teacher is employing certain instructional methods to help a particular child, it is no comfort to see the child fall further behind, even if an analysis of covariance shows that he is not as bad as would be predicted by a number of control variables.

MULTIPLE CLASSIFICATION

As was true for single-classification, *multiple-classification analysis of covariance* is analogous to multiple-classification analysis of variance, coupled with the use of regression analysis. The same general scheme is employed in both models. Thus, as in multiple analysis of variance the researcher is interested in the relationship between a dependent variable and two or more independent variables (represented by subgroups), as well as the possibility of a relationship between the dependent variable and an interaction between the independent variables. Initial differences between the groups representing the independent variables are adjusted as with single classification analysis of covariance, with one or more control variables employed. The resulting *F* value for main effects and interactions are interpreted in the usual way. Adjustments can be made in means representing all independent variable groups, in order to compensate for initial control variable differences between the groups.

All of the arguments favoring the use of multiple-classification analysis of variance models and those favoring analysis of covariance approaches can be combined to support the advocacy of multiple-classification analysis of covariance approaches for the educational researcher. It is true that the mathematical computations involved, even using a desk calculator, are somewhat lengthy. But this method is no more complex than any of the techniques studied heretofore. As may be seen in the next chapter, which is devoted to computation procedures for single- and multiple-classification analysis of covariance problems, the mathematics used in multiple-classification problems can be easily mastered.

REQUISITE ASSUMPTIONS

The assumptions which must be satisfied for valid statistical tests using analysis of covariance methods include all those for the analysis of variance (see page 183) plus one additional and important assumption: The regression coefficients (slopes) for the regression lines in the subgroup populations must be equal. (Note the parallelism of the regression lines in Figure 15.1.) Procedures for testing this assumption can be found in more advanced texts on experimental design.

Again it must be pointed out that the stringent satisfaction of these assumptions is probably not required, but the departure from them should not be too great. Because of the additional assumption of homogeneity of regression, analysis of covariance is less "robust" than an analysis of variance, that is, less able to tolerate marked departures from these assumptions. Hence, much closer attention must be paid to assumptions in the case of analysis of covariance.

REVIEW

For the educational research worker, analysis of covariance is an extremely valuable statistical technique, since it allows one to test for mean differences between two or more groups while compensating for initial differences between the groups with respect to relevant variables, thereby increasing the precision of the statistical tests.

Analysis of covariance may be used in the many school research situations when the researcher is unable, for justifiable practical reasons, to manipulate groups so that samples can be made equal on such important variables as intelligence, prior achievement, and so forth. Through analysis of covariance, differences between groups with respect to a criterion variable can be studied although the reader was warned against using such adjustment procedures on pre-existing groups without regard to the nature of the *pre-existing differences* between groups.

This important statistical tool combines analysis of variance and regression models in a particularly intriguing fashion. Essentially, control measures related to the criterion are used to generate for each subject a predicted criterion score based on his control measure scores. After subjects have been equated with respect to the controls, differences between the predicted criterion scores are then tested by analysis of variance.

Adjustments in subgroup means may be made so that one can calculate a mean difference between groups after statistically equalizing the groups on the control measures. As in the case of analysis of variance, the analysis of covariance model can be used in single-classification or multiple-classification forms.

EXERCISES

1. A school psychologist wishes to study the influence of three new curriculum plans on the history achievement of students in his junior high school. Although the groups of pupils involved were selected on a fairly random basis, the psychologist has learned that there is considerable disparity between the groups with respect to intelligence. Should he examine the subjects'

post-experiment history achievement with single-classification analysis of variance or single-classification analysis of covariance? Why?

2. Two samples have *identical* means on a criterion mathematics achievement measure, but Group A is markedly inferior to Group B with respect to intelligence and performance on a pretest of mathematics knowledge. Is it possible that with the identical means an analysis of covariance could detect a significant mean difference?

3. If criterion mean adjustments were made in the previous problem, which group's mean would become superior?

4. Is it possible that a series of mean differences between four groups which were found to be significantly different beyond the 0.01 level by analysis of variance could be tested by analysis of covariance (with an added control variable or variables) and found to be statistically insignificant?

5. Discuss the interpretation problems a researcher might encounter in using analysis of covariance procedures to test the following null hypothesis: "There is no difference in the mean performance on an arithmetic fundamentals achievement test for high, middle, and low socioeconomic student groups which have been statistically equated with respect to intelligence."

6. Construct a graph similar to that in Figure 15.1 for the case in which the three groups do *not* differ in mean score on the control variable. Does any adjustment take place? Explain.

SELECTED READINGS
Blalock, Hubert M., Jr., *Social Statistics*. New York: McGraw-Hill, 1960, chap. 20.

Edwards, Allen L., *Experimental Design in Psychological Research*. New York: Holt, Rinehart & Winston, 1960, chap. 16.

Johnson, Palmer O., and Robert W. B. Jackson, *Modern Statistical Methods: Descriptive and Inductive*. Chicago: Rand McNally, 1959, pp. 410–424.

Wert, James E., Charles O. Neidt, and J. Stanley Ahmann, *Statistical Methods in Educational and Psychological Research*. New York: Appleton-Century-Crofts, 1954, chap. 18.

16

Analysis
of
Covariance—
Computation
Procedures

As with several previous techniques, the mathematics involved in computing analysis of covariance are simple but rather time-consuming. The use of a desk calculator or similar mechanical computing device is almost a must in this instance. Fortunately, routines for analysis of covariance have been developed for most of the more elaborate high-speed computers, if the researcher has access to one.

SINGLE CLASSIFICATION

In the single-classification analysis of covariance model there is one dependent variable, one independent variable (represented by two or more groups), and at least one control variable. There may, however, be several control variables the researcher employs, for he considers them to be strongly related to the dependent variable. In such a design, he wishes to statistically compensate for differences between the independent variable groups with respect to the control variables. The criterion or dependent variable is usually represented by the symbol Y and the control variable by X, or if there is more than one by X_1, X_2, X_3, and so forth. The independent variable, of course, is represented by the groups whose criterion variable means are being tested for significance of difference.

The computation procedure for single-classification analysis of covariance can be illustrated by working with the hypothetical data for two groups presented in Table 16.1. The two samples are extremely small and are employed only for purposes of illustration. In actual research situations an investigator working with such small samples would be unable to demonstrate that the samples satisfied the requisite assumptions for analysis of covariance. Therefore, much larger samples are usually found when analysis of covariance is employed. It should also be mentioned that though the two groups are equal in size in the computational example, this need not be the case in single-classi-

Table 16.1

Scores of Two Hypothetical Programmed Instruction Groups, on a Criterion Achievement Test (Y), a Prior Mathematics Achievement Examination (X_1), and an Intelligence Test (X_2)

Subject	Y	X_1	X_2
"Small-step" group			
a	59	68	116
b	58	69	120
c	58	64	114
d	54	63	104
e	53	65	110
f	50	61	101
Σ	332	390	665
"Large-step" group			
g	56	63	114
h	51	59	102
i	51	56	103
j	49	57	100
k	48	62	111
l	47	61	110
Σ	302	358	640
Σ	634	748	1,305

fication analysis of covariance. Nor, for that matter, is the technique limited to use with only two groups.

In this example the independent variable or factor is "size of step" in a self-instruction program, that is, the difficulty gap between the items or frames composing the program. Both groups used self-instruction programmed mathematics texts for a period of two months, after which the same criterion achievement test (Y) was administered to all subjects. The program used by the "small-step" programming group was one in which the increasing level of difficulty in each item of the program was very slight. The "large-step" programming group used a program in which the difficulty level between frames was considerably greater. The null hypothesis in this example would be the following: "There is no significant difference between the achievement groups following the experimental self-instruction period (after equating on two control measures)."

The variables considered relevant to the criterion were: (1) previous mathematics achievement, as measured by a standardized achievement examination; and (2) intelligence, as measured by a group intelligence test. Data for both control variables were already at hand in the school system's records. Note from Table 16.1 that the small-step group is superior to the large-step group on both control variables.

Table 16.2

Sums and Means of the Criterion and Control Variables for Two Experimental Groups of Secondary Mathematics Pupils

Programming Method		Criterion Achievement		Controls Prior Math Achievement		Intelligence	
	n	ΣY	$\overline{Y}$	ΣX_1	$\overline{X}_1$	ΣX_2	$\overline{X}_2$
Small step	6	332	55.33	390	65.00	665	110.83
Large step	6	302	50.33	358	59.67	640	106.67
Total	12	634	52.83	748	62.33	1,305	108.67

The first step in the analysis is to set up a table similar to Table 16.2 where sums and means of the criterion and control variables are presented.

The next step in the analysis is to compute the sums of squares for the raw scores and the various crossproducts. Having done so, these quantities are then summarized in a table such as Table 16.3. These sums of squares and crossproducts are easily computed on a desk calculator.

With the data from Table 16.2 and Table 16.3, the researcher is ready to compute, *in deviation form*, the various sums of squares and crossproducts associated with: (1) the *total* variation in the sample; and (2) the amount of variation *within* the two subgroups. The reader may recall from the discussion of single-classification analysis of variance in Chapter 11 that the part of the total variation present that is not a function of the variation within groups is attributable to the differences *between* groups. In the present example one must find the deviation values, first for *total*, then for *within* groups, of Σy^2, $\Sigma x_1^2, \Sigma x_2^2, \Sigma x_2 y, \Sigma x_1 x_2$.

These values are computed as follows, where the subscripts *ss* and *ls* refer to the small-step and large-step treatment groups respectively:

Σy^2 total:

$$\Sigma y^2 = \Sigma Y^2 - \frac{(\Sigma Y)^2}{n} = 33,686 - \frac{(648)^2}{12} = 189.77$$

Σy^2 within:

$$\Sigma y^2 = \Sigma Y^2 - \left[\frac{(\Sigma Y_{ss})^2}{n_{ss}} + \frac{(\Sigma Y_{ls})^2}{n_{ls}}\right] = 33,686 - \left[\frac{(332)^2}{6} + \frac{(302)^2}{6}\right]$$

$$= 114.66$$

Σx_1^2 total:

$$\Sigma x_1^2 = \Sigma X_1^2 - \frac{(\Sigma X_1)^2}{n} = 46,796 - \frac{(748)^2}{12} = 170.67$$

Table 16.3
Summary of Squared Raw Scores and Crossproduct for 215 Mathematics Pupils

Measure	Symbols	Total for Entire Sample
Criterion achievement test	ΣY^2	33,686
Prior mathematics achievement	ΣX_1^2	46,796
Intelligence	ΣX_2^2	142,399
Crossproducts		
Prior achievement $\times$ criterion	$\Sigma X_1 Y$	39,652
Intelligence $\times$ criterion	$\Sigma X_2 Y$	69,149
Prior achievement $\times$ intelligence	$\Sigma X_1 X_2$	81,587

Σx_1^2 within:

$$\Sigma x_1^2 = \Sigma X_1^2 - \left[\frac{(\Sigma X_{1ss})^2}{n_{ss}} + \frac{(\Sigma X_{1ls})^2}{n_{ls}}\right] = 46,796 - \left[\frac{(390)^2}{6} + \frac{(358)^2}{6}\right]$$

$$= 85.33$$

Σx_2^2 total:

$$\Sigma x_2^2 = \Sigma X_2^2 - \frac{(\Sigma X_2)^2}{n} = 142,399 - \frac{(1,305)^2}{12} = 480.25$$

Σx_2^2 within:

$$\Sigma x_2^2 = \Sigma X_2^2 - \left[\frac{(\Sigma X_{2ss})^2}{n_{ss}} + \frac{(\Sigma X_{2ls})^2}{n_{ls}}\right]$$

$$= 142,399 - \left[\frac{(655)^2}{6} + \frac{(640)^2}{6}\right] = 428.16$$

$\Sigma x_1 y$ total:

$$\Sigma x_1 y = \Sigma X_1 Y - \frac{(\Sigma X_1)(\Sigma Y)}{n} = 39,652 - \frac{(748)(634)}{12} = 132.67$$

$\Sigma x_1 y$ within:

$$\Sigma x_1 y = \Sigma X_1 Y - \left[\frac{(\Sigma X_{1ss})(\Sigma Y_{ss})}{n_{ss}} + \frac{(\Sigma X_{1ls})(\Sigma Y_{ls})}{n_{ls}}\right]$$

$$= 39,652 - \left[\frac{(390)(332)}{6} + \frac{(358)(302)}{6}\right] = 52.67$$

$\Sigma x_2 y$ total:

$$\Sigma x_2 y = \Sigma X_2 Y - \frac{(\Sigma X_2)(\Sigma Y)}{n} = 69{,}149 - \frac{(1{,}305)(634)}{12} = 201.50$$

$\Sigma x_2 y$ within:

$$\Sigma x_2 y = \Sigma X_2 Y - \left[\frac{(\Sigma X_{2_{ss}})(\Sigma Y_{ss})}{n_{ss}} + \frac{(\Sigma X_{2_{ls}})(\Sigma Y_{ls})}{n_{ls}} \right]$$

$$= 69{,}149 - \left[\frac{(665)(332)}{6} + \frac{(640)(302)}{6} \right] = 139.00$$

$\Sigma x_1 x_2$ total:

$$\Sigma x_1 x_2 = \Sigma X_1 X_2 - \frac{(\Sigma X_1)(\Sigma X_2)}{n} = 81{,}587 - \frac{(748)(1{,}305)}{12} = 242.00$$

$\Sigma x_1 x_2$ within:

$$\Sigma x_1 x_2 = \Sigma X_1 X_2 - \left[\frac{(\Sigma X_{1_{ss}})(\Sigma X_{2_{ss}})}{n_{ss}} + \frac{(\Sigma X_{1_{ls}})(\Sigma X_{2_{ls}})}{n_{ls}} \right]$$

$$= 81{,}587 - \left[\frac{(39)(665)}{6} + \frac{(358)(640)}{6} \right] = 175.33$$

The reader will find it instructive to identify the source of the values used in computing the above deviation sums of squares and crossproducts. Note that, although the mathematics involved may appear to be imposing, the various values needed are first drawn from Tables 16.2 and 16.3 then inserted into the total and within formulas in a systematic fashion. The actual computation is quite simple.

The next step is to compute regression coefficients, first total then within, for each of the control variables in the analysis. This is done in a manner similar to that employed in multiple regression analysis as described in Chapter 8. The two linear equations needed to find the values of b_1 and b_2 are

$$\Sigma x_1 y = b_1 \Sigma x_1^2 + b_2 \Sigma x_1 x_2$$
$$\Sigma x_2 y = b_1 \Sigma x_1 x_2 + b_2 \Sigma x_2^2$$

These two equations are solved simultaneously, first with the total sums of squares and crossproducts, then with the within sums of squares and cross-products.

For total, the equations become

$$132.67 = b_1\,170.67 + b_2\,242.00$$
$$201.50 = b_1\,242.00 + b_2\,480.25$$

Dividing both equations by their coefficients of b_2 and then subtracting the second equation from the first (or adding if the algebraic signs of b_2 are unlike), we find the value of b_1:

$$0.54822314 = b_1\,0.70524793 + b_2$$
$$0.41957314 = b_1\,0.50390422 + b_2$$
$$0.12865000 = b_1\,0.20134371$$
$$b_1 = 0.63895713$$

We find the value of b_2 by substituting the value of b_1 in either of the equations yielded by the original division operation. Thus, substituting in the first equation above:

$$0.54822314 = (0.63895713)(0.70524793) + b_2$$
$$b_2 = 0.09759995$$

One should check these values by substituting them in one of the original equations as follows:

$$132.67 = (0.63895713)(170.67) + (0.09759995)(242.00)$$
$$132.67 = 109.0508 + 23.6192 = 132.67 \text{ (checks)}$$

By the same process the values of b_1 and b_2 for within are computed by substituting the necessary within sums of squares and crossproducts into the two linear equations.

$$52.67 = b_1\,85.33 + b_2\,175.33$$
$$139.00 = b_1\,175.33 + b_2\,428.16$$

Omitting the mathematical operations identical to those involved in finding the total b_1 and b_2, the values of the within regression coefficients are the following:

$$b_1 = -0.31404788$$
$$b_2 = 0.45324648$$

With the values of b_1 and b_2 for both total and within, the *sum of squares of residuals* may now be computed for total and within. When the within residual sums of squares has been subtracted from the total residual sum of squares, the remainder is called the *between residual sum of squares*. The between residual sum of squares represents the amount of variation attributable to differences between group means, *after* adjusting for differences between the groups with respect to the control variables. The within and between residual sums of squares are divided by their respective degrees of freedom to obtain the mean squares which, as in all forms of analysis of variance, are placed in a ratio to yield the F value by which the null hypothesis is tested.

The sum of squares of residuals for both total and within are computed[1] by use of the following equation:

$$\text{Sum of squares of residuals} = \Sigma y^2 - (b_1 \Sigma x_1 y + b_2 \Sigma x_2 y)$$

[1] When only one control variable is involved in the analysis, the residual sums of squares are found by use of the formula: Residual SS $= \Sigma y^2 - [(\Sigma xy)^2/\Sigma x^2]$.

In computing the *total* residual sum of squares, the values for the equation are the *total* regression coefficients and sums. The *within* residual sum of squares is found by using *within* values in the equation.

For total residual sum of squares, then, the equation would be as follows:

$$\text{Total SS of residuals} = 189.77 - [(0.63895713)(132.67) + (0.09759995)(201.50)]$$

$$= 85.33$$

$$\text{Within SS of residuals} = 114.66 - [(-0.31404788)(52.67) + (0.45324648)(139.00)]$$

$$= 68.20$$

The final analysis of covariance table to test the null hypothesis can now be set up. The table will take a form similar to that seen in Table 16.4.

Note that the between residual sum of squares is obtained by subtracting the within residual sum of squares from the total residual sum of squares.

The degrees of freedom used in an analysis of covariance problem are similar to those employed in analysis of variance computations with one important exception. Each control variable used takes one degree of freedom from the total degrees of freedom. Thus, for the total *df* we must subtract from the usual $n = 1$ the number of control variables employed. In the present example two control measures were used so the total degrees of freedom are $12 - 1 = 11$, less the two controls $= 9$. For any single-classification analysis of covariance problem the following degrees of freedom scheme can be employed.

Source of Variation	*Degrees of Freedom*
Total	$df = n - (1 + \text{the number of control variables})$
Between	$df = \text{number of groups} - 1$
Within	$df = df \text{ for total} - df \text{ for between}$

In the present computational example we have, for total: $df = 9$, for between: $df = 1$, for within: $df = 8$.

The *F* value obtained by dividing the between residual mean square by the within residual mean square is 2.01. An inspection of Table G reveals that with one and eight degrees of freedom an *F* of 5.32 is needed to reject the null hypothesis at the 0.05 level, so we cannot reject the null hypothesis of no mean difference between the groups.

The importance of analysis of covariance can be gauged from this example by returning to Table 16.2 where one can observe a mean difference of five points between the two experimental groups. Suppose the researcher had not attempted to adjust his data for initial differences by incorporating two control variables in an analysis of covariance scheme. The reader may be interested to learn that, *if only the criterion data* had been analyzed by a pooled variance model *t* test, the result ($t = 2.56$, $df = 10$) would have been significant beyond the 0.05 level! In other words, if the superiority of the small-step group in intelligence and prior mathematics achivement had not been taken into account, the researcher would have concluded that the small-step programming method

---

Table 16.4

Analysis of Covariance for Achievement Differences
Between Two Experimental Programmed-Instruction Groups,
Controlling for Prior Mathematics Achievement and Intelligence

Source of Variation	Degrees of Freedom	Sum of Squares	Residuals Mean Square	F
Between	1	17.13	17.13	2.01
Within	8	68.20	8.53	
Total	9	85.33		

was significantly better than the large-step method. Of course, one can now see that the two control measures employed in the covariance analysis would have acted to confound the simple *t*-test design, since one group's superiority in these relevant variables worked to the disadvantage of the other group.

Adjustment of Means

Since, in analysis of covariance, the performance of the groups on the criterion variable is related to their performance on the control variables, the researcher would like to know how each group would have performed on the criterion measure, *if* they had been equivalent at the outset with respect to the control measures. A final step in analysis of covariance permits one to adjust the criterion means to compensate for differences between the groups on the control variables.

For each group's criterion mean an adjustment term is calculated by using the within regression coefficients and the difference between the group's control variable mean and the total sample's control variable mean. This process can be illustrated by adjusting the criterion means in the previous computational example. It will be necessary to refer to Table 16.2.

The adjustment values used for $\bar{Y}$ of the small-step group are computed as follows:

$$\text{Values}_{ss} = b_1(\bar{X}_{1_{ss}} - \bar{X}_{1_t}) \text{ and } b_2(\bar{X}_{2_{ss}} - \bar{X}_{2_t})$$
$$= (-0.31404788)(65.00 - 62.33) \text{ and } (0.45324648)(110.83 - 108.75)$$
$$= -0.84 \text{ and } 0.94$$

These adjustment values are then added to or subtracted from the original value of $\bar{Y}_{ss}$ depending upon the inferiority or superiority of that group on the control measures. Since the small-step group had an advantage on both control measures, both adjustment values (regardless of the algebraic sign) are subtracted from the original value of $\bar{Y}_{ss}$. Thus the adjusted $\bar{Y}_{ss}$ is $55.33 - (0.84 + 0.94) = 53.55$.

A similar process is followed in the adjustment of $\bar{Y}$ for the large-step group:

$$\text{Values}_{ls} = b_1(\bar{X}_{1_{ls}} - \bar{X}_{1_t}) \text{ and } b_2(\bar{X}_{2_{ls}} - \bar{Y}_{2_t})$$
$$= (-0.31404788)(59.67 - 62.33) \text{ and } (0.45324648)(106.67 - 108.75)$$
$$= 0.84 \text{ and } -0.94$$

Once more the adjustment is made in terms of the original superiority or inferiority of the large-step group on the control measures. Since the large-step group's control variable means were smaller than the total control variable means in both instances, the 0.84 and 0.94 are added to the original value of $\bar{Y}_{ls}$. The adjusted $\bar{Y}_{ls}$ is $50.33 + (0.84 + 0.94) = 52.11$. Note that the adjusted $\bar{Y}_{ls}$ of 52.11 is only slightly lower than the adjusted $\bar{Y}_{ss}$ of 53.55.

It should be noted that when more than one control variable is employed there may be situations in which a group is inferior with respect to one or more control measures but superior with respect to other controls. In such cases the adjustment values usually cancel each other to a great extent, although the adjustment value which usually makes the most difference is the one based on the control variable that is most strongly related to the criterion, particularly when there is a sizeable difference between the groups on that measure. Always note the difference between the total control variable mean and the group control variable mean, then adjust accordingly.

MULTIPLE CLASSIFICATION

As in the case of analysis of variance, the basic logic of the single classification procedure can be extended to a multiple-classification scheme, where the relationship between a criterion variable and more than one independent variable (as represented by subgroups) is studied. One is able to test for group differences on the independent or main-effect variables, as well as for significant interactions between the independent variables. All these tests can be conducted in a multiple-classification analysis of covariance operation, while adjusting for differences between the independent variable groups with respect to one or more control variables considered relevant to the criterion. By this technique it is possible to refine even further the more sensitive analysis available through multiple-classification analysis of variance.

The computation procedures for multiple-classification analysis of covariance procedures can be illustrated by an example in which the two independent variables are: (1) type of instructional film, and (2) previous exposure to educational television. The dependent variable is geography achievement, and the control variables are: (1) intelligence, (2) previous overall academic achievement, and (3) pretest geography achievement.

Suppose a researcher is testing the efficacy of a unique new filmed method of teaching geography principles in contrast with a more conventional filmed approach to geography. The new method, for example, might include a number of opportunities to respond to instructional questions posed throughout the film and, subsequently, answered. Let us say that we have five films of the new type and five conventional films which treat the same topic in almost an equivalent fashion, except for the questions interspersed through the experimental films.

Suppose further that there is an educational television (ETV) project currently underway in the school in which many, but not all, students of the school are participating. If, in the researcher's opinion, previous exposure to ETV may in some way affect the response of the students to the films, he may classify his subjects so that participation in the ETV project is considered as a second independent variable.

An experiment can be conducted using the two sets of films with a sample of 40 high-school students, 20 of whom use the new films for a week and 20 of whom use the conventional films.[2] We can designate the former group as the experimental subjects and the latter group as the control subjects. In addition, subjects are selected so that 10 students in each group are participating in the educational television project.

In this experiment the researcher may use an achievement test based on the content of the films as the dependent variable, with: (1) the approach employed in the films, and (2) participation in ETV as the two independent variables. For control variables, the researcher might employ: (1) students' intelligence test scores, (2) grade-point averages earned by students during the previous semester, and (3) performance on a pretest administered before the films are used.

Having obtained the necessary data, the researcher needs a table such as Table 16.5, where the sums and means of the four subgroups are presented. Another table is also needed to summarize the experimental data for the experimental and control subjects. (See Table 16.6.)

Next, as in the single-classification model, we must compute, in deviation form, all possible sums of squares and crossproducts for the total sample and for within. In multiple-classification analysis of variance, it is also necessary to compute the deviation sums of squares and crossproducts for each main effect variable and for all possible interactions between the main effect variables. Thus, in this example we will need to compute (1) total, (2) film type, (3) ETV participation, (4) interaction, and (5) within for all of the following quantities:

$$\Sigma y^2, \Sigma x_1^2, \Sigma x_2^2, \Sigma x_3^2, \Sigma x_1 y, \Sigma x_2 y, \Sigma x_3 y, \Sigma x_1 x_2, \Sigma x_1 x_3, \Sigma x_2 x_3.$$

An example of the computation procedures to be followed for computing the sums of squares will be given here, followed by an example of the procedure for computing the crossproducts.

[2]Though disproportionate frequencies in the subgroups can be employed, extensive adjustments must be made in the analysis. Usually it is wiser to employ proportionate or equal numbers of subjects in the subgroups. For adjustment of disproportionate frequencies, see: Fei Tsao, "General Solution of the Analysis of Variance and Covariance in the Case of Unequal and Disproportionate Numbers of Observations in the Subclasses," *Psychometrika* **11** (1946): 107−128.

Table 16.5

Sums and Means of Experimental and Conventional Film-Taught Students Classified According to Participation in Educational Television Project

Group	n	Criterion Posttest Scores		Intelligence Test Scores		Controls Grade Point Averages		Pretest Scores	
		ΣY	$\bar{Y}$	ΣX_1	$\bar{X}_1$	ΣX_2	$\bar{X}_2$	ΣX_3	$\bar{X}_3$
Experimental films									
ETV participants	10	828	82.80	1,134	113.40	28.32	2.832	209	20.90
ETV nonparticipants	10	776	77.60	1,321	123.10	29.32	2.943	259	25.90
Subtotal	20	1,604	80.20	2,365	118.25	57.75	2,887	468	23.40
Conventional films									
ETV participants	10	814	81.40	1,174	117.40	27.30	2.730	239	23.90
ETV nonparticipants	10	692	69.20	1,075	107.40	27.18	2.718	232	23.20
Subtotal	20	1,506	75.30	2,248	112.40	54.48	2.724	471	23.55
Total	40	3,110	77.75	4,613	115.33	112.23	2.806	939	23.47

Table 16.6

Summary of Raw-Score Squares and Crossproducts for Criterion and Control Variables

Measure	Symbol	Total
Posttest	ΣY^2	247,847
Intelligence	ΣX_1^2	541,256
Grade-point average	ΣX_2^2	325.76
Pretest	ΣX_3^2	24,172.14
Crossproducts	$\Sigma X_1 Y$	360,483
	$\Sigma X_2 Y$	8,779.99
	$\Sigma X_3 Y$	73,920
	$\Sigma X_1 X_2$	12,999.82
	$\Sigma X_2 X_3$	2,654.34
	$\Sigma X_1 X_3$	108,603

Using the criterion variable to illustrate the computation of the five Σy^2 values, we find that

For total:
$$\Sigma y^2 = \Sigma Y^2 - \frac{(\Sigma Y)^2}{n} = 247,847 - \frac{(3,110)^2}{40} = 6,044.5$$

For films:
$$\Sigma y^2 = \frac{(\Sigma Y_e)^2}{n_e} + \frac{(\Sigma Y_c)^2}{n_c} - \frac{(\Sigma Y)^2}{n} = \frac{(1,604)^2}{20} + \frac{(1,506)^2}{20} - \frac{(3,110)^2}{40}$$

$$= 240.1$$

For ETV:

$$\Sigma y^2 = \frac{(\Sigma Y_p)^2}{n_p} + \frac{(\Sigma Y_{np})^2}{n_{np}} - \frac{(\Sigma Y)^2}{n} = \frac{(828+814)^2}{20} + \frac{(776+692)^2}{20} - \frac{(3,110)^2}{40} = 756.9$$

For interaction:

$$\Sigma y^2 = \frac{(\Sigma Y_{ep})^2}{n_{ep}} + \frac{(\Sigma Y_{enp})^2}{n_{enp}} + \frac{(\Sigma Y_{cp})^2}{n_{cp}} + \frac{(\Sigma Y_{cnp})^2}{n_{cnp}} - \frac{(\Sigma Y)^2}{n}$$

$$- (\text{SS for films} + \text{SS for ETV})$$

$$= \frac{(828)^2}{10} + \frac{(776)^2}{10} + \frac{(814)^2}{10} + \frac{(692)^2}{10} - \frac{(3,110)^2}{40} - (240.1 + 756.9) = 122.5$$

For within:

$$\Sigma y^2 = \Sigma Y^2 - \left[\frac{(\Sigma Y_{ep})^2}{n_{ep}} + \frac{(\Sigma Y_{enp})^2}{n_{enp}} + \frac{(\Sigma Y_{cp})^2}{n_{cp}} + \frac{(\Sigma Y_{cnp})^2}{n_{cnp}}\right]$$

$$= 247,847 - \left[\frac{(828)^2}{10} + \frac{(776)^2}{10} + \frac{(814)^2}{10} + \frac{(692)^2}{10}\right] = 4,925.0$$

In a similar fashion the deviation sums of squares for the control variables are computed.

The computation of deviation crossproducts is illustrated by that between the posttest criterion and the intelligence test scores:

For total:

$$\Sigma x_1 y = \Sigma X_1 Y - \frac{(\Sigma X_1)(XY)}{n} = 360,483 - \frac{(4,613)(3,110)}{40} = 1,822.25$$

For films:

$$\Sigma x_1 y = \frac{(\Sigma X_{1e})(\Sigma Y_e)}{n_e} + \frac{(\Sigma Y_{1c})(\Sigma Y_c)}{n_c} - \frac{(\Sigma X_1)(\Sigma Y)}{n}$$

$$= \frac{(2,365)(1,604)}{20} + \frac{(2,248)(1,506)}{20} - \frac{(4,613)(3,110)}{40} = 286.65$$

For ETV:

$$\Sigma x_1 y = \frac{(\Sigma X_{1p})(\Sigma Y_p)}{n_p} + \frac{(\Sigma X_{1np})(\Sigma Y_{np})}{n_{np}} - \frac{(\Sigma X_1)(\Sigma Y)}{n}$$

$$= \frac{(1,134+1,174)(828+814)}{20} + \frac{(1,231+1,074)(776+692)}{20}$$

$$- \frac{(4,613)(3,110)}{40} = 13.05$$

For interaction:

$$\Sigma x_1 y = \frac{(\Sigma X_{1ep})(\Sigma Y_{ep})}{n_{ep}} + \frac{(\Sigma X_{1enp})(\Sigma Y_{enp})}{n_{enp}} + \frac{(\Sigma X_{1cp})(\Sigma Y_{cp})}{n_{cp}}$$

$$+ \frac{(\Sigma X_{1cnp})(\Sigma Y_{cnp})}{n_{cnp}} - \frac{(\Sigma X_1)(\Sigma Y)}{n}$$

$$- (\text{SS for films} + \text{SS for ETV})$$

$$= \frac{(1{,}134)(828)}{10} + \frac{(1{,}231)(776)}{10} + \frac{(1{,}174)(814)}{10} + \frac{(1{,}074)(692)}{10}$$

$$- \frac{(4{,}613)(3{,}110)}{40} - (286.65 + 13.05) = 344.75$$

For within:

$$\Sigma x_1 y = \Sigma X_1 Y - \left[\frac{(\Sigma X_{1ep})(\Sigma Y_{ep})}{n_{ep}} + \frac{(\Sigma X_{1enp})(\Sigma Y_{enp})}{n_{enp}} \right.$$

$$\left. + \frac{(\Sigma X_{1cp})(\Sigma Y_{cp})}{n_{cp}} + \frac{(\Sigma X_{1cnp})(\Sigma Y_{cnp})}{n_{cnp}} \right]$$

$$= 360{,}483 - \left[\frac{(1{,}134)(828)}{10} + \frac{(1{,}231)(776)}{10} + \frac{(1{,}174)(814)}{10} \right.$$

$$\left. + \frac{(1{,}074)(692)}{10} \right] = 1{,}177.80$$

The reader should attempt to trace the origin of the various values in these equations back to their sources in Tables 16.5 and 16.6. Although the amount of numbers involved may seem imposing and confusing, careful consideration will reveal that each of the sums of squares and crossproducts reflects the variation in the data which can be attributed to a specific source. To do this the data are artificially reclassified or, to use the vernacular, simply "looked at in another light." In other words, the process is something akin to viewing a phenomenon from different angles in order to note the contribution made by each of several factors.

Having computed the necessary deviation values, a table similar to Table 16.7 is set up, where all deviation values are presented. In viewing Table 16.7 the reader may pause to consider the number of mathematical calculations involved in determining the 50 values presented therein. Although time consuming, the calculation of the deviation sums of squares and crossproducts by a mechanical calculator is really quite routine, since the computations for each source of variation, that is, for total, within, main effects, and interaction, are very similar. Of course, the use of a high-speed computer for this type of computation would remarkably reduce the time expenditure associated with such analyses.

Table 16.7

Deviation Values for Sums of Squares and Crossproducts

Source of Variation	Σy^2	Σx_1^2	Σx_2^2	Σx_3^2	$\Sigma x_1 y$	$\Sigma x_2 y$	$\Sigma x_3 y$	$\Sigma x_1 x_2$	$\Sigma x_2 x_3$	$\Sigma x_1 x_3$
Type of films used	240.1	344.20	0.2673	0.22	286.55	8.01	−7.35	9.57	0.25	−8.77
ETV participation	756.9	2.20	0.0245	46.22	13.05	−4.31	−187.05	0.07	1.07	−3.22
Interaction	122.5	968.25	0.0378	81.23	344.75	2.17	99.75	5.91	1.26	280.72
Within	4,925.0	7,949.10	10.5425	2,001.44	1,177.80	48.24	1,007.40	41.35	17.16	44.10
Total	6,044.5	9,263.75	10.8721	2,129.11	1,822.25	54.11	912.75	56.90	19.74	312.83

Table 16.8

Deviation Values for Sums of Squares and Crossproducts, Combined with Within

Within Plus	Σy^2	Σx_1^2	Σx_2^2	Σx_3^2	$\Sigma x_1 y$	$\Sigma x_2 y$	$\Sigma x_3 y$	$\Sigma x_1 x_2$	$\Sigma x_2 x_3$	$\Sigma x_1 x_3$
Type of films used	5,165.1	8,293.30	10.8098	2,001.66	1,464.35	56.25	1,000.05	50.92	17.41	35.33
ETV participation	5,681.9	7,951.30	10.5670	2,047.66	1,190.85	43.93	820.35	41.42	18.23	40.88
Interaction	5,047.5	8,917.35	10.5803	2,082.67	1,522.55	50.41	1,107.15	47.26	18.42	324.82

The next step in the analysis is to add the within value of each sum of squares and crossproducts to each main effect and interaction value. Thus, in the present example one would need to treat the values for Σy^2 as follows:

For within plus films used:	$4,925.0 + 240.1 = 5,165.1$
For within plus ETV participation:	$4,925.0 + 756.9 = 5,681.9$
For within plus interaction:	$4,925.0 + 122.5 = 5,047.5$

In the same fashion the within values are added to each film, ETV, and interaction sum of squares and crossproducts. These values are then summarized in a table such as Table 16.8 in which the required deviation values for the sums of squares and crossproducts are presented.

We are now at the point in our analysis where linear equations are set up to determine the regression coefficients associated with each control variable, considered separately for each source of variation. For three control variables the equations take the following form:

$$\Sigma x_1 y = b_1 \Sigma x_1{}^2 + b_2 \Sigma x_1 x_2 + b_3 \Sigma x_1 x_3$$
$$\Sigma x_2 y = b_1 \Sigma x_1 x_2 + b_2 \Sigma x_2{}^2 + b_3 \Sigma x_2 x_3$$
$$\Sigma x_3 y = b_1 \Sigma x_1 x_3 + b_2 \Sigma x_2 x_3 + b_3 \Sigma x_3{}^2$$

By substituting the values for within plus films used in the above equations the values of b_1, b_2, and b_3 for this particular source of variation can be determined. Using these regression coefficients, the sum of squares (amount of variation), attributable to the difference between the two film groups after the groups have been statistically equalized with respect to the three control variables, can then be obtained.

The within plus ETV participation values and the within plus interaction values must also be substituted in the equations in order to obtain adjusted sums of squares for these two sources of variation. Finally, an adjusted sum of squares for within alone must be calculated. This is done by substituting the required within values in the equations and solving simultaneously. In all, then, four sets of simultaneous equations must be solved. The reader who needs to be reacquainted with the solution procedures for such equations should consult the step-by-step explanation in Chapter 8.

For the within plus films used values, the equations are as follows:

$$1,464.35 = b_1\,8,293.30 + b_2\,50.92 + b_3\,35.33$$
$$56.25 = b_1\quad 50.92 + b_2\,10.8098 + b_3\,17.41$$
$$1,000.05 = b_1\quad 35.33 + b_2\,17.41 + b_3\,2,001.66$$

Simultaneous solution of the above equations yields the following regression coefficients for within plus films used:

$$b_1 = 0.15162103$$
$$b_2 = 3.74108924$$
$$b_3 = 0.46461978$$

In a similar fashion the following regression coefficients are found:

For Within Plus ETV Participation	For Within Plus Interaction	For Within Alone
$b_1 = 0.13223981$	$b_1 = 0.13561500$	$b_1 = 0.12836266$
$b_2 = 2.99838559$	$b_2 = 3.32121139$	$b_2 = 3.30372611$
$b_3 = 0.37129422$	$b_3 = 0.48107613$	$b_3 = 0.47218366$

The "within plus" residual sums of squares can now be computed for each of the four sources of variation needed for the F tests. Sometimes the residual sums of squares are called *adjusted* sums of squares. In each instance, the following equation (using "within plus" values) is solved to obtain the residual sum of squares.

$$\text{Residual SS} = \Sigma y^2 - (b_1\Sigma x_1 y + b_2\Sigma x_2 y + b_3\Sigma x_3 y)$$

Thus, for films used, we have:

$$\text{Residual SS} = 5,165.1 - [(0.15162103)(1,464.35) + 3.74108924]$$
$$(56.25) + (0.46461978)(1,000.05)] = 4,267.995$$

For ETV participation:

$$\text{Residual SS} = 5,681.9 - [(0.13223981)(1,190.85) + (2.99838559)]$$
$$(43.90) + (0.37129422)(820.35)] = 5,088.202$$

For interaction:

$$\text{Residual SS} = 5,047.5 - [(0.13561500)(1,522.55) + (3.32121139)]$$
$$(50.41) + (0.48107613)(1,107.15)] = 4,140.974$$

For within:

$$\text{Residual SS} = 4,925.0 - [(0.12836266)(1,177.80) + 3.30372611)]$$
$$(48.24) + (0.47218366)(1,007.40)] = 4,138.764$$

To arrive at the residual sums of squares which represent the amount of variation attributable to the two main effects and interaction one must subtract the within residual SS from each of the other three "within plus" sums of squares, placing the resulting values in a table similar to Table 16.9.

The degrees of freedom used in multiple analysis of covariance are determined in the same way as in the case of multiple analysis of variance (see Chapter 14), except that the number of within degrees of freedom is found by subtracting from the total *df* (39 in this example) the number of degrees of freedom for main effects and interaction (3 in the example), as well as a degree of freedom for each control variable (3 in the example). Thus, the number of degrees of freedom for within is 33.

As usual, mean squares are then obtained by dividing the sums of squares by their respective degrees of freedom. F values for each main effect and for interaction are yielded by dividing the other mean squares by the within mean squares.

As may be seen in Table 16.9, only the F value resulting from students' participation in the Educational Television Project is statistically significant.

Table 16.9
Analysis of Covariance Significance Tests

Source of Variation	Degrees of Freedom	Residuals Sum of Squares	Mean Square	F
Films used	1	129.231	129.231	1.03
ETV participation	1	949.438	949.438	7.57[a]
Interaction	1	2.210	2.210	0.02
Within	33	4,138.764	125.417	

[a]Significant beyond the 0.01 level.

This means that the following null hypothesis should be rejected: "Having statistically adjusted for initial differences in intelligence, grade-point averages, and pretest scores between students who participated in the school ETV project and those who did not, there is no significant difference between the two groups." The null hypotheses concerning the type of film used as well as interaction could not be rejected.

If one wishes to carry the analysis one step further, means are adjusted in the same fashion as was described for single-classification analysis of covariance.

REVIEW

In this chapter computation procedures for single- and multiple-classification analysis of covariance models were given along with a computational example for each. Though the extensive calculations associated with analysis of variance may seem awesome, the use of a desk calculator or some other mechanical computer makes possible relatively rapid solution of most such problems.

In essence, one computes series of deviation sums of squares and cross-products, ultimately substituting these in formulas to yield residual or adjusted sums of squares for the sources of variation typically seen in analysis of variance. The adjusted sums of squares incorporate the modifications made because of initial disparities between groups with respect to control measures.

The adjustment of criterion means was described in the chapter as a function of the differences between subgroups on the control measures, as well as the strength of relationship between the criterion and the controls.

EXERCISES

1. Two groups of elementary pupils have been involved in a semester-long experiment, in which different methods of geometry instruction have been used

with each group. At the beginning of the experiment all pupils were given a standardized arithmetic test (X_1) and a standardized group intelligence test (X_2). None of the students had experienced any formal instruction in geometry prior to the experiment. At the close of the training period both groups were given a specially designed geometry examination (Y).

Employing a single analysis of covariance model in which the arithmetic achievement and intelligence measures serve as the control variables and the geometry examination scores as the criterion, determine the value of F and decide whether the null hypothesis that Group I is not significantly different from Group II should be rejected.

Pupil	Arithmetic Achievement	Intelligence	Geometry Examination
		Group I	
1	7.1	83	82
2	4.9	77	45
3	5.8	75	19
4	6.1	74	55
5	5.6	71	22
6	8.0	67	72
7	5.3	68	33
8	4.0	66	33
9	7.2	65	31
10	4.9	64	47
11	5.9	58	51
12	4.0	55	7
		Group II	
1	7.2	76	33
2	5.2	78	24
3	6.2	75	51
4	6.8	74	60
5	5.4	73	55
6	6.8	70	43
7	4.2	66	16
8	6.4	63	31
9	5.9	62	71
10	3.6	62	14
11	5.2	56	29

2. Recognizing that the samples in this practice problem are probably too small to demonstrate that the requisite assumptions for multiple-classification analysis of covariance have been satisfied, compute the F values for the two

main effects (*A* and *B*) as well as the interaction of the two main effects
($A \times B$). Let *Y* represent the criterion variable and X_1 and X_2 the control
variables. Decide whether any of the null hypotheses associated with the
three *F* values should be rejected.

	Subject	A_1 X_1	X_2	Y	Subject	A_2 X_1	X_2	Y
	a	5	9	9	k	5	8	9
	b	5	9	6	l	4	6	9
	c	4	9	6	m	4	6	9
	d	4	8	5	n	3	7	9
B_1	e	4	8	5	o	3	5	8
	f	3	6	4	p	2	4	8
	g	3	7	4	q	1	4	8
	h	2	4	3	r	1	3	7
	i	1	4	2	s	1	3	7
	j	1	7	1	t	1	4	7
	u	7	8	6	ee	8	9	9
	v	6	8	6	ff	6	7	9
	w	6	7	5	gg	6	7	9
	x	5	6	5	hh	5	6	9
	y	5	7	4	ii	4	8	8
B_2	z	4	5	4	jj	4	2	8
	aa	4	4	4	kk	4	2	7
	bb	4	5	3	ll	4	2	7
	cc	2	5	3	mm	4	4	7
	dd	2	2	3	nn	4	3	6

SELECTED READINGS

Blalock, Hubert M., Jr., *Social Statistics*. New York: McGraw-Hill, 1960, chap. 20.

Edwards, Allen L., *Experimental Design in Psychological Research*. New York: Holt,
Rinehart & Winston, 1960, chap. 16.

Johnson, Palmer O., and Robert W. B. Jackson, *Modern Statistical Methods: Descriptive
and Inductive*. Chicago: Rand McNally, 1959, pp. 410–424.

Wert, James E., Charles O. Neidt, and J. Stanley Ahmann, *Statistical Methods in Educational and Psychological Research*. New York: Appleton-Century-Crofts, 1954,
chap. 18.

17

Some
Considerations
In
The
Use
of
Analysis
of
Variance
Procedures

Perhaps one of the major sources of confusion leading to the misuse and misinterpretation of analysis of variance (anova) procedures is the traditional association of anova procedures with *experimental design*. Almost every popular introductory text on anova procedures for the behavioral sciences has the phrase "experimental design" (or some variation) in its title. (See Selected Readings.) Although many of these are excellent textbooks on the subject containing many of the design considerations in the present chapter, the beginning student tends to lose sight of the fact that anova is a statistical tool whereas experimental design is a set of research considerations, that is, definition of experimental units, random selection of units, random assignment of units to treatment conditions, identification of important independent and dependent variables, and so forth. Some or all of these considerations have a direct bearing on three major design concepts: The *validity* of the statistical procedures and the *sensitivity* and *generalizability* of the data analysis and results. Before discussing these concepts in more detail, however, it will be helpful to briefly discuss the distinction between experimental and nonexperimental research designs in education.

EXPERIMENTAL AND EX POST FACTO ANOVA DESIGNS

Although the distinctions are not always apparent, it has been instructive to classify educational research into at least five categories: *historical*, *descriptive* (survey), *predictive* (correlational), *ex post facto*, and *experimental*.[1] Anova designs are typically employed as the quantitative methodology in the latter two types of research; and from a statistical viewpoint, the analysis in ex post facto studies is indistinguishable from that in experimental studies. The re-

[1] I. Lehman, and W. Mehrens, *Educational Research: Readings in Focus*, New York: Holt, Rinehart & Winston, 1971.

search design considerations as well as the kinds of inferences that can be made are, however, markedly different.

In ex post facto designs, the levels of the factors exist "after the fact," that is, the experimental units belong to the levels by definition. Thus, the researcher cannot assign experimental units at random to the levels of the factor. Some examples of factors which might be found in ex post facto designs where students are the experimental units are sex (levels = male; female), race/ethnicity (levels = black; white; yellow; brown; red). Clearly, the researcher is not able to randomly assign students to the levels of any of these factors. Such factors are often referred to as organismic or selection factors.

In experimental designs, however, levels of the factors do not preclude what experimental units can be assigned to them. These factors are often referred to as *treatment* factors, in so far as the levels constitute different treatments, and the researcher has control over which experimental units receive (are assigned) which treatments. Some examples of factors which might be found in experimental designs are type of programmed instruction (levels = branched; linear); drug dosage (levels = high, medium, low), instructional method (levels = inductive; deductive).

It should be clear that the crucial concept distinguishing the two types of design is that of *randomization*. This concept also lies at the heart of the distinction between causal and noncausal inferences. Consider, for example, a one-way anova design with two experimental levels: teaching methods 1 and 2. Suppose students are randomly assigned to either method and are measured on some achievement variable. Consider, also, the same situation with one exception—instead of "teaching method," the factor is "sex," having the levels males and females. In the former case, we can logically attribute significant differences in achievement between the two groups to the differences in teaching method. In the latter case, we can only infer whether a significant relationship exists—not its causal directionality. That is, significant differences in achievement between the groups could not only be attributed to sex differences, but to many other unknown (in the sense that they were not included in the study) variables related to sex differences.

Because of these distinctions, research designs other than experimental have often been referred to as *correlational*. (Recall that: "Correlation does not imply causation.") We prefer not to use this terminology, however, since establishing the relationship between the dependent and independent variables lies at the heart of any research design. The implication of causation depends on the nature of the independent variable or factor and whether it is experimental or ex post facto.[2]

Even the use of the experimental–nonexperimental design terminology is

[2]Although randomization is a logical guarantee for causal interpretations, there are methods for increasing the *plausibility* of causal interpretations when randomization has not occurred. This methodology is generally referred to as *path analysis*. See, for example, H. Blalock, *Causal Inferences in Nonexperimental Research*, Chapel Hill, N.C: University of North Carolina Press, 1961.

troublesome in view of the fact that most research designs include both experimental and ex post facto variables. An example would be a study investigating the effect of multiple-choice versus short-answer items on achievement test performance of high, middle, and low ability students. Ideally, students would be randomly assigned to either of the treatment conditions (multiple-choice or short-answer item tests) *within* the ability groupings. Then, the variance of the resulting test scores could be analyzed using a 3×2 factorial design.

Finally, we point to the use of the word "ideally" in the preceding paragraph, with respect to randomization in experimental designs. Many times (if not most) the researcher does not have the flexibility to randomly assign experimental units (students, classrooms, etc.) to treatment conditions. In this case, the procedures and resulting inferences are not truly experimental in nature. These designs are often referred to as *quasi-experimental*.[3]

VALIDITY, SENSITIVITY AND GENERALIZABILITY

Authors writing about research design have used the terms *validity*, *sensitivity*, and *generalizability* to signify a variety of concepts. For example, Campbell and Stanley (see footnote 3) use the term validity, in part, to stand for representativeness or generalizability. Their distinction between internal and external validity is a valuable one and the student is strongly advised to read Campbell and Stanley's small, but important, volume.

The intent here is not to provide universal definitions for validity, sensitivity, and generalizability, but simply to use these terms for the several specific concepts we wish to clarify.

VALIDITY

The term validity is used here in reference to potential violations of the mathematical and logical bases upon which anova procedures and resulting statistical conclusions rest. In other words, asking a question about validity is asking the question "Can I be sure that this so-called F value is really a statistic with a sampling distribution given by the F Table in the back of my book and with the degrees of freedom I think I have?" To the extent that the answer is no, the resulting probabilities (or levels of significance) that you read from the Table may be in error—the statistical decisions you make may be based more on illusion than fact.

Statistical Assumptions

Investigating the validity of an anova is a matter of looking for possible violations of the statistical assumptions detailed in Chapters 11 and 13. The assumptions of normality and homogeneity of variance can, themselves, be statistically tested; and, as was indicated in these chapters, anova is fairly "robust" with respect to violations of these assumptions. Ideally, the researcher

---

[3]For a detailed discussion see D. Campbell and J. Stanley, *Experimental and Quasi-Experimental Designs for Research*. Chicago: Rand McNally, 1963.

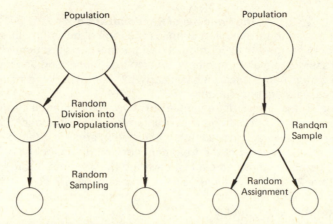

Figure 17.1   *Two equivalent conceptualizations of the process of randomization.*

pilot tests the dependent variables to investigate the shape and variability of their distributions.

The assumption of random sampling cannot be statistically tested—it is satisfied or not satisfied by the research design. Whereas the normality and homogeneity of variance assumptions guarantee the mathematical basis of the statistical tests, the random sampling assumption guarantees the logical basis of the test. That is, if our set of data was not one of any number of possible random sets of data, then our F statistic is not one of any number of possible F statistics; and using the F distribution as a sampling distribution to generate probability values would make no sense.

The concepts of *random sampling* and *randomization* (random assignment) are frequently confused as a result of their being interchanged often as the third anova assumption. Clearly, the confusion occurs because of the distinction between ex post facto and experimental factors. For example, if the factor is sex, we can easily conceptualize two distinct populations (male and female) from which we can obtain random samples. In this case, of course, no randomization takes place. (We have previously conceptualized this process in Chapter 9, Figure 9.4.)

If, on the other hand, the factor is "format of programmed text" (branching vs. linear), the conceptualization of two populations and random sampling is not immediately obvious. We first, however, conceptualize *the* population of subjects (or, in general, experimental units) to which we wish to generalize the anova results. Then we randomly split the population into two "treatment" populations. Finally, the inductive and deductive groups in our experiment are conceptualized as *random samples* from each of the treatment populations. Except in this case, random sampling implicitly randomized subjects between experimental conditions by definition of the original "treatment" populations. Figure 17.1 graphically portrays these concepts of randomization.

The Principle of Randomization

As pointed out, random sampling supplies the logical basis for valid inference in ex post facto designs. In experimental designs this basis is ultimately supplied by random assignment of experimental units to treatment conditions. The power of randomization can be seen most clearly by eliminating the need for conceptualizing treatment populations.

Consider the previous example of two experimental programmed-instruction text book formats on a curriculum unit in arithmetic. Suppose we have 20 subjects *available* (*not* sampled) for the experiment. We then randomly assign 10 subjects to each of the treatment conditions (branched or linear formats); and, using an achievement test covering the arithmetic content, we ultimately obtain 20 scores for analysis. A simple one-way anova yields an *F* statistic (on 1 and 18 *df*) which can be used to compare the mean performances of the two experimental groups.

But nowhere have we performed any random sampling. To what population, then, are we making any inference? The answer lies in the fact that we randomized subjects over treatment conditions. The "population" is all possible randomizations of the subjects (and their scores) that could have occurred under the null hypothesis of no treatment differences.

In other words, the randomization process implicitly created a sampling distribution of *F* statistics to which our particular *F* statistic belongs. We have 10 scores in each of two conditions. (See Table 17.1.) Given (a) the null hypothesis of no treatment differences and (b) the fact that we randomized subjects across treatments, we could have had, say, John's score of 18 in treatment condition B (instead of A) and Mary's score of 6 in condition A (instead of B). In fact any of the possible 184,756 rearrangements of the 10 scores in conditions A and B could have occurred.[4] In addition, we could compute the anova and resulting F statistics for each of the 184,756 possible arrangements. The set of 184,756 statistics constitutes our sampling distribution and includes our originally computed statistic.

The significance test is merely the way of determining the probability of the occurrence of our original statistic in the sampling distribution we empirically generated. We could compute this probability directly from the sampling distribution.

At this point, the reader may be wondering if all possible randomizations of data have to be analyzed every time he conducts an experiment. The answer is no, because of the following: It can be shown that sampling distributions empirically created like that above, always have the approximate properties of an *F* distribution.[5] In other words, the distribution of the 184,756 statistics

---

[4]The number of possible arrangement is determined by asking the question "In how many ways can we combine 20 scores taking 10 at a time?" Students familiar with combinatorial arithmetic will recognize the answer to be $20!/10!10! = (1 \cdot 2 \cdot 3 \cdots 20)/(1 \cdot 2 \cdot 3 \cdots 10)(1 \cdot 2 \cdot 3 \cdots 10) = 184,756$.

[5]See E. J. G. Pitman, "Significance tests which may be applied to samples of any population. III. Analysis of variance test." *Biometrika* **29** (1937): 322–325.

Table 17.1
Data for Programmed Instruction Experiment

Treatment	
Branching Format (A)	Linear Format (B)
18	11
8	4
20	12
17	5
9	13
17	13
7	6
7	12
19	5
9	4
Treatment Means	
13.1	8.5

Table 17.2
One-Way Anova for the Programmed Instruction Data of Table 17.1

Source	SS	df	MS	F
Treatments	105.80	1	105.80	4.61
Within (error)	413.40	18	22.97	

computed is closely approximated by an *F* distribution on 1 and 18 degrees of freedom. The test of significance is thus performed as usual, by looking up the original *F*-statistic in the *F* table at the back of any statistics book. (See Table 17.2)

We see, then, that in the case of experimental factors, *randomization* is the *sine qua non* for the validity of the statistical test. We need not worry about normality and homogeneity of variance assumptions, nor conceptualize a population and a random sampling process.

Selection of Experimental Units

In most of our examples of experimental designs we have used subjects or individuals as the experimental units. Unfortunately, there has occurred a subtle equation of experimental unit with individual students in much of educational research design. Many times anova procedures have been applied to scores obtained by individuals when they should have been applied to scores obtained by groups of individuals. It might be argued that the choice of experimental unit is not a topic for discussion in a section on "Validity," insofar as the anova procedures per se are immune to the meaningfulness of the data. However, the choice of experimental unit has a direct bearing upon the number of degrees of freedom in the anova and, consequently, the appropriate F-distribution for the test of significance.

Consider the following experimental design where a researcher wishes to compare the effects of presenting a certain instructional material using a series of slides versus using a film. Suppose there are 30 students in each group and they are given an achievement test at the conclusion of either the slide or film presentation. If each student was treated as the experimental unit, the anova would yield an F-value based on 1 and 58 df.

Unfortunately, the experimental unit is the smallest *independently treated* unit, which in this case, is clearly the *group*. This can be seen by considering what sources of variance will absorb the various uncontrolled effects of treatment malfunctions. For example, suppose the film broke 3 minutes into the presentation for the film group and 5 minutes were lost due to splicing and reloading. This would affect all 30 students simultaneously and, in that sense, the variability resulting from the breakdown would be reflected in the difference between treatments. The film treatment would virtually be redefined as "film plus 5-minute breakdown".

On the other hand, if the treatments were administered to each student separately in his own cubicle (complete with its own projection system), any given breakdown would be reflected in the variability among individuals *within* treatment conditions, that is, error variance. Only then could the individual be regarded as the experimental unit.

Since the group, then, is the appropriate unit for analysis, our researcher is left with but one observation in each treatment condition, namely, the mean achievement test score for the 30 students in each condition. He needs at least two such mean scores in each treatment group before he has any variance to analyze. If he did, he would obtain an F statistic on 1 and 2 df — quite a change in df from the analysis using the student as the experimental unit.

The choice of appropriate experimental units is perhaps one of the most difficult research design problems facing the educational researcher. Many times, two (or more) instructional methods are to be compared and the researcher is fortunate to gain the cooperation of two (or more) *classes*, one for each method of instruction. If the class is the appropriate unit of analysis, the researcher needs at least two more classes in order to perform the anova. In fact, depending upon the expected variability between classes, the researcher may want ten to fifteen classes for each instructional method. Given usual time, staff, and other economic restrictions prevalent in most educational systems, such allocation of resources would often be extremely difficult — if not impossible.

The point to keep in mind is this: The researcher must be aware of the decision-making purpose for which the experiment is intended and, in particular, the unit receiving the direct impact of decisions made. If it is clear that the individual student is the focus of attention, then every effort should be made to experimentally treat individuals. For example, comparing programmed-instruction text A with programmed-instruction text B, each student *should* be administered the materials on an individual basis. It may be more feasible, however, to administer the treatments to intact classrooms. In this case, where the treatments are clearly individually oriented, we suggest that the researcher can still analyze his data meaningfully on an individual score basis so long as he (1) interprets statistical probabilities with caution and (2) maintains detailed anecdotal records regarding all unintended (nontreatment-related) events occurring in the classes that could potentially contribute to mean differences between the treatment groups.

SENSITIVITY

Consider again the simple one-way anova design of the branching versus linear programmed instruction formats with 10 students in each of the treatment conditions. The total variability of the 20 arithmetic achievement test scores would be partitioned into two basic sources: the *between* source of variance reflecting the difference between the treatments and the *within* source of variance reflecting the differences between the students within the treatments. (See Table 17.2.) This latter source of variance (often called the error variance) reflects all possible independent variables other than our treatment variable that could conceivably cause individuals to differ on their scores. Any attempt to identify and control these additional sources of variability and therefore decrease the error variability, is an attempt to increase the *sensitivity* of the anova design. Sensitivity is increased when the within group or error variance is decreased, relative to the remaining systematic sources of variance. This kind of increase in sensitivity is directly reflected by the *F*-ratio, since it is the ratio of the mean square for a systematic source of variance to the mean square for the error source of variance. When the denominator decreases relative to the numerator, the ratio (or quotient) increases.

Another way to increase the *F* ratio is to bring about an increase in the numerator (systematic source) while holding the denominator (error source) relatively constant. The easiest way to increase sensitivity in this manner is to increase the sample size, as can be seen in the next section. Following that discussion, we will illustrate those design considerations that directly attempt to reduce error variation.

Sample Size

One way to increase the sensitivity of an anova design without necessarily identifying and controlling additional sources of variability is to increase the sample size, that is, the number of experimental units. From an intuitive point of view, it stands to reason that the more data sampled, the more confidence you can have in believing that the relationships observed in the sample actually occur in the population.

This can be seen more clearly by investigating the effect on the arithmetic of a simple anova table when the sample size is increased while keeping the mean differences and within group variances the same. Suppose we doubled

Table 17.3

One-Way Anova for the Programmed-Instruction Experiment When the Data in Table 17.1 Are Replicated and the Sample Size Doubled

Source	SS	df	MS	F
Treatments	211.60	1	211.60	9.73
Within (error)	826.79	39	21.76	

the number of students in the programmed-instruction experiment such that both the treatment means and within group variance remained the same.[6] In Table 17.3, we see the effect of doubling the sample size. First, the *df* for error are more than doubled resulting in a substantial decrease in the critical *F*-value needed for statistical significance. Second, the MS for the treatment source of variance is greatly increased while that for the within source remains almost the same. (Actually, the SS for the within source is doubled while the *df* are slightly more than doubled; thus, the MS for the within source is slightly less than it was originally.) The net effect, of course, is to substantially increase the *F* ratio. In this particular case, we can see that whereas the mean difference of 4.6 based on 20 cases was not significant at the 0.01 level, that same difference based on 40 cases reached significance beyond the 0.01 level.

The reader might well wonder how useful the whole notion of inference can be, if one can construct any mean difference to be significant given a large enough sample size. But remember that (1) if sampling resources were unlimited, one might as well measure every experimental unit in the population thereby eliminating the need for any inferential procedure and (2) although any mean difference could be found to be statistically significant given the right conditions, only some mean differences are large enough to be *meaningfully* considered. Again, statistical significance does not necessarily imply substantive meaningfulness.

A good anova design will contain a statement on how large a treatment difference will be considered meaningful in terms of the research content under investigation. In addition, the researcher should be able to state the maximum Type I error he is willing to risk, that is, the level of statistical significance he wishes to reach. Finally, if an estimate of the within group variance is available (e.g., from pilot testing of the dependent variable), formulas exist whereby the minimum sample size can be determined, necessary to realize the statistical significance of the desired mean differences at the desired probability level. The reader may consult any of the texts on experimental design listed at the end of the chapter for further discussion.

[6]Although this would never happen in reality, the mean treatment differences and variability among individuals within treatments would remain relatively constant to the extent that the original sample was random and representative of the population.

Table 17.4
Reorganization of the Data in Table 17.1 to Include High- and Low-Ability Blocks

| | | Treatments | | |
		Branching	Linear	Means
Ability Levels	High	18	11	
		20	12	
		17	13	15.2
		17	13	
		19	12	
	Low	8	4	
		9	5	
		7	6	6.4
		7	5	
		9	4	
	Means	13.1	8.5	

Blocking

Given a reasonably sized sample of experimental units, the best and most useful way of increasing the sensitivity of an experimental design is by identifying the important additional sources of variability and then incorporating these sources as additional factors into the experimental design. Suppose, for example, in the programmed-instruction experiment that the researcher had good reason to suspect that initial level of general, quantitative ability would substantially contribute to individual differences. Furthermore, suppose the researcher was wise enough to recognize this fact before conducting the experiment and he (1) determined those students in his sample who were high or low in quantitative ability, say 10 high-ability students and 10 low-ability students, and (2) assigned 5 students in each ability grouping *at random* to each of the treatment groups.

Now, consider the anova results in Table 17.2. The one-way analysis "hides" the potential two-way analysis, namely, the ability-by-treatment, 2×2 factorial design. The "hiding" occurs in the error or within source of variance insofar as the SS and 1 *df* for the ability grouping main effect and the SS and 1 *df* for the interaction of ability and treatment factors are included, respectively, in the SS and *df* for the within source of variance. This becomes clear when we reorganize the data of Table 17.1 in the 2×2 design (see Table 17.4). When this new design is analysed (see Table 17.5), we note the decrease in error mean square and increase in design sensitivity inasmuch as the mean difference between the linear- and branched-format treatment groups is now significant well beyond the 0.01 level.

Table 17.5
Two-Way Anova for the Programmed-Instruction Data of Table 17.4

Source	SS	df	MS	F
Treatments (T)	105.80	1	105.80	103.24
Blocks (B)	387.20	1	387.20	377.83
T × B	9.80	1	9.80	9.56
Within (Error)	16.40	16	1.02	

In addition, the researcher has bought[7] two extra hypotheses which may or may not be of substantive interest. The mean difference between high- and low-ability groups is not surprising in light of their definition. The difference does, however, support the researcher's decision to include the ability factor for the purpose of increasing sensitivity. On the other hand, the interaction (although insignificant here) could have been of theoretical interest, that is, it would not be unreasonable to hypothesize that low-ability students will profit more from the less complicated linear-programmed format whereas high-ability students will perform better using the more stimulating branched-programmed sequence.

Blocking as a means for increasing sensitivity is usually discussed under the heading of *randomized block designs* in most textbooks of experimental design. This has often led to some confusion, however, because anova procedures are basically no different than those under the heading of *factorial designs*. When a factor has been introduced in the design for the purpose of increasing its sensitivity, it is usually conceptualized as a blocking factor and, as such, is a nonexperimental factor; when a factor is present for research purposes, it is usually not regarded as a blocking factor and can be either experimental or nonexperimental. Perhaps the concept of blocking would have been better illustrated in this example using a factor called "classrooms," where we would envision the linear-branching treatment programs applied across, say, four classrooms at a given grade level in a given school. Within each classroom, students would be *randomly* assigned to the treatment conditions. The resulting data would then be analysed as a 4 × 2 factorial design.

Analysis of Covariance (Ancova)

Analysis of covariance has already been discussed in detail in Chapters 15 and 16 from the viewpoint of statistically eliminating one or more sources of bias in the interpretation of group differences. Here, we discuss the technique of analysing the variance of statistically adjusted scores with a view toward increasing sensitivity. To the extent that the researcher makes a judicious selection of covariables, the error term will generally be reduced relative to the sys-

---

[7]The unit of monetary exchange might be conceptualized as degrees of freedom.

Table 17.6
Analysis of Covariance for the Programmed-Instruction Data of Table 17.1

Source	SS	df	MS	F
Treatments	105.80	1	105.80	68.65
Within (Error)	26.20	17	1.54	

tematic sources of variance. For every covariable used in the analysis one degree of freedom is removed from the error term.

Consider again the programmed-instruction experiment. Instead of blocking on ability level, we could have performed an ancova using the general-ability measure as a covariable. In other words, the continuous arithmetic ability variable, used previously to arrive at the high–low classification, would now be used to statistically adjust the criterion, arithmetic achievement-test scores. Even as gross a scoring system as 1 for high ability and 0 for low ability students can illustrate the effect that analysis of covariance can have on sensitivity. (See Table 17.6.) Since the experiment was originally balanced in terms of ability, the adjusted treatment means are identical to the unadjusted means. Yet the adjusted ratio of the systematic to unsystematic variance is now significant well beyond the 0.01 level.

The question arises "When should one use blocking as a technique for increasing sensitivity rather than analysis of covariance?" We take the position here that the answer be "Always, except when not possible." We recommend "always" in view of the following considerations:

1. Anova assumptions are more robust in contrast to those of ancova, especially in regard to the homogeneity of regression assumption needed in ancova. In fact, the violation of this assumption implies the existence of an interaction between the covariable and one or more treatment factors—an interaction which can easily be accounted for when the covariable is included as a blocking factor in the anova design.
2. Nonlinear relationships between covariable and dependent variable cannot be handled by conventional ancova techniques, whereas the validity of blocking is not bound by any functional relationship.
3. The analysis is more straightforward with more easily interpreted results and more potentially interpretable information (additional main effects and interactions).
4. For most anova designs used in education, nearly all the information contained in a given covariable can usually be accounted for in three to five blocks.[8]

[8]Optimal numbers of blocking levels for various design conditions have been determined by L. Feldt. "A Comparison of the Precision of Three Experimental Designs Employing a Concomitant Variable." *Psychometrika* **23** (1958): 335–354.

5. The analysis of covariance is logically incapable of "equating" nonexperimental or ex post facto groups.

On the other hand, given randomization across treatment conditions, ancova may prove to be the only viable analytical technique for the following reasons:

1. It is not possible to meaningfully determine discrete blocks from a continuous covariable.
2. Even though blocks may be meaningfully determined, the researcher may not be able to randomize subjects *within* blocks before the actual experimental treatment. As a result, some cells of the blocks-by-treatment design may contain too few subjects for a valid anova.

GENERALIZABILITY

The concept of generalizability, refers to the "size" and "quality" of the "span" of inference that the researcher can make with his data. Interpreted broadly, generalizability pertains to questions of representativeness and replicability on at least three fronts: the independent variables or factors; the dependent variables or criterion measures; and the experimental units (students, classes, schools, etc.) used in the anova design. The present discussion will be restricted only to those issues concerning the experimental units and the population from which they were sampled. Equally important issues such as confounding of experimental treatments, maturation and mortality of subjects, pretest contamination, unreliability of measurement,[9] and so forth, are explicated at great length in the aforementioned work by Campbell and Stanley. (See especially the section entitled "Factors Jeopardizing Internal and External Validity.")

Random Sampling and Randomization

We have discussed the processes of random sampling and randomization as necessary conditions for the logical validity of nonexperimental and experimental designs respectively. Implicit in that discussion was the concept of *generalizability*, the intent on the part of the researcher to make statements about some larger set of experimental units using the results obtained from a subset of these units. The logical basis for this process of generalization rests upon the *random sampling* of the subset of units. (The quality of generalizability can, of course, be improved by allowing chance to operate within a structured, representative framework as in *stratified*, random sampling.)

Thus, in nonexperimental designs (males–females; retarded–normal; high–middle–low achievers; etc.) the guarantee for logical validity serves also as the basis for generalizability. If the researcher has no interest in extrapolating

---

[9]It should be noted that many of these additional sources of variance can be expected to contribute to within-cell variability and are thus important considerations in the *sensitivity* of an anova design.

from his data (i.e., his "sample" *is* his population), then he has no need for anova or any other inferential technique.

On the other hand, in experimental designs, the basis for logical validity (randomization) has no direct bearing on generalizability. Turning once more to the programmed-instruction experiment, the researcher can make a valid probability statement concerning the observed mean difference even if he considers his "sample" to be his population. If, however, he intends to generalize beyond his sample, no amount of random assignment to treatment conditions will help; he must, strictly speaking, have randomly sampled from the target population.

We have used the phrase "strictly speaking" often in this text. We reiterate here that the educational researcher is often at the mercy of his data, not being able to randomize subjects across treatment conditions or to randomly sample subjects from well-defined populations, yet he must try to make valid comparisons with general implications. We advocate that the researcher is entitled to the power of statistical methodology so long as he is well aware that many of his probability statements must be qualified with phrases such as "assuming the sample at hand is not unlike that which would have been obtained had it been randomly sampled from the population of interest." Perhaps we are distinguishing here between that branch of scientific endeavor known as *mathematical statistics* and another, named by a colleague, *heuristic statistics*.[10]

SOME ADDITIONAL CONSIDERATIONS

In this section we allude to several concepts and issues which until now we have avoided. The following discussions are intended to clue the reader into the existence of these issues and then direct him to more definitive sources.

Fixed, Random, and Mixed Models

All the examples and procedures for anova which have been illustrated thus far have contained only *fixed* factors. Factors having levels such as males versus females; inductive teaching versus deductive teaching; high versus middle versus low achievement groups; and so forth are *fixed* insofar as (1) the levels have not been sampled from a potentially larger set of levels and (2) the researcher does not intend to generalize his result beyond the levels of his included factors. Often in educational research designs, a blocking factor such as schools has levels corresponding to only a small number of the available target population of schools. A researcher investigating the relative merits of traditional and modern algebra textbooks may wish to generalize his results to all schools in a large local district. If he only has the resources for conducting his study at, say, four schools, he can choose them at random introducing a 4-level *random factor* to the design. The anova computations remain unchanged until the point of constructing the appropriate *F*-ratios since, when random factors are present, the within-groups variation is not always the appropriate

[10]Dr. Maxine Bentzen.

error term. Anova designs can contain all fixed, all random, or both fixed and random factors (*mixed* models); the procedures for determining correct error terms can be found in all the more advanced texts listed in the section of Selected Readings.

A Priori and Post Hoc Comparisons

Consider a simple one-way design with 5 levels: 3 treatment groups and 2 control groups. The procedures outlined in chapters 11 and 12 are designed to yield an *F* ratio which answers the question "Are there significant differences among the treatment means?" If the ratio is significant, we usually want to ask the next question "*Where* are these significant differences?" A descriptive analysis of the mean differences can be misleading: "Is the significant *F* ratio merely due to the discrepancy between the highest and lowest treatment means? . . . Is it due to the discrepancy between the combined effect of the 3 treatment groups and that of the 2 control groups?"

When the researcher hypothesizes these comparisons at the outset (*a priori*) he can extend the anova computations to include *specific mean contrasts*, each of which can be tested for significance. If he wishes to investigate mean differences after the fact (*post hoc*), less powerful computational routines exist to systematically test all possible pairs of treatment differences. Most of the texts mentioned at the end of this chapter contain fairly explicit guidelines for carrying out these comparisons.

Nonorthogonal Designs

All the anova designs containing two or more factors that we have considered have contained the same number of experimental units in each cell or treatment combination. When this is the case, or when proportionality exists between the cell sizes on a row-by-row (or column-by-column) basis, the computational procedures presented here are appropriate. When the cell sizes are unequal (or disproportional), these computations would lead to a source table whose sum of squares lacked orthogonality (statistical independence). Since this mathematical property is required to form valid *F*-ratios, other computational procedures (based on least-squares regression) have been developed. The computations are tedious and best left to the computer; but the interested reader can again consult the Selected Reading list.

MULTIVARIATE ANALYSIS OF VARIANCE (MANOVA)

A third complication which we have avoided thus far is the use of more than one dependent variable for any given anova design. More often than not, the educational researcher obtains several cognitive and/or affective (and perhaps even psychomotor) measures in a single research study. In the preceding example, the researcher might have also constructed an attitude questionnaire to assess student sentiment toward programmed instruction, expecting differential results depending upon the format of the program.

It has often been the case that the researcher performs and interprets separate anovas for each of his dependent variables. Unfortunately, these dependent variables are usually intercorrelated, thus "intercorrelating" the separate anovas and rendering their independent interpretations potentially misleading. If student sentiment toward programmed instruction and student ability were substantially correlated, it would not be surprising for the researcher to obtain similar results for both analyses—and it would not be particularly insightful to treat the results as two separate phenomena.

Manova is basically a technique whereby the "generalized" variance (a multidimensional analog of the common, unidimensional variance of a single variable) of two or more dependent variables considered simultaneously is analyzed and partitioned into systematic (main effects and interactions) and unsystematic (error) sources. Ratios of systematic variance to error variance are formed (analogous to the univariate F ratio), so that the significance of main effects and interactions can be determined. When a ratio of this type is significant, the computations can be further extended to determine which dependent variable (or set of dependent variables) contributes most to the significance of the main effect or interaction.

The computations involved in manova are extremely laborious and are best left to the computer. Furthermore, manova has more stringent assumptions regarding the statistical properties of the data than ordinary univariate anova techniques. The educational researcher often finds himself in the familiar position of having access to statistical methodology abounding in sophistication beyond the level of his data. If the researcher does not feel his data warrant the application of manova procedures, he should be at least compelled to interpret his univariate anovas in light of the correlations among his dependent variables. For more insight to manova, see the referenced readings by Bock and/or Tatsuoka.

RESEARCH DESIGNS TO MEASURE CHANGE

The assessment of change is particularly relevant to research in education. Educational principles and practices are investigated not so much in terms of comparing individual measurements at a single point in time, but in terms of comparing individuals on their measured growth (cognitive, affective, and psychomotor) over points in time. In our programmed-instruction experiment, the researcher should be asking the question "Which format results in better student achievement (or attitude) *than was evidenced at the start*?"

Fortunately, the traditional "posttest minus pretest" difference score analysis has been exposed as a simplistic, misleading, and statistically unsound design for the assessment of change.[11] Unfortunately, there is a great deal of controversy and difficulty in determining a useful procedure to take its place. Measuring change is closely related to the concept of sensitivity; each subject being measured more than once functionally serves as his own control, which

[11]L. J. Cronbach and L. Furby, "How Should We Measure 'Change'—Or Should We?" *Psychological Bulletin* **74** (1970): 68–80.

has the net effect of generally reducing appropriate error terms relative to systematic sources.

In fact, perhaps the best way of assessing change in the common pretest–posttest design is to block on the pretest (e.g. high–middle–low pretest-score groups) and incorporate these blocks as a factor in the design. The next best way is to perform an analysis of covariance using the pretest score as the co-variable and the posttest score as the dependent variable. The difference between posttest score and *predicted* posttest score is generally a better growth index than the raw post–minus–prescore difference.

Further complications arise when the individual is repeatedly treated over time. Anova models, commonly referred to as repeated measure designs, exist whereby these effects can be analyzed as well as possible linear and curvilinear trends across treatment means. The conceptual and analytical difficulties and possible methodologies in the assessment of change can be found in Harris' work referenced in Selected Readings.

EXERCISE

A certain state is interested in determining whether or not to adopt either of two new eleventh grade US History textbooks in lieu of the text currently in use. There are 50 school districts in the state; 10 secondary schools in each district; 4 eleventh-grade classes in each school, one teacher for every two classes; and 30 pupils in each class. The state is concerned with learning outcomes on both achievement and attitude dimensions.

Construct an experimental design to help the state make its determination and comment, when applicable, on the following design considerations:

1. Validity
2. Random sampling and/or randomization
3. Sensitivity
4. Generalizability
5. Mixed or fixed models
6. Specific treatment comparisons
7. Nature and number of dependent variables
8. Appropriate experimental units
9. Measurement of change

SELECTED READINGS

Bock, R. D. *Multivariate Statistical Methods in Behavioral Research*. To be published by McGraw-Hill in 1973.

Campbell, D., and J. Stanley, *Experimental and Quasi-Experimental Designs for Research*. Chicago: Rand-McNally, 1963. (Reprinted from *Handbook of Research on Teaching*, American Educational Research Association.)

Dayton, C. M. *The Design of Educational Experiments*. New York: McGraw-Hill, 1970.

Harris, C. W. *Problems in Measuring Change*. Madison: The University of Wisconsin Press, 1967.

Kempthorne, O. *The Design and Analysis of Experiments*. New York: Wiley, 1952.

Kirk, R. E. *Experimental Design: Procedures for the Behavioral Sciences*. Belmont, Calif.: Brooks/Cole, 1968.

Lindquist, E. F. *Design and Analysis of Experiments in Psychology and Education*. Boston: Houghton Mifflin, 1953.

Myers, J. L. *Fundamentals of Experimental Design*. Boston: Allyn and Bacon, 1966.

Tatsuoka, M. M. *Multivariate Analysis: Techniques for Educational and Psychological Research*. New York: Wiley, 1971.

Winer, B. J. *Statistical Principles in Experimental Design* (2nd ed.). New York: McGraw-Hill, 1962.

18
Factor
Analysis

With increasing frequency one encounters reports of *factor analysis* studies in educational research. The complexities of the factor analytic approach, unfortunately, prohibit an exhaustive description in this volume. Yet, those who would use the literature of educational research should understand enough about factor analysis so that they will comprehend the significance of this important tool and will not be intimidated when factor analytic terms such as "factor loadings" and "orthogonal-axes rotation" are used in educational research reports. The purpose of this chapter is to provide the reader with an extremely brief introduction to factor analysis so that he may gain a general notion of its role in educational research. In addition, hopefully, the reader will wish to pursue the topic further in more technical volumes.

Function

Factor analysis provides the researcher with a statistical tool for analyzing scores on a large number of variables in order to determine whether there are a few identifiable dimensions which can be used to describe many of the variables under analysis. In this technique the term "factor" has much the same meaning as in common speech, namely, a cause or influence which is in some measure responsible for a given phenomenon. In the case of factor analysis, a collection of intercorrelations is treated mathematically in such a way that several underlying traits, or factors, are identified and analyzed, hence giving rise to the descriptive phrase, factor analysis. It may be helpful to think of factor analysis as nothing more than an aid to the study of a table of correlations.

Starting with an elementary example, suppose a measurement specialist is working with data drawn from six subscores on an achievement examination, prepared jointly by a group of high-school social studies teachers. The teachers assert that all six parts of the test are measuring basically different achievement dimensions. Having administered the examination to a group of

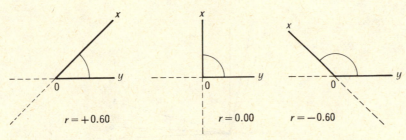

Figure 18.1 *Three correlation coefficients expressed as angles.*

students, the data are turned over to the measurement expert who quickly computes the fifteen possible intercorrelations between the six subscores. The first three subscores are highly correlated with each other but not with the other three subscores which, interestingly enough, are correlated strongly with each other.

The measurement specialist concludes that the first three parts of the test are measuring essentially the same thing, and the last three are all measuring something which is different from that measured by the first three parts. From inspection of the test items he determines that the first three parts are concerned with the student's verbal ability, and the last three parts are based on the student's mathematical ability. These two common "factors" are identified by the measurement expert as verbal ability and quantitative ability. He suggests to social studies teachers that they consider the achievement examination to be composed of only two really distinct parts.

The foregoing is an illustration of how a few underlying factors can be used to explain a number of intercorrelations between variables. It is evident that with more variables or with a situation not quite so clear-cut as the preceding example, a more sophisticated method of identifying such factors would be needed. Factor analysis is a procedure designed to deal with this problem.

Rationale

Although to understand fully the mathematical rationale of factor analysis the reader would need to consult one or more of the comprehensive references listed at the close of the chapter, some insight into the inner workings of these techniques may be provided through the following discussion based on a geometric method of exposition.

Correlation Coefficient as Angles. One way of viewing correlation is to consider the size of the angle formed by the lines of best fit which represent the two variables in standard score form. These "best fit" lines are the regression lines of $\bar{Y}$ on X and of $\bar{X}$ on Y. In Figure 18.1 three different correlation coefficients, expressed as angles, are presented. Note that the size of the acute angle on the left indicates a positive correlation, the right angle in the center indicates a correlation of zero, and the obtuse angle of the right indicates a negative

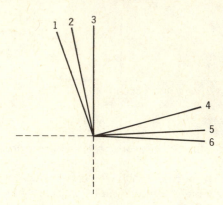

Figure 18.2 *Geometric representation of six achievement test part scores.*

correlation. In other words, up to 90°, the smaller the size of the angle between the two lines, or *vectors*, as they are usually called, the stronger is the *positive* relationship between the two variables. Beyond 90°, the relationship between the two variables becomes stronger *negatively* as the angle nears 180°.

If the previous example regarding six examination subscores will be recalled, we might find such a set of relationships depicted geometrically as in Figure 18.2, where the six parts of the test are represented as vectors. Note that three of the subscores, because of the small angles between them, are highly related to each other but not to the other three subscores. Now, if in Figure 18.2 we were to superimpose heavy lines, where the vertical and horizontal axes are located, we could use these as *factors and describe the six subscores by identifying the relationship of each to these two basic factors*. As we shall see, the size of the correlation of any variable and a factor is generally called the variable's *loading* on the factor.

Hyperspace.   As long as the intercorrelations between the variables fall nicely into place as in the preceding example, we can represent geometrically the relationships in ordinary two-dimensional space. Unfortunately, however, this is practically never the case. For example, contrast the two situations, each involving three variables, presented in Figure 18.3. On the left is presented a situation capable of being described in two-dimensional space. The particular relationships of the top of the figure can be arranged as seen on the bottom of the figure. On the right, however, the three relationships depicted on the top of the figure must result in the *three*-dimensional arrangement seen in the bottom of the figure. In other words, the three relationships in the left can be described on a flat surface, but the three relationships at the right defy such two-dimensional representation. The angles simply cannot be forced into a single two-dimensional plane.

In behavioral science research the relationships among variables are

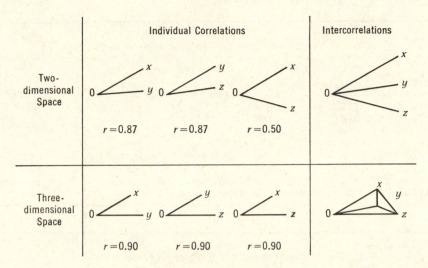

Figure 18.3 *Geometric representations and intercorrelations requiring two-dimensional space and three-dimensional space.*

usually such that the intercorrelations cannot be depicted even in three dimensions. Indeed, it is extremely rare to find *n* tests which can be represented in less than *n* dimensions. Rather, a multidimensional concept known as *hyperspace* can be used to describe intercorrelations between variables, since the sizes of the angles are such that they will not fit together in two- or three-dimensional space. The *hyperspace* concept is difficult to explain intuitively, but the reader may be able to comprehend its meaning by generalizing from the situation arising in Figure 18.3 when space for three dimensions was required. Add a fourth variable whose relationship with the other three is such that it cannot be described in the figure, thus, four-dimensional hyperspace is required.

Regardless of the number of planes or dimensions required to handle the various intercorrelations, the basis of factor-analysis principles holds true, that is, underlying factors are sought which can be used to describe or explain several "clustered" or strongly related variables.

The Correlation Matrix.   Without going into any detail, the factor analyst's first computational step is to set up a table of intercorrelations (all possible correlations) among the measures involved in the analysis. This table, known as the *correlation matrix*, is then treated by one of several mathematical procedures, such as the *centroid* or *principal-axes* methods, in order to produce a single factor which may be used to account for certain of the intercorrelations in the matrix. Once more the correlation matrix is analyzed until a second, then a third factor is produced, and so on until most of the intercorrelations of the variables can be explained or described in terms of the extracted factors.

For example, suppose a researcher is treating a battery of five different

Table 18.1

Correlation Matrix for Five Personality Tests

Test	Test 1	2	3	4	5
1	1.00	0.56	0.38	0.11	−0.19
2	0.56	1.00	0.32	−0.07	0.06
3	0.38	0.32	1.00	0.36	0.22
4	0.11	−0.07	0.36	1.00	0.49
5	−0.19	0.06	0.22	0.49	1.00

SOURCE: Adapted from J. P. Guilford, Personality, McGraw-Hill, Book Company, Inc., New York, 1959, p. 94, with the permission of the publisher.

Table 18.2

Factor Matrix for Five Personality Tests

Test	Factor Loadings I	II	III	IV
1	0.77	0.04	0.15	−0.07
2	0.45	0.29	0.19	−0.20
3	0.29	0.40	0.46	0.24
4	−0.06	0.74	0.22	0.37
5	0.02	0.46	0.09	0.25

SOURCE: Adapted from J. P. Guilford, Personality, McGraw-Hill Book Company, Inc., New York, 1959, p. 94, with the permission of the publisher.

personality tests to see what common factors seem to underlie the tests. Perhaps he can then develop a new test which will focus exclusively on these underlying factors.

First he must compute all of the possible correlations and set up a correlation matrix such as that seen in Table 18.1. Next, this matrix is subjected to certain computational operations, usually done by high-speed computers, to produce a set of factors. These factors can be used to describe the various tests by indicating the relationship or loading of the test on the factor. A *factor matrix* is then set up with the various factor loadings or correlations of each test with each factor. In the present example, four factors were extracted from the correlation matrix and are seen in the factor matrix presented in Table 18.2.

Factor Rotation. Once the factors have been identified, there is still another major problem facing the factor analyst; that of *rotating* the factors in hyperspace until a more satisfactory positioning of the factors has been found.

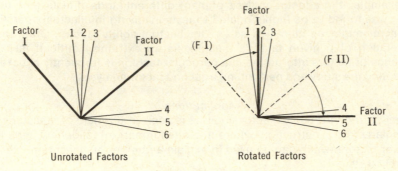

Figure 18.4 *Unrotated and rotated factors for six achievement test part scores.*

Actually, the position of the factors as a result of the factor extraction operation is quite arbitrary, and adjustments are definitely required.

The necessity for rotation, as well as the way it functions, can be briefly illustrated by the two-dimensional representation in Figure 18.4 which, the reader may recall, resembles the achievement test scores depicted earlier in Figure 18.1. It is possible that the factor extraction process could leave the two factors depicted by the heavy black line in the positions at the left of the figure. By rotating both factors slightly in a clockwise direction, we increase the strength of the relationship between the factors and the tests clustered near each, as seen at the right in Figure 18.4. Such is the general method by which factor rotation is carried out.

If the factors (or axes) can be rotated and positioned so that each factor vector (in hyperspace) has an angle of 90° with every other factor, that is, there are zero correlations between all factors, then the rotation is described as *orthogonal*. If there are correlations between the various factors, that is, if the angles between factor vectors are not 90°, then the rotation is described as *oblique*. Usually, orthogonal rotation is first attempted. Then, if by using an orthogonal approach no acceptable positioning of factors can be accomplished, the oblique approach is employed.

The rotation operation is extremely complex, and a number of different principles have been advocated for locating the best position of the factor axes. Perhaps the most commonly used is that of *simple structure* which requires, among other things, that no one factor should be related to all of the variables in the analysis. Rather, a simple structure solution would be seen when one factor might influence perhaps a fourth of the variables in the matrix and have essentially zero loadings on the rest of the variables.

Factor Interpretation.   Regardless of the principle used in reaching a decision regarding the location of the factor vectors, once they have been located, they must be interpreted by the factor analyst. The interpretation will depend on the variables to which the various factors are positively or negatively related.

For example, if in a factor analysis of many different kinds of tests, a particular factor was found to be highly related to tests involving intellectual operations, the factor might be identified as an "intellectual ability" factor. Often the interpretation of a given factor's meaning is an extremely difficult task. The existence of factors interpreted in a particular fashion is frequently checked by replicating the study and performing a second factor analysis.

Applications

The most frequent use of factor analysis is seen in the field of measurement, particularly test construction, where it is often important to identify underlying traits or factors which can be used to explain a number of measurements from different tests.

Other applications are often seen in educational research where attempts are made to parsimoniously reduce the number of dimensions needed to explain certain phenomena. For instance, a researcher might try to "boil down" a multiplicity of dimensions of teacher behavior to a few fundamental factors. An example of this type of factor analysis will be presented in the following section.

An Example from Ryans' Teacher Characteristics Study

To illustrate the form in which the reader might encounter the use of factor analysis in research literature, an excerpt is presented from David Ryans' widely quoted study on the *Characteristics of Teachers*. In this investigation teachers and their pupils were observed by individuals using a specially designed classroom observation recording form which listed a number of different dimensions. Ryans wished to reduce these dimensions to a few common factors. The description of the factor analysis for the elementary teachers and pupils, along with the interpretation of the extracted factors, is presented as follows:

> The factor analysis of assessments of elementary teacher behavior . . . was carried out with a sample consisting of third- and fourth-grade teachers from four different communities of 50,000 to 100,000 population. The number of teachers (and classrooms of pupils) observed was 275. All the teachers were women. They varied widely with regard to age, extent of teaching experience, amount and kind of training, socio-economic area in which they taught, and other factors. Each of the teachers was independently observed on different occasions by three, and in one community, four, observers who previously had undergone five weeks' training. Immediately following an observation, each teacher was assessed by the observer on each dimension of the elementary form (twenty-six first-order dimensions) of the Classroom Observation Record. Upon completion of all observation, the data of the several observers were combined to provide a composite assessment for each teacher on each dimension.

Table 18.3

Oblique Factor Matrix Based on Centroid Factors Extracted from the Intercorrelations of Composite Observer Assessments of Elementary Teacher and Pupil Behaviors

Dimension	Factor				
	I	II	III	IV	V
Pupil behavior					
Disinterested–alert	0.30	0.50	0.11	0.08	0.00
Obstructive–constructive	0.16	0.63	−0.07	0.07	0.04
Restrained–participating	0.40	0.10	0.04	0.00	0.18
Rude–self-controlled	−0.01	0.66	0.10	0.16	−0.05
Apathetic–initiating	0.60	0.29	0.05	−0.08	0.02
Dependent–responsible	0.46	0.49	0.19	−0.03	−0.10
Teacher behavior					
Partial–fair	0.11	0.06	0.39	0.30	0.00
Autocratic–democratic	0.42	−0.11	0.35	0.13	−0.01
Aloof (G-responsive)[a]	0.00	−0.09	0.03	0.59	−0.02
Restricted–understanding	0.27	−0.06	0.44	0.24	0.03
Unattractive–attractive	0.00	0.02	0.02	0.03	0.35
Disorganized–systematic	−0.01	0.56	0.12	−0.15	0.28
Inarticulate–fluent	0.00	0.33	−0.04	0.02	0.36
Inflexible–adaptable	0.36	0.02	0.26	0.21	−0.04
Harsh–kindly	0.25	0.08	0.37	0.43	−0.30
Apathetic–alert	0.05	0.08	−0.40	0.23	0.36
Aloof (I-responsive)[b]	−0.02	−0.10	0.05	0.62	−0.01
Stereotyped–original	0.52	0.14	−0.05	−0.03	0.09
Changeable–constant	−0.04	0.54	0.43	−0.10	0.17
Excitable–calm	0.00	0.36	0.58	0.05	0.01
Uncertain–confident	−0.02	0.44	0.08	0.04	0.28
Irresponsible–responsible	0.04	0.60	−0.06	0.03	0.14
Pessimistic–optimistic	0.05	0.04	−0.02	0.53	0.03
Infantile–mature	0.21	0.44	0.04	0.14	−0.04

[a]To group.
[b]To individuals.

Product-moment coefficients...were computed among twenty-four of the dimensions.... The resulting table of inter-correlations was factor-analyzed by the centroid method and both orthogonal and oblique rotations were attempted. Five centroid factors were extracted. Orthogonal rotation of these factors did not yield an acceptable solution. The oblique factors shown in Table [18.3], however, provided a solution that more satisfactorily met the customary criteria of simple structure.

Factor I is related to both pupil behavior and teacher behavior and appears to be associated with the teacher's ability to encourage pupil participation and initiative. The teacher who is assessed high on Factor I is characterized by descriptions such as original, resourceful, imaginative, adaptable, flexible, democratic, "puts pupils on their own," and "encourages pupil initiative." From the standpoint of observable teacher behaviors, Factor I appears to be defined in terms of originality and adaptability.

Factor II is also derived from both pupil and teacher behaviors. Pupil traits which have high loadings on this factor seem to relate to constructive, responsible, cooperative, controlled pupil activity. With regard to observable teacher behaviors, Factor II seems to refer to responsible, systematic, businesslike vs. unplanned, slipshod classroom procedure. The teacher who is assessed high on Factor II frequently is described as systematic, well prepared, definite, consistent, thorough, responsible, and self-controlled.

Rationally interpreted, Factor III seems to involve two clusters of teacher behaviors, one having to do with an understanding, kindly, warm classroom manner and another with a tendency for the teacher to be composed, calm, and perhaps easygoing. The teacher who is assessed high on Factor III probably is liked by others for such human traits as kindliness, patience, and understanding.

Factor IV appears to relate to sociability. The teacher who is high on Factor IV probably likes people and enjoys contacts with them (the social environment consisting of eight-to ten-year-old children in this case). Such a teacher is described as approachable, friendly, tactful, gregarious, cooperative, genial, good-natured, and "looks on the bright side."

Factor V evidently stems from such qualities as animation and buoyancy, a pleasing voice, expressive speech, personal charm, and grooming. This factor may be interpreted as having to do with dramatic qualities, or the "stage appearance" of the teacher with the more obvious characteristics of a person, such as his physique, voice, and expressive movements.

It is of interest to note that the pupil behavior traits contribute significantly to Factors I and II, but these traits have only slight loadings on Factors III, IV, and V. This might suggest that, in the elementary schools, pupil behavior in class may be to a considerable extent a function of the teacher's ability (a) to stimulate the pupils and (b) to maintain situations in which the pupils are alert and responsible and are participating in constructive activities.[1]

In conclusion to this extremely brief introduction to factor analysis, it should be pointed out that the entire factor-analytic field is tremendously

[1]David G. Ryans, *Characteristics of Teachers*. Menasha, Wisc.: George Banta Co., 1960, with permission of author and publishers.

technical. Major arguments abound regarding small but important points. Yet with all its complexities, factor analysis is undoubtedly one of the research worker's more important weapons.

REVIEW

Factor analysis is a formidable statistical tool used to detect common traits or dimensions that underly many intercorrelated variables. By analyzing the correlations between a host of measures, the factor analyst can usually produce several factors to which some, but not all, of the measures are highly correlated. These factors are then rotated in such a way that the clusters of measures which have high correlations with a factor are well reflected by it. The factors are subsequently interpreted and labeled so that they may be of value in further research. During the analysis many somewhat subjective decisions and classifications must be made by the researcher.

Factor analysis is most frequently employed in the field of measurement where one often wishes to reduce many test measures to a few more meaningful dimensions.

EXERCISES

1. In a factor analysis designed to detect common dimensions in a group of twelve vocational interest tests, intercorrelations indicate that there are three groups of four tests each, which tend to correlate highly with one another but not with the eight tests in the other two groups. How many factors will probably result from the factor analysis?

2. If a particular test has a high loading on a particular factor, does it have a strong or weak correlation with the factor?

3. Having analyzed a correlation matrix so that six factors have been produced, a statistician attempts to rotate the factors so that each factor is located in a dimension of hyperspace with a negligible or zero correlation with all other factors. However, no matter how he rotates them, moderate correlations between his factors persist. Will he use an orthogonal or an oblique solution to the rotation problem?

4. With the use of a high-speed computer an educator has located and satisfactorily rotated three factors yielded from scores on 14 supposedly distinct observation categories regarding teacher–pupil rapport. He now begins to interpret and name the three factors. Can he use the computer to assist him in this task? Why?

SELECTED READINGS

Cattell, R. B., Factor Analysis: An Introduction and Manual for the Psychologist and Social Scientist. New York: Harper & Row, 1952, chap. 1.
Fruchter, Benjamin, Introduction to Factor Analysis. New York: Van Nostrand, Reinhold, 1954.

Guertin, Wilson H. and Bailey Jr., John P., *Introduction to Modern Factor Analysis*. Ann Arbor, Michigan: Edwards Bros., 1970.

Guilford J. P., *Psychometric Methods*. New York: McGraw-Hill, 1954, chap. 16.

Harman, Harry H., *Modern Factor Analysis*. Chicago: University of Chicago Press, 1960.

Horst, Paul, *Factor Analysis of Data Matrices*. New York: Holt, Rinehart & Winston, 1965.

Thompson, Sir Godfrey, *The Factorial Analysis of Human Ability*. London: University of London Press, 1951.

Thurstone, L. L., *Multiple-Factor Analysis: A Development and Expansion of the Vectors of Mind*. Chicago: University of Chicago Press, 1947.

19
Nonparametric Statistics

To this point the inferential techniques described have all been of the *parametric* type, in contrast to the *nonparametric* procedures discussed in this and the following chapter. The chief distinction between parametric and nonparametric techniques hinges upon the assumptions which must be made regarding population parameters. In the case of most parametric procedures, such as the *t* test and analysis of variance in general, certain assumptions are made regarding the nature of the population data from which the sample data under analysis were drawn. For example, it is assumed in the case of the *t* test that the parent populations are distributed normally and with equal variability.

PARAMETER ASSUMPTIONS

Nonparametric techniques require far fewer assumptions about population data. For that matter, these techniques have often been referred to as "distribution-free" procedures. Actually, it is somewhat misleading to think of nonparametric tests as though they could be legitimately conducted without considering population data. Though never requiring population normality, in some instances nonparametric tests do involve limited assumptions regarding the nature of population distributions. It is certainly true, however, that the assumptions associated with nonparametric statistical tests are much weaker than those demanded by many parametric tests. Statisticians generally agree that when the researcher is working with data which *seriously* violate the parameter assumptions required by appropriate parametric tests, nonparametric procedures are suitable alternatives.

MEASUREMENT LEVEL

Another distinction is sometimes made between parametric and nonparametric procedures on the basis of the measurement level of the data to be analyzed. A brief examination of three different measurement levels follows.

The least powerful level of measurement, a *nominal scale*, exists when symbols or numbers are used to identify different categories of a variable. We simply attach a name (*nomen*) to categories on the scale. For example, the numbers on football players' jerseys represent a nominal scale. For that matter, any classification scheme we employ, such as "rural" or "urban," which labels objects, characteristics, or persons without signifying any ordered relationship between the categories is a nominal scale. Some authors argue that this level of measurement, as it only involves the categorization of individuals according to certain qualitative differences, should not really be considered a measurement scale.[1]

Whereas a nominal scale carries no notion of order, the *ordinal scale* implies actual rank order. Not only is there a difference between categories, there is an *ordered* relationship between the categories. Such ordered relationships are frequently designated by the *carat* (>) which is usually interpreted as "greater than." For example, the rank system employed in the military would constitute an ordinal scale, for sergeant > corporal > private. Note that there is *no notion of equidistance* between points (or categories) on the scale, only a notion of rank order. In other words, the distance between sergeant and corporal may not be the same as the distance between corporal and private, *but* all sergeants are ranked higher than either corporals or privates. In educational research, a common example of data gathered on an ordinal scale is seen when observers are asked to rate teachers or pupils in terms such as "good," "average," or "poor."

An *interval scale* possesses all of the characteristics of an ordinal scale and, in addition, is composed of units which are equal. For example, the distance between points 55 and 65 on the scale must be the same as the distance between points 38 and 48. Thus, an equal distance *numerically* is assumed to be an equal distance in *fact*. Examples of interval scales involve latency measures such as how long in seconds it takes a subject to respond to an experimental stimulus.

Educational research workers are divided in their opinions as to whether most of the measurement scales used in education, for example, those produced by intelligence tests, achievement tests, and interest tests, should be treated as ordinal or interval scales. There is, however, a growing tendency to consider such data as though they were somewhere *between* ordinal and interval scales.

It has been argued by several authors[2] that, unless data have been measured on a scale of at least interval strength, parametric techniques such as analysis of variance should not be used. These individuals contend that one of the prime considerations in selecting a particular statistical test is whether the

---

[1]See, for example, Quinn McNemar, *Psychological Statistics*, 3rd ed. (New York: Wiley, 1962), p. 374.

[2]Sidney Siegel, *Nonparametric Statistics for the Behavioral Sciences* (New York: McGraw-Hill, 1956). Also, Virginia Senders, *Measurement and Statistics* (New York: Oxford University Press, 1958).

data to be treated are nominal, ordinal, or interval in nature. The principal reason for this concern over measurement scales is a belief that only certain types of mathematical operations are permissible with data of a given measurement strength. Ordinal data, it is argued, should not be subjected to the mathematical operations (addition, subtraction, multiplication, division) which are used in parametric analyses, since such operations require equidistance between the points on the scale being used. These individuals believe that most of the data dealt with in educational research are measured on scales which are probably not so strong as an interval scale; hence such data should be treated by nonparametric rather than parametric procedures. Proponents of this point of view often conclude that *most* data analyses in educational research should be made through the use of nonparametric techniques.

The view expressed in the preceding paragraph has been rejected by most statisticians on the grounds that it confuses a measurement question with a statistical question. It is not true that parametric analyses such as a *t* test cannot be *computed* on data which are only ordinal in nature. Actually, parametric procedures can be computed whenever the data are represented in numerical form. One could, for example, compute a *t* test to determine whether the numbers on the basketball uniforms of one team were significantly larger than the numbers on the basketball uniforms of another team. The question, however, would be whether there would be any sense in such an analysis.

The researcher always tries to find data which accurately reflect the variables they represent. Having done so, he then subjects his data to some kind of statistical analysis. A number of empirical studies have demonstrated that, when parametric procedures have been employed with *ordinal* data, they rarely distort a relationship between variables which may be present in the data. More often than not, such parametric analysis results are nearly identical to those yielded by nonparametric procedures. Since the majority of data encountered in educational research probably falls somewhere between ordinal and interval strength, the educational researcher is usually on safe grounds when he applies parametric tests to numerical (ordinal or interval) data. This rule requires, of course, that other assumptions of the particular parametric test have been satisfied.

PARAMETRICS VERSUS NONPARAMETRICS

There are several advantages of parametric methods over nonparametric methods. For one thing, the parametric techniques, particularly analysis of variance, offer more analysis flexibility to the researcher. The ability to categorize variables in such a way as to simultaneously study relationships between a dependent variable and many different independent variables, as well as interaction relationships between such variables, is tremendously advantageous. In addition, parametric procedures are often markedly more powerful than their nonparametric counterparts. That is, generally a parametric procedure will more frequently reject a null hypothesis than will a nonparametric test designed to perform the same function. This can be attributed to the parametric procedure's using more of the available information, such as the deviations from the mean of the scores in the analysis. Nonparametric procedures more frequently rely upon frequency count and ranking procedures, thus discarding some of the information available in the data.

With respect to the power differences of parametric and nonparametric techniques, an important point should be noted concerning the generality of findings from the less powerful nonparametric tests. To illustrate, if a difference is highly significant by using the sign test, a popular nonparametric technique, then it has a very high probability of being significant when using parametric statistics. However, the reverse is not true. Consequently, if a researcher can show a high level of significance with a rather weak statistical test, this makes his findings much more general over other possible ways of analyzing the data.

There are, however, certain advantages of nonparametric techniques. For one thing, nonparametric tests are usually much easier to compute. But, as has been pointed out by others, most researchers who have invested considerable time in conducting investigations are reluctant to use a simple analysis merely because it takes less time, if a more complex analysis, requiring a few more computation hours, might detect subtle relationships between variables. Classroom teachers, however, find their hours for research investigation are at a premium, and they are ordinarily concerned with only differences or relationships of considerable magnitude—the kind that would be detected by the less powerful nonparametric test. Such teachers will find recourse to nonparametric techniques a time-saving way of dealing with classroom questions which are amenable to statistical analysis.

Another unique value of certain nonparametric procedures is that they can be used to treat data which have been measured on nominal, or classificatory, scales. Such data cannot, on any logical basis, be ordered numerically, hence there is no possibility of using parametric statistical tests which require numerical data.

To reiterate, the primary reason for using nonparametric procedures rests upon the fact that certain parametric methods require strong assumptions regarding the nature of population data, whereas nonparametric procedures generally do not. There have been numerous theoretical articles written in recent years which debate the validity of using parametric procedures with ordinal data. As indicated earlier, the conclusion of leading statisticians is generally in favor of using parametric procedures with ordinal as well as interval data.

Since the researcher will encounter certain nonparametric procedures in reports of educational research and, on occasion, may have opportunities to use them, several of the more prominent nonparametric tests will be described.

The general pattern of nonparametric procedures is much like that seen with parametric tests, namely, certain sample data are treated by a statistical model which yields a numerical value or statistic. This value is then interpreted for the likelihood of its chance occurrence according to some type of statistical probability distribution. If the value is such that it would occur very infrequently by chance, then the sample phenomenon that produced it (the variable relationship under analysis) is assumed to be a product of a nonchance factor. In other words, the relationship under investigation is assumed to be real and the null hypothesis is rejected.

Though the discussion of nonparametric procedures in this volume will of necessity be brief, touching only on the more prominent procedures, the topic of nonparametric statistics has been ably treated by Siegel.[3] Although Siegel's treatment of nonparametric techniques has been the subject of some controversy,[4] it is a well-organized and highly readable account of the rationale, method, and application of many nonparametric tests, presented with computational examples. Thus, the reader wishing to study this topic is urged to consult the Siegel text.

RELATIONSHIPS AND DIFFERENCES

Though most inferential statistic procedures are ultimately designed to test relationships between variables, it is convenient to consider these procedures in terms of difference tests or relationship tests. In the use of difference techniques one tests for the existence of a relationship between a dependent variable, such as pupil achievement, and an independent variable *represented by two or more classifications*, such as two groups taught by different methods of instruction. In the parametric realm, for example, one might *test* for a significant *difference* between the two groups by a *t* test. If a significant difference were found, the researcher would conclude that the *variables* of achievement and instructional method were *related*. In other words, difference tests are also concerned with relationships.

On the other hand, the relationship techniques such as product-moment correlation and the various point coefficients assess relationships in a different fashion. If a statistician obtains an *r* of 0.89 when correlating two variables, he says that the variables are strongly related. Relationship tests can give us a notion not only of the existence of a relationship, but also an estimate of its magnitude.

At any rate, we have seen that the *t* test, analysis of variance, and analysis of covariance were parametric difference-testing procedures, while the correlation measures were parametric relationship-testing procedures. The same distinction can be drawn in the field of nonparametric methods and, as long as the reader remembers that, in the final analysis, inferential statistical techniques are really concerned with relationships between variables, the following description of these two types of techniques may prove helpful.

It must be noted that the tests described in the remainder of the chapter in no way exhaust the nonparametric procedures suitable for particular purposes. The tests discussed, however, are representative of similar procedures of a nonparametric nature. Some of the tests can be used with nominal and

[3]Siegel, *op. cit.*
[4]Richard J. Savage, "Nonparametric Statistics," *J. Am. Statist. Assoc.* **52**, no. 332 (1957).

stronger data while other techniques require ordinal or interval data. Deeper insight into any of the procedures described in this chapter can be secured by consulting the computational treatment of the procedure in the following chapter.

CONFIDENCE INTERVALS

As with parametric procedures, it is possible to develop confidence intervals for nonparametric tests. Although not widely used, methods for computing nonparametric confidence intervals have been described by several authors.[5]

DIFFERENCE TESTS

Difference tests can be classified according to whether they are concerned with one, two, or more than two samples, as well as whether the samples are related.

One-Sample Case

Chi-Square Test.   Often a researcher is concerned with the question of whether his sample data are distributed in a particular fashion such as in the shape of the normal curve. For example, he can check the assumption of a particular population's normality, by seeing whether a sample drawn from that population departs significantly from the shape of a normal distribution. Then too, we have occasions to see whether sample data are distributed in other ways, such as in other kinds of probability distributions or, perhaps, according to previously established empirical distributions.

A nonparametric technique which may be used to test the difference between the distribution of one sample and some other hypothetical or known distribution is the *chi-square* (χ^2) *test*. The χ^2 test can be used with data measured on nominal or stronger scales. Essentially, this procedure involves a "goodness of fit" test wherein the sample frequencies actually falling within certain categories are contrasted with those which might be expected on the basis of the hypothetical distribution. If a marked difference exists between the *observed* or *actual* frequencies falling in each category and the frequencies *expected* to fall in each category on the basis of chance or a previously established distribution, then the χ^2 test will yield a numerical value large enough to be interpreted as statistically significant.

To provide an example of this process, suppose an educator wished to determine whether a set of students' achievement scores were distributed in a nonnormal fashion. If there were a range of achievement scores from 40 to 90 and a large enough number of subjects, the scores could be classified into categories or intervals of five points 40–44, 45–49, 50–54, and so on. Now the frequencies of the scores *actually* falling within each of these categories would be counted. Next, a table of the normal curve could be consulted and, in terms

[5]See, for example, W. Allen Wallis and Harry V. Roberts, *Statistics: A New Approach* (New York: Free Press, 1956).

of the mean and standard deviation of the sample, it could be determined how many scores would be *expected* to fall within each of the five-point categories *if the distribution were perfectly normal*. By contrasting the observed or actual frequencies with these *expected* or *hypothetical frequencies*, one can determine through the χ^2 test whether the sample departs significantly from normality.

In brief, the χ^2 test yields a value which is produced by the disparity in each of the data categories or cells between expected and observed frequencies. If the sample distribution were *perfectly* normal, there would be no difference in any category between expected and observed frequencies and the resulting value of χ^2 would be zero. The greater the disparity between the observed and the expected frequencies the larger χ^2 becomes. As usual, the final value of this statistical test is interpreted for significance from a probability curve, in this instance from a set of χ^2 curves. Each χ^2 value is interpreted according to the number of degrees of freedom in the analysis in a fashion similar to use of the several *t*-test curves. The table of χ^2 is then used to secure the probability level of the χ^2 value yielded by the analysis. In this book χ^2 values at various levels of significance are contained in Table I.

The chi-square one-sample test can also be used to determine whether a data sample departs significantly from a previously established distribution. For example, a researcher might wish to determine whether the proportion of a particular high school's 1964 senior class who continued their formal education after graduation was essentially the same as the proportions in previous years. By checking follow-up data for the past five years, the researcher could determine that 29 percent of the previous seniors had continued their formal educations while 71 percent had not. This previously established ratio, that is, 29:71, determines the *expected* frequencies for the χ^2 test. The *actual* frequencies are drawn from the follow-up data for the 1963 senior class. As in all chi-squares analyses, the actual frequencies are contrasted with the expected frequencies in such a way as to yield a χ^2 value which is subsequently checked for statistical significance according to a chi-square probability curve.

Additional Tests. Another test suitable for the one-sample case involving nominal data is the *binominal test*. With ordinal data, appropriate one-sample tests are the *Kolmogorov–Smirnov test* and the *one-sample runs test*. These techniques are described by Siegel.[6]

Two Related Samples

Wilcoxon Matched-Pairs Signed-Ranks Test. When a research worker contrasts the performance of two groups he must first pose the question: "Are the two samples independent?" If the two groups consist of matched pairs or two measures on the same individuals, as in pre- and posttests comparisons, the answer is "no." In such cases, statistical techniques are used which take this

[6]Siegel, *op. cit.*

relationship into consideration. In parametric procedures, for example, special modifications of the *t* test are employed. In nonparametric tests, a frequently used procedure for testing differences between related samples is the *Wilcoxon matched-pairs signed-ranks test.*

The Wilcoxon test uses not only the *direction* of differences between pairs (when two measures for the same individual are taken, these are considered to represent a "pair"), but also the relative *magnitude* of the differences. Hence, the Wilcoxon test requires numerical data and could not be employed when the data are only classificatory in nature.

In essence, the Wilcoxon matched-pairs signed-ranks test is based on the notion that researchers can determine whether one member of a pair exceeds the other, and by roughly how much. If most of the *major* differences between pairs favor one group, then that group is significantly superior to the other. If the null hypothesis is true, then the number and magnitude of differences favoring the group will be about the same as those favoring the other group.

In computing the Wilcoxon test simply note the difference between each pair, rank the differences irrespective of algebraic sign, then total the ranks with the *less frequent* sign. The resulting value is called *T* and is interpreted for statistical probability from a statistical table. In this text, the critical values of *T* are given in Table J.

Consideration of the process involved will reveal that the smaller the value of *T* is, the greater is the preponderance of differences between pairs in favor of one group, hence the more significant. If the two related samples were perfectly identical, there would be an equal quantity and magnitude of negative ranks and positive ranks; thus the value of *T* would be large. To put it another way, if the members of *each* pair in one group exceed their matched counterparts in the other group, the value of the less frequent rank sum, that is, *T*, would be zero and, of course, quite significant.

Sign Test. The *sign test* is frequently used in testing for differences between two related samples but, since it only utilizes the direction and not the magnitude of the differences between pairs, it is less powerful than the Wilcoxon test. The sign test also requires data measured by at least an ordinal scale. This very useful test has a wide range of applications and is extremely simple to compute. The basic rationale of the sign test is that if two groups of related subjects are contrasted when the null hypothesis holds true, there should be approximately half of one group judged better than or greater than the other group. If a markedly greater proportion of one group is favored, the sign test detects the existence of a significant difference.

A Nominal Data Test. A model suitable for checking differences between related samples when the data are only nominal, the *McNemar test for the significance of changes*, is described in Siegel's[7] volume on nonparametrics.

[7]*Ibid.*

Two Independent Samples

Mann–Whitney U Test.   If the two samples involved do not consist of matched pairs, the researcher has a variety of nonparametric difference tests at his disposal. If the data are numerical in nature, the *Mann–Whitney U test* is frequently employed. The *U* test is a powerful nonparametric technique and may frequently be employed in place of the parametric *t* test with little loss in power efficiency.

Briefly, the *U* test is based on the notion that, if scores of two similar groups are ranked together (as though the two groups were one), there will be a considerable intermingling of the two groups' rankings; but, if one group significantly exceeds the other, then most of the superior group's rankings will be higher than those of the inferior group. The value of *U* is computed after the combined ranking by concentrating on the lower ranked group and counting the number of ranks of the higher group which fall *below* the lower ranked group. Thus, if *all* of the higher ranked group exceeded all of the lower ranked group, there would be none of the superior group's rankings below those of the inferior group and the value of *U* would be zero. Once more, as in the Wilcoxon tests, this is an instance where the lower the value of the statistic yielded by the test, the more significant it is.

The *Mann–Whitney* test can be used with extremely small samples. Probability tables are available (in this text, Tables K and L) for samples as small as three subjects in one group and only one subject in the second group.

Statistical analyses involving the Mann–Whitney *U* test have been seen with increasing frequency in the literature of educational research during the past few years.

The Chi-Square Test.   When the data from two independent samples are only nominal, then one may again use the χ^2 test to detect significant differences. For two samples the χ^2 analysis follows a pattern similar to that described earlier in the one-sample goodness of fit test. In the case of the two-sample application, however, the expected frequencies are not drawn from some hypothetical distribution, but directly from the actual or observed frequencies themselves. To illustrate the process, the hypothetical data in Table 19.1 have been presented in which the performance of men and women on their initial automobile operator's license driving test is contrasted.

In this example the independent variable is sex, as represented by the male and female groups; the dependent variable is performance on the driving test, classified into categories of "pass" or "fail." The figures in the table represent the *actual* or observed scores of the 100 persons taking the driving test. To indicate how the *expected* frequencies are determined in such a two-sample case, it will be helpful if the reader will study Table 19.1, where it can be seen that 60 of the 100 persons involved passed the driving test, and 40 failed. Note also the subtotals for men and women are 50, or exactly half of the total of 100 subjects. Now according to simple logic, since 50 percent of the subjects were male, we should expect that 50 percent of the 60 persons who passed the test

Table 19.1

Hypothetical Performance of 50 Men and 50 Women in Their Initial Automobile Operator's License Driving Test

	Passed	Failed	Subtotal
Men	40	10	50
Women	20	30	50
Subtotal	60	40	100 Total

should be males. Thus, the *expected* frequency for males who passed the test is 50 percent of 60, or 30. Similarly, for females who should have passed the test, the expected frequency is 30. For males who failed the test, the expected frequency is 20 (50 percent of the 40 subjects who failed), and for females who failed, the expected frequency is also 20.

The value of χ^2 depends upon the *disparity* between the actual frequencies and the expected frequencies, with χ^2 becoming larger as the disparity increases. In other words, if the value of χ^2 is large enough to be statistically significant, there is a considerable difference between the *category proportions* of two independent variable groups with respect to the dependent variable.

For example, in the hypothetical example given in Table 19.1, the value of χ^2 is 15.04 which is significant beyond the 0.01 level. This result indicates that there is indeed a difference of considerable consequence between the males and females in the example. (Of course, it must be reemphasized that the illustration employed is totally hypothetical and, though it may reflect the authors' subconscious bias regarding the competence of female drivers, cannot be used to support the respective merits of either men or women drivers.)

Additional Tests. When nominal data are involved, differences may also be assessed by the *Fisher exact probability test*. If ordinal data are available, differences between two independent groups may be tested by the *median test*, the *Kolmogorov–Smirnov two-sample test*, the *Wald–Wolfowitz runs test*, and the *Moses test of extreme reactions*. All of these techniques are explained further by Siegel.[8]

More Than Two Related Samples

Friedman Two-Way Analysis of Variance. When one wishes to determine if three or more of *matched* samples differ significantly with respect to data measured at least on an ordinal scale, the *Friedman two-way analysis of variance* may be employed. This technique is applied whenever the researcher is working with sets of matched subjects or when the same subjects have been exposed to different treatment conditions.

For example, suppose we wished to see whether there were any

[8]*Ibid.*

significant performance differences between physical education students who were taught by three different methods to play a new kind of game. Their performance in the new game could be determined by the combined ratings of five judges who could rate the performance of each student without knowing which method of instruction had been used to teach him the game skill. Essentially, then, the research is designed to discover the existence, or lack of existence, of a relationship between performance (as reflected by judges' ratings) and method of instruction (as represented by the three groups of students).

Because physical ability and intelligence are variables which are probably related to the success of the subjects in mastering the new skill, the researcher might assemble five *sets* of three subjects with each one of the subjects in a given set matched with the other members on the bases of IQ score and previous performance on a test of physical aptitude. The three subjects in each set could then be assigned, on a random basis, to one of the three instructional methods.

After receiving instruction via one of the three methods, the performance of each subject would then be rated by the judges in such a fashion that during the analysis stage *his rank within his set of three subjects* could be determined. Now, if one of the three instructional methods is markedly superior to the other two, one might expect that the students taught by that method would receive rankings of "1" rather than rankings of "2" or "3." As a result, the total of ranks for the superior instructional method would be only five, since each subject in the five matched sets who had been taught by that method would be ranked higher than the two members of his set who were exposed to the other methods. In other words, the total of ranks for the superior method would be much smaller than the total of ranks for the inferior methods.

In contrast to this, if the three instructional methods are about equally effective, the ranks within each of the five sets will be fairly well scattered, and the sum of the ranks for each instructional method will be similar.

To summarize, then, the rationale of the Friedman two-way analysis of variance is based on the fact that, if matched sets of subjects (or the same subjects exposed to differential treatments) are assigned to different groups representing an independent variable, their *within-sets* rankings that are based on the dependent variable will be distributed in a fairly random pattern when the null hypothesis is tenable. When the null hypothesis is untenable, that is, when there are differences between two or more of the groups representing the independent variable, there will be a marked disparity between the sums of ranks for the independent variable groups.

To test for significant differences between the condition (independent variable) groups, the several sums of ranks are inserted in a formula which yields a value (χ_r^2) to be subsequently interpreted for significance according to a chi-square table. If the value is sufficiently large, the null hypothesis is rejected and it is concluded that significant differences between the condition groups exist. Special probability tables must be used for this test when the number of subjects and conditions is particularly small.

More Than Two Independent Samples

If one wishes to test for significant differences between more than two independent samples which are not related, the parametric analysis of variance model is the usual choice. However, if the sample data appear to markedly depart from the requisite assumptions of this test, the researcher may turn to nonparametric techniques.

Kruskal-Wallis One-Way Analysis of Variance. If the dependent variable data are numerical in nature, the *Kruskal-Wallis* test may be employed. This technique requires that the dependent variable under analysis is continuously distributed, that is, has no extended "gaps" where no scores appear.

The basic rationale for the test is quite simple. If there are no differences among the several groups representing the independent variable, then when all scores are ranked, irrespective of groups, from highest to lowest, the average sum of ranks for each group should be roughly comparable. If there are significant differences among the groups, then a marked disparity among the several group's average sums of ranks will exist.

For example, suppose a school psychologist wished to contrast the scores of youngsters from three grade levels on a personality test. He would first compute ranks for the entire set of subjects, then sum the ranks for each of the three grade level groups, and average the sum according to how many subjects were in each group. If these average sums of ranks are relatively similar, then it is likely that no significant difference exists among students from the three grade levels. On the other hand, if marked differences do exist among the several average sums of ranks, then the null hypothesis should be rejected and grade level should be taken into consideration when interpreting scores of the personality test.

The sums of ranks are inserted in a formula which yields a value known as *H*. When the number of samples and subjects is small, a special table of probabilities (Table H in the Appendix) is used to interpret the significance of *H*. When the number of samples and subjects is larger, *H* is interpreted for significance from a chi-square table.

The Chi-Square Test. When the data are only nominal in nature, once again a chi-square analysis is used to test for differences between more than two independent samples. The procedure involved is simply an extension of that seen in the case of two independent samples where the observed frequencies are contrasted with expected frequencies drawn from row and column totals. If the disparity between expected and observed frequencies is quite large, this reflects a significant difference between the groups. The larger the value of chi square, the greater the difference between the groups.

Chi square can also be applied to ordinal and interval data, but it then represents a markedly less powerful test than those designated for use with numerical data.

RELATIONSHIP TESTS

Thus far this chapter has explored only statistical models designed to test for differences between: (1) a sample and a hypothetical distribution; (2) two samples, either related or independent; and (3) more than two samples, either related or independent. A nonparametric procedure comparable to the parametric product-moment correlational procedure has not yet been treated. There is such a technique, designed to be used with ranked data, which has been widely used for a number of years.

Spearman Rank-Order Correlation Coefficient. The Spearman rank-order coefficient (r_s), or *rho* as it is sometimes called, is frequently encountered in the literature of educational research. It can be employed to determine the degree of relationship between two ordinally measured variables. For example, if we were to assess the degree of relationship between students' academic rank in high-school and their rank on a test of attitudes toward study habits, the Spearman correlational method would be an appropriate technique.

The rationale for the Spearman rank-order correlation coefficient is based upon the notion of *differences* between ranks of individuals on two measures. For example, if a perfect positive relationship between the two variables is present, then an individual who ranked first on one measure would also rank first on the second measure, and so on. In each instance the difference between the two ranks of each individual would be zero. If the relationship between the variables is less than perfect, we would find that an individual who ranked first on one measure might rank seventh in the second measure with a resulting difference of six points between his two ranks. An index of the disagreement in ranks, or, rephrasing, the lack of relationship between the two variables is drawn from the size and number of these differences. To remove the negative sign from certain differences which occur between ranks, all differences are squared, then summed. The sum of squared differences is the crucial value in the formula which yields the Spearman coefficient. If the sum of the squared differences is small, then a strong relationship exists. If the sum of the square differences is moderately large, a low order relationship exists. If the sum of the squared differences is extremely large, a negative relationship exists.

When inserted in the formula which yields the Spearman coefficient, a sum of squared differences of zero (from a perfect positive relationship) would yield a coefficient of $+1.00$. A perfect negative relationship would occur if the ranks were perfectly reversed, with the resulting large sum of squared differences, yielding a coefficient of -1.00. It can be seen, then, that the range and meaning of the Spearman coefficient are identical to those of the Pearson product-moment correlation coefficient. Generally speaking, r_s can be interpreted in the same way as r.

The significance of r_s for samples from 4 to 30 subjects can be ascertained readily from a specially prepared probability table (Table E in Appendix). For larger samples, a formula which yields a t value is used to check the significance of the Spearman coefficient.

In reality the Spearman coefficient is nothing more than the Pearson product-moment formula applied to the two sets of ranks.

Additional Tests. Other nonparametric relationship techniques, particularly a set of coefficients developed by Kendall, have been described by Siegel.[9]

REVIEW

Nonparametric statistical tests require far less stringent assumptions than parametric tests such as analysis of variance. Although the argument is not fashionable these days, it is held by some that the use of parametric procedures with much educational data yields spurious results, so nonparametric techniques should be employed. Yet, because of their greater power and flexibility, parametric procedures should ordinarily be used when there is a choice between a nonparametric and a parametric test. However, in cases where parametric assumptions are seriously violated or where the samples are so small that it would be difficult to demonstrate the satisfaction of parametric assumptions, nonparametric techniques have their place.

In viewing the many parametric tests, the reader was urged to think of the procedures as difference-testing or relationship-testing models. Representative nonparametric models were discussed for the more common educational research analysis requirements.

For testing differences between one sample and a hypothetical distribution, the chi square was described. Because it may be applied to nominal or classificatory data, the χ^2 test is widely used.

With ordinal or stronger data, the difference between two related (matched) samples can be tested by the Wilcoxon matched-pairs signed-ranks model. A less powerful test for the same situation is the sign test.

For two independent samples with ordinal or stronger data the Mann–Whitney U test is an excellent choice. With only nominal data the χ^2 test for two independent groups may be used.

For three or more related groups with data of at least ordinal strength, the Friedman two-way analysis of variance is a suitable model. With three or more independent samples and ordinal or stronger data, the Kruskal-Wallis one-way analysis of variance model was recommended. Chi square can be used with three or more independent groups and data of only nominal strength.

The Spearman rank-order correlation coefficient was described as a relationship technique suitable for dealing with data of ordinal or greater strength. This coefficient is interpreted in much the same way as the standard product-moment correlation coefficient.

During the discussion Siegel's[10] lucid treatment of nonparametric methods was strongly recommended.

[9]*Ibid.*
[10]*Ibid.*

EXERCISES

1. In general will a nonparametric or parametric test, each designed to accomplish the same analytic function, more frequently reject the null hypothesis?

2. If an educator wished to use a *t* test to contrast differences between two independent groups but found that the assumptions of the *t* test could not be satisfied, which nonparametric test should he employ?

3. A researcher wishes to test for a relationship between two sets of ranked data. Which nonparametric test should he use?

4. To test the null hypothesis that three large groups of students are different with respect to their religious affiliation (i.e., Protestant, Catholic, other) which statistical model may be used?

5. A teacher wishes to test for pretest and posttest differences in scores on an attitude scale for her class which has just seen a lengthy movie on the problems of racial intolerance. Which two nonparametric tests might be employed in this situation? Which of the two is the more powerful test?

6. Which nonparametric technique would a researcher use to test whether a large set of data was distributed in a significantly nonnormal fashion?

7. Five sets of three matched subjects have been exposed to three different attitude modification self-instruction programs. Each subject has obtained a "gain" score based on the difference between his performances on a pre-experiment and postexperiment attitude inventory. Which nonparametric test might be used to test for differences in the effectiveness of the three self-instruction programs?

8. An educator wishes to test for differences between four independent groups. With nominal data which nonparametric test should he use? With ordinal data which nonparametric test should he use?

SELECTED READINGS

Anderson, Norman H., "Scales and Statistics: Parametric and Nonparametric," *Psychol. Bull.* **58** (July 1961): 305–316.

Blalock, Hubert M., Jr., *Social Statistics*. New York: McGraw-Hill, 1960, chaps. 2, 14 and 15.

Edward, Allen L., *Statistical Methods for the Behavioral Sciences*. New York: Holt, Rinehart & Winston, 1957, chaps. 18 and 19.

McNemar, Quinn, *Psychological Statistics*. New York: Wiley, 1962, chap. 19.

Siegel, Sidney, *Nonparametric Statistics for the Behavioral Sciences*. New York: McGraw-Hill, 1956.

20
Nonparametric Statistics— Computation Procedures

Computation procedures are outlined in this chapter for those nonparametric tests which were described in some detail in the previous chapter, namely, the *chi-square test*, the *Wilcoxon matched-pairs signed-ranks test*, the *sign test*, the *Mann-Whitney U test*, the *Friedman two-way analysis of variance*, the *Kruskal-Wallis one-way analysis of variance*, and the *Spearman rank order correlation coefficient*. Only a brief reiteration of the purposes of these various tests will be supplied in the present chapter. For a more extensive discussion of the rationale and purpose of a particular technique, the reader is urged to consult the previous chapter or the references cited at the close of the chapter.

CHI SQUARE

The chi-square (χ^2) test is undoubtedly the most important member of the nonparametric family. This test can be used with data which are only nominal in strength such as categories representing college major or parental occupation. Chi square is employed to test the difference between an actual sample and another hypothetical or previously established distribution. Chi square can also be used to test differences between two or more actual samples. The computation procedures for χ^2 are basically the same in either of these two situations; only slight computational differences exist.

Though χ^2 can be used to treat data which are classified into nominal nonordered categories, it can also be employed with numerical data. The researcher may wish, however, to analyze such data with more powerful parametric tests. But for nominal data, few alternatives to χ^2 analysis exist.

The basic computation equation for chi square is seen in Formula 20.1.

$$\chi^2 = \sum \frac{(\text{Observed frequency} - \text{Expected frequency})^2}{\text{Expected frequency}} \qquad (20.1)$$

Table 20.1

District Teachers Hired Last Year and During the Preceding Ten Years, Classified According to Whether They Were Graduated from a State-Supported or Private College

	State College Graduate	Private College Graduate
Number of teachers employed last year	30	20
Percentage of teachers employed in preceding 10 years	40%	60%

The use of this formula and the subsequent interpretation of the significance of χ^2 will be illustrated both in the one-sample case and in the case of two or more samples.

It should be noted that whenever χ^2 is calculated from 1×2 or 2×2 cell tables (instances in which there is but one degree of freedom) an adjustment known as Yates (1934) correction for continuity must be employed. To use this correction a value of 0.5 is subtracted from the absolute value (irrespective of algebraic sign) of the numerator contribution of each cell to Formula 20.1. Therefore each cell makes this sort of contribution

$$\frac{(|\text{Observed frequency} - \text{Expected frequency}| - 0.5)^2}{\text{Expected frequency}}$$

to the total value of chi square. This will be illustrated shortly.

One-Sample Case

Researchers often wish to know whether a sample departs significantly from some known or hypothetical distribution. For example, a school superintendent of a large school system may wish to know whether his recently employed first-year teachers are being drawn from state-supported or private colleges in a proportion significantly different from the pattern seen in the previous decade. The administrator may use an χ^2 analysis to settle this issue. In this instance the basic analytic task is to contrast the proportion of state-supported and private college graduates between: (1) the recently employed teachers, and (2) an established proportion drawn from district records over the past ten years. The recently employed teachers in this case represent the *observed* frequencies, and the previously established proportion serves as the basis for calculating the expected frequencies. In any one-sample case application of χ^2, the sample which is to be contrasted with the known or hypothetical distribution constitutes the observed frequencies. The data to be used in the present example are summarized in Table 20.1.

The expected frequencies needed for the χ^2 formula (20.1) are calculated as follows: First, the proportion between state and private college graduates in the previously established distribution is noted, namely, 40 percent state

---

Table 20.2
Observed and Expected Frequencies[a] for the One-Sample χ^2 Analysis Example

State College Graduates	Private College Graduates
(20)	(30)
30	20

---

[a]Expected frequencies in parentheses.

college graduates to 60 percent private college graduates. Then this proportion is applied to the 50 recently employed teachers for, according to the previously established distribution, it would be "expected" that 40 percent, or 20, of the 50 new teachers would be state college graduates, and 60 percent, or 30, or the 50 new teachers would be private college graduates. Since the observed frequencies are the actual frequencies of the sample in question, the observed and expected frequencies can be set up in a table such as Table 20.2, where the expected frequencies are in parentheses.

The quantities necessary for the solution of the chi-square analysis are now available and are placed in Formula 20.1 and solved. Remember that in calculating χ^2 from 1×2 or 2×2 tables, Yates correction should be used.

$$\chi^2 = \frac{(|30-20|-0.5)^2}{20} + \frac{(|20-30|-0.5)^2}{30}$$
$$= 4.5 + 3.0$$
$$= 7.5$$

This χ^2 value of 7.5, as in all previous inferential significance tests, is interpreted from a table of probability values, in this case based on the χ^2 distribution. It is necessary to enter the table with the appropriate number of degrees of freedom. For a one-sample case, in which expected proportions need *not* be calculated from the sample data, *df* is always the number of cells (as seen in Table 20.2) less one. In this example there are two cells, so $df = 2 - 1 = 1$. Now consult Table I in the Appendix and note that with one degree of freedom a χ^2 value equal to or greater than 3.84 is needed to reject the null hypothesis at the 0.05 level, while a χ^2 value of 6.64 or greater is needed to reject the null hypothesis at the 0.01 level. Since the obtained χ^2 value of 7.5 exceeds both of these, the null hypothesis that the recently employed teachers are being drawn from state and private colleges in the same proportion as in previous years is rejected. The district administrator may now begin to search for reasons behind this statistically significant departure from previous practices.

Goodness of Fit

Basically, the χ^2 one-sample case is an instance of checking the "goodness of fit" between an actual sample and some known or hypothetical distribution.

Frequently, the educational researcher wants to check the assumption of normality by seeing if the sample data (ordinal or interval) depart significantly from the shape of a normal distribution. This can be accomplished through a chi-square analysis by assessing the degree to which the sample data "fit" a normal shape.

The procedure is essentially the same as in the previous example, except that the expected frequencies are calculated on the basis of the normal curve rather than the records of previously employed teachers; thus, two additional degrees of freedom are lost due to the need for estimating the parameters (mean and standard deviation) of the hypothetical normal curve. First, the actual sample data, that is, the observed frequencies, are cast in a number of categories. The optimal number of categories will be described later. Then, in terms of the mean and standard deviation of the sample, the researcher checks the normal curve table to see what proportion of the distribution should fall in a particular category if the distribution were perfectly normal. For example, suppose there were a number of five-point categories, an equal proportion above and below the sample mean, which were being used for a sample whose actual standard deviation was 10.0. The normal curve table would reveal that in the first five-point category above the mean, since it consisted of one-half standard deviation unit distance, there should be 19 percent of the sample distribution. In the next five-unit category or cell there should be 15 percent of the sample distribution, if it were perfectly normal, and so on. Now these hypothetical proportions can be multiplied by the actual number of cases in the sample with the result representing the expected frequencies. The observed and expected frequencies are then used in Formula 20.1 as in the previous example except with *df* now equaling the number of categories or cells less three.

How Many Categories?

The question of number of categories is important and, while there is some controversy among statisticians, the following guidelines are generally accepted. In some cases the researcher has relatively little control over the number of categories in his analysis, for they consist of some type of unique nominal classes such as "living" or "deceased." In most cases, however, a certain amount of control over categories can be exercised. For instance, five attitude inventory categories such as "strongly agree," "agree," "neutral," "disagree," and "strongly disagree" could be regrouped into three categories: "agree," "neutral," "disagree." Similarly, a range of IQ scores could be subdivided into a variety of categories ranging from two such as "100 and above" and "below 100" to a host of categories with two- or three-point ranges in each. Even nominal scale categories can be recategorized under new more or less inclusive headings.

The general rule in setting up χ^2 categories is to have as many as possible, for the test will then be more sensitive. (Clearly, when testing for "goodness of fit," at least four categories must be used to have at least one *df* for the statistical test.) The limitation is that no more than 20 percent of the cells have an

Table 20.3

Responses of 200 Boys and Girls to a Question Regarding the Value of Extracurricular Student Activities

	Very Valuable	Uncertain	Of Little Value	Row Subtotal
Boys	40	40	20	100
Girls	60	20	20	100
Column subtotal	100	60	40	200 Total

expected frequency smaller than 5.0, and no cell has an *expected* frequency smaller than 1.0. This does not mean that the observed or actual frequencies should not be small, only the expected frequencies. If too many small expected frequencies exist, the categories should be combined, unless such combinations are meaningless. For example, a category of "agreement" should not be combined with one of "disagreement." This rule means that when only two-, three-, or four-cell χ^2 analyses are set up, *no* cell can have an expected frequency of less than 5.0.

If categories are combined to the point, where there are only two categories and still an expected frequency of less than 5.0 exists, χ^2 should not be used. Instead, the *binominal test*[1] may be used to treat the data. The same rules about the required magnitude of expected frequencies apply to the two or more sample cases to be described next.

Two or More Sample Cases

In contrasting differences between two or more samples by a chi-square test, the same principles apply as in the one-sample application. Only the methods of determining expected frequencies and the number of degrees of freedom vary.

Difference Between Two Samples. A computational example will illustrate the procedure for testing the null hypothesis that two samples are drawn from the same population. Suppose an investigator wishes to see if boys and girls respond differently to an attitudinal question regarding the educational value of extracurricular student activities. In Table 20.3 the responses of 100 boys and 100 girls to such a question have been summarized, as well as row and column subtotals.

The expected frequencies for such a problem are determined in a logical fashion. Note that since there are equal numbers of boys and girls, as seen in the row subtotals, we should *expect* equal proportions of the column subtotals to be divided between the boys and girls thus, 50 percent of the 100 frequencies

[1]Sidney Siegel, *Nonparametric Statistics for the Behavioral Sciences*. New York: McGraw-Hill, 1956, pp. 36–42.

Table 20.4
Responses of 200 Boys and Girls to a Question Regarding the Value of Extracurricular Activities[a]

	Very Valuable	Uncertain	Of Little Value	Row Subtotal
Boys	(50) 40	(30) 40	(20) 20	100
Girls	(50) 60	(30) 20	(20) 20	100
Column subtotal	100	60	40	200 Total

[a]Expected frequencies in parentheses.

in the "very valuable" column would be expected to go to the girls and 50 percent to the boys. Similarly the 60 "uncertain" and 40 "of little value" frequencies should be divided equally between the boys and girls. The expected frequencies for this example have been added parenthetically to Table 20.4.

If the reader is unclear about how the expected frequencies were computed, tables 20.3 and 20.4 should be studied carefully. Briefly, to obtain the expected frequency for the upper left corner cell, the proportion of upper *row subtotal* to *total* (100/200) is multiplied by the left *column subtotal* (100) to yield the desired quantity (50). Expected frequencies for other cells are computed in a similar fashion.

The observed and expected frequencies are then inserted into the χ^2 calculation formula (19.1) as follows and solved accordingly:

$$\chi^2 = \frac{(40-50)^2}{50} + \frac{(40-30)^2}{30} + \frac{(20-20)^2}{20} + \frac{(60-50)^2}{50} + \frac{(20-30)^2}{30}$$

$$+ \frac{(20-20)^2}{20}$$

$$= 2.0 + 3.3 + 0 + 2.0 + 3.3 + 0$$

$$= 10.6$$

For two or more samples, the degrees of freedom necessary to interpret χ^2 values, such as the above, are always determined from the frequency table by the number of rows minus one times the number of columns minus one $(r-1)(c-1) = df$. In this case, $(2-1)(3-1) = 2df$.

Examination of Table I reveals that with two degrees of freedom a χ^2 value of 10.6 is significant beyond the 0.01 level. If this satisfies the previously set rejection level, the result indicates that the null hypothesis should be considered untenable and that there is a relationship between sex and response to the question. *The actual nature of the relationship must be discerned by a visual inspection of the frequency table.*

Table 20.5
Annual Truancy Reports for Three High Schools[a]

School	None	1–3	4–6	More than 6	Row Subtotal
	(400)	(87.5)	(50)	(62.5)	
A	400	100	50	50	600
	(266.6)	(58.3)	(33.3)	(41.7)	
B	300	50	25	25	400
	(133.3)	(29.2)	(16.7)	(20.8)	
	100	25	25	50	200
Column subtotal	800	175	100	125	1200 Total

Number of Truancy Reports by Individuals

[a]Expected frequencies in parentheses.

Differences Between More Than Two Samples. The technique for computing a chi-square analysis in which three or more samples are involved is quite similar to the two-sample case. In Table 20.5 a set of data is represented for three secondary schools in a lower socioeconomic metropolitan school district in which the number of yearly truancy reports for three student samples is cited. Note that the categories for the truancy reports are not perfectly equal, but are derived in a fairly logical fashion. Expected frequencies have been added in parentheses.

The expected frequencies are computed as before. To illustrate, the expected frequency for the upper right corner cell is determined by taking the proportion between the upper *row subtotal* and the *total* (600/1200) and multiplying it by the right *column subtotal* (125) to yield the expected frequency (62.5). The expected and observed frequencies are then inserted in Formula 20.1 and χ^2 is produced as follows:

$$\chi^2 = \frac{(400-400)^2}{400} + \frac{(100-87.5)^2}{87.5} + \frac{(50-50)^2}{50} + \frac{(50-62.5)^2}{62.5}$$

$$+ \frac{(300-266.6)^2}{266.6} + \frac{(50-58.3)^2}{58.3} + \frac{(25-33.3)^2}{33.3} + \frac{(25-41.7)^2}{41.7}$$

$$+ \frac{(100-133.3)^2}{133.3} + \frac{(25-29.2)^2}{29.2} + \frac{(25-16.7)^2}{16.7} + \frac{(50-20.8)^2}{20.8}$$

$$= 0 + 1.79 + 0 + 2.50 + 4.18 + 1.18 + 2.07 + 6.69 + 8.32 + 0.60 + 4.13 + 40.99$$

$$= 72.45$$

This value of the square is interpreted for statistical significance from Table I with degrees of freedom equaling $(r-1)(c-1) = (3-1)(4-1) = 6$. The χ^2 value of 72.45 is well beyond that needed for significance at the 0.001 level;

thus the null hypothesis should be rejected. It is necessary to consult the frequency table to discover the precise manner in which the truancy reports of the three high-schools differ. An examination of the frequencies reveals that School C has a markedly greater proportion of truancy reports than the other two schools.

When interpreting the meaning of a significant χ^2 value, it is often helpful to note the contribution made by each cell in the frequency table to the total χ^2 value. Observe, in this example, for instance, that the lower right cell makes a contribution of 40.99 to the final χ^2 of 72.45. Such observations can prove valuable in explaining the relationship indicated by the significant χ^2.

When computing χ^2 values by the method described here, the researcher should be careful to check that the subtotal of the expected frequencies in any row or column equals the subtotal of the observed frequencies in the same row or column. The trivial differences between the expected and observed frequency subtotals created by rounding should be disregarded.

WILCOXON MATCHED-PAIRS SIGNED-RANKS TEST

The Wilcoxon matched-pairs signed-ranks test is used to assess the significance of difference between two samples consisting of matched pairs of subjects. Matched pairs of subjects would include two measures taken on the same subject as in a pre- and posttest comparison of individuals. This test is the nonparametric counterpart of the *t* test for correlated data. As most nonparametric techniques, the Wilcoxon test is quite simple to compute. The computation procedures can be illustrated by the following hypothetical example.

An educational research worker has carefully matched eight pairs of subjects so that both members of each pair have equivalent scores on an intelligence test and a physics achievement test. Over a two-week period one of the groups is shown a series of filmed lectures covering a rather esoteric topic in the field of physics. These students are given no other instruction on the topic which, incidentally, is so uncommon that students would have difficulty securing additional study materials. After each film a twenty-item multiple choice examination is given to the subjects, but the students are not given the correct answers nor do they receive corrected test papers.

The second group receives the same treatment as the former group with one exception. At the conclusion of each twenty-item examination, the second group's papers are quickly corrected and returned to the students. The second group, therefore, receives *knowledge of results* regarding their performance while the first group does not. At the close of the experimental period an extensive examination is administered to both groups. The scores on the test are then analyzed by the Wilcoxon matched-pairs signed-ranks test.

The data from this example are summarized in Table 20.6 where in the second and third columns the posttraining test scores of the eight matched pairs are cited. In the remaining three columns at the right of the table, all of the operations are depicted which are necessary to compute *T*, the statistic on which the Wilcoxon test is based.

Table 20.6

Posttraining Test Scores of Two Groups of Matched Students, Classified According to Whether They Received "Knowledge of Results"

Pair	Knowledge of Results	No Knowledge of Results	Difference	Rank of Difference	Rank with Less Frequent Sign
1	65	61	4	2.5	
2	72	59	13	7	
3	58	63	−5	−4	4
4	48	41	7	5	
5	62	64	−2	−1	1
6	59	55	4	2.5	
7	74	54	20	8	
8	69	60	9	6	
					$\overline{T=5}$

The first step in computing T is to calculate all of the differences, either positive or negative, between the pairs by subtracting the scores of those who had no knowledge of results from their matched counterparts. These differences are then listed in a separate column.

Next the differences are ranked *regardless of algebraic sign*, giving a rank of 1 to the smallest difference, a rank of 2 to the next smallest difference, and so forth. To repeat, the ranking is done without considering algebraic signs, so that a difference of -3 is given a *lower* rank than either -4 or $+4$. Pairs whose difference is zero are dropped from the analysis. If more than one pair has an identical difference, all of the pairs are given the mean of the totaled rankings, as in the case of pairs one and six in the example when each difference was assigned a ranking of 2.5.

Having ranked the differences regardless of algebraic sign, the sign is now affixed once more to the rank of the differences. Essentially, this identifies which ranks arose from negative differences and which arose from positive differences.

Now T is obtained merely by summing the smaller number of the like-signed ranks. In this example the negative ranks are fewer, so T equals 5. The significance of T, if the number of pairs is 25 or less, can be determined by consulting Table J in the Appendix. In this example, n was 8 so we find that a T value of 4 or less is needed to yield significance at the 0.05 level, and a T of zero is needed for significance at the 0.01 level. (Both of these values refer to two-tailed tests.) Note that unlike many other statistics, the smaller T is, the more significant it is.

It can be noted that Table J only covers cases involving from six to 25 pairs. When n exceeds 25, Formula 20.2 is used and the significance of T is determined from the table of the normal curve, given in Table C in the Appendix.

$$z = \frac{T - \frac{n(n+1)}{4}}{\sqrt{\frac{n(n+1)(2n+1)}{24}}} \qquad (20.2)$$

To indicate how satisfactory this formula is, even for small samples, we may use the value of T and n from the previous example and compute the value of z. Substituting $T = 5$ and $n = 8$ in the formula, z is found as follows:

$$z = \frac{5 - \frac{8(8+1)}{4}}{\sqrt{\frac{8(8+1)(2)(8+1)}{24}}}$$

$$= -1.77$$

Notice that a z of -1.77 nears statistical significance at the 0.05 level (a z of ± 1.96 would be required for a two-tailed hypothesis test) but does not quite reach it. This is basically the same as the result noted in Table J where the obtained T of 5 barely missed the required T of 4.

The computation procedure followed for the Wilcoxon matched-pairs signed-ranks tests, as can be seen, is quite simple. Once again, if n is 25 or less Table J can be used to interpret the probability of T. If n exceeds 25, Formula 20.2 is used and the resulting z value interpreted from Table C.

SIGN TEST

The sign test is used in situations similar to those for which the Wilcoxon test is employed but may be utilized when only the direction, not the size, of difference between matched pairs can be determined. For example, suppose matched pairs are subjected to an experimental condition so that one member of the pair can be identified as superior to the other, but no notion of the degree of superiority can be obtained. This is an ideal situation for the application of the sign test.

The computation of the widely used nonparametric procedure can be illustrated by an example drawn from a high-school wrestling class, where twelve pairs of boys, matched on previously administered tests of physical strength and coordination, were taught a particular wrestling stunt by two different instructional methods. Following training, the boys performed their stunt in pairs before judges who, without knowing which member of each pair was taught by which method, rated the performance of one member of the pair as superior to that of the other pair member. Data from the study are summarized in Table 20.7. In this table the member of each pair is identified (by teaching method) who was rated superior by the judges. A sign has been given to each difference in the column at the right depending on the direction of difference. In the event that no direction of difference can be discerned between a pair, such individuals are dropped from the analysis as in the Wilcoxon test.

Table 20.7

Performance Ratings of 12 Pairs of Boys Taught by Method A and Method B

Pair	Teaching Method Used with Boy Judged Superior	Sign
1	A	+
2	A	+
3	B	−
4	B	−
5	A	+
6	A	+
7	A	+
8	B	−
9	A	+
10	A	+
11	A	+
12	A	+
		$x = 3$

The symbol x is used to represent the number of the fewer signs. In this case the value of x is 3.

For samples of 25 or fewer pairs, Table K can be used to interpret the probability of x. As can be seen in the table, with n equal to 12, an x of 3 has a one-tailed probability occurrence of 0.073 and, accordingly, a two-tailed probability of 0.146. The null hypothesis would, therefore, be considered tenable.

With ns larger than 25, the significance of the sign test is determined in a manner similar to that seen in the Wilcoxon test, namely, through the use of Formula 20.3 which yields a z value.

$$z = \frac{(x \pm 0.5) - \frac{1}{2}n}{\frac{1}{2}\sqrt{n}} \tag{20.3}$$

In this formula $x + 0.5$ is used when x is less than $\frac{1}{2}n$, and $x - 0.5$ is used when x is greater than $\frac{1}{2}n$. The use of Formula 20.3 can be illustrated by data from 36 matched pairs, where the number of fewer difference signs was 8, thus $n = 36$ and $x = 8$. Since x is less than $\frac{1}{2}n$, $x + 0.5$ is used in the formula.

$$z = \frac{(8 + 0.5) - 18}{\frac{1}{2}\sqrt{36}}$$

$$= -3.17$$

A z value of -3.17, interpreted from Table C, is significant beyond the 0.01 level, and the null hypothesis would be rejected.

MANN-WHITNEY U TEST

When the difference between two independent or nonmatched groups is to be assessed, the Mann-Whitney U test represents a powerful alternative to the parametric t test for uncorrelated samples. The U test needs data which can be ranked. With small samples, U can be calculated in an extremely brief manner. The statistic on which this test is based, that is, U, is interpreted for statistical significance in one of three different ways, depending upon the size of the sample involved. This will be demonstrated shortly. Before proceeding, however, it will be necessary to define n_1 as the number of cases in the smaller of the two groups and n_2 as number of cases in the larger of the two groups.

Very Small Samples

When n_1 and n_2 are very small, U is computed as follows. First, the scores of the two groups are ranked together but retaining each score's identity as to the group from which it was drawn. For example, with the eight scores presented below, the ranking is conducted in order of increasing size as follows:

Group A Scores: 4, 6, 7, 12, 15

Group B Scores: 3, 8, 9

Now in combined ranking:

Rank	3	4	6	7	8	9	12	15
Group	B	A	A	A	B	B	A	A

Next, focus on the B group and count the number of A scores which are ranked below or precede each score in the B group. For the B score of 3, no A score is ranked lower. For the B score of 8, three A scores precede, as is the case with the B score of 9. Hence, $U = 0 + 3 + 3 = 6$, that is, the number of times an A score preceded a B score.

When neither n_1 or n_2 is larger than 8, Table L of the Appendix may be used to determine the probability of the occurrence of U. To use Table L, the separate subtable is consulted which has n_2 equal to the number of cases in the larger sample. In the present example, $n_2 = 5$, so the subtable for $n_2 = 5$ is consulted. Next, the value of n_1 is located in the top row of the table. The column of probability values below the appropriate n_1 indicates the significance level for the U values in the column at the extreme left. In the present example a U of 6, when $n_2 = 5$ and $n_1 = 3$, has a 0.393 probability of occurrence. *All probability values in Table L are for one-tailed tests*, so the two-tailed probability of this U would be 0.786. The researcher would consider the null hypothesis tenable under the circumstances. In the U test we once again see an example of a statistical test where the smaller the statistic is, the more significant it is.

It sometimes happens that the value of U is so large that it is not cited in the appropriate subtable. This situation occurs when the researcher has focused on the "wrong" group to determine U. A value of U too large for the table is called U'. In the present example U' would have been obtained had we used the values of B scores that were ranked below the values of A scores. To illustrate, U would then have been $1+1+1+3+3 = 9$. The subtable where $n_2 = 5$ shows that when $n_1 = 3$, there is no probability value of a U of 9. Thus, we know that this U is actually U'. Now U' can quickly be converted to U by the use of Formula 20.4.

$$U = n_1 n_2 - U' \qquad (20.4)$$

In the present example, Formula 20.4 would be used as follows to obtain the U originally found by counting the number of B scores that preceded A scores.

$$U = (3)(5) - 9 = 6$$

Moderately Large Samples

When n_2 is between 9 and 20, Table L is not used to determine the significance of U. Instead, Table M in the Appendix is used. This table gives critical values for U for one- and two-tailed tests at commonly used significance levels. The researcher must use the particular subtable of Table M which is appropriate for the significance level he employs. For example, if $n_1 = 8$ and $n_2 = 16$ in a two-tailed null hypothesis test where the rejection level has been preset at 0.05, a U value of 31 or less is needed to reject the null hypothesis.

Once more, the researcher may occasionally compute the value of U'. This can be quickly ascertained by inserting the obtained value in Formula 20.4 and computing a second U value. The smaller of the two U values is U, while the larger is U'.

Large Samples

When n_2 is larger than 20, a special formula has been developed for interpreting the probability of U by a z value and the normal curve. This formula (20.5) is as follows:

$$z = \frac{U - \dfrac{n_1 n_2}{2}}{\sqrt{\dfrac{(n_1)(n_2)(n_1 + n_2 + 1)}{12}}} \qquad (20.5)$$

Formula 20.5, like some of the nonparametric formulas seen previously for treating large samples, yields a z value whose probability of occurrence is determined through use of the normal curve table in the Appendix.

With large or even moderately large samples, the computation of U by the counting method described earlier is far too time-consuming. A procedure which yields identical results is carried out by considering the scores in both groups as though they were in one group and then ranking all scores, giving a 1

Table 20.8
Behavior Rigidity Scores of Nine Experimental and Six Control Students

Experimental Group		Control Group	
Score	Rank	Score	Rank
49	13	59	15
47	11	56	14
41	9	48	12
39	9	46	10
35	6	37	7
30	5	26	2
29	4		
28	3		
24	1		
			$R_1 = 60$

---

to the lowest score, a 2 to the next lowest, and so forth. Then, if R_1 equals the sum of the ranks assigned to the n_1 group,

$$U = n_1 n_2 + \frac{n_l(n_1 + 1)}{2} - R_1 \qquad (20.6)$$

Through the use of Formula 20.6 with large groups, *or with moderately large groups*, U can be readily computed. Once again, the obtained value should be inserted in the transformation formula (20.4) to see if U' rather than U has been obtained noting that the smaller value is U.

Use of Formulas 20.5 and 20.6 can be illustrated by the hypothetical data presented in Table 20.8, where behavioral rigidity scores and ranks of an experimental and a control group of students are presented.

The first step is to give overall rankings to the scores, considering them as a combined group. The rankings of the smaller group are then summed, in this example to yield an R_1 of 60. This value is then inserted, along with n_1 and n_2 into Formula 20.6 as follows:

$$U = (6)(9) + \frac{(6)(6 + 1)}{2} - 60$$

$$= 15$$

To be certain that this value is U rather than U', Formula 20.4 is used:

$$U = (6)(9) - 15$$

$$= 39$$

The smaller of these values is U, hence we know that $U = 15$, and $U' = 39$.

The next step in the analysis is to insert U, n_1, and n_2 into Formula 20.5 and solve for z.

$$z = \frac{15 - \dfrac{(6)(9)}{2}}{\sqrt{\dfrac{(6)(9)(6 + 9 + 1)}{12}}}$$

$$= \frac{-12}{8.49}$$

$$= -1.41$$

Since a z value of -1.41, as interpreted from the table of the normal curve, is not significant at the 0.05 level, the null hypothesis would not be rejected.

In computing U through Formula 20.6, ties-in ranks are assigned the average of the tied ranks. If the tied ranks are many and U is close to the previously decided rejection level, a special correction formula[2] which takes ties into account may be used. The effect of this correction is to slightly increase the value of z, thus making it more significant.

FRIEDMAN TWO-WAY ANALYSIS OF VARIANCE

The Friedman two-way analysis of variance by ranks is designed to test the null hypothesis that several matched samples have been drawn from the same population. The matched samples may be the same group of subjects who have been exposed to several conditions, or they may be sets of individuals who have been matched on relevant variables and are randomly assigned to different conditions. In either situation the condition represents the independent variable while the criterion data, which must be amenable to ranking, represent the dependent variable.

The use of the Friedman test will be illustrated by the data presented in Table 20.9, where four elementary-school pupils, who have each been exposed to three different programmed instruction methods, have ranked each method according to how "interesting" they believed it to be.

In this instance the most interesting method was ranked 1, the next most interesting method ranked 2, and the least interesting method ranked 3. It makes no difference in the Friedman test whether rankings are from lowest to highest or highest to lowest. Tied ranks in the Friedman test are assigned the average rank of the ties. The next step is to sum the ranks in each of the columns as has been done in Table 20.9. We are now ready to use Formula 20.7 which yields the statistic upon which the Friedman test is based, χ_r^2. Although the formula may appear formidable, its computation is really quite simple.

$$\chi_r^2 = \frac{12}{Nk(k+1)} \Sigma (R_j)^2 - 3N(k+1) \tag{20.7}$$

[2]*Ibid.*, pp. 123–126.

Table 20.9

Ranks of Three Programmed Instruction Methods by Four Elementary-School Pupils

| Pupil | Programming Method | | |
	I	II	III
A	2	1	3
B	3	1	2
C	1	2	3
D	2	1	3
	$R_1 = 8$	$R_2 = 5$	$R_3 = 11$

where

N = the number of rows
k = the number of columns
$(R_j)^2$ directs one to first square, then sum all column rank totals

Thus, we may insert the necessary values in Formula 20.7 and solve as follows:

$$\chi_r^2 = \frac{12}{(4)(3)(3+1)} \left[(8)^2 + (5)^2 + (11)^2 \right] - 3(4)(3+1)$$

$$= 4.5$$

The probability of χ_r^2 is generally determined by using the standard χ^2 table (Table I) with df = the number of columns less one. However, when the number of columns is 3 and the number of rows 2–9, or when the number of columns is 4 and the number of rows 2–4, Table N of the Appendix should be used. Since in this example there are only three columns and four rows, we consult Table N to see that when $k = 3$ and $N = 4$, a χ_r^2 value of 4.5 is significant at the 0.125 level; thus, the null hypothesis would not be rejected.

KRUSKAL–WALLIS ONE-WAY ANALYSIS OF VARIANCE

The Kruskal–Wallis one-way analysis of variance by ranks is designed to test the null hypothesis that several independent samples are drawn from the same population. This test, then, is basically designed to test for differences between three or more groups when the data involved are capable of being ranked. The test can be applied to situations involving extremely small samples. In fact, probability values are available for three samples involving as few as one, one, and two subjects.

Computation procedures to be used with the test will be illustrated by an example, where three small samples of public school special services personnel are contrasted with respect to their performance on an attitude inventory designed to measure likeliness of establishing good rapport with colleagues. Scores and ranks of the subjects are presented in Table 20.10.

The first step in the computation procedure is to consider all scores as

---

Table 20.10

Scores of Three Groups of Public School Special Services Personnel on a Test of Potential Rapport with Colleagues

School Nurses		Counselors		Psychometricians	
Score	Rank	Score	Rank	Rank	Score
64	9	72	13	66	11
59	8	70	12	49	5
56	6	65	10	48	5
47	3	57	7	42	1
44	2				
$R_1 = 28$		$R_2 = 42$		$R_3 = 21$	

---

though they were drawn from one group and assign ranks to each score. This has been done in Table 20.10 in the columns adjacent to the three score columns. These ranks are then summed for each column. In the present example, this operation yielded $R_1 = 28$, $R_2 = 42$, and $R_3 = 21$. We are now ready to use the formula (20.8) for the Kruskal–Wallis test.

$$H = \frac{12}{n(n+1)} \sum \frac{R_j^2}{n_j} - 3(n+1) \qquad (20.8)$$

where

n = the number of cases in all the samples combined

$\sum \dfrac{R_j^2}{n_j}$ directs one to square each sum of column ranks, divide each of these squares by the number of ranks in the column, then add the resulting quantities together

Thus, the value of H in the present example would be computed as follows:

$$H = \frac{12}{13(13+1)} \left[\frac{(28)^2}{5} + \frac{(42)^2}{4} + \frac{(21)^2}{4} \right] - 3(13+1)$$

$$= 4.73$$

When the number of cases in each sample exceeds five, H may be interpreted for level of statistical significance from a chi-square table (Table I in the Appendix) with df = the number of columns, or samples, less one. However, when there are only three samples and the number of cases per sample is five or less, then Table H of the Appendix should be used to interpret the probability of the occurrence of H. This situation exists in the present example where $n_1 = 5$, $n_2 = 4$, and $n_3 = 4$. From Table H we find that with samples of this size an H of 4.73 has a probability of occurrence significant at the 0.10 level (where H must equal or exceed 4.6187) but not at the 0.05 level (where H must equal or exceed 5.6176). Thus, had the researcher previously set his null hypothesis rejection level at 0.05, the null hypothesis would have to be considered tenable.

This result indicates that on the basis of these samples, at least, there was no significant difference between the three groups of special services personnel with respect to scores on the test of potential rapport with colleagues.

The reader may note from the data, however, that there are apparently certain score differences between the three samples. With larger n's in the groups, if the trend of these differences persisted, the results would definitely be statistically significant. This situation, therefore, illustrates how the factor of sample size is so instrumental in yielding probabilistic significance.

SPEARMAN RANK-ORDER CORRELATION COEFFICIENT

The Spearman rank-order correlation coefficient is one of the most widely used nonparametric techniques. Often referred to as *rho*, this statistic will be designated as r_S in this discussion. The function of r_S is essentially the same as that of the Pearson product-moment correlation coefficient, namely, to assess the degree of relationship between two variables. However, while the Pearson r requires that certain assumptions such as homoscedasticity be satisfied, the Spearman coefficient does not. Thus, it may be used in certain instances when the researcher finds it impossible to apply r. As it is computed rapidly with small samples, r_S is often used by persons who wish to secure a quick estimate of relationship between variables.

In computing r_S, first list all scores of the subjects on both of the variables. Next, ranks should be assigned to each subject, first for X scores and then for the Y scores. The difference between the two ranks for each subject is then listed in a new column. These squares of these differences are listed in a separate column and then summed. The necessary values are now available so that r_S can be readily computed by the use of Formula 20.9.

$$r_S = 1 - \frac{6\Sigma d^2}{n^3 - n} \tag{20.9}$$

where
$n =$ the number of subjects
$\Sigma d^2 =$ the sum of the squared differences between subjects' ranks

The use of Formula 20.9 can be illustrated from the hypothetical attitude scale data presented in Table 20.11, when the previously described procedure for ranking, obtaining differences, and squaring these differences has been accomplished. Note that tied scores are assigned the average of the ranks. Though quite a large number of tied ranks can be tolerated without affecting the size of r_S, a correction for an excessive number of ties is described elsewhere.[3] The sum of the squared differences (Σd^2) in this case is 8.5. Inserting this quantity and the number of subjects, Formula 20.9 yields r_S as follows:

$$r_S = 1 - \frac{6(8.5)}{7^3 - 7}$$

$$= 0.85$$

[3]*Ibid.*

Table 20.11
Scores and Ranks of Seven Subjects on Two Attitude Inventories

Subject	Attitude Inventory X Score	Rank	Attitude Inventory Y Score	Rank	d	d^2
a	124	1	62	2	−1	1
b	123	2	59	3	−1	1
c	119	3	67	1	2	4
d	117	4	57	4.5	0.5	0.25
e	110	5	57	4.5	0.5	0.25
f	104	6	50	7	−1	1
g	94	7	52	6	1	1
						$\Sigma d^2 = 8.5$

The Spearman coefficient is interpreted in basically the same way as the standard product-moment r, where a coefficient near +1.00 reflects a strong positive relationship, a coefficient near −1.00 reflects a strong negative relationship, and a coefficient near zero reflects little or no relationship.

Significance of r_s

The statistical significance of r_s can be determined quite readily with small samples of 4 to 30 cases through the use of Table E in the Appendix, where one-tailed significance levels are supplied for critical values of r_s at the 0.05 and 0.01 levels. To illustrate the use of Table E, we can note that with the r_s of 0.887 obtained in the foregoing example, where $n = 7$, a one-tailed significance level of 0.05 has been reached. The tabled 0.05 critical value with this size sample was 0.714 while the 0.01 critical value was 0.893.

When n is 10 or greater, the significance of the Spearman coefficient may be tested by the use of Formula 20.10 which yields a t value, interpreted from the t table (Table F in the Appendix), where $df = n - 2$.

$$t = r_s \sqrt{\frac{n-2}{1-r_s^2}}$$

(20.10)

To illustrate the use of Formula 20.10 we can insert a Spearman coefficient value of 0.70, where the number of subjects involved was 32. The formula is then set up and computed as follows:

$$t = 0.70 \sqrt{\frac{32-2}{1-(0.70)^2}}$$

$$= 5.37$$

With 30df ($n-2$) it may be seen from Table F that the obtained t value of 5.37 is significant beyond the 0.01 level.

REVIEW

In this chapter computation procedures and examples were given for the chi-square test, the Wilcoxon matched-pairs signed-ranks test, the sign test, the Mann–Whitney U test, the Friedman two-way analysis of variance, the Kruskal–Wallis one-way analysis of variance, and the Spearman rank-order correlation coefficient.

Because of the widespread use in goodness of fit tests, as well as difference tests between two or more samples, considerable attention was given to the χ^2 test, particularly to its expected frequency requirements. Suggestions for regrouping chi-square categories were given.

It was seen that almost all of these tests can be quickly calculated and readily interpreted, a point of some importance to time-pressed teachers and administrators.

EXERCISES

1. During seven previous years the average percentage of students electing particular foreign languages in a metropolitan high-school has been the following: French, 35%; Spanish, 40%; German, 15%; Latin, 10%. This year the school counselors note an apparently marked divergence from previous enrollments, for the 500 students electing foreign languages are distributed as follows: French, 200; Spanish, 150; German, 100; Latin, 50. Using a χ^2 analysis, determine whether this year's enrollment in foreign languages is significantly different (at the 0.01 level) from the average distribution pattern during the seven previous years.

2. Determine by a χ^2 goodness of fit test whether the following distribution of scores can be considered to depart significantly from the shape of a normal distribution. Remember that a score such as 17 actually represents an interval from $16.5 - 17.5$. Set up at $1 \times 8 \, \chi^2$ table and compute the expected frequencies based on the normal curve table.

Score	Frequency
20	20
19	40
18	60
17	80
16	80
15	60
14	40
13	20

3. Below are responses of two groups of students to a questionnaire item.

Using a chi-square two-sample test determine whether the null hypotheses regarding group differences should be rejected.

	A	B	C	D
Group X	60	50	40	50
Group Y	0	10	30	30

4. Fifty first-year elementary teachers and fifty first-year secondary teachers have completed an attitude inventory regarding professional organizations in education. Their responses have been summarized in the 2×5 table below. If necessary, combine categories of scores, so that χ^2 can be applied without violating generally accepted notions regarding minimum expected frequencies. Compute a chi-square value to see whether the two samples of teachers can be considered to have been drawn from the same population.

	Attitude Inventory Score				
	40 and Below	41–50	51–60	61–70	71 and Above
Elementary teachers	4	10	12	18	6
Secondary teachers	3	11	13	15	8

5. Two samples consisting of matched pairs of elementary pupils have been given different sets of spelling materials. The two students in each pair were matched in IQ and scores on an extensive spelling pretest. Below are their scores in a posttraining spelling examination. Using a Wilcoxon matched-pairs signed-ranks test determine whether the performance of the groups using spelling materials X is significantly different beyond the 0.05 level from the group using spelling materials Z.

Pair Number	Spelling Examination Score	
	Materials X	Materials Z
1	28	31
2	33	35
3	40	39
4	36	39
5	40	43
6	14	21
7	16	19
8	21	26
9	32	30
10	43	56

6. Twelve matched pairs of primary grade students have undergone a month-long reading-improvement training session, with one group using conventional reading improvement materials and the other group using an approach based on a modified form of our alphabet symbols known as the *Augmented Roman Alphabet*. At the conclusion of the training period 10 of the 12 pupils in the Augmented Roman Alphabet group exceed the performance of their material counterparts on a standardized reading test. Using a sign test, determine whether this difference is significant beyond the 0.05 level.

7. By employing a Mann–Whitney test determine the value of U and decide whether Group I significantly out-performed Group II at the 0.05 level. Assume that you have made a prediction in advance of the data-gathering that Group I will perform better (that is, secure higher scores) than Group II, hence are entitled to use a one-tailed test.

Group I scores	2	3	5	6	9	9	10
Group II scores	1	1	4	4			

8. Test the null hypothesis that the following scores of 20 boys and 18 girls are not significantly different from one another on an inventory of interest in social welfare work. Use the Mann–Whitney U test Formulas 20.5 and 20.6 to analyze the data.

Boys	Girls	Boys	Girls
42	54	33	41
40	53	30	41
40	50	30	41
39	48	30	38
38	48	28	34
37	47	28	33
36	47	27	30
35	46	26	30
35	46	25	
34	43	24	

9. Using a Friedman two-way analysis of variance model, determine the value of χ_r^2 and decide whether to reject the null hypothesis at the 0.01 level for the following data, where three matched sets of subjects have been trained by four different instructional techniques and subsequently ranked in terms of performance.

Subject Set	Instructional Technique 1	2	3	4
A	4	2	1	3
B	4	3	1	2
C	4	3	1	1

10. The following are personality test scores for three groups of secondary teachers, whose college majors were English, psychology, and sociology. Using the Kruskal–Wallis one-way analysis of variance, determine the value of *H* and decide whether the three samples should be considered part of the same population.

Psychology	English	Sociology
64	65	59
63	42	42
58	39	29
43	30	
40		

11. Compute a Spearman rank order correlation coefficient on the data given in exercise 7 on page 98. Note how r_s compares with the product-moment *r* of 0.35.

12. Determine the size of r_s for the following two sets of rankings by two teachers of a set of essay examinations. Assuming that r_s will be positive and, therefore, using a one-tailed test, is r_s significant beyond the 0.05 level?

Test Paper	Ranking by Teacher I	Ranking by Teacher II
1	1	1
2	3	2
3	2	3
4	5	4
5	4	5
6	6	6
7	7	7

SELECTED READINGS

Blalock, Hubert M., Jr., *Social Statistics*. New York: McGraw-Hill, 1960, chaps. 2, 14, and 15.

Edwards, Allen L., *Statistical Methods for the Behavioral Sciences*. New York: Holt, Rinehart & Winston, 1957, chaps. 18 and 19.

McNemar, Quinn, *Psychological Statistics*. New York: Wiley, 1962, chap. 19.

Siegel, Sidney, *Nonparametric Statistics for the Behavioral Sciences*. New York: McGraw-Hill, 1956.

Tate, Merle W., and Richard C. Clelland, *Nonparametric and Short-cut Statistics*. Danville, Ill.: Interstate Printers and Publishers, 1957.

Yates, F., "Contingency Tables Involving Small Numbers and the χ^2 Test," *J. Roy. Statist. Soc. Suppl.* **1** (1934): 217–235.

21
Choosing
the
Appropriate
Technique

This chapter is designed to accomplish two purposes. For the reader who will actually be selecting statistical procedures for analyzing research data, the following pages will provide both information and practice helpful in choosing the correct analysis technique for different research tasks. For those who will only be reading about research studies, practice in selecting the appropriate statistical technique will markedly aid in a conceptual understanding of the purposes for which these techniques are commonly used.

The scheme employed is quite simple. A hypothetical educational situation will be presented representing a general class of research designs that might be encountered by an educator. Following the hypothetical situation, the reader will be asked to select from several choices the statistical technique most appropriate for the analysis of the situation at hand. If the correct choice is made, the reader will be so informed without delay and will be presented with another hypothetical situation. If the incorrect choice is made, additional information will be presented in order to clarify the reasons why another technique is more suitable. The reader will then be allowed to choose another statistical technique for the situation.

DIRECTIONS FOR READING THIS CHAPTER

The pages in the following section are numbered as usual *but are not to be read consecutively*. In proceeding from one page to the next, you will respond to a multiple-choice question by turning to the page indicated to the left of your answer section. The page to which you turn will either be the "right answer page" and will contain an additional multiple-choice question, or it will be a "wrong answer page" and will include directions regarding which page should be selected next. At the bottom of each page, in italicized print, selections of the text are cited which may be profitably reviewed by the reader. Please begin on page 309.

A pilot experiment, designed to test the effectiveness of a new approach to spelling proficiency, has been conducted over a semester-long period in a junior high school. Two different classes of 29 seventh-grade pupils participated in the study. Students in Group *X* received their formal spelling instructions from Mr. Jordan, an experienced teacher. Mr. Jordan employed conventional methods of spelling instruction such as are commonly used in upper elementary grades. While he met with Group *X* five times each week for a period of one hour, only one hour per week was devoted to spelling instruction. Group *Y* also met with Mr. Jordan daily, but while they devoted an hour per week to spelling instruction, all formal spelling teaching employed the newly developed programmed spelling lessons that were presented to the student through the use of self-instruction "teaching machines." Since all of the students involved in the pilot study had been preselected for purposes of the research, subjects in the two groups had been matched in pairs with respect to intellectual ability and pre-experiment performance on an orally administered spelling quiz of 150 words. At the conclusion of the semester's experiment, the spelling quiz was readministered to both groups.

Which of the statistical procedures presented below should be selected to test whether there is a significant difference between Mr. Jordan's conventional instruction techniques and the programmed method of teaching spelling as determined by postexperiment performance on the spelling quiz?

Page 310   Product-Moment Correlation
Page 312   *t* Test
Page 314   Analysis of Covariance

To review the distinction between "difference-testing" and "relationship-testing" procedures, see pp. 45–46.

YOUR ANSWER
Product-Moment Correlation

Well, let's see. We have learned that correlation procedures are used to determine the degree of relationship between two variables. In order to calculate a relationship between the two variables, we must have two measures for the same subjects. Now the measures available in the situation under consideration are pre-experiment spelling scores, postexperiment spelling scores, and intelligence test scores. We could, then, compute correlation coefficients between any two of these measures. Which correlation coefficient, however, would tell us anything about the effectiveness of the two methods of teaching spelling? Would the correlation between pre- and postexperiment spelling indicate anything about the value of the new approach to spelling, even if we considered the groups one at a time? No, we could gain little insight into the efficacy of the new method by correlating student's scores on any of the available measures.

We need a statistical technique that will indicate if those who studied spelling by the new method *exceeded* the performance of those who studied by the conventional method. A *difference-testing* technique is called for in this situation, not product-moment correlation. In light of this additional information, return to page 309 and select the correct technique.

To review the function of product-moment correlation, see pp. 64–66.

YOUR ANSWER
Determination of a Confidence Interval

As you may recall, confidence intervals are used to estimate, from sample statistics, the limits within which population parameters such as means, correlation coefficients, and mean differences probably fall. Estimation of such intervals or ranges is an extremely important operation in educational research. However, the task facing the researcher in this instance is to determine whether a statistically significant difference exists between any of the four groups. Having determined that a significant difference exists, the next step might be to determine the confidence interval.

In selecting a technique to use in the present situation, the researcher must choose a statistical model capable of testing for mean differences between two or more groups. Now return to page 312 and select the most appropriate technique.

To review the purposes of estimation procedures, see pp. 54–59.

YOUR ANSWER
t Test

Correct. The problem at hand is to test the null hypothesis that the post-experiment performance of the two matched groups is equivalent. Since the groups have been matched on measures considered relevant to the criterion, the major remaining factor which is potentially related to the criterion is type of treatment, i.e., mode of instruction. Because the groups consist of matched pairs, the correlated *t* model should be used. If the null hypothesis is tenable, as indicated by a nonsignificant *t* value, then one would conclude that no difference favoring the new method of teaching spelling exists, at least on the basis of this pilot study. If the null hypothesis is untenable, as manifested by a significant *t* value, and the group favored by the mean differences is the experimental group, the evidence to support the use of the new method has been provided by the pilot study. Further large-scale experimentation to assess the relative efficacy of the new method is probably warranted.

Taking another somewhat comparable situation, assume that *three* new methods of teaching spelling are being contrasted with a conventional method. Once more, only one instructor is involved in the experiment. Four groups of fifteen pupils, randomly drawn from a large number of potential subjects, have been equated with respect to pre-experiment spelling scores, intelligence test scores, and previous scholastic performance in school. If one wished to determine whether there were significant differences in the scores of the four groups (three experimental, one control) on a postexperiment spelling test, which of the following statistical procedures would be most appropriate?

Page 311   Determination of a Confidence Interval
Page 315   Single-Classification Analysis of Variance
Page 316   Chi Square

To review the different types of t test models, see pp. 130–131.

YOUR ANSWER
Spearman Rank-Order Correlation Coefficient

The Spearman rank-order correlation approach yields an index of the relationship between two ranked variables. As such, it is often employed in situations when the assumptions of the product-moment r cannot be satisfied. It is true in the present prediction problem that the counselor would have a better idea of whom to recommend for university work if he knew more about the general nature of relationships between the variable of college grade performance and the potential prediction variables he has at his disposal such as students' high-school grade averages, 9th grade IQ scores, and college entrance examination scores. Yet, while the Spearman r_S will provide such a general estimate of the strength and direction of relationships between prediction variables and the criterion variable, it does not provide a method for making appropriate predictions for *individual* students.

Such a technique is needed in the present instance, that is, a model which makes it possible to set up a prediction equation which, when an individual's scores on the predictor variables are inserted, will yield an estimate of his performance on the criterion measure—in this case, university grades. Return to page 315 and select the appropriate technique.

To review the purposes of the Spearman rank-order correlation coefficient, see pp. 280–281.

YOUR ANSWER
Analysis of Covariance

You have probably recalled that analysis of covariance may be used to test for differences among two or more groups, while statistically controlling for group differences on variables which are relevant to the criterion variable under consideration. In the situation described, the criterion measure is student performance on the post-experiment spelling examination. Available measures which are relevant are undoubtedly pre-experiment spelling scores and intelligence test scores. However, there is really no need of statistically equating group differences on these relevant variables, for subjects in the two groups *were already matched* before the experiment was commenced. Hence, while analysis of covariance *could* be employed in the situation to yield the necessary information regarding the efficacy of the experimental method, a technique which did not involve the computation associated with the statistical equalization of groups would be more economical and probably a better choice under these circumstances. Return to page 309 and select the correct technique.

To review the function of analysis of covariance, see pp. 204–206.

YOUR ANSWER
Single-Classification Analysis of Variance

Correct. When testing for mean differences between several randomly drawn samples, single-classification analysis of variance is appropriate, if only one independent variable is employed in the design. In the present situation, the single independent variable is method of instruction as represented by the four groups, and the dependent variable is performance on the spelling test.

Turning to another problem, a high-school counselor is faced with the task of setting up a systematic procedure for predicting the likely success of his school's seniors at a nearby private university. In previous years, students with a grade point average lower than B+, regardless of intelligence or any other factors, have been advised not to enroll in the University on the grounds that they would probably fail to maintain university grade standards.

Both the admission officials at the University and the administrators at the school have requested the counseling office to develop a more precise scheme for predicting potential University success. Certain of the high school's graduates, each with C averages throughout high school, have entered the University (against advisement) and maintained excellent scholastic records.

The counselor is given complete access to records at the University, as well as the high school, for all of the students who were graduated from the high school and entered the University. Records are quite complete for the past twelve years. Included in the University records are college grades and entrance examination scores. The high-school records have high-school grades, scores on a standardized intelligence test administered during the ninth grade, as well as certain personal data such as sex, church affiliation, and so forth.

Which of the following statistical devices should the counselor use to develop the prediction scheme which will permit more precise advisement of his high school's university aspirants?

Page 313   Spearman Rank-Order Correlation Coefficient
Page 318   Regression
Page 319   Standard Deviation

To review the assumptions underlying analysis of variance, see pp. 166–168.

YOUR ANSWER
Chi Square

There are research situations quite similar to the present one in which chi square might be used to test for differences between several groups. Yet, since χ^2 is a nonparametric statistical model and uses only frequency count data rather than deviations from the mean, it is a markedly less *powerful* statistical test than its parametric counterparts. Chi square can be used to test for differences between two or more groups, when the criterion data appear only in classificatory, rather than numerical form.

In the present example, the postexperiment spelling scores of the subjects are numerical, thus a parametric approach is probably preferable to chi square. The researcher should select a parametric model which will test for mean differences between two or more samples. Return to page 312 and pick the appropriate statistical technique.

To review the applications of the chi-square model, see pp. 273–274 and 276–277.

YOUR ANSWER
Single-Classification Analysis of Variance

Let's see whether an analysis of variance model fits this type of situation. Analysis of variance techniques permit the researcher to tell whether two or more groups differ with respect to a criterion variable. The groups under analysis are usually considered to represent an independent variable such as marital status, for example, *never married*, *married*, or *formerly married but now single*. When this is the case, the researcher is essentially testing the *relationship* between the independent variable and the dependent variable, even though he is employing a difference-testing technique.

In the example being considered at present, the measurement specialist is not searching for differences between the scores of groups on any of the creativity tests. Instead he is trying to see if scores of groups or "clusters" of tests are related strongly enough, so that the tests in the cluster can be explained in terms of the degree to which the tests correlate with a single dimension. It is necessary to locate dimensions which are not too highly correlated with other tests, or else the explanatory function of the analysis is not well served. Considerable computational treatment of data would be required for the appropriate analysis. Such computational operations are usually performed by a high-speed computer. With this additional information in mind, return to page 318 and select the appropriate technique.

To review the purposes of single-classification analysis of variance, see pp. 152–154.

YOUR ANSWER
Regression

Correct. Through the use of a linear regression model the counselor could set up a prediction equation so that by inserting a student's score on one or more prediction variables, such as his IQ, a predicted college grade point average could be determined, with certain known error limits for inaccurate predictions. To secure the data necessary for the development of a regression prediction equation, the counselor would have to consider his school's previous graduates who entered the University as his regression sample. On the basis of the relationships between their performance on the criterion and one or more predictive variables, the prediction equation could be set up.

Consider a different type of research situation. Suppose an educational measurement specialist is faced with the task of developing a new test of verbal "creativity" that encompasses the various kinds of creativity identified in other tests, such as the ability to use common words in an unusual fashion. He has at his disposal test scores for 200 elementary pupils on nine supposedly different measures of creativity. He wishes to identify a few underlying dimensions which can be used to account for the various facets of verbal creativity and, having done so, to design a new measuring device which is based exclusively on these few traits. Which of the following techniques should be selected to assist in this type of research?

Page 317   Single-Classification Analysis of Variance
Page 320   Factor Analysis
Page 322   Friedman Two-Way Analysis of Variance

To review the assumptions which should be satisfied before using regression procedures, see pp. 100–101.

YOUR ANSWER
Standard Deviation

The standard deviation, like the mean, median, and variance, is a descriptive statistic, suitable for describing a certain facet of a set of data. More specifically, the standard deviation is an index of the variability of a set of data. Though it is in some cases desirable to know something about how widely scores diverge from the mean of a distribution, the particular task faced by the counselor is to select a rigorous predictive model. For these purposes, standard deviation would not suffice. Now return to page 315 and select the appropriate *predictive* statistical model.

To review the differences between description and inferential statistics, see pp. 4–5.

YOUR ANSWER
Factor Analysis

Correct. Through a factor analytic approach, the measurement expert could locate a few underlying factors which could be used to account for the different kinds of verbal creativity ostensibly measured by the nine different creativity tests. Having located these factors and rotated them, either by orthogonal or oblique rotation procedures, until an appropriate positioning has been found, he can interpret the factors according to their actual correlations with the various tests. He is then in a position to develop his new test based on these isolated dimensions.

For the next hypothetical situation, imagine that a teacher wishes to demonstrate that two forms of an achievement test she has developed are "parallel" or relatively equivalent. If so, she can administer one form as a pretest and the second as a posttest in a study of certain new instructional procedures she wishes to introduce to her class. The actual experiment she wishes to conduct involves a comparison of the achievement of three matched groups of pupils who have been taught a series of concepts by three relatively distinct instructional procedures. The results of the experiment will assist the teacher in deciding which of the instructional procedures to use with future classes.

Anticipating this project, the teacher prepared a large number of test items during the preceding semester and randomly divided them into two sets of items which represented two forms of the test. Having instructed her class by using a combination of the three new instructional procedures, she administered the two forms to 110 pupils in four sections (classes) of the same course at the close of the instructional period. She notes with pleasure that the means for the two test forms are practically identical. By employing which of the following techniques can the teacher now secure a statistical notion of the degree to which the forms of the test are equivalent?

Page 323   Multiple-Classification Analysis of Variance
Page 324   *t* Test
Page 326   Product-Moment Correlation

To review the varied applications of factors analysis, see pp. 256–257.

YOUR ANSWER
Single-Classification Analysis of Variance

Single-classification analysis of variance allows the researcher to test the null hypothesis that means of several samples have been drawn from the same population. To phrase it another way, single-classification analyses of variance permits one to tell whether there are any significant mean differences between two or more groups. The administrator's problem is somewhat the same, for he wants to learn if there is a significant difference in the responses of the two groups composed of males and females. But there are no *means* of the two groups to analyze. Instead of numerical criterion data from which one could compute means and standard deviations, we have here a set of nominal, or classificatory data where there are three classes of responses to the questionnaire item. In this instance the difference between the two samples will be determined by the *frequency* of the responses to the three categories. Analysis of variance models cannot be used with such data. Instead, a nonparametric difference-testing technique is required. Now return to page 326 and select the appropriate technique.

To review the measurement-level requirements of nonparametric tests, see pp. 268–270.

YOUR ANSWER
Friedman Two-Way Analysis of Variance

Actually, the Friedman test is a very useful nonparametric device which may be employed to test the significance of differences between several matched samples or between subjects who have been exposed to different treatment conditions. In the present problem the measurement specialist is not dealing with subjects who have been matched, but it is true that each subject has been exposed to every different test. However, the measurement expert's quest is for the magnitude of relationship between scores on the various tests under analysis. He is not interested in *differences* between the scores of various subjects in the study. Thus the Friedman technique, since it tests for differences, is inappropriate.

An appropriate technique for this type of situation must be one which will be able to isolate certain features common to several but not all of the tests. Now return to page 318 and select the appropriate technique.

To review the functions of the Friedman test, see pp. 277–278.

YOUR ANSWER
Multiple-Classification Analysis of Variance

Multiple-classification analysis of variance is a particularly powerful tool at the disposal of the educational researcher, and there are a variety of situations in which it can be appropriately used. Unfortunately, this is not one of them. Multiple-classification analysis of variance allows the researcher to determine whether there are differences between two or more sets of groups (representing independent variables) with respect to a dependent variable. It is also possible to detect a significant interaction effect of two or more independent variables upon a dependent variable.

For example, with achievement test scores as a dependent or criterion measure, we could see if there were: (1) any difference between scores of males and females; as well as (2) any difference between bright, average, and dull pupils. In such a design the two independent variables would be sex and intelligence. It would also be possible to see if an interaction between sex and intelligence resulted in any achievement score differences.

What the teacher in the present example needs is an index of the relationship, not difference, between her previous pupils' scores on the two test forms. *Now return to page 320 and select the appropriate technique.*

To review the applications of multiple-classification analysis of variance, see pp. 176–178.

324

YOUR ANSWER
t Test

Well, at first glance this might appear to be a situation where a *t* test could be appropriately used, for a *t* test does allow the researcher to tell whether two sample means are significantly different. And there are two scores for each of the 110 pupils, so one could consider each set of scores to represent a different sample. By means of a *t* test we could determine whether the means of the scores for the two forms were significantly different. But is this what the teacher really wants to know?

Since the means of the scores on the forms are practically identical, it is a foregone conclusion that a *t* test will allow one to consider the null hypothesis tenable. Does this help us, however? Such an occurrence might result from a situation where a number of students obtained high scores on Form A and low scores on Form B, but a similar number of students had low scores on Form A and high scores on Form B. In other words the two forms might not be yielding similar scores for individual pupils; only their means would be similar. Whereas the teacher would want to know whether one form is more difficult than the other, what she really needs to know is whether a student who scores high on one form tends to score high on the other and, conversely, whether a low scorer on one form is also a low scorer on the other. To discover how an individual's scores on both forms are *related* in the quest of the teacher in this situation. Now return to page 320 and select the appropriate technique.

To review the purposes of the t test, see pp. 124–126.

YOUR ANSWER
Chi Square

Correct. To conduct a chi-square analysis of these data we would cast the responses into a 2×3 (sex by questionnaire item categories) frequency table and determine whether the pattern of boys' responses departed significantly from the pattern of girls' responses. Chi square can be used, of course, in a variety of related situations ranging from one sample tests (a sample vs. a known or hypothetical distribution) to *k* sample tests, where a host of different groups are contrasted with respect to response frequencies in nominal categories.

For the next problem, consider the case of an educational investigator who wished to test whether there are any significant differences between the achievement scores of three samples of students taught by three rather distinctive varieties of lecture instruction. The first lecture approach features a multitude of rhetorical, but unanswered, questions designed to stimulate the students to think about the content of the lecture. The second lecture approach embodies many rhetorical questions, which the lecturer himself quickly answers. The final lecture technique has few, if any, rhetorical questions.

The investigator also wishes to see if the student's level of intelligence interacts in any significant fashion with the performance under the three varieties of lecture techniques. He gathers posttest achievement scores for three sets of subjects who have been exposed to the different lecture methods. Intelligence-test data are also secured for each subject so that the total sample of 300 students (100 taught by each method) can be classified as "above average intelligence," "average intelligence," or "below average intelligence."

In order to test the null hypotheses (1) that there are no significant achievement differences between students taught by the three lecture methods, and (2) that there is no significant interaction of intelligence level and lecture method on achievement, which of the following techniques should the researcher select?

Page 327   *t* Test
Page 330   Single-Classification Analysis of Variance
Page 332   Multiple-Classification Analysis of Variance

To review the requirements for chi-square tests, see pp. 284–291.

YOUR ANSWER
Product-Moment Correlation

Correct. The teacher needs to know the type and strength of the relationship, if any, between the 110 pupils' scores on the two test forms. What she would like to result is a strong positive *r*, perhaps in the neighborhood of 0.80 or 0.90. Such a coefficient would indicate that an individual who scored high on one form would very likely score high on the other, as would be true conversely with low scorers. A markedly lower *r* would suggest that further work needs to be done in equating the two forms. An inspection of the means for the two forms has revealed that neither form is more difficult than the other. By studying the difficulty and discrimination efficiency of individual items over a period of time, the teacher should be able to increase the comparability of the two test forms.

In the next hypothetical research situation we find a school administrator studying the results of a year's tryout of team-teaching. Though achievement standards have been as high as in previous years, he is puzzled by results from a postcourse questionnaire which was administered to the 95 pupils who took part in the team-teaching project. In particular, he is perplexed by responses to one question:

(7) Which type of teaching situation do you prefer?	Number checking
Team-teaching with more students per group	12
Team-teaching with fewer students per group	57
Conventional teaching with one teacher per 25–35 pupils	26

Of the 26 students who chose conventional teaching, all but 5 were boys. The administrator wonders whether the fact that all 3 teachers constituting the teaching team were women might be important. Specifically, he speculates that there may be a significant difference between the responses to question seven of the 55 boys and 40 girls in the group. Which of the following should be used?

Page 321   Single-Classification Analysis of Variance
Page 325   Chi Square
Page 328   Spearman Rank-Order Correlation Coefficient

To review the assumptions required for the product-moment correlation method, see p. 75.

YOUR ANSWER
t Test

Well, a *t* test might be used to test one of the null hypotheses under consideration, that is, the hypothesis that there is no significant achievement differential between the three groups. But, since a *t* test can only be used with two groups at a time, one would have to compute three *t* tests to tell whether there were any mean differences between the three lecture groups. Further, *t* tests offer no hope of detecting *interaction* effects of two or more independent variables upon a dependent variable. Thus, a *t* test would not be a suitable choice for this situation. Return to page 325 and select the appropriate technique.

To review the functions of the t test, see pp. 124–126.

YOUR ANSWER
Spearman Rank-Order Correlation Coefficient

To the extent that this situation requires a nonparametric technique you are correct. However, the Spearman correlation approach requires data of ordinal or interval strength. What we have here are nominal data represented by the three classes of response to the questionnaire item. Further, the Spearman rank-order correlation coefficient is a *relationship-testing* technique rather than a *difference-testing* technique. What the administrator needs here is a nonparametric technique suitable for use with nominal data, which can be used to test for differences between two groups. Return to page 326 and select such a technique.

To review the measurement-level requirements of the Spearman correlational method, see pp. 301–302.

YOUR ANSWER
Kruskal–Wallis One-Way Analysis of Variance

The Kruskal–Wallis test is an excellent alternative to single classification analysis of variance, when the assumptions of the more powerful parametric test cannot be met or when the samples are very small. In the present situation, however, a statistical test is needed which can be used to control, or statistically compensate for, differences in relevant variables between two or more groups. Since the Kruskal–Wallis one-way analysis of variance has no such potential, we must turn to another model with built-in provisions for handling initial differences between groups on important variables. Return to page 332 and select the appropriate technique.

To review the function of the Kruskal–Wallis test, see p. 279.

YOUR ANSWER
Single-Classification Analysis of Variance

Well, a single-classification analysis of variance model could be used to test the null hypothesis that there were no significant mean differences between the three student samples taught by different lecture methods. But what about the second null hypothesis regarding *interaction* between intelligence level and lecture approach? Single-classification analysis of variance cannot cope with this kind of question. Thus, a more sophisticated analysis of variance model is required for this situation. Return to page 325 and select such a model.

To review the meaning of interaction, see p. 181.

YOUR ANSWER
Mann–Whitney* U *Test

Correct. To test for differences between two samples, the Mann–Whitney U test is an extremely powerful model. The U test compares favorably, in fact, with the parametric t-test but can be applied to situations where the assumptions of the t test cannot be satisfied. The present situation where nonnormal population data precluded the use of the t test is an illustration of an instance in which the Mann–Whitney test should be used.

For the final problem in the chapter, consider the predicament of a large school system's curriculum-instruction committee which is faced with the task of recommending for district adoption a set of remedial reading materials for use in intermediate elementary grades. After several months of study, the committee has narrowed the choice to two sets of such materials. Several short-term experimental studies have been conducted by the committee in which the gain performance of two material groups, each using different materials, was contrasted. Results of these projects, several of which detected significant performance differences, strongly suggest that one set of the reading materials does yield somewhat better achievement than the competing materials. Unfortunately, these superior materials are also more expensive. Since the committee is obliged to consider the relevant economic factors, they are undecided as to which of the two sets of materials should be endorsed. One member of the committee proposes that the experimental data previously gathered by the committee be subjected to additional analysis in such a way as to help make the impending decision a more intelligent one. Which of the following statistical procedures did he probably have in mind?

Page 336   Sign Test
Page 338   Product-Moment Correlation
Page 339   Determination of a Confidence Interval

To review the function of the U test, see p. 276.

YOUR ANSWER
Multiple-Classification Analysis of Variance

Correct. By the use of this powerful model, the researcher could test both of his null hypotheses. Incidentally, he could easily test a third hypothesis regarding performance difference between achievement level groups. The results of such an analysis, however, are a foregone conclusion, that is, the brighter students will outperform their peers. Yet there are many occasions when a researcher tests for criterion mean differences between groups representing one independent variable, then a second independent variable, and finally the interaction effect of the two independent variables.

In the next problem, suppose a school psychologist is studying the influence of nondirective versus directive teaching approaches on the social studies achievement of 200 high-school juniors. Three teachers have participated in the experimental project, each teaching one class by a highly directive approach, where the instructor assumes primary responsibility for the student's learning. Each of the three teachers also instructs a second class through use of a nondirective approach where the student is urged to take the chief responsibility for his learning. At the beginning and the end of a three-month instructional period where all three instructors cover identical content in their courses, achievement examinations are administered to all students. In addition, a test of intellectual aptitude is administered to all pupils midway through the experiment.

The school psychologist, since he had to use as subjects those pupils who were assigned to the three participating teachers, wants to rule out differences between the directively taught and nondirectively taught pupils with respect to intelligence and pretest achievement level. Having done so, he wishes to see if there is significant achievement difference between the two groups. Which of the following techniques should he select?

Page 329   Kruskal–Wallis One-Way Analysis of Variance
Page 334   Regression
Page 337   Analysis of Covariance

To review the assumptions required for multiple-classification analysis of variance, see p. 183.

YOUR ANSWER
Wilcoxon Matched-Pairs Signed-Rank Test

The Wilcoxon test, an important nonparametric test, can be used to test for differences between two groups. However, the subjects in the two groups must consist of matched pairs. In the present situation, the two groups are composed of randomly drawn, therefore *independent* subjects. Now return to page 337 and choose the technique that can be used with two smaller independent samples.

To review the function of the Wilcoxon matched-pairs signed-ranks test, see pp. 274–275.

YOUR ANSWER
Regression

To some extent, regression analysis could be used in the present situation, for we need to predict what a pupil's criterion (posttest) achievement score would be if he were equal to all other students regarding pretest score and intelligence test score. But there is a more complex parametric technique which *combines* regression analysis with the analysis of variance model to perform this operation while testing for mean differences between the *statistically equalized* groups. Return to page 332 and select the technique.

To review the purposes of regression analysis, see pp. 96–97.

YOUR ANSWER
Chi Square

It is true that chi square might be considered appropriate in the present situation, for one can test differences between two groups by means of χ^2. Yet, the chi-square approach is a less powerful technique than several other nonparametric tests which can perform the same function, so if an alternative exists, the more powerful test is usually selected.

Another limitation of the present situation which would preclude the use of chi square is the small number of subjects involved. The reader may recall that chi-square analyses require that the expected frequencies in most cells of a chi-square table be five or larger. Certainly six subjects in the two groups presently being considered, even in a two by two chi-square table, would lead to insufficient expected frequencies.

Now return to page 337 and select the appropriate technique.

To review the data requirements of chi-square models, see pp. 284–291.

YOUR ANSWER
Sign Test

The sign test might seem like an appropriate choice for this type of situation, for it is a difference-testing technique which may be used with matched pairs of subjects. However, the curriculum-instruction committee does not merely need to know whether one set of reading materials is superior to the other. This, evidently, has already been established. They need an estimate or *how much* better the superior materials are likely to be in continued usage. This type of information is needed to weigh against the higher cost of the superior materials.

In other words, a hypothesis-testing technique is not needed here, for it only answers the questions "Is there a difference?" or "Is there a relationship?" What the committee needs is a statistical method of estimating from sample data the probable magnitude of mean difference in the population. Now return to page 331 and select such a procedure.

To review the function of the sign test, see p. 275.

YOUR ANSWER
Analysis of Covariance

Correct. Through analysis of covariance the differences between the two groups in pretest achievement and intelligence could be statistically adjusted so that a test between means of the directive and nondirective groups could be computed, *as if* there were no intellectual or pretest achievement disparity between the groups. Because of its utility in school research situations such as this where "intact" groups must often be used, analysis of covariance is an invaluable implement in the educational researcher's statistical tool kit.

For the next problem situation, imagine that an educational experimenter has studied the influence of a number of instructional variables on certain aspects of students' attitudes toward school and study activities. Using a newly developed attitude inventory, the researcher has sampled a large number of pupils, attempting to establish norms for the inventory. From these early studies, he is convinced that the attitude scores yielded by the inventory, are not normally distributed in the student population. Rather, samples of the numerical scores acquired through use of the inventory are always negatively skewed. The experimenter thus reasons that analyses of such data should not be conducted with those parametric techniques which require relatively normal population distributions.

He is currently conducting an experiment in which two groups of six pupils have been exposed to different instructional procedures. All twelve pupils were randomly selected and randomly assigned to one of the two groups. At the conclusion of the instructional period, both groups were given the attitude inventory. Which of the following techniques should be used to test whether the attitude scores of the two groups are significantly different?

Page 331   Mann–Whitney *U* Test
Page 333   Wilcoxon Matched-Pairs Signed-Rank Test
Page 335   Chi Square

To review the assumptions required for the use of analysis of covariance, see pp. 211–212.

YOUR ANSWER
Product-Moment Correlation

Although product-moment correlation methods frequently are employed in varied aspects of educational research, the present situation does not call for this approach. Recall that correlation indicates the strength and direction of the relationship between two variables, whereas the present situation is more amenable to treatment by a difference-testing technique. Yet, a difference-testing technique is needed which will reveal whether students exposed to one set of reading materials perform better than students exposed to the other set. Further, an estimate is needed of *how much* better one set of materials is, because the performance differential must be considered against the higher cost of the superior materials. Product-moment correlation is not suitable for supplying answers to such questions; hence a different technique is required for this situation. Return to page 331 and select it.

To review the function of product-moment correlation, see pp. 64–66.

YOUR ANSWER
Determination of a Confidence Interval

Correct.   Use of an estimation approach to assist the educational decision-maker is a most suitable choice. In this particular situation, a confidence interval should be determined for the difference between performance means of the subject using the two different sets of intervals. For example, a 95 percent confidence interval for mean difference could be developed so that the committee could tell, with odds of 95 to 5, the probable student mean performance superiority that could be expected by using the better, but more expensive reading materials. With such estimates, perhaps computed for each experimental study which has been previously conducted by the group, the committee is in a far better position to reach a prudent decision regarding the remedial reading materials.

Estimation procedures are strongly recommended as a statistical operation, carried out after hypothesis testing, which will assist one in evaluating the import of statistically significant results.

This is the final page in the chapter.

To review the role of estimation in educational research, see pp. 54–59.

Answers
to
Exercises

Minor differences in answers to numerical questions may occur because of differences in rounding procedures.

Chapter 2, pages 21–23

1. $X = 38.40$

2. $\overline{X} = 110.80$

3. (a) 99.5
   (b) 8.0
   (c) 25.5

4. (a) $X =$ 6.81
   (b) $\overline{X} = 26.75$
   (c) $\overline{X} = 47.13$

5. Range $= 28$ Mode $= 118$

6. $s = 2.81$

7. $s^2 = 32.78$ $s = 5.73$

8. (a) Group A: $\overline{X} = 52.05$ Median $= 54$ $s = 7.62$ Range $= 30$
      Group B: $\overline{X} = 60.00$ Median $= 61$ $s = 6.10$ Range $= 21$
   (b) Group B
   (c) Group A
   (d) Group B

9. Because of the truncated distribution, the median should be used.

10. Who can tell? We must determine precisely which measure of central tendency is being employed before attaching any interpretation to such phrases as "average man."

11. (a) Period two class
(b) Period two class
(c) Because of its greater heterogeneity, probably the period four class for both highest and lowest scores.

Chapter 3, pages 35–37

1. Approximately 16 percent

2. Positively skewed, or skewed to the right. (This assumes that low to high scores are represented, as is customary, from left to right.)

3. Matched centiles and z scores

Percentile	z
84th	1.0
50th	0
16th	-1.0
98th	2.0
2nd	-2.0

4. (a) $z = 2.0$ (b) $z = -1.0$ (c) $z = 1.0$ (d) $z = -2.0$

5. (a) $z = -1.39$ (c) $z = -1.08$ (e) $z = 1.13$
(b) $z = 0.02$ (d) $z = 1.06$ (f) $z = 0.36$

6. (a) 2 As; 7 Bs; 11 Cs; 7 Ds; 2 Fs
(b) 9, 11, 13, 15

7. (a) $Z = 36.1$ (c) $Z = 39.2$ (e) $Z = 61.3$
(b) $Z = 50.2$ (d) $Z = 60.6$ (f) $Z = 53.6$

8. (a) 50th   (b) 84th   (c) 98th   (d) 16th

9. He could transform all of the IQ scores into standard scores (z or Z) on the basis of the standardization data for each intelligence test, then match on the basis of the standard scores.

10. Nothing. No percentage interpretations should be made from standard scores in nonnormal distributions.

11. (a) 67th   (b) 80th   (c) 97th   (d) 14th

12. (a) 55.2   (b) 68.8   (c) 45.0   (d) 50.0

Chapter 4, pages 60–61

1. Reject it.

2. Accept it.

3. No, a 0.05 level of significance signifies that what has been observed in these samples (in this instance, a difference between means) would occur *by chance alone* only five times in one hundred.

4. Reject it because of the extremely improbable (by chance alone) z value.

5. (a) Reject   (d) Reject only if p is less than 0.05, for example, 0.02
   (b) Accept   (e) Accept
   (c) Reject   (f) Reject

6. Yes

7. One-tailed test

8. 0.10

9. Type I

10. Because he is now more interested in the question "How much difference?" than the question "Is there a difference?" He is more concerned with estimation procedures.

11. (a) 95%: 19.4 to 21.8   99%: 19.1 to 22.1
    (b) 95%: 18.9 to 22.3   99%: 18.4 to 22.8
    The more data sampled, the more reliable the estimate and the tighter the interval of estimation.

Chapter 5, pages 80–82

1. $r = -0.71$

2. (a) r should not be used, for the assumption of homoscedasticity cannot be satisfied.
   (b) r can be used, for the assumptions of homoscedasticity and linearity appear to be satisfied.
   (c) r should not be used, for the assumption of a linear relationship cannot be satisfied.

3. Remembering that in using Table D, df = number of pairs minus two,
   (a) Reject null hypothesis.
   (b) Accept null hypothesis.
   (c) Reject null hypothesis.
   (d) Reject null hypothesis.
   (e) Accept null hypothesis.

4. Product-moment correlation coefficient

5. Point biserial coefficient (continuous variable *versus* dichotomous variable)

6. Correlation ratio

7. Multiple correlation

8. Partial correlation

9. The psychologist should compute a 95 percent confidence interval for the r of 0.53. For example, a range of 0.40–0.66 for r might indicate that by using a similar process the population r can be assumed to fall within such limits 95 percent of the time.

Chapter 6, pages 91–93

1. $r = 0.86$

2. Yes   From Table D, $p < 0.01$.

3. $r = 0.67$

4. No, although an r of 0.67 with 8 df is significant beyond the 0.05 level.

5. $r = 0.49$

6. Yes

7. $r = 0.35$ No, $p > 0.05$

8. (a) $R_{x \cdot yx} = 0.22$ (b) $R_{y \cdot xz} = 0.18$ (c) $R_{z \cdot xy} = 0.19$

9. (a) $r_{xy \cdot z} = 0.16$ (b) $r_{yz \cdot x} = 0.12$ (c) $r_{xz \cdot y} = -0.17$

10. 0.76 to 0.83

11. 0.25 to 0.86

Chapter 7, pages 107–108

1. Regression

2. No, variables may serve as criteria in certain instances and as predictors in others. For example, while college academic achievement is usually a criterion variable, it might serve as a predictor variable for success in various post-college endeavors.

3. Because the whole scheme of regression prediction is predicated on the notion that the relationship between criterion and prediction in the sample can serve as a guide for making estimates in subsequent cases, if the individual for whom the prediction is to be made is markedly unlike those in the regression sample, the relationship between criterion and predictor will be less likely to hold for him.

4. Situation *A*

5. 43.5

6. $s_{y \cdot x} = 8.4$

7. Multiple regression

Chapter 8, pages 120–122

1. $a = -9.55$ $b = 0.585$

2. (a) 18.53   (c) 13.85   (e) 8.59
   (b) 15.02   (d) 12.68   (f) 6.83

3. $\tilde{Y} = 20.12 + 1.946X$

4. (a) 136.88   (c) 127.15   (e) 101.85
   (b) 134.93   (d) 113.53   (f) 97.96

5. $s_{y \cdot x} = 10.78$

6. Approximately 32 times in 100, since 68 percent of the time the actual score will fall within a range ± one standard error of estimate (10.78).

7. $\tilde{Y} = 12.93 + 1.488X$

8. (a) 62.53   (c) 65.74   (e) 38.12
   (b) 63.68   (d) 59.79

9. $\tilde{X} = 2.80 + 1.20Y - 0.30Z$

Chapter 9, pages 134–135

1. Researcher B

2. Researcher A

3. Researcher B

4. $t = 2.25$ and $df = 30$

5. No, because the mean difference represents only the numerator of the *t* model. Other factors such as sample size may produce a much larger *t* value for a smaller mean difference.

6. $t = -2.42$, for it is the absolute value of *t* which determines its probability level.

7. (1) a one-tailed t test with $t = 1.90$ and $df = 9$ allows one to reject the null hypothesis at the 0.05 probability level (which is indicated under the 0.10 column in Table F).

Chapter 10, pages 147–149

1. (a) Use pooled variance formula; $df = 37$.
   (b) Use either pooled variance formula or separate variance formula; $df = 13$.
   (c) Use pooled variance formula; $df = 34$.
   (d) Use separate variance formula; df is a special case involving interpolation. See discussion in the chapter. The t value needed for rejection of null hypothesis at 0.05 level is 2.00.

2. (a) $t = -3.23$ Reject the null hypothesis.
   (b) $t = 2.52$ Reject the null hypothesis.
   (c) $t = 1.10$ Accept the null hypothesis.
   (d) $t = 2.11$ Reject the null hypothesis.

3. (a) $F_{14,13} = 1.42$ Consider groups homogeneous.
   (b) $F_{50,61} = 1.73$ Consider groups heterogeneous.
   (c) $F_{9,9} = 1.55$ Consider groups homogeneous.
   (d) $F_{99,50} = 3.25$ Consider groups heterogeneous.
   (e) $F_{60,40} = 2.53$ Consider groups heterogeneous.

4. Use pooled variance t model. $df = 14$ $t = 1.45$ Accept the null hypothesis.

5. Use pooled variance t model. $df = 18$ $t = 1.01$ Accept the null hypothesis.

6. $t = 11.15$ Reject the null hypothesis.

7. $r = 0.845$ $t = 29.93$ Reject the null hypothesis.

8. Null hypothesis should be rejected. When using t table be sure to halve probability values for one-tailed tests.

9. Consistent with his one-tailed prediction test he must accept the null hypothesis. Under the circumstances, the study should undoubtedly be replicated and results treated with a two-tailed significance test.

Chapter 11, pages 162–163

1. The null hypothesis will be accepted.

2. Analysis of variance

3. Analysis *A*

4. No, the significant *F* indicates that such mean differences exist, but additional analysis (such as described by Tukey and Duncan, page 000) is required to locate the individual means which are significantly disparate.

5. Yes

Chapter 12, pages 171–173

1. $F = 13.33$ Reject the null hypothesis.

2. (a) Yes   (b) Yes   (c) No

3. (a) Yes   (b) Yes   (c) Yes

4. Total SS $= 563.73$
   Within SS $= 446.00$
   Between SS $= 117.73$

5. The largest variance is for Group *X* where $s_x^2 = 49.8$ while the smallest variance is for Group *Y* where $s_y^2 = 23.5$. Dividing the smaller variance into the larger variance, an *F* of 2.12 is produced. With 4 and 4 degrees of freedom this *F* is not large enough to reject the null hypothesis, so the variances may be considered homogeneous.

6. Within MS $= 7.88$ Between MS $= 77.62$ $F_{3,24} = 9.85$

7. $F_{2,27} = 9.13$ ($p < 0.05$)

8. Between MS $= 215.76$ Within MS $= 32.63$ $F_{2,42} = 9.85$

Chapter 13, page 186

1. Single-classification analysis of variance

2. Multiple-classification analysis of variance

3. Yes

4. Yes, because with each additional source of variation such as an independent variable the error term in the denominator of all the *F* ratios in the problem is reduced, thereby increasing the probability of significant *F* values. This is why a multiple-classification analysis of variance model is such a powerful statistical technique.

5. Tenable, for all *F* values will be less than one.

Chapter 14, pages 201–202

1. Methods MS $= 0.05$ $F_{2,54} = 0.005$ Accept the null hypothesis.
   Sex MS $= 2.4$ $F_{1,54} = 0.23$ Accept the null hypothesis.
   Interaction MS $= 149.45$ $F_{2,54} = 14.09$ Reject the null hypothesis.

2. (a) Instructional method $F_{2,72} = 22.61, p < 0.05$
   (b) Ability level $F_{2,72} = 29.63, p < 0.05$
   (c) Interaction $F_{4,72} = 0.99, p > 0.05$

3. For A: $F_{2,107} = 14.15$ ($p < 0.01$); for B: $F_{1,107} = 0.32$ ($p > 0.05$); for C: $F_{1,107} = 0.04$ ($p > 0.05$); for $A \times B$: $F_{2,107} = 1.57$ ($p > 0.05$); for $A \times C$: $F = 3.03$ ($p > 0.05$); for $B \times C$: $F_{1,107} = 5.70$ ($p > 0.05$); for $A \times B \times C$: $F_{2,107} = 0.70$ ($p > 0.05$)

Chapter 15, pages 212–213

1. Analysis of covariance. By employing this model the school psychologist can statistically compensate for the initial intellectual differences between the groups. Single-classification analysis of variance does not possess this analysis capacity.

2. Yes

3. Group A

4. Yes

Chapter 16, pages 232–234

1. $F_{1,20} = 0.12$ Accept the null hypothesis.

2. For A, $F = 150.46$ Reject the null hypothesis.
   For B, $F = 9.22$ Reject the null hypothesis.
   For $A \times B$, $F = 2.35$ Accept the null hypothesis.

Chapter 18, page 265

1. Three

2. Strong

3. Oblique

4. No. The interpretation of the meaning of factors is a test involving human judgment. Of course, the computer analysis is of great assistance, but in the final analysis it is the task of the researcher to give meaningful interpretations to such factors.

Chapter 19, page 282

1. Because of its greater power, the parametric test.

2. Mann–Whitney U Test

3. The Spearman rank-order correlation coefficient

4. The chi-square test

5. The sign test and the Wilcoxon matched-pairs signed-ranks test, with the latter being the most powerful

6 The chi-square test

7. The Friedman two-way analysis of variance

8. With nominal data, the chi-square test
   With ordinal data, the Kruskal–Wallis one-way analysis of variance

Chapter 20, pages 303–306

1. $\chi^2 = 24.40$ ($df = 3$), $p < 0.01$. This year's foreign language enrollment is indeed significantly different from the average distribution of previous years' enrollments.

2.

	13	14	15	16	17	18	19	20
Observed Frequencies	20	40	60	80	80	60	40	20
Expected Frequencies	19.8[a]	34.5	62.2	83.5	83.5	62.2	34.5	19.8[a]

[a]Expected frequencies in the extreme two cells were calculated on the basis of the proportion of the normal curve that was not already covered by the other six cells, that is, 0.0495 in each cell.

$\chi^2 = 2.21$ ($df = 5$), $p > 0.80$ The distribution does not depart significantly from normality.

3. $\chi^2 = 40.12$ ($df = 3$), $p < 0.01$ Reject the null hypothesis.

4. Regrouping into a 2×4 table so that the categories are "50 and below, 51–60, 61–70, 71 and above," $\chi^2 = 0.60$ ($df = 3$), $p > 0.80$ The two samples can be considered to have been drawn from the same population.

5. $T = 3.5$, $p < 0.05$

6. With the number of less frequent signs (x) equaling two, $p < 0.05$. Thus, the difference between the two groups is significant at the required level.

7. $U = 4$, $p < 0.05$ (one-tailed). The performance of Group I can be judged significantly superior to that of Group II.

8. $U = 52.5, z = -3.73, p < 0.01$ The null hypothesis should be rejected.

9. $\chi_r{}^2 = 5.4, p > 0.05$ Accept the null hypothesis.

10. $H = 1.51$ With samples of 5, 4, 3 an H value of 5.66 is needed to reject the null hypothesis at the 0.05 level, so the three samples should be considered part of the same population.

11. $r_S = 0.25$

12. $r_S = 0.93, p < 0.05$

Appendix

TABLE A. Table of Squares and Square Roots

Number	Square	Square root	Number	Square	Square root
1	1	1.0000	31	9 61	5.5678
2	4	1.4142	32	10 24	5.6569
3	9	1.7321	33	10 89	5.7446
4	16	2.0000	34	11 56	5.8310
5	25	2.2361	35	12 25	5.9161
6	36	2.4495	36	12 96	6.0000
7	49	2.6458	37	13 69	6.0828
8	64	2.8284	38	14 44	6.1644
9	81	3.0000	39	15 21	6.2450
10	1 00	3.1623	40	16 00	6.3246
11	1 21	3.3166	41	16 81	6.4031
12	1 44	3.4641	42	17 64	6.4807
13	1 69	3.6056	43	18 49	6.5574
14	1 96	3.7417	44	19 36	6.6332
15	2 25	3.8730	45	20 25	6.7082
16	2 56	4.0000	46	21 16	6.7823
17	2 89	4.1231	47	22 09	6.8557
18	3 24	4.2426	48	23 04	6.9282
19	3 61	4.3589	49	24 01	7.0000
20	4 00	4.4721	50	25 00	7.0711
21	4 41	4.5826	51	26 01	7.1414
22	4 84	4.6904	52	27 04	7.2111
23	5 29	4.7958	53	28 09	7.2801
24	5 76	4.8990	54	29 16	7.3485
25	6 25	5.0000	55	30 25	7.4162
26	6 76	5.0990	56	31 36	7.4833
27	7 29	5.1962	57	32 49	7.5498
28	7 84	5.2915	58	33 64	7.6158
29	8 41	5.3852	59	34 81	7.6811
30	9 00	5.4772	60	36 00	7.7460

SOURCE: H. Sorenson, *Statistics for Students of Psychology and Education,* McGraw-Hill Book Company, Inc., New York, 1936, table 72, pp. 347–359, with the kind permission of the author and publisher.

TABLE A. (*Continued*)

Number	Square	Square root	Number	Square	Square root
61	37 21	7.8102	101	1 02 01	10.0499
62	38 44	7.8740	102	1 04 04	10.0995
63	39 69	7.9373	103	1 06 09	10.1489
64	40 96	8.0000	104	1 08 16	10.1980
65	42 25	8.0623	105	1 10 25	10.2470
66	43 56	8.1240	106	1 12 36	10.2956
67	44 89	8.1854	107	1 14 49	10.3441
68	46 24	8.2462	108	1 16 64	10.3923
69	47 61	8.3066	109	1 18 81	10.4403
70	49 00	8.3666	110	1 21 00	10.4881
71	50 41	8.4261	111	1 23 21	10.5357
72	51 84	8.4853	112	1 25 44	10.5830
73	53 29	8.5440	113	1 27 69	10.6301
74	54 76	8.6023	114	1 29 96	10.6771
75	56 25	8.6603	115	1 32 25	10.7238
76	57 76	8.7178	116	1 34 56	10.7703
77	59 29	8.7750	117	1 36 89	10.8167
78	60 84	8.8318	118	1 39 24	10.8628
79	62 41	8.8882	119	1 41 61	10.9087
80	64 00	8.9443	120	1 44 00	10.9545
81	65 61	9.0000	121	1 46 41	11.0000
82	67 24	9.0554	122	1 48 84	11.0454
83	68 89	9.1104	123	1 51 29	11.0905
84	70 56	9.1652	124	1 53 76	11.1355
85	72 25	9.2195	125	1 56 25	11.1803
86	73 96	9.2736	126	1 58 76	11.2250
87	75 69	9.3274	127	1 61 29	11.2694
88	77 44	9.3808	128	1 63 84	11.3137
89	79 21	9.4340	129	1 66 41	11.3578
90	81 00	9.4868	130	1 69 00	11.4018
91	82 81	9.5394	131	1 71 61	11.4455
92	84 64	9.5917	132	1 74 24	11.4891
93	86 49	9.6437	133	1 76 89	11.5326
94	88 36	9.6954	134	1 79 56	11.5758
95	90 25	9.7468	135	1 82 25	11.6190
96	92 16	9.7980	136	1 84 96	11.6619
97	94 09	9.8489	137	1 87 69	11.7047
98	96 04	9.8995	138	1 90 44	11.7473
99	98 01	9.9499	139	1 93 21	11.7898
100	1 00 00	10.0000	140	1 96 00	11.8322

TABLE A. (*Continued*)

Number	Square	Square root	Number	Square	Square root
141	1 98 81	11.8743	181	3 27 61	13.4536
142	2 01 64	11.9164	182	3 31 24	13.4907
143	2 04 49	11.9583	183	3 34 89	13.5277
144	2 07 36	12.0000	184	3 38 56	13.5647
145	2 10 25	12.0416	185	3 42 25	13.6015
146	2 13 16	12.0830	186	3 45 96	13.6382
147	2 16 09	12.1244	187	3 49 69	13.6748
148	2 19 04	12.1655	188	3 53 44	13.7113
149	2 22 01	12.2066	189	3 57 21	13.7477
150	2 25 00	12.2474	190	3 61 00	13.7840
151	2 28 01	12.2882	191	3 64 81	13.8203
152	2 31 04	12.3288	192	3 68 64	13.8564
153	2 34 09	12.3693	193	3 72 49	13.8924
154	2 37 16	12.4097	194	3 76 36	13.9284
155	2 40 25	12.4499	195	3 80 25	13.9642
156	2 43 36	12.4900	196	3 84 16	14.0000
157	2 46 49	12.5300	197	3 88 09	14.0357
158	2 49 64	12.5698	198	3 92 04	14.0712
159	2 52 81	12.6095	199	3 96 01	14.1067
160	2 56 00	12.6491	200	4 00 00	14.1421
161	2 59 21	12.6886	201	4 04 01	14.1774
162	2 62 44	12.7279	202	4 08 04	14.2127
163	2 65 69	12.7671	203	4 12 09	14.2478
164	2 68 96	12.8062	204	4 16 16	14.2829
165	2 72 25	12.8452	205	4 20 25	14.3178
166	2 75 56	12.8841	206	4 24 36	14.3527
167	2 78 89	12.9228	207	4 28 49	14.3875
168	2 82 24	12.9615	208	4 32 64	14.4222
169	2 85 61	13.0000	209	4 36 81	14.4568
170	2 89 00	13.0384	210	4 41 00	14.4914
171	2 92 41	13.0767	211	4 45 21	14.5258
172	2 95 84	13.1149	212	4 49 44	14.5602
173	2 99 29	13.1529	213	4 53 69	14.5945
174	3 02 76	13.1909	214	4 57 96	14.6287
175	3 06 25	13.2288	215	4 62 25	14.6629
176	3 09 76	13.2665	216	4 66 56	14.6969
177	3 13 29	13.3041	217	4 70 89	14.7309
178	3 16 84	13.3417	218	4 75 24	14.7648
179	3 20 41	13.3791	219	4 79 61	14.7986
180	3 24 00	13.4164	220	4 84 00	14.8324

TABLE A. *(Continued)*

Number	Square	Square root	Number	Square	Square root
221	4 88 41	14.8661	261	6 81 21	16.1555
222	4 92 84	14.8997	262	6 86 44	16.1864
223	4 97 29	14.9332	263	6 91 69	16.2173
224	5 01 76	14.9666	264	6 96 96	16.2481
225	5 06 25	15.0000	265	7 02 25	16.2788
226	5 10 76	15.0333	266	7 07 56	16.3095
227	5 15 29	15.0665	267	7 12 89	16.3401
228	5 19 84	15.0997	268	7 18 24	16.3707
229	5 24 41	15.1327	269	7 23 61	16.4012
230	5 29 00	15.1658	270	7 29 00	16.4317
231	5 33 61	15.1987	271	7 34 41	16.4621
232	5 38 24	15.2315	272	7 39 84	16.4924
233	5 42 89	15.2643	273	7 45 29	16.5227
234	5 47 56	15.2971	274	7 50 76	16.5529
235	5 52 25	15.3297	275	7 56 25	16.5831
236	5 56 96	15.3623	276	7 61 76	16.6132
237	5 61 69	15.3948	277	7 67 29	16.6433
238	5 66 44	15.4272	278	7 72 84	16.6733
239	5 71 21	15.4596	279	7 78 41	16.7033
240	5 76 00	15.4919	280	7 84 00	16.7332
241	5 80 81	15.5242	281	7 89 61	16.7631
242	5 85 64	15.5563	282	7 95 24	16.7929
243	5 90 49	15.5885	283	8 00 89	16.8226
244	5 95 36	15.6205	284	8 06 56	16.8523
245	6 00 25	15.6525	285	8 12 25	16.8819
246	6 05 16	15.6844	286	8 17 96	16.9115
247	6 10 09	15.7162	287	8 23 69	16.9411
248	6 15 04	15.7480	288	8 29 44	16.9706
259	6 20 01	15.7797	289	8 35 21	17.0000
250	6 25 00	15.8114	290	8 41 00	17.0294
251	6 30 01	15.8430	291	8 46 81	17.0587
252	6 35 04	15.8745	292	8 52 64	17.0880
253	6 40 09	15.9060	293	8 58 49	17.1172
254	6 45 16	15.9374	294	8 64 36	17.1464
255	6 50 25	15.9687	295	8 70 25	17.1756
256	6 55 36	16.0000	296	8 76 16	17.2047
257	6 60 49	16.0312	297	8 82 09	17.2337
258	6 65 64	16.0624	298	8 88 04	17.2627
259	6 70 81	16.0935	299	8 94 01	17.2916
260	6 76 00	16.1245	300	9 00 00	17.3205

TABLE A. (*Continued*)

Number	Square	Square root	Number	Square	Square root
301	9 06 01	17.3494	341	11 62 81	18.4662
302	9 12 04	17.3781	342	11 69 64	18.4932
303	9 18 09	17.4069	343	11 76 49	18.5203
304	9 24 16	17.4356	344	11 83 36	18.5472
305	9 30 25	17.4642	345	11 90 25	18.5742
306	9 36 36	17.4929	346	11 97 16	18.6011
307	9 42 49	17.5214	347	12 04 09	18.6279
308	9 48 64	17.5499	348	12 11 04	18.6548
309	9 54 81	17.5784	349	12 18 01	18.6815
310	9 61 00	17.6068	350	12 25 00	18.7083
311	9 67 21	17.6352	351	12 32 01	18.7350
312	9 73 44	17.6635	352	12 39 04	18.7617
313	9 79 69	17.6918	353	12 46 09	18.7883
314	9 85 96	17.7200	354	12 53 16	18.8149
315	9 92 25	17.7482	355	12 60 25	18.8414
316	9 98 56	17.7764	356	12 67 36	18.8680
317	10 04 89	17.8045	357	12 74 49	18.8944
318	10 11 24	17.8326	358	12 81 64	18.9209
319	10 17 61	17.8606	359	12 88 81	18.9473
320	10 24 00	17.8885	360	12 96 00	18.9737
321	10 30 41	17.9165	361	13 03 21	19.0000
322	10 36 84	17.9444	362	13 10 44	19.0263
323	10 43 29	17.9722	363	13 17 69	19.0526
324	10 49 76	18.0000	364	13 24 96	19.0788
325	10 56 25	18.0278	365	13 32 25	19.1050
326	10 62 76	18.0555	366	13 39 56	19.1311
327	10 69 29	18.0831	367	13 46 89	19.1572
328	10 75 84	18.1108	368	13 54 24	19.1833
329	10 82 41	18.1384	369	13 61 61	19.2094
330	10 89 00	18.1659	370	13 69 00	19.2354
331	10 95 61	18.1934	371	13 76 41	19.2614
332	11 02 24	18.2209	372	13 83 84	19.2873
333	11 08 89	18.2483	373	13 91 29	19.3132
334	11 15 56	18.2757	374	13 98 76	19.3391
335	11 22 25	18.3030	375	14 06 25	19.3649
336	11 28 96	18.3303	376	14 13 76	19.3907
337	11 35 69	18.3576	377	14 21 29	19.4165
338	11 42 44	18.3848	378	14 28 84	19.4422
339	11 49 21	18.4120	379	14 36 41	19.4679
340	11 56 00	18.4391	380	14 44 00	19.4936

TABLE A. (*Continued*)

Number	Square	Square root	Number	Square	Square root
381	14 51 61	19.5192	421	17 72 41	20.5183
382	14 59 24	19.5448	422	17 80 84	20.5426
383	14 66 89	19.5704	423	17 89 29	20.5670
384	14 74 56	19.5959	424	17 97 76	20.5913
385	14 82 25	19.6214	425	18 06 25	20.6155
386	14 89 96	19.6469	426	18 14 76	20.6398
387	14 97 69	19.6723	427	18 23 29	20.6640
388	15 05 44	19.6977	428	18 31 84	20.6882
389	15 13 21	19.7231	429	18 40 41	20.7123
390	15 21 00	19.7484	430	18 49 00	20.7364
391	15 28 81	19.7737	431	18 57 61	20.7605
392	15 36 64	19.7990	432	18 66 24	20.7846
393	15 44 49	19.8242	433	18 74 89	20.8087
394	15 52 36	19.8494	434	18 83 56	20.8327
395	15 60 25	19.8746	435	18 92 25	20.8567
396	15 68 16	19.8997	436	19 00 96	20.8806
397	15 76 09	19.9249	437	19 09 69	20.9045
398	15 84 04	19.9499	438	19 18 44	20.9284
399	15 92 01	19.9750	439	19 27 21	20.9523
400	16 00 00	20.0000	440	19 36 00	20.9762
401	16 08 01	20.0250	441	19 44 81	21.0000
402	16 16 04	20.0499	442	19 53 64	21.0238
403	16 24 09	20.0749	443	19 62 49	21.0476
404	16 32 16	20.0998	444	19 71 36	21.0713
405	16 40 25	20.1246	445	19 80 25	21.0950
406	16 48 36	20.1494	446	19 89 16	21.1187
407	16 56 49	20.1742	447	19 98 09	21.1424
408	16 64 64	20.1990	448	20 07 04	21.1660
409	16 72 81	20.2237	449	20 16 01	21.1896
410	16 81 00	20.2485	450	20 25 00	21.2132
411	16 89 21	20.2731	451	20 34 01	21.2368
412	16 97 44	20.2978	452	20 43 04	21.2603
413	17 05 69	20.3224	453	20 52 09	21.2838
414	17 13 96	20.3470	454	20 61 16	21.3073
415	17 22 25	20.3715	455	20 70 25	21.3307
416	17 30 56	20.3961	456	20 79 36	21.3542
417	17 38 89	20.4206	457	20 88 49	21.3776
418	17 47 24	20.4450	458	20 97 64	21.4009
419	17 55 61	20.4695	459	21 06 81	21.4243
420	17 64 00	20.4939	460	21 16 00	21.4476

TABLE A. (*Continued*)

Number	Square	Square root	Number	Square	Square root
461	21 25 21	21.4709	501	25 10 01	22.3830
462	21 34 44	21.4942	502	25 20 04	22.4054
463	21 43 69	21.5174	503	25 30 09	22.4277
464	21 52 96	21.5407	504	25 40 16	22.4499
465	21 62 25	21.5639	505	25 50 25	22.4722
466	21 71 56	21.5870	506	25 60 36	22.4944
467	21 80 89	21.6102	507	25 70 49	22.5167
468	21 90 24	21.6333	508	25 80 64	22.5389
469	21 99 61	21.6564	509	25 90 81	22.5610
470	22 09 00	21.6795	510	26 01 00	22.5832
471	22 18 41	21.7025	511	26 11 21	22.6053
472	22 27 84	21.7256	512	25 21 44	22.6274
473	22 37 29	21.7486	513	26 31 69	22.6495
474	22 46 76	21.7715	514	26 41 96	22.6716
475	22 56 25	21.7945	515	26 52 25	22.6936
476	22 65 76	21.8174	516	22 62 56	22.7156
477	22 75 29	21.8403	517	26 72 89	22.7376
478	22 84 84	21.8632	518	26 83 24	22.7596
479	22 94 41	21.8861	519	26 93 61	22.7816
480	23 04 00	21.9089	520	27 04 00	22.8035
481	23 13 61	21.9317	521	27 14 41	22.8254
482	23 23 24	21.9545	522	27 24 84	22.8473
483	23 32 89	21.9773	523	27 35 29	22.8692
484	23 42 56	22.0000	524	27 45 76	22.8910
485	23 52 25	22.0227	525	27 56 25	22.9129
486	23 61 96	22.0454	526	27 66 76	22.9347
487	23 71 69	22.0681	527	27 77 29	22.9565
488	23 81 44	22.0907	528	27 87 84	22.9783
489	23 91 21	22.1133	529	27 98 41	23.0000
490	24 01 00	22.1359	530	28 09 00	23.0217
491	24 10 81	22.1585	531	28 19 61	23.0434
492	24 20 64	22.1811	532	28 30 24	23.0651
493	24 30 49	22.2036	533	28 40 89	23.0868
494	24 40 36	22.2261	534	28 51 56	23.1084
495	24 50 25	22.2486	535	28 62 25	23.1301
496	24 60 16	22.2711	536	28 72 96	23.1517
497	24 70 09	22.2935	537	28 83 69	23.1733
498	24 80 04	22.3159	538	28 94 44	23.1948
499	24 90 01	22.3383	539	29 05 21	23.2164
500	25 00 00	22.3607	540	29 16 00	23.2379

TABLE A. *(Continued)*

Number	Square	Square root	Number	Square	Square root
541	29 26 81	23.2594	581	33 75 61	24.1039
542	29 37 64	23.2809	582	33 87 24	24.1247
543	29 48 49	23.3024	583	33 98 89	24.1454
544	29 59 36	23.3238	584	34 10 56	24.1661
545	29 70 25	23.3452	585	34 22 25	24.1868
546	29 81 16	23.3666	586	34 33 96	24.2074
547	29 92 09	23.3880	587	34 45 69	24.2281
548	30 03 04	23.4094	588	34 57 44	24.2487
549	30 14 01	23.4307	589	34 69 21	24.2693
550	30 25 00	23.4521	590	34 81 00	24.2899
551	30 36 01	23.4734	591	34 92 81	24.3105
552	30 47 04	23.4947	592	35 04 64	24.3311
553	30 58 09	23.5160	593	35 16 49	24.3516
554	30 69 16	23.5372	594	35 28 36	24.3721
555	30 80 25	23.5584	595	35 40 25	24.3926
556	30 91 36	23.5797	596	35 52 16	24.4131
557	31 02 49	23.6008	597	35 64 09	24.4336
558	31 13 64	23.6220	598	35 76 04	24.4540
559	31 24 81	23.6432	599	35 88 01	24.4745
560	31 36 00	23.6643	600	36 00 00	24.4949
561	31 47 21	23.6854	601	36 12 01	24.5153
562	31 58 44	23.7065	602	36 24 04	24.5357
563	31 69 69	23.7276	603	36 36 09	24.5561
564	31 80 96	23.7487	604	36 48 16	24.5764
565	31 92 25	23.7697	605	36 60 25	24.5967
566	32 03 56	23.7908	606	36 72 36	24.6171
567	32 14 89	23.8118	607	36 84 49	24.6374
568	32 26 24	23.8328	608	36 96 64	24.6577
569	32 37 61	23.8537	609	37 08 81	24.6779
570	32 49 00	23.8747	610	37 21 00	24.6982
571	32 60 41	23.8956	611	37 33 21	24.7184
572	32 71 84	23.9165	612	37 45 44	24.7385
573	32 83 29	23.9374	613	37 57 69	24.7588
574	32 94 76	23.9583	614	37 69 96	24.7790
575	33 06 25	23.9792	615	37 82 25	24.7992
576	33 17 76	24.0000	616	37 94 56	24.8193
577	33 29 29	24.0208	617	38 06 89	24.8395
578	33 40 84	24.0416	618	38 19 24	24.8596
579	33 52 41	24.0624	619	38 31 61	24.8797
580	33 64 00	24.0832	620	38 44 00	24.8998

TABLE A. (*Continued*)

Number	Square	Square root	Number	Square	Square root
621	38 56 41	24.9199	661	43 69 21	25.7099
622	38 68 84	24.9399	662	43 82 44	25.7294
623	38 81 29	24.9600	663	43 95 69	25.7488
624	38 93 76	24.9800	664	44 08 96	25.7682
625	39 06 25	25.0000	665	44 22 25	25.7876
626	39 18 76	25.0200	666	44 35 56	25.8070
627	39 31 29	25.0400	667	44 48 89	25.8263
628	39 43 84	25.0599	668	44 62 24	25.8457
629	39 56 41	25.0799	669	44 75 61	25.8650
630	39 69 00	25.0998	670	44 89 00	25.8844
631	39 81 61	25.1197	671	45 02 41	25.9037
632	39 94 24	25.1396	672	45 15 84	25.9230
633	40 06 89	25.1595	673	45 29 29	25.9422
634	40 19 56	25.1794	674	45 42 76	25.9615
635	40 32 25	25.1992	675	45 56 25	25.9808
636	40 44 96	25.2190	676	45 69 76	26.0000
637	40 57 69	25.2389	677	45 83 29	26.0192
638	40 70 44	25.2587	678	45 96 84	26.0384
639	40 83 21	25.2784	679	46 10 41	26.0576
640	40 96 00	25.2982	680	46 24 00	26.0768
641	41 08 81	25.3180	681	46 37 61	26.0960
642	41 21 64	25.3377	682	46 51 24	26.1151
643	41 34 49	25.3574	683	46 64 89	26.1343
644	41 47 36	25.3772	684	46 78 56	26.1534
645	41 60 25	25.3969	685	46 92 25	26.1725
646	41 73 16	25.4165	686	47 05 96	26.1916
647	41 86 09	25.4362	687	47 19 69	26.2107
648	41 99 04	25.4558	688	47 33 44	26.2298
649	42 12 01	25.4755	689	47 47 21	26.2488
650	42 25 00	25.4951	690	47 61 00	26.2679
651	42 38 01	25.5147	691	47 74 81	26.2869
652	42 51 04	25.5343	692	47 88 64	26.3059
653	42 64 09	25.5539	693	48 02 49	26.3249
654	42 77 16	25.5734	694	48 16 36	26.3439
655	42 90 25	25.5930	695	48 30 25	26.3629
656	43 03 36	25.6125	696	48 44 16	26.3818
657	43 16 49	25.6320	697	48 58 09	26.4008
658	43 29 64	25.6515	698	48 72 04	26.4197
659	43 42 81	25.6710	699	48 86 01	26.4386
660	43 56 00	25.6905	700	49 00 00	26.4575

TABLE A. (*Continued*)

Number	Square	Square root	Number	Square	Square root
701	49 14 01	26.4764	741	54 90 81	27.2213
702	49 28 04	26.4953	742	55 05 64	27.2397
703	49 42 09	26.5141	743	55 20 49	27.2580
704	49 56 16	26.5330	744	55 35 36	27.2764
705	49 70 25	26.5518	745	55 50 25	27.2947
706	49 84 36	26.5707	746	55 65 16	27.3130
707	49 98 49	26.5895	747	55 80 09	27.3313
708	50 12 64	26.6083	748	55 95 04	27.3496
709	50 26 81	26.6271	749	56 10 01	27.3679
710	50 41 00	26.6458	750	56 25 00	27.3861
711	50 55 21	26.6646	751	56 40 01	27.4044
712	50 69 44	26.6833	752	56 55 04	27.4226
713	50 83 69	26.7021	753	56 70 09	27.4408
714	50 97 96	26.7208	754	56 85 16	27.4591
715	51 12 25	26.7395	755	57 00 25	27.4773
716	51 26 56	26.7582	756	57 15 36	27.4955
717	51 40 89	26.7769	757	57 30 49	27.5136
718	51 55 24	26.7955	758	57 45 64	27.5318
719	51 69 61	26.8142	759	57 60 81	27.5500
720	51 84 00	26.8328	760	57 76 00	27.5681
721	51 98 41	26.8514	761	57 91 21	27.5862
722	52 12 84	26.8701	762	58 06 44	27.6043
723	52 27 29	26.8887	763	58 21 69	27.6225
724	52 41 76	26.9072	764	58 36 96	27.6405
725	52 56 25	26.9258	765	58 52 25	27.6586
726	52 70 76	26.9444	766	58 67 56	27.6767
727	52 85 29	26.9629	767	58 82 89	27.6948
728	52 99 84	26.9815	768	58 98 24	27.7128
729	53 14 41	27.0000	769	59 13 61	27.7308
730	53 29 00	27.0185	770	59 29 00	27.7489
731	53 43 61	27.0370	771	59 44 41	27.7669
732	53 58 24	27.0555	772	59 59 84	27.7849
733	53 72 89	27.0740	773	59 75 29	27.8029
734	53 87 56	27.0924	774	59 90 76	27.8209
735	54 02 25	27.1109	775	60 06 25	27.8388
736	54 16 96	27.1293	776	60 21 76	27.8568
737	54 31 69	27.1477	777	60 37 29	27.8747
738	54 46 44	27.1662	778	60 52 84	27.8927
739	54 61 27	27.1846	779	60 68 41	27.9106
740	54 76 00	27.2029	780	60 84 00	27.9285

TABLE A. (*Continued*)

Number	Square	Square root	Number	Square	Square root
781	60 99 61	27.9464	821	67 40 41	28.6531
782	61 15 24	27.9643	822	67 56 84	28.6705
783	61 30 89	27.9821	823	67 73 29	28.6880
784	61 46 56	28.0000	824	67 89 76	28.7054
785	61 62 25	28.0179	825	68 06 25	28.7228
786	61 77 96	28.0357	826	68 22 76	28.7402
787	61 93 69	28.0535	827	68 39 29	28.7576
788	62 09 44	28.0713	828	68 55 84	28.7750
789	62 25 21	28.0891	829	68 72 41	28.7924
790	62 41 00	28.1069	830	68 89 00	28.8097
791	62 56 81	28.1247	831	69 05 61	28.8271
792	62 72 64	28.1425	832	69 22 24	28.8444
793	62 88 49	28.1603	833	69 38 89	28.8617
794	63 04 36	28.1780	834	69 55 56	28.8791
795	63 20 25	28.1957	835	69 72 25	28.8964
796	63 36 16	28.2135	836	69 88 96	28.9137
797	63 52 09	28.2312	837	70 05 69	28.9310
798	63 68 04	28.2489	838	70 22 44	28.9482
799	63 84 01	28.2666	839	70 39 21	28.9655
800	64 00 00	28.2843	840	70 56 00	28.9828
801	64 16 01	28.3019	841	70 72 81	29.0000
802	64 32 04	28.3196	842	70 89 64	29.0172
803	64 48 09	28.3373	843	71 06 49	29.0345
804	64 64 16	28.3549	844	71 23 36	29.0517
805	64 80 25	28.3725	845	71 40 25	29.0689
806	64 96 36	28.3901	846	71 57 16	29.0861
807	65 12 49	28.4077	847	71 74 09	29.1033
808	65 28 64	28.4253	848	71 91 04	29.1204
809	65 44 81	28.4429	849	72 08 01	29.1376
810	65 61 00	28.4605	850	72 25 00	29.1548
811	65 77 21	28.4781	851	72 42 01	29.1719
812	65 93 44	28.4956	852	72 59 04	29.1890
813	66 09 69	28.5132	853	72 76 09	29.2062
814	66 25 96	28.5307	854	72 93 16	29.2233
815	66 42 25	28.5482	855	73 10 25	29.2404
816	66 58 56	28.5657	856	73 27 36	29.2575
817	66 74 89	28.5832	857	73 44 49	29.2746
818	66 91 24	28.6007	858	73 61 64	29.2916
819	67 07 61	28.6082	859	73 78 81	29.3087
820	67 24 00	28.6356	860	73 96 00	29.3258

TABLE A. *(Continued)*

Number	Square	Square root	Number	Square	Square root
861	74 13 21	29.3428	901	81 18 01	30.0167
862	74 30 44	29.3598	902	81 36 04	30.0333
863	74 47 69	29.3769	903	81 54 09	30.0500
864	74 64 96	29.3939	904	81 72 16	30.0666
865	74 82 25	29.4109	905	81 90 25	30.0832
866	74 99 56	29.4279	906	82 08 36	30.0998
867	75 16 89	29.4449	907	82 26 49	30.1164
868	75 34 24	29.4618	908	82 44 64	30.1330
869	75 51 61	29.4788	909	82 62 81	30.1496
870	75 69 00	29.4958	910	82 81 00	30.1662
871	75 86 41	29.5127	911	82 99 21	30.1828
872	76 03 84	29.5296	912	83 17 44	30.1993
873	76 21 29	29.5466	913	83 35 69	30.2159
874	76 38 76	29.5635	914	83 53 96	30.2324
875	76 56 25	29.5804	915	83 72 25	30.2490
876	76 73 76	29.5973	916	83 90 56	30.2655
877	76 91 29	29.6142	917	84 08 89	30.2820
878	77 08 84	29.6311	918	84 27 24	30.2985
879	77 26 41	29.6479	919	84 45 61	30.3150
880	77 44 00	29.6648	920	84 64 00	30.3315
881	77 61 61	29.6816	921	84 82 41	30.3480
882	77 79 24	29.6985	922	85 00 84	30.3645
883	77 96 89	29.7153	923	85 19 29	30.3809
884	78 14 56	29.7321	924	85 37 76	30.3974
885	78 32 25	29.7489	925	85 56 25	30.4138
886	78 49 96	29.7658	926	85 74 76	30.4302
887	78 67 69	29.7825	927	85 93 29	30.4467
888	78 85 44	29.7993	928	86 11 84	30.4631
889	79 03 21	29.8161	929	86 30 41	30.4795
890	79 21 00	29.8329	930	86 49 00	30.4959
891	79 38 81	29.8496	931	86 67 61	30.5123
892	79 56 64	29.8664	932	86 86 24	30.5287
893	79 74 49	29.8831	933	87 04 89	30.5450
894	79 92 36	29.8998	934	87 23 56	30.5614
895	80 10 25	29.9166	935	87 42 25	30.5778
896	80 28 16	29.9333	936	87 60 96	30.5941
897	80 46 09	29.9500	937	87 79 69	30.6105
898	80 64 04	29.9666	938	87 98 44	30.6268
899	80 82 01	29.9833	939	88 17 21	30.6431
900	81 00 00	30.0000	940	88 36 00	30.6594

TABLE A. (Continued)

Number	Square	Square root	Number	Square	Square root
941	88 54 81	30.6757	971	94 28 41	31.1609
942	88 73 64	30.6920	972	94 47 84	31.1769
943	88 92 49	30.7083	973	94 67 29	31.1929
944	89 11 36	30.7246	974	94 86 76	31.2090
945	89 30 25	30.7409	975	95 06 25	31.2250
946	89 49 16	30.7571	976	95 25 76	31.2410
947	89 68 09	30.7734	977	95 45 29	31.2570
948	89 87 04	30.7896	978	95 64 84	31.2730
949	90 06 01	30.8058	979	95 84 41	31.2890
950	90 25 00	30.8221	980	96 04 00	31.3050
951	90 44 01	30.8383	981	96 23 61	31.3209
952	90 63 04	30.8545	982	96 43 24	31.3369
953	90 82 09	30.8707	983	96 62 89	31.3528
954	91 01 16	30.8869	984	96 82 56	31.3688
955	91 20 25	30.9031	985	97 02 25	31.3847
956	91 39 36	30.9192	986	97 21 96	31.4006
957	91 58 49	30.9354	987	97 41 69	31.4166
958	91 77 64	30.9516	988	97 61 44	31.4325
959	91 96 81	30.9677	989	97 81 21	31.4484
960	92 16 00	30.9839	990	98 01 00	31.4643
961	92 35 21	31.0000	991	98 20 81	31.4802
962	92 54 44	31.0161	992	98 40 64	31.4960
963	92 73 69	31.0322	993	98 60 49	31.5119
964	92 92 96	31.0483	994	98 80 36	31.5278
965	93 12 25	31.0644	995	99 00 25	31.5436
966	93 31 56	31.0805	996	99 20 16	31.5595
967	93 50 89	31.0966	997	99 40 09	31.5753
968	93 70 24	31.1127	998	99 60 04	31.5911
969	93 89 61	31.1288	999	99 80 01	31.6070
970	94 09 00	31.1448	1000	100 00 00	31.6228

TABLE B. Table of Random Numbers

COLUMN NUMBER

1st Thousand

Row	00000 01234	00000 56789	11111 01234	11111 56789	22222 01234	22222 56789	33333 01234	33333 56789
00	23157	54859	01837	25993	76249	70886	95230	36744
01	05545	55043	10537	43508	90611	83744	10962	21343
02	14871	60350	32404	36223	50051	00322	11543	80834
03	38976	74951	94051	75853	78805	90194	32428	71695
04	97312	61718	99755	30870	94251	25841	54882	10513
05	11742	69381	44339	30872	32797	33118	22647	06850
06	43361	28859	11016	45623	93009	00499	43640	74036
07	93806	20478	38268	04491	55751	18932	58475	52571
08	49540	13181	08429	84187	69538	29661	77738	09527
09	36768	72633	37948	21569	41959	68670	45274	83880
10	07092	52392	24627	12067	06558	45344	67338	45320
11	43310	01081	44863	80307	52555	16148	89742	94647
12	61570	06360	06173	63775	63148	95123	35017	46993
13	31352	83799	10779	18941	31579	76448	62584	86919
14	57048	86526	27795	93692	90529	56546	35065	32254
15	09243	44200	68721	07137	30729	75756	09298	27650
16	97957	35018	40894	88329	52230	82521	22532	61587
17	93732	59570	43781	98885	56671	66826	95996	44569
18	72621	11225	00922	68264	35666	59434	71687	58167
19	61020	74418	45371	20794	95917	37866	99536	19378
20	97839	85474	33055	91718	45473	54144	22034	23000
21	89160	97192	22232	90637	35055	45489	88438	16361
22	25966	88220	62871	79265	02823	52862	84919	54883
23	81443	31719	05049	54806	74690	07567	65017	16543
24	11322	54931	42362	34386	08624	97687	46245	23245

SOURCE: M. G. Kendall and B. B. Smith, "Randomness and Random Sampling Numbers," *J. Roy. Statist. Soc.* 101, 147–166 (1938). By permission of the Royal Statistical Society.

TABLE B. (Continued)

COLUMN NUMBER

2nd Thousand

Row	00000 01234	00000 56789	11111 01234	11111 56789	22222 01234	22222 56789	33333 01234	33333 56789
00	64755	83885	84122	25920	17696	15655	95045	95947
01	10302	52289	77436	34430	38112	49067	07348	23328
02	71017	98495	51308	50374	66591	02887	53765	69149
03	60012	55605	88410	34879	79655	90169	78800	03666
04	37330	94656	49161	42802	48274	54755	44553	65090
05	47869	87001	31591	12273	60626	12822	34691	61212
06	38040	42737	64167	89578	39323	49324	88434	38706
07	73508	30908	83054	80078	86669	30295	56460	45336
08	32623	46474	84061	04324	20628	37319	32356	43969
09	97591	99549	36630	35106	62069	92975	95320	57734
10	74012	31955	59790	96982	66224	24015	96749	07589
11	56754	26457	13351	05014	90966	33674	69096	33488
12	49800	49908	54831	21998	08528	26372	92923	65026
13	43584	89647	24878	56670	00221	50193	99591	62377
14	16653	79664	60325	71301	35742	83636	73058	87229
15	48502	69055	65322	58748	31446	80237	31252	96367
16	96765	54692	36316	86230	48296	38352	23816	64094
17	38923	61550	80357	81784	23444	12463	33992	28128
18	77958	81694	25225	05587	51073	01070	60218	61961
19	17928	28065	25586	08771	02641	85064	65796	48170
20	94036	85978	02318	04499	41054	10531	87431	21596
21	47460	60479	56230	48417	14372	85167	27558	00368
22	47856	56088	51992	82439	40644	17170	13463	18288
23	57616	34653	92298	62018	10375	76515	62986	90756
24	08300	92704	66752	66610	57188	79107	54222	22013

TABLE B. (Continued)

COLUMN NUMBER

3rd Thousand

Row	00000 01234	00000 56789	11111 01234	11111 56789	22222 01234	22222 56789	33333 01234	33333 56789
00	89221	02362	65787	74733	51272	30213	92441	39651
01	04005	99818	63918	29032	94012	42363	01261	10650
02	98546	38066	50856	75045	40645	22841	53254	44125
03	41719	84401	59226	01314	54581	40398	49988	65579
04	28733	72489	00785	25843	24613	49797	85567	84471
05	65213	83927	77762	03086	80742	24395	68476	83792
06	65553	12678	90906	90466	43670	26217	69900	31205
07	05668	69080	73029	85746	58332	78231	45986	92998
08	39302	99718	49757	79519	27387	76373	47262	91612
09	64592	32254	45879	29431	38320	05981	18067	87137
10	07513	48792	47314	83660	68907	05336	82579	91582
11	86593	68501	56638	99800	82839	35148	56541	07232
12	83735	22599	97977	81248	36838	99560	32410	67614
13	08595	21826	54655	08204	87990	17033	56258	05384
14	41273	27149	44293	69458	16828	63962	15864	35431
15	00473	75908	56238	12242	72631	76314	47252	06347
16	86131	53789	81383	07868	89132	96182	07009	86432
17	33849	78359	08402	03586	03176	88663	08018	22546
18	61870	41657	07468	08612	98083	97349	20775	45091
19	43898	65923	25078	86129	78491	97653	91500	80786
20	29939	39123	04548	45985	60952	06641	28726	46473
21	38505	85555	14388	55077	18657	94887	67831	70819
22	31824	38431	67125	25511	72044	11562	53279	82268
23	91430	03767	13561	15597	06750	92552	02391	38753
24	38635	68976	25498	97526	96458	03805	04116	63514

Table B. (Continued)

COLUMN NUMBER

4th Thousand

Row	00000 01234	00000 56789	11111 01234	11111 56789	22222 01234	22222 56789	33333 01234	33333 56789
00	02490	54122	27944	39364	94239	72074	11679	54082
01	11967	36469	60627	83701	09253	30208	01385	37482
02	48256	83465	49699	24079	05403	35154	39613	03136
03	27246	73080	21481	23536	04881	89977	49484	93071
04	32532	77265	72430	70722	86529	18457	92657	10011
05	66757	98955	92375	93431	43204	55825	45443	69265
06	11266	34545	76505	97746	34668	26999	26742	97516
07	17872	39142	45561	80146	93137	48924	64257	59284
08	62561	30365	03408	14754	51798	08133	61010	97730
09	62796	30779	35497	70501	30105	08133	00997	91970
10	75510	21771	04339	33660	42757	62223	87565	48468
11	87439	01691	63517	26590	44437	07217	98706	39032
12	97742	02621	10748	78803	38837	65226	92149	59051
13	98811	06001	21571	02875	21828	83912	85188	61624
14	51264	01852	64607	92553	29004	26695	78583	62998
15	40239	93376	10419	68610	49120	02941	80035	99317
16	26936	59186	51667	27645	46329	44681	94190	66647
17	88502	11716	98299	40974	42394	62200	69094	81646
18	63499	38093	25593	61995	79867	80569	01023	38374
19	36379	81206	03317	78710	73828	31083	60509	44091
20	93801	22322	47479	57017	59334	30647	43061	26660
21	29856	87120	56311	50053	25365	81265	22414	02431
22	97720	87931	88265	13050	71017	15177	06957	92919
23	85237	09105	74601	46377	59938	15647	34177	92753
24	75746	75268	31727	95773	72364	87324	36879	06802

TABLE B. (*Continued*)

COLUMN NUMBER

5th Thousand

Row	00000 01234	00000 56789	11111 01234	11111 56789	22222 01234	22222 56789	33333 01234	33333 56789
00	29935	06971	63175	52579	10478	89379	61428	21363
01	15114	07126	51890	77787	75510	13103	42942	48111
02	03870	43225	10589	87629	22039	94124	38127	65022
03	79390	39188	40756	45269	65959	20640	14284	22960
04	30035	06915	79196	54428	64819	52314	48721	81594
05	29039	99861	28759	79802	68531	39198	38137	24373
06	78196	08108	24107	49777	09599	43569	84820	94956
07	15847	85493	91442	91351	80130	73752	21539	10986
08	36614	62248	49194	97209	92587	92053	41021	80064
09	40549	54884	91465	43862	35541	44466	88894	74180
10	40878	08997	14286	09982	90308	78007	51587	16658
11	10229	49282	41173	31468	59455	18756	08908	06660
12	15918	76787	30624	25928	44124	25088	31137	71614
13	13403	18796	49909	94404	64979	41462	18155	98335
14	66523	94596	74908	90271	10009	98648	17640	68909
15	91665	36469	68343	17870	25975	04662	21272	50620
16	67415	87515	08207	73729	73201	57593	96917	69699
17	76527	96996	23724	33448	63392	32394	60887	90617
18	19815	47789	74348	17147	10954	34355	81194	54407
19	25592	53587	76384	72575	84347	68918	05739	57222
20	55902	45539	63646	31609	95999	82887	40666	66692
21	02470	58376	79794	22482	42423	96162	47491	17264
22	18630	53263	13319	97619	35859	12350	14632	87659
23	89673	38230	16063	92007	59503	38402	76450	33333
24	62986	67364	06595	17427	84623	14565	82860	57300

TABLE C. Areas and Ordinates of the Normal Curve in Terms of x/σ

(1) z STANDARD SCORE $\left(\dfrac{x}{\sigma}\right)$	(2) A AREA FROM MEAN TO $\dfrac{x}{\sigma}$	(3) B AREA IN LARGER PORTION	(4) C AREA IN SMALLER PORTION	(5) y ORDINATE AT $\dfrac{x}{\sigma}$
0.00	.0000	.5000	.5000	.3989
0.01	.0040	.5040	.4960	.3989
0.02	.0080	.5080	.4920	.3989
0.03	.0120	.5120	.4880	.3988
0.04	.0160	.5160	.4840	.3986
0.05	.0199	.5199	.4801	.3984
0.06	.0239	.5239	.4761	.3982
0.07	.0279	.5279	.4721	.3980
0.08	.0319	.5319	.4681	.3977
0.09	.0359	.5359	.4641	.3973
0.10	.0398	.5398	.4602	.3970
0.11	.0438	.5438	.4562	.3965
0.12	.0478	.5478	.4522	.3961
0.13	.0517	.5517	.4483	.3956
0.14	.0557	.5557	.4443	.3951
0.15	.0596	.5596	.4404	.3945
0.16	.0636	.5636	.4364	.3939
0.17	.0675	.5675	.4325	.3932
0.18	.0714	.5714	.4286	.3925
0.19	.0753	.5753	.4247	.3918
0.20	.0793	.5793	.4207	.3910
0.21	.0832	.5832	.4168	.3902
0.22	.0871	.5871	.4129	.3894
0.23	.0910	.5910	.4090	.3885
0.24	.0948	.5948	.4052	.3876
0.25	.0987	.5987	.4013	.3867
0.26	.1026	.6026	.3974	.3857
0.27	.1064	.6064	.3936	.3847
0.28	.1103	.6103	.3897	.3836
0.29	.1141	.6141	.3859	.3825
0.30	.1179	.6179	.3821	.3814
0.31	.1217	.6217	.3783	.3802
0.32	.1255	.6255	.3745	.3790
0.33	.1293	.6293	.3707	.3778
0.34	.1331	.6331	.3669	.3765

SOURCE: A. L. Edwards' *Statistical Methods for the Behavioral Sciences*, Holt, Rinehart and Winston, Inc., © 1954, pp. 490–499.

TABLE C. (*Continued*)

(1) z STANDARD SCORE $\left(\frac{x}{\sigma}\right)$	(2) A AREA FROM MEAN TO $\frac{x}{\sigma}$	(3) B AREA IN LARGER PORTION	(4) C AREA IN SMALLER PORTION	(5) y ORDINATE AT $\frac{x}{\sigma}$
0.35	.1368	.6368	.3632	.3752
0.36	.1406	.6406	.3594	.3739
0.37	.1443	.6443	.3557	.3725
0.38	.1480	.6480	.3520	.3712
0.39	.1517	.6517	.3483	.3697
0.40	.1554	.6554	.3446	.3683
0.41	.1591	.6591	.3409	.3668
0.42	.1628	.6628	.3372	.3653
0.43	.1664	.6664	.3336	.3637
0.44	.1700	.6700	.3300	.3621
0.45	.1736	.6736	.3264	.3605
0.46	.1772	.6772	.3228	.3589
0.47	.1808	.6808	.3192	.3572
0.48	.1844	.6844	.3156	.3555
0.49	.1879	.6879	.3121	.3538
0.50	.1915	.6915	.3085	.3521
0.51	.1950	.6950	.3050	.3503
0.52	.1985	.6985	.3015	.3485
0.53	.2019	.7019	.2981	.3467
0.54	.2054	.7054	.2946	.3448
0.55	.2088	.7088	.2912	.3429
0.56	.2123	.7123	.2877	.3410
0.57	.2157	.7157	.2843	.3391
0.58	.2190	.7190	.2810	.3372
0.59	.2224	.7224	.2776	.3352
0.60	.2257	.7257	.2743	.3332
0.61	.2291	.7291	.2709	.3312
0.62	.2324	.7324	.2676	.3292
0.63	.2357	.7357	.2643	.3271
0.64	.2389	.7389	.2611	.3251
0.65	.2422	.7422	.2578	.3230
0.66	.2454	.7454	.2546	.3209
0.67	.2486	.7486	.2514	.3187
0.68	.2517	.7517	.2483	.3166
0.69	.2549	.7549	.2451	.3144

TABLE C. (*Continued*)

(1) z STANDARD SCORE $\left(\frac{x}{\sigma}\right)$	(2) A AREA FROM MEAN TO $\frac{x}{\sigma}$	(3) B AREA IN LARGER PORTION	(4) C AREA IN SMALLER PORTION	(5) y ORDINATE AT $\frac{x}{\sigma}$
0.70	.2580	.7580	.2420	.3123
0.71	.2611	.7611	.2389	.3101
0.72	.2642	.7642	.2358	.3079
0.73	.2673	.7673	.2327	.3056
0.74	.2704	.7704	.2296	.3034
0.75	.2734	.7734	.2266	.3011
0.76	.2764	.7764	.2236	.2989
0.77	.2794	.7794	.2206	.2966
0.78	.2823	.7823	.2177	.2943
0.79	.2852	.7852	.2148	.2920
0.80	.2881	.7881	.2119	.2897
0.81	.2910	.7910	.2090	.2874
0.82	.2939	.7939	.2061	.2850
0.83	.2967	.7967	.2033	.2827
0.84	.2995	.7995	.2005	.2803
0.85	.3023	.8023	.1977	.2780
0.86	.3051	.8051	.1949	.2756
0.87	.3078	.8078	.1922	.2732
0.88	.3106	.8106	.1894	.2709
0.89	.3133	.8133	.1867	.2685
0.90	.3159	.8159	.1841	.2661
0.91	.3186	.8186	.1814	.2637
0.92	.3212	.8212	.1788	.2613
0.93	.3238	.8238	.1762	.2589
0.94	.3264	.8264	.1736	.2565
0.95	.3289	.8289	.1711	.2541
0.96	.3315	.8315	.1685	.2516
0.97	.3340	.8340	.1660	.2492
0.98	.3365	.8365	.1635	.2468
0.99	.3389	.8389	.1611	.2444
1.00	.3413	.8413	.1587	.2420
1.01	.3438	.8438	.1562	.2396
1.02	.3461	.8461	.1539	.2371
1.03	.3485	.8485	.1515	.2347
1.04	.3508	.8508	.1492	.2323

TABLE C. (*Continued*)

(1) z Standard Score $\left(\frac{x}{\sigma}\right)$	(2) A Area from Mean to $\frac{x}{\sigma}$	(3) B Area in Larger Portion	(4) C Area in Smaller Portion	(5) y Ordinate at $\frac{x}{\sigma}$
1.05	.3531	.8531	.1469	.2299
1.06	.3554	.8554	.1446	.2275
1.07	.3577	.8577	.1423	.2251
1.08	.3599	.8599	.1401	.2227
1.09	.3621	.8621	.1379	.2203
1.10	.3643	.8643	.1357	.2179
1.11	.3665	.8665	.1335	.2155
1.12	.3686	.8686	.1314	.2131
1.13	.3708	.8708	.1292	.2107
1.14	.3729	.8729	.1271	.2083
1.15	.3749	.8749	.1251	.2059
1.16	.3770	.8770	.1230	.2036
1.17	.3790	.8790	.1210	.2012
1.18	.3810	.8810	.1190	.1989
1.19	.3830	.8830	.1170	.1965
1.20	.3849	.8849	.1151	.1942
1.21	.3869	.8869	.1131	.1919
1.22	.3888	.8888	.1112	.1895
1.23	.3907	.8907	.1093	.1872
1.24	.3925	.8925	.1075	.1849
1.25	.3944	.8944	.1056	.1826
1.26	.3962	.8962	.1038	.1804
1.27	.3980	.8980	.1020	.1781
1.28	.3997	.8997	.1003	.1758
1.29	.4015	.9015	.0985	.1736
1.30	.4032	.9032	.0968	.1714
1.31	.4049	.9049	.0951	.1691
1.32	.4066	.9066	.0934	.1669
1.33	.4082	.9082	.0918	.1647
1.34	.4099	.9099	.0901	.1626
1.35	.4115	.9115	.0885	.1604
1.36	.4131	.9131	.0869	.1582
1.37	.4147	.9147	.0853	.1561
1.38	.4162	.9162	.0838	.1539
1.39	.4177	.9177	.0823	.1518

TABLE C. *(Continued)*

(1) z STANDARD SCORE $\left(\dfrac{x}{\sigma}\right)$	(2) A AREA FROM MEAN TO $\dfrac{x}{\sigma}$	(3) B AREA IN LARGER PORTION	(4) C AREA IN SMALLER PORTION	(5) y ORDINATE AT $\dfrac{x}{\sigma}$
1.40	.4192	.9192	.0808	.1497
1.41	.4207	.9207	.0793	.1476
1.42	.4222	.9222	.0778	.1456
1.43	.4236	.9236	.0764	.1435
1.44	.4251	.9251	.0749	.1415
1.45	.4265	.9265	.0735	.1394
1.46	.4279	.9279	.0721	.1374
1.47	.4292	.9292	.0708	.1354
1.48	.4306	.9306	.0694	.1334
1.49	.4319	.9319	.0681	.1315
1.50	.4332	.9332	.0668	.1295
1.51	.4345	.9345	.0655	.1276
1.52	.4357	.9357	.0643	.1257
1.53	.4370	.9370	.0630	.1238
1.54	.4382	.9382	.0618	.1219
1.55	.4394	.9394	.0606	.1200
1.56	.4406	.9406	.0594	.1182
1.57	.4418	.9418	.0582	.1163
1.58	.4429	.9429	.0571	.1145
1.59	.4441	.9441	.0559	.1127
1.60	.4452	.9452	.0548	.1109
1.61	.4463	.9463	.0537	.1092
1.62	.4474	.9474	.0526	.1074
1.63	.4484	.9484	.0516	.1057
1.64	.4495	.9495	.0505	.1040
1.65	.4505	.9505	.0495	.1023
1.66	.4515	.9515	.0485	.1006
1.67	.4525	.9525	.0475	.0989
1.68	.4535	.9535	.0465	.0973
1.69	.4545	.9545	.0455	.0957
1.70	.4554	.9554	.0446	.0940
1.71	.4564	.9564	.0436	.0925
1.72	.4573	.9573	.0427	.0909
1.73	.4582	.9582	.0418	.0893
1.74	.4591	.9591	.0409	.0878

TABLE C. (*Continued*)

(1) z STANDARD SCORE $\left(\frac{x}{\sigma}\right)$	(2) A AREA FROM MEAN TO $\frac{x}{\sigma}$	(3) B AREA IN LARGER PORTION	(4) C AREA IN SMALLER PORTION	(5) y ORDINATE AT $\frac{x}{\sigma}$
1.75	.4599	.9599	.0401	.0863
1.76	.4608	.9608	.0392	.0848
1.77	.4616	.9616	.0384	.0833
1.78	.4625	.9625	.0375	.0818
1.79	.4633	.9633	.0367	.0804
1.80	.4641	.9641	.0359	.0790
1.81	.4649	.9649	.0351	.0775
1.82	.4656	.9656	.0344	.0761
1.83	.4664	.9664	.0336	.0748
1.84	.4671	.9671	.0329	.0734
1.85	.4678	.9678	.0322	.0721
1.86	.4686	.9686	.0314	.0707
1.87	.4693	.9693	.0307	.0694
1.88	.4699	.9699	.0301	.0681
1.89	.4706	.9706	.0294	.0669
1.90	.4713	.9713	.0287	.0656
1.91	.4719	.9719	.0281	.0644
1.92	.4726	.9726	.0274	.0632
1.93	.4732	.9732	.0268	.0620
1.94	.4738	.9738	.0262	.0608
1.95	.4744	.9744	.0256	.0596
1.96	.4750	.9750	.0250	.0584
1.97	.4756	.9756	.0244	.0573
1.98	.4761	.9761	.0239	.0562
1.99	.4767	.9767	.0233	.0551
2.00	.4772	.9772	.0228	.0540
2.01	.4778	.9778	.0222	.0529
2.02	.4783	.9783	.0217	.0519
2.03	.4788	.9788	.0212	.0508
2.04	.4793	.9793	.0207	.0498
2.05	.4798	.9798	.0202	.0488
2.06	.4803	.9803	.0197	.0478
2.07	.4808	.9808	.0192	.0468
2.08	.4812	.9812	.0188	.0459
2.09	.4817	.9817	.0183	.0449

TABLE C. (*Continued*)

(1) *z* Standard Score $\left(\frac{x}{\sigma}\right)$	(2) *A* Area from Mean to $\frac{x}{\sigma}$	(3) *B* Area in Larger Portion	(4) *C* Area in Smaller Portion	(5) *y* Ordinate at $\frac{x}{\sigma}$
2.10	.4821	.9821	.0179	.0440
2.11	.4826	.9826	.0174	.0431
2.12	.4830	.9830	.0170	.0422
2.13	.4834	.9834	.0166	.0413
2.14	.4838	.9838	.0162	.0404
2.15	.4842	.9842	.0158	.0396
2.16	.4846	.9846	.0154	.0387
2.17	.4850	.9850	.0150	.0379
2.18	.4854	.9854	.0146	.0371
2.19	.4857	.9857	.0143	.0363
2.20	.4861	.9861	.0139	.0355
2.21	.4864	.9864	.0136	.0347
2.22	.4868	.9868	.0132	.0339
2.23	.4871	.9871	.0129	.0332
2.24	.4875	.9875	.0125	.0325
2.25	.4878	.9878	.0122	.0317
2.26	.4881	.9881	.0119	.0310
2.27	.4884	.9884	.0116	.0303
2.28	.4887	.9887	.0113	.0297
2.29	.4890	.9890	.0110	.0290
2.30	.4893	.9893	.0107	.0283
2.31	.4896	.9896	.0104	.0277
2.32	.4898	.9898	.0102	.0270
2.33	.4901	.9901	.0099	.0264
2.34	.4904	.9904	.0096	.0258
2.35	.4906	.9906	.0094	.0252
2.36	.4909	.9909	.0091	.0246
2.37	.4911	.9911	.0089	.0241
2.38	.4913	.9913	.0087	.0235
2.39	.4916	.9916	.0084	.0229
2.40	.4918	.9918	.0082	.0224
2.41	.4920	.9920	.0080	.0219
2.42	.4922	.9922	.0078	.0213
2.43	.4925	.9925	.0075	.0208
2.44	.4927	.9927	.0073	.0203

TABLE C. (*Continued*)

(1) z STANDARD SCORE $\left(\frac{x}{\sigma}\right)$	(2) A AREA FROM MEAN TO $\frac{x}{\sigma}$	(3) B AREA IN LARGER PORTION	(4) C AREA IN SMALLER PORTION	(5) y ORDINATE AT $\frac{x}{\sigma}$
2.45	.4929	.9929	.0071	.0198
2.46	.4931	.9931	.0069	.0194
2.47	.4932	.9932	.0068	.0189
2.48	.4934	.9934	.0066	.0184
2.49	.4936	.9936	.0064	.0180
2.50	.4938	.9938	.0062	.0175
2.51	.4940	.9940	.0060	.0171
2.52	.4941	.9941	.0059	.0167
2.53	.4943	.9943	.0057	.0163
2.54	.4945	.9945	.0055	.0158
2.55	.4946	.9946	.0054	.0154
2.56	.4948	.9948	.0052	.0151
2.57	.4949	.9949	.0051	.0147
2.58	.4951	.9951	.0049	.0143
2.59	.4952	.9952	.0048	.0139
2.60	.4953	.9953	.0047	.0136
2.61	.4955	.9955	.0045	.0132
2.62	.4956	.9956	.0044	.0129
2.63	.4957	.9957	.0043	.0126
2.64	.4959	.9959	.0041	.0122
2.65	.4960	.9960	.0040	.0119
2.66	.4961	.9961	.0039	.0116
2.67	.4962	.9962	.0038	.0113
2.68	.4963	.9963	.0037	.0110
2.69	.4904	.9964	.0036	.0107
2.70	.4965	.9965	.0035	.0104
2.71	.4966	.9966	.0034	.0101
2.72	.4967	.9967	.0033	.0099
2.73	.4968	.9968	.0032	.0096
2.74	.4969	.9969	.0031	.0093
2.75	.4970	.9970	.0030	.0091
2.76	.4971	.9971	.0029	.0088
2.77	.4972	.9972	.0028	.0086
2.78	.4973	.9973	.0027	.0084
2.79	.4974	.9974	.0026	.0081

TABLE C. (*Continued*)

(1) z STANDARD SCORE $\left(\frac{x}{\sigma}\right)$	(2) A AREA FROM MEAN TO $\frac{x}{\sigma}$	(3) B AREA IN LARGER PORTION	(4) C AREA IN SMALLER PORTION	(5) y ORDINATE AT $\frac{x}{\sigma}$
2.80	.4974	.9974	.0026	.0079
2.81	.4975	.9975	.0025	.0077
2.82	.4976	.9976	.0024	.0075
2.83	.4977	.9977	.0023	.0073
2.84	.4977	.9977	.0023	.0071
2.85	.4978	.9978	.0022	.0069
2.86	.4979	.9979	.0021	.0067
2.87	.4979	.9979	.0021	.0065
2.88	.4980	.9980	.0020	.0063
2.89	.4981	.9981	.0019	.0061
2.90	.4981	.9981	.0019	.0060
2.91	.4982	.9982	.0018	.0058
2.92	.4982	.9982	.0018	.0056
2.93	.4983	.9983	.0017	.0055
2.94	.4984	.9984	.0016	.0053
2.95	.4984	.9984	.0016	.0051
2.96	.4985	.9985	.0015	.0050
2.97	.4985	.9985	.0015	.0048
2.98	.4986	.9986	.0014	.0047
2.99	.4986	.9986	.0014	.0046
3.00	.4987	.9987	.0013	.0044
3.01	.4987	.9987	.0013	.0043
3.02	.4987	.9987	.0013	.0042
3.03	.4988	.9988	.0012	.0040
3.04	.4988	.9988	.0012	.0039
3.05	.4989	.9989	.0011	.0038
3.06	.4989	.9989	.0011	.0037
3.07	.4989	.9989	.0011	.0036
3.08	.4990	.9990	.0010	.0035
3.09	.4990	.9990	.0010	.0034
3.10	.4990	.9990	.0010	.0033
3.11	.4991	.9991	.0009	.0032
3.12	.4991	.9991	.0009	.0031
3.13	.4991	.9991	.0009	.0030
3.14	.4992	.9992	.0008	.0029

TABLE C. (*Continued*)

(1) z STANDARD SCORE $\left(\frac{x}{\sigma}\right)$	(2) A AREA FROM MEAN TO $\frac{x}{\sigma}$	(3) B AREA IN LARGER PORTION	(4) C AREA IN SMALLER PORTION	(5) y ORDINATE AT $\frac{x}{\sigma}$
3.15	.4992	.9992	.0008	.0028
3.16	.4992	.9992	.0008	.0027
3.17	.4992	.9992	.0008	.0026
3.18	.4993	.9993	.0007	.0025
3.19	.4993	.9993	.0007	.0025
3.20	.4993	.9993	.0007	.0024
3.21	.4993	.9993	.0007	.0023
3.22	.4994	.9994	.0006	.0022
3.23	.4994	.9994	.0006	.0022
3.24	.4994	.9994	.0006	.0021
3.30	.4995	.9995	.0005	.0017
3.40	.4997	.9997	.0003	.0012
3.50	.4998	.9998	.0002	.0009
3.60	.4998	.9998	.0002	.0006
3.70	.4999	.9999	.0001	.0004

TABLE D. Values of the Correlation Coefficient for Different Levels of Significance

df	P = .10	.05	.02	.01
1	.988	.997	.9995	.9999
2	.900	.950	.980	.990
3	.805	.878	.934	.959
4	.729	.811	.882	.917
5	.669	.754	.833	.874
6	.622	.707	.789	.834
7	.582	.666	.750	.798
8	.549	.632	.716	.765
9	.521	.602	.685	.735
10	.497	.576	.658	.708
11	.476	.553	.634	.684
12	.458	.532	.612	.661
13	.441	.514	.592	.641
14	.426	.497	.574	.623
15	.412	.482	.558	.606
16	.400	.468	.542	.590
17	.389	.456	.528	.575
18	.378	.444	.516	.561
19	.369	.433	.503	.549
20	.360	.423	.492	.537
21	.352	.413	.482	.526
22	.344	.404	.472	.515
23	.337	.396	.462	.505
24	.330	.388	.453	.496
25	.323	.381	.445	.487
26	.317	.374	.437	.479
27	.311	.367	.430	.471
28	.306	.361	.423	.463
29	.301	.355	.416	.456
30	.296	.349	.409	.449
35	.275	.325	.381	.418
40	.257	.304	.358	.393
45	.243	.288	.338	.372
50	.231	.273	.322	.354
60	.211	.250	.295	.325
70	.195	.232	.274	.302
80	.183	.217	.256	.283
90	.173	.205	.242	.267
100	.164	.195	.230	.254

SOURCE: Table D is reprinted from Table V.A. of Fisher & Yates, *Statistical Methods for Research Workers*, published by Oliver and Boyd Ltd., Edinburgh, and by permission of the author and publishers.

NOTE: The probabilities given are for a two-tailed test of significance, that is with the sign of r ignored. For a one-tailed test of significance, the tabled probabilities should be halved.

TABLE D. (*Continued*)

Additional Values of r at the 5 and 1 Per Cent Levels of Significance

df	.05	.01	df	.05	.01	df	.05	.01
32	.339	.436	48	.279	.361	150	.159	.208
34	.329	.424	55	.261	.338	175	.148	.193
36	.320	.413	65	.241	.313	200	.138	.181
38	.312	.403	75	.224	.292	300	.113	.148
42	.297	.384	85	.211	.275	400	.098	.128
44	.291	.376	95	.200	.260	500	.088	.115
46	.284	.368	125	.174	.228	1,000	.062	.081

TABLE E. Table of Critical Values of r_s, the Spearman Rank Correlation Coefficient

N	Significance level (one-tailed test)	
	.05	.01
4	1.000	
5	.900	1.000
6	.829	.943
7	.714	.893
8	.643	.833
9	.600	.783
10	.564	.746
12	.506	.712
14	.456	.645
16	.425	.601
18	.399	.564
20	.377	.534
22	359	.508
24	.343	.485
26	.329	.465
28	.317	.448
30	.306	.432

SOURCE: E. G. Olds, "Distributions of Sums of Squares of Rank Differences for Small Numbers of Individuals," *Ann. Math. Statist.* **9**, 133–148 (1938).

TABLE F. Distribution of *t*

df	Level of significance for one-tailed test					
	.10	.05	.025	.01	.005	.0005
	Level of significance for two-tailed test					
	.20	.10	.05	.02	.01	.001
1	3.078	6.314	12.706	31.821	63.657	636.619
2	1.886	2.920	4.303	6.965	9.925	31.598
3	1.638	2.353	3.182	4.541	5.841	12.941
4	1.533	2.132	2.776	3.747	4.604	8.610
5	1.476	2.015	2.571	3.365	4.032	6.859
6	1.440	1.943	2.447	3.143	3.707	5.959
7	1.415	1.895	2.365	2.998	3.499	5.405
8	1.397	1.860	2.306	2.896	3.355	5.041
9	1.383	1.833	2.262	2.821	3.250	4.781
10	1.372	1.812	2.228	2.764	3.169	4.587
11	1.363	1.796	2.201	2.718	3.106	4.437
12	1.356	1.782	2.179	2.681	3.055	4.318
13	1.350	1.771	2.160	2.650	3.012	4.221
14	1.345	1.761	2.145	2.624	2.977	4.140
15	1.341	1.753	2.131	2.602	2.947	4.073
16	1.337	1.746	2.120	2.583	2.921	4.015
17	1.333	1.740	2.110	2.567	2.898	3.965
18	1.330	1.734	2.101	2.552	2.878	3.922
19	1.328	1.729	2.093	2.539	2.861	3.883
20	1.325	1.725	2.086	2.528	2.845	3.850
21	1.323	1.721	2.080	2.518	2.831	3.819
22	1.321	1.717	2.074	2.508	2.819	3.792
23	1.319	1.714	2.069	2.500	2.807	3.767
24	1.318	1.711	2.064	2.492	2.797	3.745
25	1.316	1.708	2.060	2.485	2.787	3.725
26	1.315	1.706	2.056	2.479	2.779	3.707
27	1.314	1.703	2.052	2.473	2.771	3.690
28	1.313	1.701	2.048	2.467	2.763	3.674
29	1.311	1.699	2.045	2.462	2.756	3.659
30	1.310	1.697	2.042	2.457	2.750	3.646
40	1.303	1.684	2.021	2.423	2.704	3.551
60	1.296	1.671	2.000	2.390	2.660	3.460
120	1.289	1.658	1.980	2.358	2.617	3.373
∞	1.282	1.645	1.960	2.326	2.576	3.291

SOURCE: Table F is abridged from Table III of Fisher & Yates: *Statistical Tables for Biological, Agricultural, and Medical Research,* published by Oliver & Boyd Ltd., Edinburgh, and by permission of the authors and publishers.

TABLE G. The Five (Roman Type) and One (Boldface Type) Per Cent Points for the Distribution of F

n_1 degrees of freedom (for greater mean square)

n_2	1	2	3	4	5	6	7	8	9	10	11	12	14	16	20	24	30	40	50	75	100	200	500	∞
1	161 / 4,052	200 / 4,999	216 / 5,403	225 / 5,625	230 / 5,764	234 / 5,859	237 / 5,928	239 / 5,981	241 / 6,022	242 / 6,056	243 / 6,082	244 / 6,106	245 / 6,142	246 / 6,169	248 / 6,208	249 / 6,234	250 / 6,258	251 / 6,286	252 / 6,302	253 / 6,323	253 / 6,334	254 / 6,352	254 / 6,361	254 / 6,366
2	18.51 / 98.49	19.00 / 99.00	19.16 / 99.17	19.25 / 99.25	19.30 / 99.30	19.33 / 99.33	19.36 / 99.34	19.37 / 99.36	19.38 / 99.38	19.39 / 99.40	19.40 / 99.41	19.41 / 99.42	19.42 / 99.43	19.43 / 99.44	19.44 / 99.45	19.45 / 99.46	19.46 / 99.47	19.47 / 99.48	19.47 / 99.48	19.48 / 99.49	19.49 / 99.49	19.49 / 99.49	19.50 / 99.50	19.50 / 99.50
3	10.13 / 34.12	9.55 / 30.82	9.28 / 29.46	9.12 / 28.71	9.01 / 28.24	8.94 / 27.91	8.88 / 27.67	8.84 / 27.49	8.81 / 27.34	8.78 / 27.23	8.76 / 27.13	8.74 / 27.05	8.71 / 26.92	8.69 / 26.83	8.66 / 26.69	8.64 / 26.60	8.62 / 26.50	8.60 / 26.41	8.58 / 26.35	8.57 / 26.27	8.56 / 26.23	8.54 / 26.18	8.54 / 26.14	8.53 / 26.12
4	7.71 / 21.20	6.94 / 18.00	6.59 / 16.69	6.39 / 15.98	6.26 / 15.52	6.16 / 15.21	6.09 / 14.98	6.04 / 14.80	6.00 / 14.66	5.96 / 14.54	5.93 / 14.45	5.91 / 14.37	5.87 / 14.24	5.84 / 14.15	5.80 / 14.02	5.77 / 13.93	5.74 / 13.83	5.71 / 13.74	5.70 / 13.69	5.68 / 13.61	5.66 / 13.57	5.65 / 13.52	5.64 / 13.48	5.63 / 13.46
5	6.61 / 16.26	5.79 / 13.27	5.41 / 12.06	5.19 / 11.39	5.05 / 10.97	4.95 / 10.67	4.88 / 10.45	4.82 / 10.27	4.78 / 10.15	4.74 / 10.05	4.70 / 9.96	4.68 / 9.89	4.64 / 9.77	4.60 / 9.68	4.56 / 9.55	4.53 / 9.47	4.50 / 9.38	4.46 / 9.29	4.44 / 9.24	4.42 / 9.17	4.40 / 9.13	4.38 / 9.07	4.37 / 9.04	4.36 / 9.02
6	5.99 / 13.74	5.14 / 10.92	4.76 / 9.78	4.53 / 9.15	4.39 / 8.75	4.28 / 8.47	4.21 / 8.26	4.15 / 8.10	4.10 / 7.98	4.06 / 7.87	4.03 / 7.79	4.00 / 7.72	3.96 / 7.60	3.92 / 7.52	3.87 / 7.39	3.84 / 7.31	3.81 / 7.23	3.77 / 7.14	3.75 / 7.09	3.72 / 7.02	3.71 / 6.99	3.69 / 6.94	3.68 / 6.90	3.67 / 6.88
7	5.59 / 12.25	4.74 / 9.55	4.35 / 8.45	4.12 / 7.85	3.97 / 7.46	3.87 / 7.19	3.79 / 7.00	3.73 / 6.84	3.68 / 6.71	3.63 / 6.62	3.60 / 6.54	3.57 / 6.47	3.52 / 6.35	3.49 / 6.27	3.44 / 6.15	3.41 / 6.07	3.38 / 5.98	3.34 / 5.90	3.32 / 5.85	3.29 / 5.78	3.28 / 5.75	3.25 / 5.70	3.24 / 5.67	3.23 / 5.65
8	5.32 / 11.26	4.46 / 8.65	4.07 / 7.59	3.84 / 7.01	3.69 / 6.63	3.58 / 6.37	3.50 / 6.19	3.44 / 6.03	3.39 / 5.91	3.34 / 5.82	3.31 / 5.74	3.28 / 5.67	3.23 / 5.56	3.20 / 5.48	3.15 / 5.36	3.12 / 5.28	3.08 / 5.20	3.05 / 5.11	3.03 / 5.06	3.00 / 5.00	2.98 / 4.96	2.96 / 4.91	2.94 / 4.88	2.93 / 4.86
9	5.12 / 10.56	4.26 / 8.02	3.86 / 6.99	3.63 / 6.42	3.48 / 6.06	3.37 / 5.80	3.29 / 5.62	3.23 / 5.47	3.18 / 5.35	3.13 / 5.26	3.10 / 5.18	3.07 / 5.11	3.02 / 5.00	2.98 / 4.92	2.93 / 4.80	2.90 / 4.73	2.86 / 4.64	2.82 / 4.56	2.80 / 4.51	2.77 / 4.45	2.76 / 4.41	2.73 / 4.36	2.72 / 4.33	2.71 / 4.31
10	4.96 / 10.04	4.10 / 7.56	3.71 / 6.55	3.48 / 5.99	3.33 / 5.64	3.22 / 5.39	3.14 / 5.21	3.07 / 5.06	3.02 / 4.95	2.97 / 4.85	2.94 / 4.78	2.91 / 4.71	2.86 / 4.60	2.82 / 4.52	2.77 / 4.41	2.74 / 4.33	2.70 / 4.25	2.67 / 4.17	2.64 / 4.12	2.61 / 4.05	2.59 / 4.01	2.56 / 3.96	2.55 / 3.93	2.54 / 3.91
11	4.84 / 9.65	3.98 / 7.20	3.59 / 6.22	3.36 / 5.67	3.20 / 5.32	3.09 / 5.07	3.01 / 4.88	2.95 / 4.74	2.90 / 4.63	2.86 / 4.54	2.82 / 4.46	2.79 / 4.40	2.74 / 4.29	2.70 / 4.21	2.65 / 4.10	2.61 / 4.02	2.57 / 3.94	2.53 / 3.86	2.50 / 3.80	2.47 / 3.74	2.45 / 3.70	2.42 / 3.66	2.41 / 3.62	2.40 / 3.60
12	4.75 / 9.33	3.88 / 6.93	3.49 / 5.95	3.26 / 5.41	3.11 / 5.06	3.00 / 4.82	2.92 / 4.65	2.85 / 4.50	2.80 / 4.39	2.76 / 4.30	2.72 / 4.22	2.69 / 4.16	2.64 / 4.05	2.60 / 3.98	2.54 / 3.86	2.50 / 3.78	2.46 / 3.70	2.42 / 3.61	2.40 / 3.56	2.36 / 3.49	2.35 / 3.46	2.32 / 3.41	2.31 / 3.38	2.30 / 3.36
13	4.67 / 9.07	3.80 / 6.70	3.41 / 5.74	3.18 / 5.20	3.02 / 4.86	2.92 / 4.62	2.84 / 4.44	2.77 / 4.30	2.72 / 4.19	2.67 / 4.10	2.63 / 4.02	2.60 / 3.96	2.55 / 3.85	2.51 / 3.78	2.46 / 3.67	2.42 / 3.59	2.38 / 3.51	2.34 / 3.42	2.32 / 3.37	2.28 / 3.30	2.26 / 3.27	2.24 / 3.21	2.22 / 3.18	2.21 / 3.16

SOURCE: Table G is reproduced from G. W. Snedecor, *Statistical Methods*, 5th ed., Iowa State University Press, Ames, Iowa, by permission of the author and publisher.

TABLE G. (Continued)

n_1 degrees of freedom (for greater mean square)

n_2	1	2	3	4	5	6	7	8	9	10	11	12	14	16	20	24	30	40	50	75	100	200	500	∞
14	4.60 8.86	3.74 6.51	3.34 5.56	3.11 5.03	2.96 4.69	2.85 4.46	2.77 4.28	2.70 4.14	2.65 4.03	2.60 3.94	2.56 3.86	2.53 3.80	2.48 3.70	2.44 3.62	2.39 3.51	2.35 3.43	2.31 3.34	2.27 3.26	2.24 3.21	2.21 3.14	2.19 3.11	2.16 3.06	2.14 3.02	2.13 3.00
15	4.54 8.68	3.68 6.36	3.29 5.42	3.06 4.89	2.90 4.56	2.79 4.32	2.70 4.14	2.64 4.00	2.59 3.89	2.55 3.80	2.51 3.73	2.48 3.67	2.43 3.56	2.39 3.48	2.33 3.36	2.29 3.29	2.25 3.20	2.21 3.12	2.18 3.07	2.15 3.00	2.12 2.97	2.10 2.92	2.08 2.89	2.07 2.87
16	4.49 8.53	3.63 6.23	3.24 5.29	3.01 4.77	2.85 4.44	2.74 4.20	2.66 4.03	2.59 3.89	2.54 3.78	2.49 3.69	2.45 3.61	2.42 3.55	2.37 3.45	2.33 3.37	2.28 3.25	2.24 3.18	2.20 3.10	2.16 3.01	2.13 2.96	2.09 2.89	2.07 2.86	2.04 2.80	2.02 2.77	2.01 2.75
17	4.45 8.40	3.59 6.11	3.20 5.18	2.96 4.67	2.81 4.34	2.70 4.10	2.62 3.93	2.55 3.79	2.50 3.68	2.45 3.59	2.41 3.52	2.38 3.45	2.33 3.35	2.29 3.27	2.23 3.16	2.19 3.08	2.15 3.00	2.11 2.92	2.08 2.86	2.04 2.79	2.02 2.76	1.99 2.70	1.97 2.67	1.96 2.65
18	4.41 8.28	3.55 6.01	3.16 5.09	2.93 4.58	2.77 4.25	2.66 4.01	2.58 3.85	2.51 3.71	2.46 3.60	2.41 3.51	2.37 3.44	2.34 3.37	2.29 3.27	2.25 3.19	2.19 3.07	2.15 3.00	2.11 2.91	2.07 2.83	2.04 2.78	2.00 2.71	1.98 2.68	1.95 2.62	1.93 2.59	1.92 2.57
19	4.38 8.18	3.52 5.93	3.13 5.01	2.90 4.50	2.74 4.17	2.63 3.94	2.55 3.77	2.48 3.63	2.43 3.52	2.38 3.43	2.34 3.36	2.31 3.30	2.26 3.19	2.21 3.12	2.15 3.00	2.11 2.92	2.07 2.84	2.02 2.76	2.00 2.70	1.96 2.63	1.94 2.60	1.91 2.54	1.90 2.51	1.88 2.49
20	4.35 8.10	3.49 5.85	3.10 4.94	2.87 4.43	2.71 4.10	2.60 3.87	2.52 3.71	2.45 3.56	2.40 3.45	2.35 3.37	2.31 3.30	2.28 3.23	2.23 3.13	2.18 3.05	2.12 2.94	2.08 2.86	2.04 2.77	1.99 2.69	1.96 2.63	1.92 2.56	1.90 2.53	1.87 2.47	1.85 2.44	1.84 2.42
21	4.32 8.02	3.47 5.78	3.07 4.87	2.84 4.37	2.68 4.04	2.57 3.81	2.49 3.65	2.42 3.51	2.37 3.40	2.32 3.31	2.28 3.24	2.25 3.17	2.20 3.07	2.15 2.99	2.09 2.88	2.05 2.80	2.00 2.72	1.96 2.63	1.93 2.58	1.89 2.51	1.87 2.47	1.84 2.42	1.82 2.38	1.81 2.36
22	4.30 7.94	3.44 5.72	3.05 4.82	2.82 4.31	2.66 3.99	2.55 3.76	2.47 3.59	2.40 3.45	2.35 3.35	2.30 3.26	2.26 3.18	2.23 3.12	2.18 3.02	2.13 2.94	2.07 2.83	2.03 2.75	1.98 2.67	1.93 2.58	1.91 2.53	1.87 2.46	1.84 2.42	1.81 2.37	1.80 2.33	1.78 2.31
23	4.28 7.88	3.42 5.66	3.03 4.76	2.80 4.26	2.64 3.94	2.53 3.71	2.45 3.54	2.38 3.41	2.32 3.30	2.28 3.21	2.24 3.14	2.20 3.07	2.14 2.97	2.10 2.89	2.04 2.78	2.00 2.70	1.96 2.62	1.91 2.53	1.88 2.48	1.84 2.41	1.82 2.37	1.79 2.32	1.77 2.28	1.76 2.26
24	4.26 7.82	3.40 5.61	3.01 4.72	2.78 4.22	2.62 3.90	2.51 3.67	2.43 3.50	2.36 3.36	2.30 3.25	2.26 3.17	2.22 3.09	2.18 3.03	2.13 2.93	2.09 2.85	2.02 2.74	1.98 2.66	1.94 2.58	1.89 2.49	1.86 2.44	1.82 2.36	1.80 2.33	1.76 2.27	1.74 2.23	1.73 2.21
25	4.24 7.77	3.38 5.57	2.99 4.68	2.76 4.18	2.60 3.86	2.49 3.63	2.41 3.46	2.34 3.32	2.28 3.21	2.24 3.13	2.20 3.05	2.16 2.99	2.11 2.89	2.06 2.81	2.00 2.70	1.96 2.62	1.92 2.54	1.87 2.45	1.84 2.40	1.80 2.32	1.77 2.29	1.74 2.23	1.72 2.19	1.71 2.17
26	4.22 7.72	3.37 5.53	2.98 4.64	2.74 4.14	2.59 3.82	2.47 3.59	2.39 3.42	2.32 3.29	2.27 3.17	2.22 3.09	2.18 3.02	2.15 2.96	2.10 2.86	2.05 2.77	1.99 2.66	1.95 2.58	1.90 2.50	1.85 2.41	1.82 2.36	1.78 2.28	1.76 2.25	1.72 2.19	1.70 2.15	1.69 2.13

TABLE G. (Continued)

n_1 degrees of freedom (for greater mean square)

n_2	1	2	3	4	5	6	7	8	9	10	11	12	14	16	20	24	30	40	50	75	100	200	500	∞
27	4.21 / 7.68	3.35 / 5.49	2.96 / 4.60	2.73 / 4.11	2.57 / 3.79	2.46 / 3.56	2.37 / 3.39	2.30 / 3.26	2.25 / 3.14	2.20 / 3.06	2.16 / 2.98	2.13 / 2.93	2.08 / 2.83	2.03 / 2.74	1.97 / 2.63	1.93 / 2.55	1.88 / 2.47	1.84 / 2.38	1.80 / 2.33	1.76 / 2.25	1.74 / 2.21	1.71 / 2.16	1.68 / 2.12	1.67 / 2.10
28	4.20 / 7.64	3.34 / 5.45	2.95 / 4.57	2.71 / 4.07	2.56 / 3.76	2.44 / 3.53	2.36 / 3.36	2.29 / 3.23	2.24 / 3.11	2.19 / 3.03	2.15 / 2.95	2.12 / 2.90	2.06 / 2.80	2.02 / 2.71	1.96 / 2.60	1.91 / 2.52	1.87 / 2.44	1.81 / 2.35	1.78 / 2.30	1.75 / 2.22	1.72 / 2.18	1.69 / 2.13	1.67 / 2.09	1.65 / 2.06
29	4.18 / 7.60	3.33 / 5.42	2.93 / 4.54	2.70 / 4.04	2.54 / 3.73	2.43 / 3.50	2.35 / 3.33	2.28 / 3.20	2.22 / 3.08	2.18 / 3.00	2.14 / 2.92	2.10 / 2.87	2.05 / 2.77	2.00 / 2.68	1.94 / 2.57	1.90 / 2.49	1.85 / 2.41	1.80 / 2.32	1.77 / 2.27	1.73 / 2.19	1.71 / 2.15	1.68 / 2.10	1.65 / 2.06	1.64 / 2.03
30	4.17 / 7.56	3.32 / 5.39	2.92 / 4.51	2.69 / 4.02	2.53 / 3.70	2.42 / 3.47	2.34 / 3.30	2.27 / 3.17	2.21 / 3.06	2.16 / 2.98	2.12 / 2.90	2.09 / 2.84	2.04 / 2.74	1.99 / 2.66	1.93 / 2.55	1.89 / 2.47	1.84 / 2.38	1.79 / 2.29	1.76 / 2.24	1.72 / 2.16	1.69 / 2.13	1.66 / 2.07	1.64 / 2.03	1.62 / 2.01
32	4.15 / 7.50	3.30 / 5.34	2.90 / 4.46	2.67 / 3.97	2.51 / 3.66	2.40 / 3.42	2.32 / 3.25	2.25 / 3.12	2.19 / 3.01	2.14 / 2.94	2.10 / 2.86	2.07 / 2.80	2.02 / 2.70	1.97 / 2.62	1.91 / 2.51	1.86 / 2.42	1.82 / 2.34	1.76 / 2.25	1.74 / 2.20	1.69 / 2.12	1.67 / 2.08	1.64 / 2.02	1.61 / 1.98	1.59 / 1.96
34	4.13 / 7.44	3.28 / 5.29	2.88 / 4.42	2.65 / 3.93	2.49 / 3.61	2.38 / 3.38	2.30 / 3.21	2.23 / 3.08	2.17 / 2.97	2.12 / 2.89	2.08 / 2.82	2.05 / 2.76	2.00 / 2.66	1.95 / 2.58	1.89 / 2.47	1.84 / 2.38	1.80 / 2.30	1.74 / 2.21	1.71 / 2.15	1.67 / 2.08	1.64 / 2.04	1.61 / 1.98	1.59 / 1.94	1.57 / 1.91
36	4.11 / 7.39	3.26 / 5.25	2.86 / 4.38	2.63 / 3.89	2.48 / 3.58	2.36 / 3.35	2.28 / 3.18	2.21 / 3.04	2.15 / 2.94	2.10 / 2.86	2.06 / 2.78	2.03 / 2.72	1.98 / 2.62	1.93 / 2.54	1.87 / 2.43	1.82 / 2.35	1.78 / 2.26	1.72 / 2.17	1.69 / 2.12	1.65 / 2.04	1.62 / 2.00	1.59 / 1.94	1.56 / 1.90	1.55 / 1.87
38	4.10 / 7.35	3.25 / 5.21	2.85 / 4.34	2.62 / 3.86	2.46 / 3.54	2.35 / 3.32	2.26 / 3.15	2.19 / 3.02	2.14 / 2.91	2.09 / 2.82	2.05 / 2.75	2.02 / 2.69	1.96 / 2.59	1.92 / 2.51	1.85 / 2.40	1.80 / 2.32	1.76 / 2.22	1.71 / 2.14	1.67 / 2.08	1.63 / 2.00	1.60 / 1.97	1.57 / 1.90	1.54 / 1.86	1.53 / 1.84
40	4.08 / 7.31	3.23 / 5.18	2.84 / 4.31	2.61 / 3.83	2.45 / 3.51	2.34 / 3.29	2.25 / 3.12	2.18 / 2.99	2.12 / 2.88	2.07 / 2.80	2.04 / 2.73	2.00 / 2.66	1.95 / 2.56	1.90 / 2.49	1.84 / 2.37	1.79 / 2.29	1.74 / 2.20	1.69 / 2.11	1.66 / 2.05	1.61 / 1.97	1.59 / 1.94	1.55 / 1.88	1.53 / 1.84	1.51 / 1.81
42	4.07 / 7.27	3.22 / 5.15	2.83 / 4.29	2.59 / 3.80	2.44 / 3.49	2.32 / 3.26	2.24 / 3.10	2.17 / 2.96	2.11 / 2.86	2.06 / 2.77	2.02 / 2.70	1.99 / 2.64	1.94 / 2.54	1.89 / 2.46	1.82 / 2.35	1.78 / 2.26	1.73 / 2.17	1.68 / 2.08	1.64 / 2.02	1.60 / 1.94	1.57 / 1.91	1.54 / 1.85	1.51 / 1.80	1.49 / 1.78
44	4.06 / 7.24	3.21 / 5.12	2.82 / 4.26	2.58 / 3.78	2.43 / 3.46	2.31 / 3.24	2.23 / 3.07	2.16 / 2.94	2.10 / 2.84	2.05 / 2.75	2.01 / 2.68	1.98 / 2.62	1.92 / 2.52	1.88 / 2.44	1.81 / 2.32	1.76 / 2.24	1.72 / 2.15	1.66 / 2.06	1.63 / 2.00	1.58 / 1.92	1.56 / 1.88	1.52 / 1.82	1.50 / 1.78	1.48 / 1.75
46	4.05 / 7.21	3.20 / 5.10	2.81 / 4.24	2.57 / 3.76	2.42 / 3.44	2.30 / 3.22	2.22 / 3.05	2.14 / 2.92	2.09 / 2.82	2.04 / 2.73	2.00 / 2.66	1.97 / 2.60	1.91 / 2.50	1.87 / 2.42	1.80 / 2.30	1.75 / 2.22	1.71 / 2.13	1.65 / 2.04	1.62 / 1.98	1.57 / 1.90	1.54 / 1.86	1.51 / 1.80	1.48 / 1.76	1.46 / 1.72
48	4.04 / 7.19	3.19 / 5.08	2.80 / 4.22	2.56 / 3.74	2.41 / 3.42	2.30 / 3.20	2.21 / 3.04	2.14 / 2.90	2.08 / 2.80	2.03 / 2.71	1.99 / 2.64	1.96 / 2.58	1.90 / 2.48	1.86 / 2.40	1.79 / 2.28	1.74 / 2.20	1.70 / 2.11	1.64 / 2.02	1.61 / 1.96	1.56 / 1.88	1.53 / 1.84	1.50 / 1.78	1.47 / 1.73	1.45 / 1.70

TABLE G. (Continued)

n_1 degrees of freedom (for greater mean square)

n_1	1	2	3	4	5	6	7	8	9	10	11	12	14	16	20	24	30	40	50	75	100	200	500	∞
50	4.03 / 7.17	3.18 / 5.06	2.79 / 4.20	2.56 / 3.72	2.40 / 3.41	2.29 / 3.18	2.20 / 3.02	2.13 / 2.88	2.07 / 2.78	2.02 / 2.70	1.98 / 2.62	1.95 / 2.56	1.90 / 2.46	1.85 / 2.39	1.78 / 2.26	1.74 / 2.18	1.69 / 2.10	1.63 / 2.00	1.60 / 1.94	1.55 / 1.86	1.52 / 1.82	1.48 / 1.76	1.46 / 1.71	1.44 / 1.68
55	4.02 / 7.12	3.17 / 5.01	2.78 / 4.16	2.54 / 3.68	2.38 / 3.37	2.27 / 3.15	2.18 / 2.98	2.11 / 2.85	2.05 / 2.75	2.00 / 2.66	1.97 / 2.59	1.93 / 2.53	1.88 / 2.43	1.83 / 2.35	1.76 / 2.23	1.72 / 2.15	1.67 / 2.06	1.61 / 1.96	1.58 / 1.90	1.52 / 1.82	1.50 / 1.78	1.46 / 1.71	1.43 / 1.66	1.41 / 1.64
60	4.00 / 7.08	3.15 / 4.98	2.76 / 4.13	2.52 / 3.65	2.37 / 3.34	2.25 / 3.12	2.17 / 2.95	2.10 / 2.82	2.04 / 2.72	1.99 / 2.63	1.95 / 2.56	1.92 / 2.50	1.86 / 2.40	1.81 / 2.32	1.75 / 2.20	1.70 / 2.12	1.65 / 2.03	1.59 / 1.93	1.56 / 1.87	1.50 / 1.79	1.48 / 1.74	1.44 / 1.68	1.41 / 1.63	1.39 / 1.60
65	3.99 / 7.04	3.14 / 4.95	2.75 / 4.10	2.51 / 3.62	2.36 / 3.31	2.24 / 3.09	2.15 / 2.93	2.08 / 2.79	2.02 / 2.70	1.98 / 2.61	1.94 / 2.54	1.90 / 2.47	1.85 / 2.37	1.80 / 2.30	1.73 / 2.18	1.68 / 2.09	1.63 / 2.00	1.57 / 1.90	1.54 / 1.84	1.49 / 1.76	1.46 / 1.71	1.42 / 1.64	1.39 / 1.60	1.37 / 1.56
70	3.98 / 7.01	3.13 / 4.92	2.74 / 4.08	2.50 / 3.60	2.35 / 3.29	2.23 / 3.07	2.14 / 2.91	2.07 / 2.77	2.01 / 2.67	1.97 / 2.59	1.93 / 2.51	1.89 / 2.45	1.84 / 2.35	1.79 / 2.28	1.72 / 2.15	1.67 / 2.07	1.62 / 1.98	1.56 / 1.88	1.53 / 1.82	1.47 / 1.74	1.45 / 1.69	1.40 / 1.62	1.37 / 1.56	1.35 / 1.53
80	3.96 / 6.96	3.11 / 4.88	2.72 / 4.04	2.48 / 3.56	2.33 / 3.25	2.21 / 3.04	2.12 / 2.87	2.05 / 2.74	1.99 / 2.64	1.95 / 2.55	1.91 / 2.48	1.88 / 2.41	1.82 / 2.32	1.77 / 2.24	1.70 / 2.11	1.65 / 2.03	1.60 / 1.94	1.54 / 1.84	1.51 / 1.78	1.45 / 1.70	1.42 / 1.65	1.38 / 1.57	1.35 / 1.52	1.32 / 1.49
100	3.94 / 6.90	3.09 / 4.82	2.70 / 3.98	2.46 / 3.51	2.30 / 3.20	2.19 / 2.99	2.10 / 2.82	2.03 / 2.69	1.97 / 2.59	1.92 / 2.51	1.88 / 2.43	1.85 / 2.36	1.79 / 2.26	1.75 / 2.19	1.68 / 2.06	1.63 / 1.98	1.57 / 1.89	1.51 / 1.79	1.48 / 1.73	1.42 / 1.64	1.39 / 1.59	1.34 / 1.51	1.30 / 1.46	1.28 / 1.43
125	3.92 / 6.84	3.07 / 4.78	2.68 / 3.94	2.44 / 3.47	2.29 / 3.17	2.17 / 2.95	2.08 / 2.79	2.01 / 2.65	1.95 / 2.56	1.90 / 2.47	1.86 / 2.40	1.83 / 2.33	1.77 / 2.23	1.72 / 2.15	1.65 / 2.03	1.60 / 1.94	1.55 / 1.85	1.49 / 1.75	1.45 / 1.68	1.39 / 1.59	1.36 / 1.54	1.31 / 1.46	1.27 / 1.40	1.25 / 1.37
150	3.91 / 6.81	3.06 / 4.75	2.67 / 3.91	2.43 / 3.44	2.27 / 3.14	2.16 / 2.92	2.07 / 2.76	2.00 / 2.62	1.94 / 2.53	1.89 / 2.44	1.85 / 2.37	1.82 / 2.30	1.76 / 2.20	1.71 / 2.12	1.64 / 2.00	1.59 / 1.91	1.54 / 1.83	1.47 / 1.72	1.44 / 1.66	1.37 / 1.56	1.34 / 1.51	1.29 / 1.43	1.25 / 1.37	1.22 / 1.33
200	3.89 / 6.76	3.04 / 4.71	2.65 / 3.88	2.41 / 3.41	2.26 / 3.11	2.14 / 2.90	2.05 / 2.73	1.98 / 2.60	1.92 / 2.50	1.87 / 2.41	1.83 / 2.34	1.80 / 2.28	1.74 / 2.17	1.69 / 2.09	1.62 / 1.97	1.57 / 1.88	1.52 / 1.79	1.45 / 1.69	1.42 / 1.62	1.35 / 1.53	1.32 / 1.48	1.26 / 1.39	1.22 / 1.33	1.19 / 1.28
400	3.86 / 6.70	3.02 / 4.66	2.62 / 3.83	2.39 / 3.36	2.23 / 3.06	2.12 / 2.85	2.03 / 2.69	1.96 / 2.55	1.90 / 2.46	1.85 / 2.37	1.81 / 2.29	1.78 / 2.23	1.72 / 2.12	1.67 / 2.04	1.60 / 1.92	1.54 / 1.84	1.49 / 1.74	1.42 / 1.64	1.38 / 1.57	1.32 / 1.47	1.28 / 1.42	1.22 / 1.32	1.16 / 1.24	1.13 / 1.19
1000	3.85 / 6.66	3.00 / 4.62	2.61 / 3.80	2.38 / 3.34	2.22 / 3.04	2.10 / 2.82	2.02 / 2.66	1.95 / 2.53	1.89 / 2.43	1.84 / 2.34	1.80 / 2.26	1.76 / 2.20	1.70 / 2.09	1.65 / 2.01	1.58 / 1.89	1.53 / 1.81	1.47 / 1.71	1.41 / 1.61	1.36 / 1.54	1.30 / 1.44	1.26 / 1.38	1.19 / 1.28	1.13 / 1.19	1.08 / 1.11
∞	3.84 / 6.64	2.99 / 4.60	2.60 / 3.78	2.37 / 3.32	2.21 / 3.02	2.09 / 2.80	2.01 / 2.64	1.94 / 2.51	1.88 / 2.41	1.83 / 2.32	1.79 / 2.24	1.75 / 2.18	1.69 / 2.07	1.64 / 1.99	1.57 / 1.87	1.52 / 1.79	1.46 / 1.69	1.40 / 1.59	1.35 / 1.52	1.28 / 1.41	1.24 / 1.36	1.17 / 1.25	1.11 / 1.15	1.00 / 1.00

TABLE H. Table of Probabilities Associated with Values as Large as
Observed Values of H in the Kruskal-Wallis One-Way Analysis
of Variance by Ranks

Sample sizes			H	p	Sample sizes			H	p
n_1	n_2	n_3			n_1	n_2	n_3		
2	1	1	2.7000	.500	4	3	2	6.4444	.008
								6.3000	.011
2	2	1	3.6000	.200				5.4444	.046
								5.4000	.051
2	2	2	4.5714	.067				4.5111	.098
			3.7143	.200				4.4444	.102
3	1	1	3.2000	.300					
					4	3	3	6.7455	.010
3	2	1	4.2857	.100				6.7091	.013
			3.8571	.133				5.7909	.046
								5.7273	.050
3	2	2	5.3572	.029				4.7091	.092
			4.7143	.048				4.7000	.101
			4.5000	.067					
			4.4643	.105	4	4	1	6.6667	.010
								6.1667	.022
3	3	1	5.1429	.043				4.9667	.048
			4.5714	.100				4.8667	.054
			4.0000	.129				4.1667	.082
								4.0667	.102
3	3	2	6.2500	.011					
			5.3611	.032	4	4	2	7.0364	.006
			5.1389	.061				6.8727	.011
			4.5556	.100				5.4545	.046
			4.2500	.121				5.2364	.052
3	3	3	7.2000	.004				4.5545	.098
			6.4889	.011				4.4455	.103
			5.6889	.029					
			5.6000	.050	4	4	3	7.1439	.010
			5.0667	.086				7.1364	.011
			4.6222	.100				5.5985	.049
								5.5758	.051
4	1	1	3.5714	.200				4.5455	.099
								4.4773	.102
4	2	1	4.8214	.057					
			4.5000	.076	4	4	4	7.6538	.008
			4.0179	.114				7.5385	.011
								5.6923	.049
4	2	2	6.0000	.014				5.6538	.054
			5.3333	.033				4.6539	.097
			5.1250	.052				4.5001	.104
			4.4583	.100					
			4.1667	.105	5	1	1	3.8571	.143

SOURCE: W. H. Kruskal and W. A. Wallis, "Use of Ranks in One-Criterion
Variance Analysis," *J. Am. Statist. Assoc.*, **47**, 614–617 (1952) with the kind
permission of the authors and the publisher.

TABLE H. (*Continued*)

Sample sizes			H	p	Sample sizes			H	p
n_1	n_2	n_3			n_1	n_2	n_3		
4	3	1	5.8333	.021	5	2	1	5.2500	.036
			5.2083	.050				5.0000	.048
			5.0000	.057				4.4500	.071
			4.0556	.093				4.2000	.095
			3.8889	.129				4.0500	.119
5	2	2	6.5333	.008					
			6.1333	.013				5.6308	.050
			5.1600	.034				4.5487	.099
			5.0400	.056				4.5231	.103
			4.3733	.090	5	4	4	7.7604	.009
			4.2933	.122				7.7440	.011
5	3	1	6.4000	.012				5.6571	.049
			4.9600	.048				5.6176	.050
			4.8711	.052				4.6187	.100
			4.0178	.095				4.5527	.102
			3.8400	.123	5	5	1	7.3091	.009
5	3	2	6.9091	.009				6.8364	.011
			6.8218	.010				5.1273	.046
			5.2509	.049				4.9091	.053
			5.1055	.052				4.1091	.086
			4.6509	.091				4.0364	.105
			4.4945	.101	5	5	2	7.3385	.010
5	3	3	7.0788	.009				7.2692	.010
			6.9818	.011				5.3385	.047
			5.6485	.049				5.2462	.051
			5.5152	.051				4.6231	.097
			4.5333	.097				4.5077	.100
			4.4121	.109	5	5	3	7.5780	.010
5	4	1	6.9545	.008				7.5429	.010
			6.8400	.011				5.7055	.046
			4.9855	.044				5.6264	.051
			4.8600	.056				4.5451	.100
			3.9873	.098				4.5363	.102
			3.9600	.102	5	5	4	7.8229	.010
5	4	2	7.2045	.009				7.7914	.010
			7.1182	.010				5.6657	.049
			5.2727	.049				5.6429	.050
			5.2682	.050				4.5229	.099
			4.5409	.098				4.5200	.101
			4.5182	.101	5	5	5	8.0000	.009
5	4	3	7.4449	.010				7.9800	.010
			7.3949	.011				5.7800	.049
			5.6564	.049				5.6600	.051
								4.5600	.100
								4.5000	.102

TABLE I. Distribution of χ^2

Probability

df	.99	.98	.95	.90	.80	.70	.50	.30	.20	.10	.05	.02	.01	.001
1	.0^{3}157	.0^{2}628	.00393	.0158	.0642	.148	.455	1.074	1.642	2.706	3.841	5.412	6.635	10.827
2	.0201	.0404	.103	.211	.446	.713	1.386	2.408	3.219	4.605	5.991	7.824	9.210	13.815
3	.115	.185	.352	.584	1.005	1.424	2.366	3.665	4.642	6.251	7.815	9.837	11.341	16.268
4	.297	.429	.711	1.064	1.649	2.195	3.357	4.878	5.989	7.779	9.488	11.668	13.277	18.465
5	.554	.752	1.145	1.610	2.343	3.000	4.351	6.064	7.289	9.236	11.070	13.388	15.086	20.517
6	.872	1.134	1.635	2.204	3.070	3.828	5.348	7.231	8.558	10.645	12.592	15.033	16.812	22.457
7	1.239	1.564	2.167	2.833	3.822	4.671	6.346	8.383	9.803	12.017	14.067	16.622	18.475	24.322
8	1.646	2.032	2.733	3.490	4.594	5.527	7.344	9.524	11.030	13.362	15.507	18.168	20.090	26.125
9	2.088	2.532	3.325	4.168	5.380	6.393	8.343	10.656	12.242	14.684	16.919	19.679	21.666	27.877
10	2.558	3.059	3.940	4.865	6.179	7.267	9.342	11.781	13.442	15.987	18.307	21.161	23.209	29.588
11	3.053	3.609	4.575	5.578	6.989	8.148	10.341	12.899	14.631	17.275	19.675	22.618	24.725	31.264
12	3.571	4.178	5.226	6.304	7.807	9.034	11.340	14.011	15.812	18.549	21.026	24.054	26.217	32.909
13	4.107	4.765	5.892	7.042	8.634	9.926	12.340	15.119	16.985	19.812	22.362	25.472	27.688	34.528
14	4.660	5.368	6.571	7.790	9.467	10.821	13.339	16.222	18.151	21.064	23.685	26.873	29.141	36.123
15	5.229	5.985	7.261	8.547	10.307	11.721	14.339	17.322	19.311	22.307	24.996	28.259	30.578	37.697
16	5.812	6.614	7.962	9.312	11.152	12.624	15.338	18.418	20.465	23.542	26.296	29.633	32.000	39.252
17	6.408	7.255	8.672	10.085	12.002	13.531	16.338	19.511	21.615	24.769	27.587	30.995	33.409	40.790
18	7.015	7.906	9.390	10.865	12.857	14.440	17.338	20.601	22.760	25.989	28.869	32.346	34.805	42.312
19	7.633	8.567	10.117	11.651	13.716	15.352	18.338	21.689	23.900	27.204	30.144	33.687	36.191	43.820
20	8.260	9.237	10.851	12.443	14.578	16.266	19.337	22.775	25.038	28.412	31.410	35.020	37.566	45.315
21	8.897	9.915	11.591	13.240	15.445	17.182	20.337	23.858	26.171	29.615	32.671	36.343	38.932	46.797
22	9.542	10.600	12.338	14.041	16.314	18.101	21.337	24.939	27.301	30.813	33.924	37.659	40.289	48.268
23	10.196	11.293	13.091	14.848	17.187	19.021	22.337	26.018	28.429	32.007	35.172	38.968	41.638	49.728
24	10.856	11.992	13.848	15.659	18.062	19.943	23.337	27.096	29.553	33.196	36.415	40.270	42.980	51.179
25	11.524	12.697	14.611	16.473	18.940	20.867	24.337	28.172	30.675	34.382	37.652	41.566	44.314	52.620
26	12.198	13.409	15.379	17.292	19.820	21.792	25.336	29.246	31.795	35.563	38.885	42.856	45.642	54.052
27	12.879	14.125	16.151	18.114	20.703	22.719	26.336	30.319	32.912	36.741	40.113	44.140	46.963	55.476
28	13.565	14.847	16.928	18.939	21.588	23.647	27.336	31.391	34.027	37.916	41.337	45.419	48.278	56.893
29	14.256	15.574	17.708	19.768	22.475	24.577	28.336	32.461	35.139	39.087	42.557	46.693	49.588	58.302
30	14.953	16.306	18.493	20.599	23.364	25.508	29.336	33.530	36.250	40.256	43.773	47.962	50.892	59.703

For larger values of df, the expression $\sqrt{2\chi^2} - \sqrt{2df - 1}$ may be used as a normal deviate with unit variance, remembering that the probability for χ^2 corresponds with that of a single tail of the normal curve.

SOURCE: Table I is reprinted from Table IV of Fisher & Yates: *Statistical Tables for Biological, Agricultural, and Medical Research,* published by Oliver & Boyd Ltd., Edinburgh, and by permission of the authors and publishers.

TABLE J. Table of Critical Values of T in the Wilcoxon Matched-Pairs Signed-Ranks Test

N	Level of significance, direction predicted		
	.025	.01	.005
	Level of significance, direction not predicted		
	.05	.02	.01
6	0	—	—
7	2	0	—
8	4	2	0
9	6	3	2
10	8	5	3
11	11	7	5
12	14	10	7
13	17	13	10
14	21	16	13
15	25	20	16
16	30	24	20
17	35	28	23
18	40	33	28
19	46	38	32
20	52	43	38
21	59	49	43
22	66	56	49
23	73	62	55
24	81	69	61
25	89	77	68

SOURCE: F. Wilcoxon, *Some Rapid Approximate Statistical Procedures,* American Cyanamid Company, New York, 1949, table I, p. 13, with the kind permission of the author and publisher.

TABLE K. Table of Probabilities Associated with Values as Small as Observed Values of x in the Binomial Test

Given in the body of this table are one-tailed probabilities under H_0 for the binomial test when $P = Q = \frac{1}{2}$. To save space, decimal points are omitted in the p's.

N	0	1	2	3	4	5	6	7	8	9	10	11	12	13	14	15
5	031	188	500	812	969	†										
6	016	109	344	656	891	984	†									
7	008	062	227	500	773	938	992	†								
8	004	035	145	363	637	855	965	996	†							
9	002	020	090	254	500	746	910	980	998	†						
10	001	011	055	172	377	623	828	945	989	999	†					
11		006	033	113	274	500	726	887	967	994	†	†				
12		003	019	073	194	387	613	806	927	981	997	†	†			
13		002	011	046	133	291	500	709	867	954	989	998	†	†		
14		001	006	029	090	212	395	605	788	910	971	994	999	†	†	
15			004	018	059	151	304	500	696	849	941	982	996	†	†	†
16			002	011	038	105	227	402	598	773	895	962	989	998	†	†
17			001	006	025	072	166	315	500	685	834	928	975	994	999	†
18			001	004	015	048	119	240	407	593	760	881	952	985	996	999
19				002	010	032	084	180	324	500	676	820	916	968	990	998
20				001	006	021	058	132	252	412	588	748	868	942	979	994
21				001	004	013	039	095	192	332	500	668	808	905	961	987
22					002	008	026	067	143	262	416	584	738	857	933	974
23					001	005	017	047	105	202	339	500	661	798	895	953
24					001	003	011	032	076	154	271	419	581	729	846	924
25						002	007	022	054	115	212	345	500	655	788	885

SOURCE: Table IV, B, of Helen Walker and J. Lev, *Statistical Inference*, New York, Holt, Rinehart and Winston, Inc., 1953, p. 458, with the kind permission of the authors and publisher.

† 1.0 or approximately 1.0.

TABLE L. Table of Probabilities Associated with Values as Small as Observed Values of U in the Mann-Whitney Test

$n_2 = 3$

U \ n_1	1	2	3
0	.250	.100	.050
1	.500	.200	.100
2	.750	.400	.200
3		.600	.350
4			.500
5			.650

$n_2 = 4$

U \ n_1	1	2	3	4
0	.200	.067	.028	.014
1	.400	.133	.057	.029
2	.600	.267	.114	.057
3		.400	.200	.100
4		.600	.314	.171
5			.429	.243
6			.571	.343
7				.443
8				.557

$n_2 = 5$

U \ n_1	1	2	3	4	5
0	.167	.047	.018	.008	.004
1	.333	.095	.036	.016	.008
2	.500	.190	.071	.032	.016
3	.667	.286	.125	.056	.028
4		.429	.196	.095	.048
5		.571	.286	.143	.075
6			.393	.206	.111
7			.500	.278	.155
8			.607	.365	.210
9				.452	.274
10				.548	.345
11					.421
12					.500
13					.579

$n_2 = 6$

U \ n_1	1	2	3	4	5	6
0	.143	.036	.012	.005	.002	.001
1	.286	.071	.024	.010	.004	.002
2	.428	.143	.048	.019	.009	.004
3	.571	.214	.083	.033	.015	.008
4		.321	.131	.057	.026	.013
5		.429	.190	.086	.041	.021
6		.571	.274	.129	.063	.032
7			.357	.176	.089	.047
8			.452	.238	.123	.066
9			.548	.305	.165	.090
10				.381	.214	.120
11				.457	.268	.155
12				.545	.331	.197
13					.396	.242
14					.465	.294
15					.535	.350
16						.409
17						.469
18						.531

SOURCE: H. B. Mann, and D. R. Whitney, "On a Test of Whether One of Two Random Variables Is Stochastically Larger than the Other," *Ann. Math. Statist.* **18**, 52–54 (1947), with the kind permission of the authors and the publisher.

TABLE L. (*Continued*)

$n_2 = 7$

n_1 / U	1	2	3	4	5	6	7
0	.125	.028	.008	.003	.001	.001	.000
1	.250	.056	.017	.006	.003	.001	.001
2	.375	.111	.033	.012	.005	.002	.001
3	.500	.167	.058	.021	.009	.004	.002
4	.625	.250	.092	.036	.015	.007	.003
5		.333	.133	.055	.024	.011	.006
6		.444	.192	.082	.037	.017	.009
7		.556	.258	.115	.053	.026	.013
8			.333	.158	.074	.037	.019
9			.417	.206	.101	.051	.027
10			.500	.264	.134	.069	.036
11			.583	.324	.172	.090	.049
12				.394	.216	.117	.064
13				.464	.265	.147	.082
14				.538	.319	.183	.104
15					.378	.223	.130
16					.438	.267	.159
17					.500	.314	.191
18					.562	.365	.228
19						.418	.267
20						.473	.310
21						.527	.355
22							.402
23							.451
24							.500
25							.549

TABLE L. (*Continued*)

$n_2 = 8$

U \ n_1	1	2	3	4	5	6	7	8	t	Normal
0	.111	.022	.006	.002	.001	.000	.000	.000	3.308	.001
1	.222	.044	.012	.004	.002	.001	.000	.000	3.203	.001
2	.333	.089	.024	.008	.003	.001	.001	.000	3.098	.001
3	.444	.133	.042	.014	.005	.002	.001	.001	2.993	.001
4	.556	.200	.067	.024	.009	.004	.002	.001	2.888	.002
5		.267	.097	.036	.015	.006	.003	.001	2.783	.003
6		.356	.139	.055	.023	.010	.005	.002	2.678	.004
7		.444	.188	.077	.033	.015	.007	.003	2.573	.005
8		.556	.248	.107	.047	.021	.010	.005	2.468	.007
9			.315	.141	.064	.030	.014	.007	2.363	.009
10			.387	.184	.085	.041	.020	.010	2.258	.012
11			.461	.230	.111	.054	.027	.014	2.153	.016
12			.539	.285	.142	.071	.036	.019	2.048	.020
13				.341	.177	.091	.047	.025	1.943	.026
14				.404	.217	.114	.060	.032	1.838	.033
15				.467	.262	.141	.076	.041	1.733	.041
16				.533	.311	.172	.095	.052	1.628	.052
17					.362	.207	.116	.065	1.523	.064
18					.416	.245	.140	.080	1.418	.078
19					.472	.286	.168	.097	1.313	.094
20					.528	.331	.198	.117	1.208	.113
21						.377	.232	.139	1.102	.135
22						.426	.268	.164	.998	.159
23						.475	.306	.191	.893	.185
24						.525	.347	.221	.788	.215
25							.389	.253	.683	.247
26							.433	.287	.578	.282
27							.478	.323	.473	.318
28							.522	.360	.368	.356
29								.399	.263	.396
30								.439	.158	.437
31								.480	.052	.481
32								.520		

TABLE M. Table of Critical Values or U in the Mann-Whitney Test

Critical Values of U for a One-tailed Test at $\alpha = .001$ or for a Two-tailed Test at $\alpha = .002$

n_1 \ n_2	9	10	11	12	13	14	15	16	17	18	19	20
1												
2												
3									0	0	0	0
4		0	0	0	1	1	1	2	2	3	3	3
5	1	1	2	2	3	3	4	5	5	6	7	7
6	2	3	4	4	5	6	7	8	9	10	11	12
7	3	5	6	7	8	9	10	11	13	14	15	16
8	5	6	8	9	11	12	14	15	17	18	20	21
9	7	8	10	12	14	15	17	19	21	23	25	26
10	8	10	12	14	17	19	21	23	25	27	29	32
11	10	12	15	17	20	22	24	27	29	32	34	37
12	12	14	17	20	23	25	28	31	34	37	40	42
13	14	17	20	23	26	29	32	35	38	42	45	48
14	15	19	22	25	29	32	36	39	43	46	50	54
15	17	21	24	28	32	36	40	43	47	51	55	59
16	19	23	27	31	35	39	43	48	52	56	60	65
17	21	25	29	34	38	43	47	52	57	61	66	70
18	23	27	32	37	42	46	51	56	61	66	71	76
19	25	29	34	40	45	50	55	60	66	71	77	82
20	26	32	37	42	48	54	59	65	70	76	82	88

SOURCE: Tables 1, 3, 5, and 7 of D. Auble, "Extended Tables for the Mann-Whitney Statistic," *Bull. Inst. Educ. Res. Indiana Univ.* **1**, No. 2 (1953), with the kind permission of the author and the publisher.

TABLE M. (*Continued*)

Critical Values of U for a One-tailed Test at α = .01 or for a Two-tailed Test at α = .02

n_1 \ n_2	9	10	11	12	13	14	15	16	17	18	19	20
1												
2					0	0	0	0	0	0	1	1
3	1	1	1	2	2	2	3	3	4	4	4	5
4	3	3	4	5	5	6	7	7	8	9	9	10
5	5	6	7	8	9	10	11	12	13	14	15	16
6	7	8	9	11	12	13	15	16	18	19	20	22
7	9	11	12	14	16	17	19	21	23	24	26	28
8	11	13	15	17	20	22	24	26	28	30	32	34
9	14	16	18	21	23	26	28	31	33	36	38	40
10	16	19	22	24	27	30	33	36	38	41	44	47
11	18	22	25	28	31	34	37	41	44	47	50	53
12	21	24	28	31	35	38	42	46	49	53	56	60
13	23	27	31	35	39	43	47	51	55	59	63	67
14	26	30	34	38	43	47	51	56	60	65	69	73
15	28	33	37	42	47	51	56	61	66	70	75	80
16	31	36	41	46	51	56	61	66	71	76	82	87
17	33	38	44	49	55	60	66	71	77	82	88	93
18	36	41	47	53	59	65	70	76	82	88	94	100
19	38	44	50	56	63	69	75	82	88	94	101	107
20	40	47	53	60	67	73	80	87	93	100	107	114

T A B L E M. (*Continued*)

Critical Values of U for a One-tailed Test at $\alpha = .025$ or for a Two-tailed
Test at $\alpha = .05$

n_1 \ n_2	9	10	11	12	13	14	15	16	17	18	19	20
1												
2	0	0	0	1	1	1	1	1	2	2	2	2
3	2	3	3	4	4	5	5	6	6	7	7	8
4	4	5	6	7	8	9	10	11	11	12	13	13
5	7	8	9	11	12	13	14	15	17	18	19	20
6	10	11	13	14	16	17	19	21	22	24	25	27
7	12	14	16	18	20	22	24	26	28	30	32	34
8	15	17	19	22	24	26	29	31	34	36	38	41
9	17	20	23	26	28	31	34	37	39	42	45	48
10	20	23	26	29	33	36	39	42	45	48	52	55
11	23	26	30	33	37	40	44	47	51	55	58	62
12	26	29	33	37	41	45	49	53	57	61	65	69
13	28	33	37	41	45	50	54	59	63	67	72	76
14	31	36	40	45	50	55	59	64	67	74	78	83
15	34	39	44	49	54	59	64	70	75	80	85	90
16	37	42	47	53	59	64	70	75	81	86	92	98
17	39	45	51	57	63	67	75	81	87	93	99	105
18	42	48	55	61	67	74	80	86	93	99	106	112
19	45	52	58	65	72	78	85	92	99	106	113	119
20	48	55	62	69	76	83	90	98	105	112	119	127

TABLE M. (*Continued*)

Critical Values of U for a One-tailed Test at $\alpha = .05$ or for a Two-tailed Test at $\alpha = .10$

n_2 \ n_1	9	10	11	12	13	14	15	16	17	18	19	20
1											0	0
2	1	1	1	2	2	2	3	3	3	4	4	4
3	3	4	5	5	6	7	7	8	9	9	10	11
4	6	7	8	9	10	11	12	14	15	16	17	18
5	9	11	12	13	15	16	18	19	20	22	23	25
6	12	14	16	17	19	21	23	25	26	28	30	32
7	15	17	19	21	24	26	28	30	33	35	37	39
8	18	20	23	26	28	31	33	36	39	41	44	47
9	21	24	27	30	33	36	39	42	45	48	51	54
10	24	27	31	34	37	41	44	48	51	55	58	62
11	27	31	34	38	42	46	50	54	57	61	65	69
12	30	34	38	42	47	51	55	60	64	68	72	77
13	33	37	42	47	51	56	61	65	70	75	80	84
14	36	41	46	51	56	61	66	71	77	82	87	92
15	39	44	50	55	61	66	72	77	83	88	94	100
16	42	48	54	60	65	71	77	83	89	95	101	107
17	45	51	57	64	70	77	83	89	96	102	109	115
18	48	55	61	68	75	82	88	95	102	109	116	123
19	51	58	65	72	80	87	94	101	109	116	123	130
20	54	62	69	77	84	92	100	107	115	123	130	138

TABLE N. Table of Probabilities Associated with Values as Large as
Observed Values of $\chi_r{}^2$ in the Friedman Two-Way Analysis
of Variance by Ranks

$N = 2$		$N = 3$		$N = 4$		$N = 5$	
$\chi_r{}^2$	p	$\chi_r{}^2$	p	$\chi_r{}^2$	p	$\chi_r{}^2$	p
0	1.000	.000	1.000	.0	1.000	.0	1.000
1	.833	.667	.944	.5	.931	.4	.954
3	.500	2.000	.528	1.5	.653	1.2	.691
4	.167	2.667	.361	2.0	.431	1.6	.522
		4.667	.194	3.5	.273	2.8	.367
		6.000	.028	4.5	.125	3.6	.182
				6.0	.069	4.8	.124
				6.5	.042	5.2	.093
				8.0	.0046	6.4	.039
						7.6	.024
						8.4	.0085
						10.0	.00077

SOURCE: M. Friedman, "The use of ranks to avoid the assumption of
normality implicit in the analysis of variance," *J. Am. Statist. Assoc.* **32**, 688–
689 (1937), with the kind permission of the author and publisher.

TABLE N. (*Continued*)

$k = 3$

$\chi_r{}^2$	p	$\chi_r{}^2$	p	$\chi_r{}^2$	p	$\chi_r{}^2$	p

\multicolumn{2}{N=6}		N = 7		N = 8		N = 9	
$\chi_r{}^2$	p	$\chi_r{}^2$	p	$\chi_r{}^2$	p	$\chi_r{}^2$	p
.00	1.000	.000	1.000	.00	1.000	.000	1.000
.33	.956	.286	.964	.25	.967	.222	.971
1.00	.740	.857	.768	.75	.794	.667	.814
1.33	.570	1.143	.620	1.00	.654	.889	.865
2.33	.430	2.000	.486	1.75	.531	1.556	.569
3.00	.252	2.571	.305	2.25	.355	2.000	.398
4.00	.184	3.429	.237	3.00	.285	2.667	.328
4.33	.142	3.714	.192	3.25	.236	2.889	.278
5.33	.072	4.571	.112	4.00	.149	3.556	.187
6.33	.052	5.429	.085	4.75	.120	4.222	.154
7.00	.029	6.000	.052	5.25	.079	4.667	.107
8.33	.012	7.143	.027	6.25	.047	5.556	.069
9.00	.0081	7.714	.021	6.75	.038	6.000	.057
9.33	.0055	8.000	.016	7.00	.030	6.222	.048
10.33	.0017	8.857	.0084	7.75	.018	6.889	.031
12.00	.00013	10.286	.0036	9.00	.0099	8.000	.019
		10.571	.0027	9.25	.0080	8.222	.016
		11.143	.0012	9.75	.0048	8.667	.010
		12.286	.00032	10.75	.0024	9.556	.0060
		14.000	.000021	12.00	.0011	10.667	.0035
				12.25	.00086	10.889	.0029
				13.00	.00026	11.556	.0013
				14.25	.000061	12.667	.00066
				16.00	.0000036	13.556	.00035
						14.000	.00020
						14.222	.000097
						14.889	.000054
						16.222	.000011
						18.000	.0000006

TABLE N. (*Continued*)

$$k = 4$$

$\chi_r{}^2$	p	$\chi_r{}^2$	p	$\chi_r{}^2$	p	$\chi_r{}^2$	p
	N = 2		N = 3			N = 4	
.0	1.000	.2	1.000	.0	1.000	5.7	.141
.6	.958	.6	.958	.3	.992	6.0	.105
1.2	.834	1.0	.910	.6	.928	6.3	.094
1.8	.792	1.8	.727	.9	.900	6.6	.077
2.4	.625	2.2	.608	1.2	.800	6.9	.068
3.0	.542	2.6	.524	1.5	.754	7.2	.054
3.6	.458	3.4	.446	1.8	.677	7.5	.052
4.2	.375	3.8	.342	2.1	.649	7.8	.036
4.8	.208	4.2	.300	2.4	.524	8.1	.033
5.4	.167	5.0	.207	2.7	.508	8.4	.019
6.0	.042	5.4	.175	3.0	.432	8.7	.014
		5.8	.148	3.3	.389	9.3	.012
		6.6	.075	3.6	.355	9.6	.0069
		7.0	.054	3.9	.324	9.9	.0062
		7.4	.033	4.5	.242	10.2	.0027
		8.2	.017	4.8	.200	10.8	.0016
		9.0	.0017	5.1	.190	11.1	.00094
				5.4	.158	12.0	.000072

TABLE O. Conversion of a Pearson r into a Corresponding Fisher's z_r Coefficient

r	z	r	z	r	z	r	z	r	z	r	z
.25	.26	.40	.42	.55	.62	.70	.87	.85	1.26	.950	1.83
.26	.27	.41	.44	.56	.63	.71	.89	.86	1.29	.955	1.89
.27	.28	.42	.45	.57	.65	.72	.91	.87	1.33	.960	1.95
.28	.29	.43	.46	.58	.66	.73	.93	.88	1.38	.965	2.01
.29	.30	.44	.47	.59	.68	.74	.95	.89	1.42	.970	2.09
.30	.31	.45	.48	.60	.69	.75	.97	.90	1.47	.975	2.18
.31	.32	.46	.50	.61	.71	.76	1.00	.905	1.50	.980	2.30
.32	.33	.47	.51	.62	.73	.77	1.02	.910	1.53	.985	2.44
.33	.34	.48	.52	.63	.74	.78	1.05	.915	1.56	.990	2.65
.34	.35	.49	.54	.64	.76	.79	1.07	.920	1.59	.995	2.99
.35	.37	.50	.55	.65	.78	.80	1.10	.925	1.62		
.36	.38	.51	.56	.66	.79	.81	1.13	.930	1.66		
.37	.39	.52	.58	.67	.81	.82	1.16	.935	1.70		
.38	.40	.53	.59	.68	.83	.83	1.19	.940	1.74		
.39	.41	.54	.60	.69	.85	.84	1.22	.945	1.78		

SOURCE: The values in this table were derived from Table VB in Fisher & Yates: *Statistical Methods for Research Workers,* published by Oliver & Boyd Ltd., Edinburgh, and by permission of the authors and publishers.

NOTE: For all values of r below .25, $r = z$ to two decimal places.

INDEX